Contents

1: Overview   1

2: Housing Expenditure   10

List of tables

1: Overview

2: Housing Expenditure

3: Equivalised Income

4: Trends in household expenditure over time

5: Household expenditure by Output Area Classification

Appendix A

**Household expenditure tables can be accessed via the links given in
Appendix A**

Appendix B

List of Figures

Overview

Housing expenditure

Equivalised income

Trends in household expenditure over time

Household expenditure by Output Area Classification

Symbols and conventions used in this report

[ ]　　　　Figures should be used with extra caution because based on fewer than 20 reporting households.

..　　　　The data is suppressed if the unweighted sample counts are less than ten reporting households.

-　　　　No figures are available because there are no reporting households.

Rounding　　Individual figures have been rounded independently. The sum of component items does not therefore necessarily add to the totals shown.

Averages　　These are averages (means) for all households included in the column or row, and, unless specified, are not restricted to those households reporting expenditure on a particular item or income of a particular type.

Period covered: Calendar year 2009 (1 January 2009 to 31 December 2009).

List of contributors

Editor: Giles Horsfield

Authors: Chris Payne

                     Laura Keyse

                     Louise Skilton

                     Paul Hossack

                     Rebecca Ayres

Living Costs and   James Boyde

Food Survey team   Karen Carter

                     Karen Watkins

                     Linda Williams

                     Sarah Skinner

                     Scott Symons

                     Sian Wilson

                     Tracy Lane

                     Field Team and Interviewers

                     Coders and Editors

Reviewers: Andrew Barnard

                     Gareth Clancy

                     Mike Prestwood

Acknowledgements

A large scale survey is a collaborative effort and the authors wish to thank the interviewers and other ONS staff who contributed to the study. The survey would not be possible without the co-operation of the respondents who gave up their time to be interviewed and keep a diary of their spending. Their help is gratefully acknowledged.

Introduction

This report presents the latest information from the Living Costs and Food Survey for the 2009 calendar year (January to December). The Expenditure and Food Survey (EFS) was renamed as the Living Costs and Food Survey (LCF) in 2008 when it became a module of the Integrated Household Survey (IHS).

The current LCF is the result of the amalgamation of the Family Expenditure and National Food Surveys (FES and NFS). Both surveys were well established and important sources of information for government and the wider community, charting changes and patterns in Britain's spending and food consumption since the 1950s. The Office for National Statistics (ONS) has overall project management and financial responsibility for the LCF while the Department for Environment, Food and Rural Affairs (DEFRA) sponsors the specialist food data.

The survey continues to be primarily used to provide information for the Retail Prices Index; National Accounts estimates of household expenditure; the analysis of the effect of taxes and benefits, and trends in nutrition. However, the results are multi purpose, providing an invaluable supply of economic and social data.

The 2009 survey

In 2009 5,223 households in Great Britain took part in the LCF survey. The response rate was 50 per cent in Great Britain and 56 per cent in Northern Ireland. The fieldwork was undertaken by the Office for National Statistics and the Northern Ireland Statistics and Research Agency. Further details about the conduct of the survey are given in Appendix B.

The format of the Family Spending publication changed in 2003–04 so that the tables of key results which were found in the main body of the report are now in Appendix A. This year's report includes an overview chapter outlining key findings, two detailed chapters focusing upon expenditure on housing and the impact of equivalising income when calculating results, a fourth chapter looking at trends in household expenditure over time and finally a chapter on expenditure by Output Area Classification (OAC).

Data quality and definitions

The results shown in this report are of the data collected by the LCF, following a process of validation and adjustment for non-response using weights that control for a number of factors. These issues are discussed in the section on reliability in Appendix B.

Figures in the report are subject to sampling variability. Standard errors for detailed expenditure items are presented in relative terms in Table A1 and are described in Appendix B, section B6. Figures shown for particular groups of households (for example income groups or household composition groups), regions or other sub-sets of the sample are subject to larger sampling variability, and are more sensitive to possible extreme values than are figures for the sample as a whole.

The definitions used in the report are set out in Appendix B, section B4, and changes made since 1991 are described in section B5. Note particularly that Housing Benefit and Council Tax Rebate (rates rebate in Northern Ireland), unlike other social security benefits, are not included in income but are shown as a reduction in housing costs.

Income and Expenditure Balancing

The LCF is designed primarily as a survey of household expenditure on goods and services. It also gathers information about the income of household members, and is an important and detailed source of income data. However, the survey is not designed to produce a balance sheet of income and expenditure either for individual households or groups of households. For further information on the balancing of income and expenditure figures, see 'Description and response rate of the survey', page 215

Related data sources

Details of household consumption expenditure within the context of the UK National Accounts are produced as part of Consumer Trends (www.statistics.gov.uk/statbase/Product.asp?vlnk=242). This publication includes all expenditure by members of UK resident households. National Accounts figures draw on a number of sources including the LCF: figures shown in this report are therefore not directly comparable to National Accounts data. National Accounts data may be more appropriate for deriving long term trends on expenditure.

More detailed income information is available from the Family Resources Survey (FRS), conducted for the Department for Work and Pensions. Further information about food consumption, and in particular details of food quantities, is available from the Department for Environment, Food and Rural Affairs, who are continuing to produce their own report of the survey (www.defra.gov.uk/evidence/statistics/foodfarm/food/familyfood/index.htm).

In Northern Ireland, a companion survey to the GB LCF is conducted by the Central Survey Unit of the Northern Ireland Statistics and Research Agency (NISRA). Households in Northern Ireland are over-sampled so that separate analysis can be carried out, however these cases are given less weight when UK data are analysed.

Additional tabulations

This report gives a broad overview of the results of the survey, and provides more detailed information about some aspects of expenditure. However, many users of LCF data have very specific data requirements that may not appear in the desired form in this report. The ONS can provide more detailed analysis of the tables in this report, and can also provide additional tabulations to meet specific requests. A charge will be made to cover the cost of providing additional information.

The tables in Family Spending 2009 are available as Excel spreadsheets.

Anonymised microdata from the Living Costs and Food Survey (LCF), the Expenditure and Food Survey (EFS) and the Family Expenditure Survey (FES) are available from the United Kingdom Data Archive. Details on access arrangements and associated costs can be found at www.data-archive.ac.uk or by telephoning 01206 872143.

Overview

This chapter presents the key findings of the 2009 Living Costs and Food Survey (LCF), formerly the Expenditure and Food Survey. The chapter provides an overview of household income and expenditure, characterised by different household types and regions, as well as a summary of the ownership of a limited range of durable goods. All estimates in this publication have not been adjusted for inflation unless otherwise stated.

All of the tables (except Table 1.1) referred to in this chapter can be found in Appendix A of the report (page 113).

Household expenditure

Table 1.1 shows total weekly household expenditure in the United Kingdom (UK) by the 12 Classification of Individual COnsumption by Purpose (COICOP)[1] categories. In 2009 average weekly household expenditure in the UK was £455.00, less than in 2008 when it was £471.00. As in previous years, spending was highest on transport at £58.40 per week. This was £5.00 less than in 2008, a drop of 8 per cent.

Recreation and culture (£57.90 per week) and housing, fuel and power (£57.30) were the next highest categories of expenditure, although the gap between these two categories narrowed between 2008 and 2009, with average spending on recreation and culture previously at £60.10 and average spending on housing, fuel and power at £53.00. The average weekly expenditure on food and non-alcoholic drinks in 2009 was £52.20.

Table 1.1 Expenditure by COICOP category and total household expenditure, 2009

COICOP category	£ per week
Transport	58.40
Recreation and culture	57.90
Housing, fuel and power	57.30
Food and non-alcoholic drinks	52.20
Restaurants and hotels	38.40
Miscellaneous goods and services	35.00
Household goods and services	27.90
Clothing and footwear	20.90
Communication	11.70
Alcoholic drinks, tobacco and narcotics	11.20
Education	7.00
Health	5.30
Total COICOP expenditure	383.10
Other expenditure items	71.80
Total expenditure	455.00

Totals may not add up due to the independent rounding of component categories

Of the £58.40 spent on transport each week, half (50 per cent) was spent on the operation of personal transport (£29.30), see Table A1. This was a drop of 8 per cent on the previous year, in line with the overall drop observed in spending on transport. As in 2008 petrol, diesel and other motor oils (£19.20 per week) was the largest expenditure in the operation of personal transport category.

The expenditure within most categories under the heading transport fell between 2008 and 2009, including purchase of vehicles, which decreased from £21.10 to £19.50 per week in 2009. In particular, households spent less on outright purchase of second hand cars or vans (£8.00 per week compared to £9.80 per week in 2008). Households spent on average £9.60 per week on transport services, including rail, tube and bus fares, compared to £10.50 in 2008.

Approximately a third (32 per cent) of spending on recreation and culture (£18.70 per week) was spent on recreational and cultural services; sports admissions, leisure class fees and equipment hire accounted for £5.00 per week; cinema, theatre and museums etc £2.30 per week; TV, video, satellite rental, cable subscriptions, TV licenses and internet £5.90 per week; and gambling payments £4.10 per week.

Spending on package holidays fell from £14.70 per week in 2008 to £13.20 in 2009. Of this, £12.30 was spent on holidays abroad, £1.30 less than in 2008. Spending on audio-visual, photographic and information processing equipment (£7.00 per week) and other recreational items and equipment, gardens and pets (£10.50 per week) remained relatively constant. In particular, the average weekly spend on TV, video and computers remained at £4.80. (Table A1).

Of the £52.20 average weekly spend on food and non-alcoholic drinks, £6.70 was spent on fresh fruit and vegetables; £2.90 on fruit and £3.80 on vegetables; £11.40 was spent on meat, the highest proportion (47 per cent) of which was spent on other meat and meat preparations (£5.40 per week); £5.00 was spent on bread, rice and cereals; £3.20 was spent on buns, cakes, biscuits, etc; and £4.10 was spent on non-alcoholic drinks (Table A1). Almost three-quarters (72 per cent, £37.70 per week) of food and non-alcoholic drinks were purchased from large supermarket chains (Table A3), an increase of £1.20 on the previous year.

Alcohol bought and consumed on licensed premises (£7.20 per week) accounted for slightly more than half (55 per cent) of all expenditure on alcoholic drink (£14.00 per week). Of the remaining £6.80 spent on alcohol, £4.60 was spent at large supermarket chains and £2.20 was spent at other off-licence outlets (Table A2).

Household expenditure by income

Household incomes have been ranked in ascending order and divided into decile groups in order to examine expenditure patterns between different income groups. Households with the smallest income lie in the first decile group and those with the largest income lie in the top (tenth) decile group. Average weekly household expenditure in 2009 ranged from £162.70 in the lowest of the 10 income decile groups to £922.10 in the highest (Figure 1.1, Table A6); expenditure in this highest decile was £122.80 lower than in 2008.

Figure 1.1   **Household expenditure by gross income decile group, 2009**

£ per week

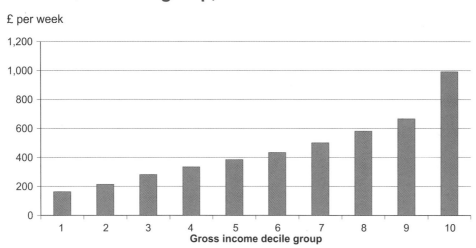

Gross income decile group

Households in the lowest income decile group spent a larger proportion of their total average weekly expenditure on housing, fuel and power (23 per cent), and food and non-alcoholic drinks (16 per cent), than those in the highest income decile group (8 per cent in both cases). Similarly, the lowest income decile group spent a larger proportion of expenditure on education (3 per cent) than some of the higher income decile groups (1 per cent in the seventh, eighth and ninth decile groups). However, households in the highest income decile group spent a greater proportion on transport (13 per cent) and recreation and culture (14 per cent) than those in the lowest income decile group (9 and 10 per cent respectively) (Table A7).

Household expenditure by age

Average weekly expenditure varied with the age of the household reference person (HRP). As in 2008, households whose HRP was aged 30 to 49 years had the highest average expenditure (£558.80 per week) while those with an HRP aged 75 years and over had the lowest average household expenditure (£236.40 per week). It should be noted that households with an HRP aged 30 to 49 years contained an average of 2.9 people, whereas households with an HRP aged 75 years and over contained an average of 1.4 people (Table A11).

Spending on housing, fuel and power in households whose HRP was aged less than 30 years increased from £76.20 in 2008 to £97.30, an increase of 28 per cent (Table A11). This corresponds to 23 per cent of total household expenditure for households with a HRP aged less than 30, whereas households with an HRP aged 75 years or over spent 17 per cent of their total household expenditure on housing, fuel and power (Table A12).

The proportion of expenditure spent on food and non-alcoholic drinks increased with age, from 9 per cent among households with an HRP aged less than 30 years to 16 per cent among households with an HRP aged 75 years and over.

The pattern of spending on restaurants and hotels, as a proportion of total expenditure, was relatively constant among age groups, with the percentage of total expenditure ranging from 9 per cent among households with an HRP aged between 30 and 64, to 6 per cent among households with an HRP aged 75 years and over (Table A12). When the amount spent is considered, household expenditure on restaurants and hotels was greatest in households with an HRP aged between 30 and 49 (£49.70 per week), but much lower in households with HRP over 75 (£13.10 per week). This compares with an average expenditure across all ages of £38.40 (Table A13).

Expenditure on recreation and culture, as a proportion of total spending, varied from 9 per cent among households with an HRP aged less than 30 years to a maximum of 14 per cent among households with an HRP aged 50 to 74 years (Table A12).

Figure 1.2 Expenditure on selected items as a proportion of total spending by age of the HRP, 2009

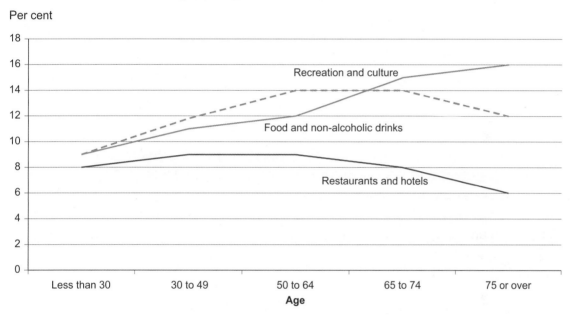

Household expenditure by economic activity and socio-economic classification

This analysis uses the National Statistics Socio-Economic Classification (NS-SEC), see Appendix B, page 133.

Household spending varied with the economic status of the HRP. The average weekly expenditure of households where the HRP was in employment (£568.50 per week) was more than twice that of households where the HRP was unemployed (£229.00 per week), and just under twice that of households where the HRP was economically inactive (£286.40 per week) (Table A19).

In households where the HRP was in employment, spending was greatest on transport (£77.00 per week) and recreation and culture (£72.30 per week). Among households where the HRP was unemployed, spending on housing, fuel and power was greatest (£42.50 per week), followed by food and non-alcoholic drinks (£31.90 per week) (Table A19).

Average weekly expenditure was highest among households where the HRP was in the 'large employers and higher managerial' occupational group, at £877.70 per week. An average weekly expenditure of £398.90 was recorded for households where the HRP was in a 'routine' occupation (Table A24).

Household expenditure by household composition

Generally, household expenditure increased with the size of the household. Thus, average weekly household expenditure was lowest among retired one-person households who were mainly dependent on the state pension (£148.90) and highest among households containing three or more adults with children (£710.90) (Table A25).

Household expenditure by region

Overall, average household expenditure in the UK was £461.70 per week for the years 2007–09 combined. There were five regions in which expenditure over this period was higher than the UK average: expenditure was highest in London (552.30), followed by the South East (£523.90 per week), the East (£487.70), Northern Ireland (£485.80) and the South West (£474.10). Spending was lowest among households in the North East (£387.20), Wales (£396.10), and Yorkshire and the Humber (£400.70) (Figure 1.3, Table A35).

Figure 1.3   **Household expenditure by region, 2007 to 2009**

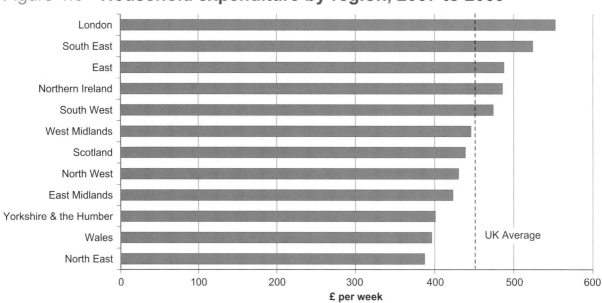

During the three-year period, 2007–2009, spending on transport was highest among households in the South East (£75.30 per week) and lowest among those in the North East (£49.00 per week). Households in London spent the most on housing, fuel and power (£80.10 per week) compared with the UK national average of £54.00 per week (Table A37). Housing expenditure is looked at in more detail in chapter two.

Households in rural areas had higher overall expenditure (£500.00 per week) than those in urban areas (£450.20 per week). This was reflected in expenditure on transport, where spending was highest (£75.70 in rural areas and £57.00 in urban areas), and recreation and culture (£65.80 in rural areas and £56.40 in urban areas). However, expenditure on housing, fuel and power was slightly higher in urban areas (£54.90 per week) than in rural areas (£52.00 per week) (Table A38).

Household income

Income within the survey is defined as the gross weekly cash income current at the time of interview. Gross income includes salaries and wages, income from self employment, benefits and pensions. See Appendix B for further details on income.

Average gross weekly household income in the UK in 2009 was £683.00, £30.00 less than in 2008 (£713.00 per week). Besides wages and salaries (66 per cent), social security benefits formed the largest proportion of income (14 per cent), followed by self-employment income, and income from annuities and pensions at 8 per cent (Figure 1.4, Table A40).

Figure 1.4   **Percentage of gross weekly household income by source of income, 2009**

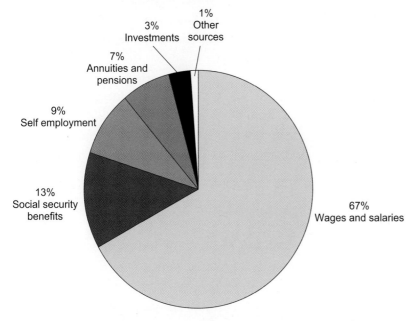

Household income by age

Households with an HRP aged 30 to 49 recorded the highest gross weekly income: £873 per week. Of this, 79 per cent was acquired from wages and salaries.

Households whose HRP was aged less than 30 years received the highest proportion of their average gross weekly income from wages and salaries (83 per cent), however this age group earned considerably less (£575 per week) than households whose HRP was aged 30 to 64 years.

Households with a household reference person (HRP) aged less than 65 years of age had a higher average weekly gross income than those with an HRP aged 65 years and over. The lowest gross weekly income was recorded by households with an HRP aged 75 years or over (£331 an increase of £41.00 from the previous year) with 54 per cent of their income gained through social security benefits. It is worth noting that households with an HRP aged 65 to 74 years and households with an HRP aged 75 years or over had a higher disposable (gross income minus direct taxes) proportion of their gross weekly income (91 and 93 per cent respectively) than households with an HRP aged less than 65 years (Table A41).

Household income by region

There were three English regions that exceeded the 2007–2009 UK national average income of £685 per week. They were London (£940), the South East (£797) and the East (£732). Income was lowest among households in the North East (£561 per week) and Yorkshire and the Humber (£565 per week).

Among UK countries, households in England had the highest average gross weekly income (£698), whereas those in Wales had the lowest average income at £585 per week (Table A44).

Household income by economic activity and socio-economic classification

Households where the HRP was in the 'large employers and higher managerial' occupational group had an average gross weekly income of £1,647, almost three times the income of households where the HRP worked in a 'routine' occupation (£560). These incomes were acquired mainly from wages and salaries (87 and 82 per cent respectively).

Households with an HRP in the 'lower supervisory' occupational group received the highest proportion of their average gross weekly income (£738) from wages and salaries (89 per cent). By contrast, those households with an HRP in the 'long-term unemployed' occupational group obtained 85 per cent of their average gross weekly income (£204) from social security benefits (Table A46).

Ownership of durable goods

Overall, 75 per cent of households had a home computer and 71 per cent had an internet connection at home, an increase of 3 and 5 percentage points, respectively, from 2008 (Table A50). Among households in the highest income decile group, 98 per cent had a home computer and 97 per cent an internet connection, compared with only 38 and 30 per cent of households in the lowest income decile group. This does, however, represent a 5 percentage point increase in households with a home computer and a 4 percentage point increase on households with an internet connection in the lowest income decile group from 2008 (Table A51).

In general, households with children were more likely to have an internet connection than those without. Overall, 89 per cent of two-adult, non-retired households owned a home computer, with 86 per cent having an internet connection (Table A51).

Connection to the internet was lowest among households in Northern Ireland (57 per cent) and highest in the South East and London (both 72 per cent). Ownership of a mobile phone was lowest among households in Wales (49 per cent) and highest in the West Midlands and South West at 85 per cent (Table A53).

More than three-quarters (76 per cent) of all households owned a car or van, with 33 per cent owning two or more. Ownership of at least one car or van varied from 33 per cent in the lowest income decile, to 96 per cent in the highest (Table A52).

Ownership of a car or van was highest among households in the East (83 per cent), the South West (82 per cent) and the South East (81 per cent), and lowest among households in London (64 per cent) and the North East (68 per cent) (Table A53).

1   From 2001-02, the Classification of Individual COnsumption by Purpose (COICOP) was introduced as a new coding frame for expenditure items. COICOP is the internationally agreed classification system for reporting household consumption expenditure. Total expenditure is made up from the total of the COICOP expenditure groups (1 to 12) plus 'Other expenditure items (13)'. Other expenditure items are those items excluded from the narrower COICOP classifications, such as mortgage interest payments, council tax, domestic rates, holiday spending, cash gifts and charitable donations.

Housing expenditure

Background

This chapter presents housing-related costs such as rent, mortgage payments, repair and maintenance, and home improvements. The first section outlines the definitions of housing expenditure: the Classification Of Individual COnsumption by Purpose (COICOP) definition, followed by the definition used in the analysis of this chapter, which includes expenditure not present in COICOP. This chapter also examines housing expenditure over time and by income, region, and household characteristics. The final section explores housing costs for renters, and for mortgage holders in more depth.

Definitions of housing expenditure

The COICOP system has been used to classify expenditure on the Living Costs and Food Survey LCF (and previously the Family expenditure Survey (EFS)) since 2001/02. COICOP is an internationally agreed system of classification for reporting consumption expenditure within National Accounts and is used by other household budget surveys across the European Union. Further information on COICOP can be found on the United Nations Statistics Division website: **http://unstats.un.org/unsd/cr/registry/regct.asp?Lg=1**.

Under COICOP, household consumption expenditure is categorised into the following 12 headings:
1. Food & non-alcoholic drinks
2. Alcoholic drinks, tobacco & narcotics
3. Clothing & footwear
4. Housing (net), fuel & power
5. Household goods & services
6. Health
7. Transport
8. Communication
9. Recreation & culture
10. Education
11. Restaurants & hotels
12. Miscellaneous goods & services

It is important to note that COICOP classified housing costs do not include what is considered to be non-consumption expenditure, for example, mortgage interest, mortgage capital repayments, mortgage protection premiums, council tax and domestic rates.

In addition to the 12 COICOP expenditure categories, the tables contained in Appendix A include a category called 'other expenditure items' under which certain non-consumption expenditures can be found. This category includes the following housing-related costs: mortgage interest payments; mortgage protection premiums; council tax; and domestic rates. Housing costs that are not included in either the COICOP definition of housing or the 'other expenditure item' category are captured within the 'other items recorded' category that can be viewed in Table A1 in Appendix A.

For the purpose of this chapter all data relating to housing expenditure have been combined to facilitate an understanding of total housing costs. This comprehensive definition of housing expenditure is made up from three types of expenditure detailed in Table 2.1: expenditure included in COICOP, housing costs included in the 'other expenditure items' and 'other items recorded' categories of *Family Spending*.

It should also be noted that throughout *Family Spending*, including this chapter, rent excluding service charges and benefit receipts associated with housing (net rent) has been used when calculating total expenditure. This convention ensures that rebates, benefits and allowances are excluded from the calculation of total household expenditure on rent.

Table 2.1 **Definition of total housing expenditure**

Housing costs which are included in the COICOP classification:

- Actual rentals for housing
  - net rent (gross rent *less* housing benefit, rebates and allowances received)
  - second dwelling rent
- Maintenance and repair of dwelling
  - central heating maintenance and repair
  - house maintenance and repair
  - paint, wallpaper, timber
  - equipment hire, small materials
- Water supply and miscellaneous services relating to dwelling
  - water charges
  - other regular housing payments including service charge for rent
  - refuse collection, including skip hire.
- Household Insurances
  - structural insurance
  - contents insurance
  - insurance for household appliances.

Housing costs which are included as 'other expenditure items' but excluded from COICOP classification:

- Housing: mortgage interest payments etc
  - mortgage interest payments
  - mortgage protection premiums
  - council tax, domestic rates
  - council tax, mortgage, insurance (second dwelling).

Housing costs which are included as 'other items recorded' and are excluded from COICOP classification:

- Purchase or alteration of dwellings (contracted out), mortgages
  - outright purchase of houses, flats etc. including deposits
  - capital repayment of mortgage
  - central heating installation
  - DIY improvements: double glazing, kitchen units, sheds etc
  - home improvements (contracted out)
  - bathroom fittings
  - purchase of materials for capital improvements
  - purchase of second dwelling.

Housing expenditure

Table 2.2 shows expenditure on the items included in the comprehensive definition of housing expenditure. It also displays total household expenditure, which includes all expenditure items covered by the survey. The total expenditure figure reported here is therefore greater than the expenditure totals shown in the tables in Appendix A, as these exclude certain non-consumption costs.

Under the comprehensive definition of housing expenditure, UK households spent on average £139.30 a week on housing in 2009, which equates to just over a fifth (21 per cent) of total weekly expenditure. The COICOP definition of housing expenditure (excluding fuel and power) on the other hand, gave an average of £36.00 per week for each household (see Table A1).

In 2009 spending was highest on mortgages (interest payments, protection premiums and capital repayments) at £48.70 a week. The next highest expenditure was on charges (council tax or domestic rates, water charges, refuse collection and other regular services) at £26.50 a week. This was followed by net rent at £21.70 a week and household alterations and improvements at £21.10 per week. Figure 2.1 provides a breakdown of housing expenditure items as a proportion of housing expenditure.

Figure 2.1 **Housing expenditure items as a percentage of total housing expenditure, 2009**

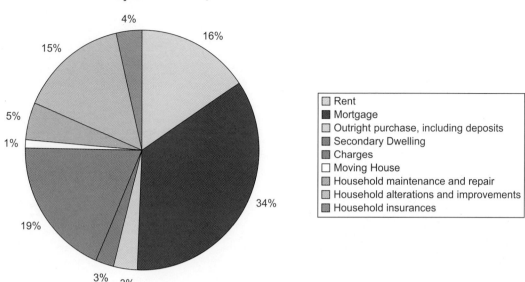

Housing expenditure over time

Overall, expenditure on housing has decreased over the last three years, from £142.00 in 2007 to £139.30 per week in 2009. There was a slight increase of £1.40 per week from 2007 to 2008, which was followed by a decrease between 2008 and 2009 where average weekly expenditure on housing fell by around £4. However, housing expenditure as a percentage of total expenditure has remained stable, decreasing by only 1 percentage point from 2007 (22 per cent) to 2009 (21 per cent). See Table 2.2 for a comparison of housing expenditure from 2007 to 2009.

Figure 2.2 presents the average weekly spend on each category of housing expenditure from 2007 to 2009. The largest decrease was seen in the mortgages category, which has decreased from £53.30 in 2007 to £48.70 in 2009. Spending has remained relatively consistent for most other categories, with slight downward trends continuing for household maintenance and repair, and moving house costs.

Figure 2.2 **Housing expenditure 2007 to 2009**

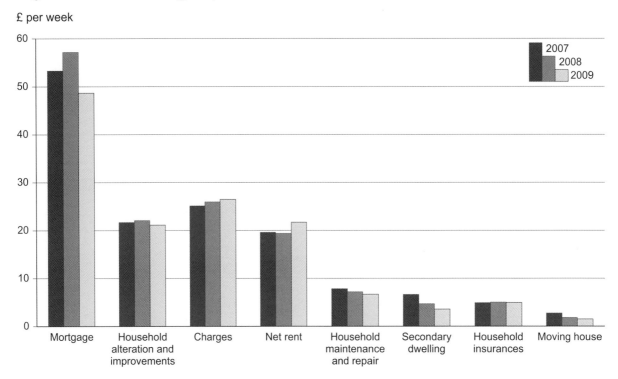

£ per week

Legend: 2007, 2008, 2009

Categories: Mortgage, Household alteration and improvements, Charges, Net rent, Household maintenance and repair, Secondary dwelling, Household insurances, Moving house

Expenditure by gross income

Table 2.3 presents housing expenditure by gross income decile group (a decile is one-tenth of the distribution). Overall, spending on housing increased with income. The highest income group spent £351.30 per week; more than twice the average for all income groups (£139.30); and more than eight times that of the lowest income group (£40.40).

The two categories that showed the greatest variation by income are mortgages, and housing alteration and improvements. Figure 2.3 shows expenditure on mortgages to be consistently higher through income deciles, up to a weekly average of £145.20 in the highest income decile. Expenditure on housing alteration and improvements showed a less consistent increase with income, but still displayed a sharp increase in the 10th decile group to £91.30 per week.

Figure 2.3 **Expenditure on selected items by gross income decile group, 2009**

£ per week

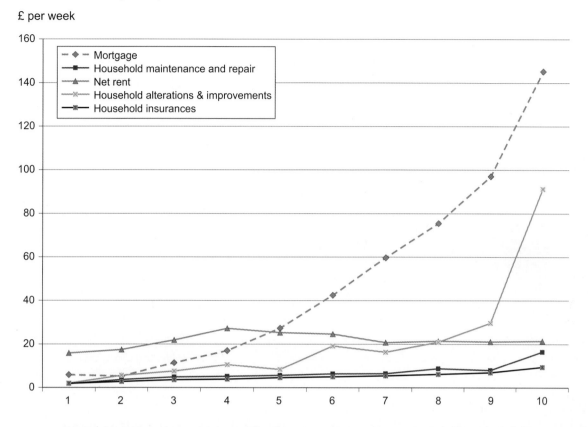

A very different pattern can be seen when looking at net rent by income decile group; households in the first decile group spent the least on net rent at £15.90 per week while households in the fourth decile group spent the most at £27.20 per week.

Expenditure on household insurances and on household maintenance and repairs increased slightly with income, but the increase was far less pronounced than for other categories.

Expenditure by age of the household reference person

Figure 2.4 presents the average weekly spend on the top three housing expenditure categories by age of the household reference person (HRP) (HRP is defined in Appendix B). Average weekly expenditure on mortgages peaked at £89.30 for households with an HRP aged 30 to 49. Average weekly expenditure for households with an HRP under the age of 30, and of the age range 50 to 64, was lower at around £40. Similarly, the average weekly spend for household alterations and improvements was highest for households with an HRP aged 30 to 49 at £30.50. Net rent expenditure decreased as the age of the HRP increased. Average weekly expenditure for households with an HRP under the age of 30 was £72.00, compared with £25.50 for households with an HRP aged between 30 and 49, and £7.50 for households with an HRP aged over 75.

Figure 2.5 shows that expenditure on net rent for households with an HRP aged under 30 has increased from £51.70 in 2008 to £72 in 2009. There has been little or no increase for HRP age groups over 30.

Figure 2.4 **Expenditure on selected items by age of household reference person, 2009**

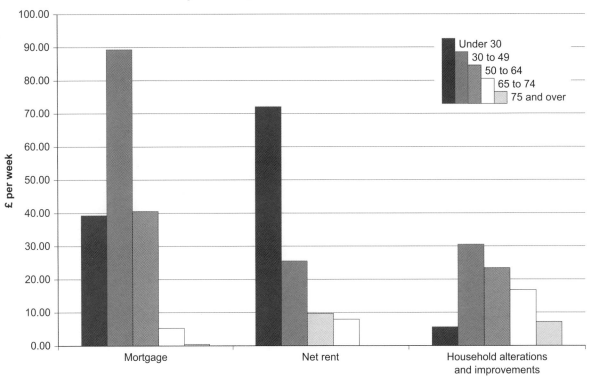

Figure 2.5 **Expenditure on net rent by age of household reference person, 2008 and 2009**

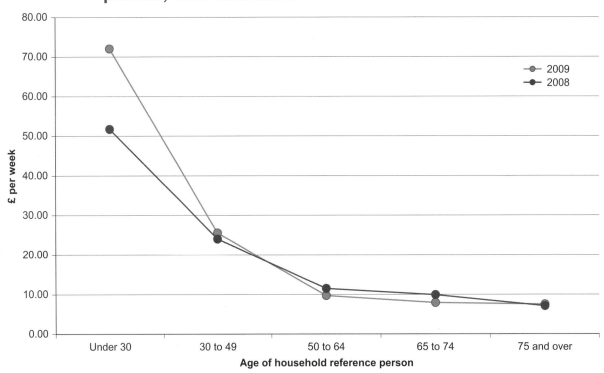

Expenditure by region

Table 2.5, Figure 2.6, and Figure 2.7 show housing expenditure by country and Government Office Region. Looking first at expenditure by country (Figure 2.6, households in England spent the most on housing at £143.80 a week, followed by Scotland (£127.90), Wales (£109.90) and Northern Ireland (£91.30).

Figure 2.6 Housing expenditure by country, 2009

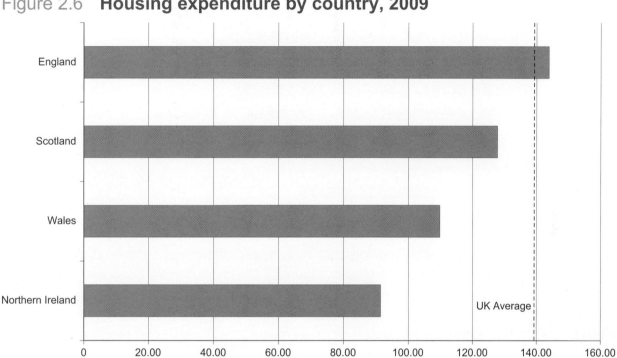

Figure 2.7 shows housing expenditure by Government Office Region and country (excluding England). Three English regions had average weekly household spends that were greater than the UK average. Housing expenditure was greatest in London at £199.30 a week, followed by the South East (198.70) and East (157.30). Expenditure was lowest in Northern Ireland with an average spend of £91.30. The lowest spending in England was in the North East, where average weekly housing costs were £98.80.

Figure 2.7   **Housing expenditure by region, 2009**

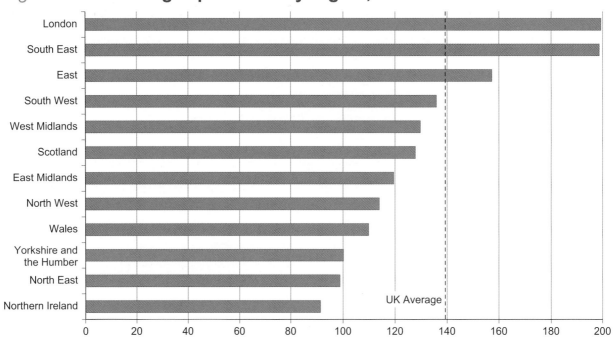

Variations in the total spending on housing are largely due to differences between regions in the average amount spent on rent and mortgages. Figures 2.8 and 2.9 present the percentage difference in each region from the UK average for net rent and mortgages, respectively. It is important to note that these figures include all households. Average expenditure on rent only by renters, and mortgages only by mortgage holders is examined later in the chapter.

Figure 2.8 shows that average weekly expenditure on net rent for households in London was £50.60, which was the only region to exceed the UK average of £21.70. Spending on net rent was lowest in the North East of England with an average weekly expenditure of £12.50, closely followed by Wales where the average weekly net rent was £14.90.

Figure 2.8   **Percentage difference compared with UK average for net rent by UK Countries and Government Office Regions, 2009**

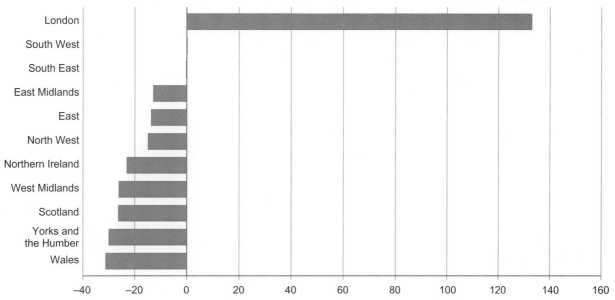

Figure 2.9 shows London, the South East and the East of England had average mortgage payments above the UK average of £48.70; all other regions spent less on mortgages than the UK average. Expenditure on mortgages was lowest in Wales with average weekly mortgage payments of £38.10.

Figure 2.9   **Percentage difference compared with UK average for mortgage payments by UK Countries and Government Office Regions, 2009**

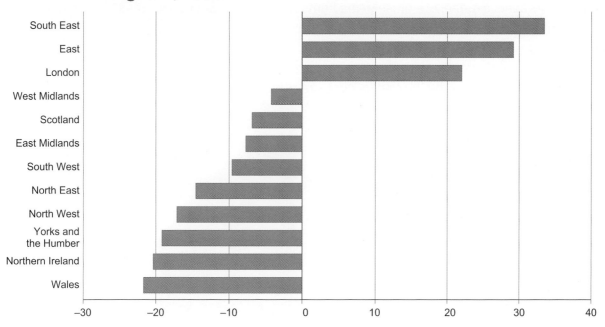

Expenditure by socio-economic classification

Figure 2.10 and Table 2.6 present housing expenditure by socio-economic classification of the household reference person (HRP). Households with an HRP in the 'large employer and higher managerial' occupation group spent the most, at £316.20 per week: twice that of households with an HRP in the 'routine' occupation group, where the average weekly spend was £119.90.

Figure 2.10 **Housing expenditure by socio-economic classification of household reference person, 2009**

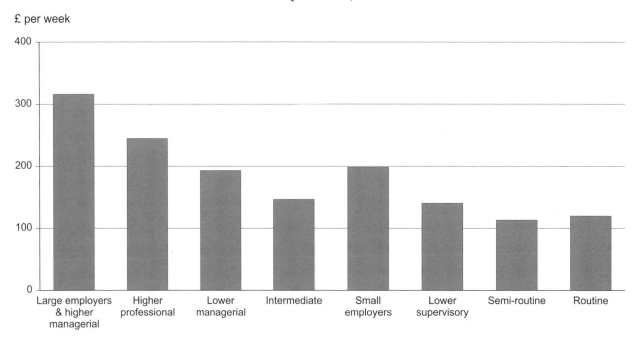

Figure 2.11 presents expenditure on selected items by the socio-economic classification of the HRP. Overall, expenditure followed a similar pattern as described above, with those with an HRP classified as 'large employer and higher managerial' spending more than those in 'routine' occupations. The exception to this was net rent where the opposite pattern is observed and the highest expenditure was for the 'routine' occupation group, reflecting the high number of renters in this group.

Figure 2.11 **Expenditure on selected items by socio-economic classification of household reference person, 2009**

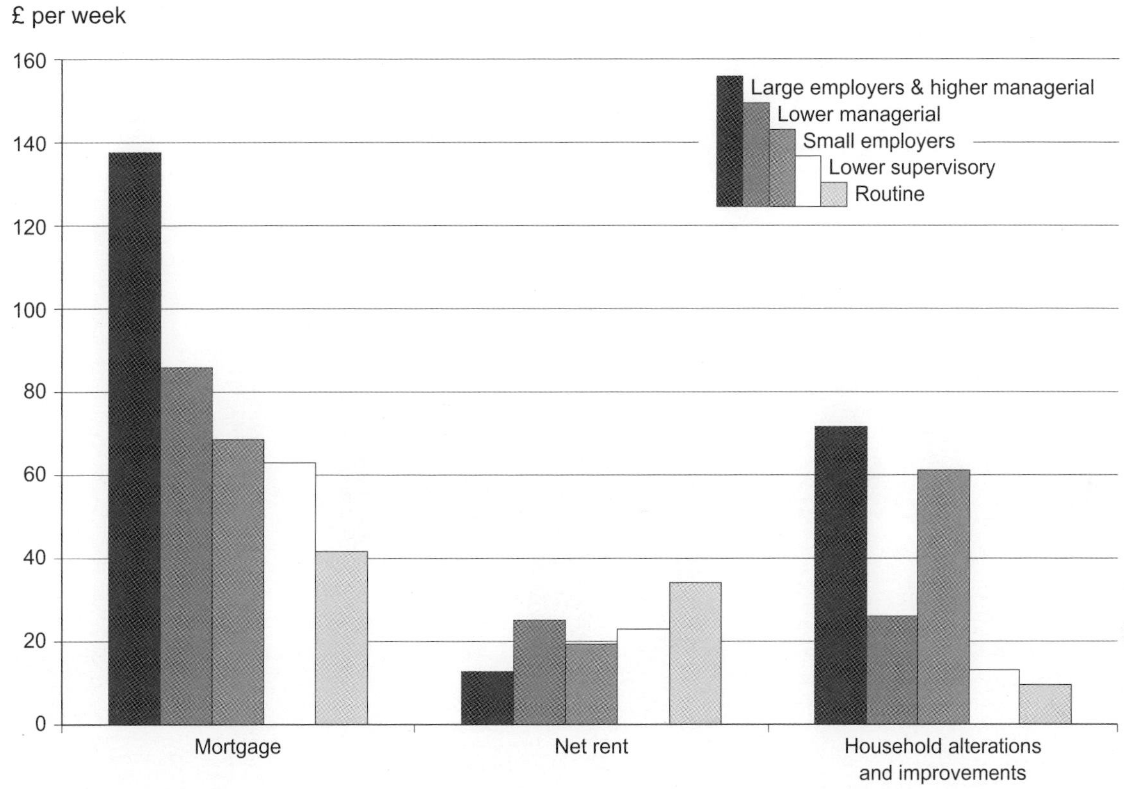

£ per week

Legend:
- Large employers & higher managerial
- Lower managerial
- Small employers
- Lower supervisory
- Routine

Categories: Mortgage, Net rent, Household alterations and improvements

Analysis of housing costs for renters and mortgage holders

The following analysis looks at average expenditure on net rent for households that report spending on net rent and average expenditure on mortgages for mortgage holders. This is the only place in *Family Spending* where averages are not across all households. Excluding households with nil expenditure for net rent and mortgages provides a more informative picture of expenditure on these items.

Table 2.8 provides expenditure on rent over the last three years. In 2009 renters spent on average £70.70 per week on net rent. Table 2.9 provides expenditure on mortgages over the last three years. In 2009 the average weekly expenditure on mortgages by mortgage holders was £133.00.

Table 2.10 and Figure 2.12 present average weekly expenditure for the relevant households by income decile group for mortgage holders and renters. Figure 2.12 shows a steady increase in net rent as the income decile increases. Households in the first income decile spent £24.90 on net rent, compared with £149.80 in the ninth income decile and £240.10 in the tenth income decile. It should be noted, however, that a relatively small number of households in the highest income group paid rent. The estimate of net costs for this income group should therefore be viewed with caution. Average expenditure for mortgages followed a roughly similar pattern to net rent, increasing towards the higher income deciles. The fluctuations in the lower decile groups may be due to a low number of mortgage holders in this decile group, and should be viewed with caution.

Figure 2.12 **Expenditure on net rent and mortgages by renters and mortgage holders by gross income decile group, 2009**

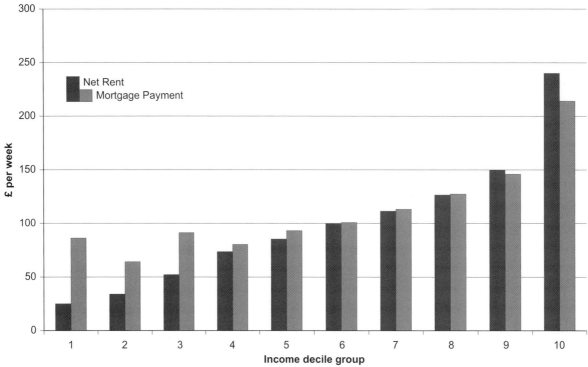

Table 2.11, Figure 2.13, and Figure 2.14 show net rent and mortgage expenditure, respectively, averaged across renters and mortgage holders, by country and Government Office Region.

Figure 2.13 **Expenditure on net rent[1] by UK Countries and GORs, 2009**

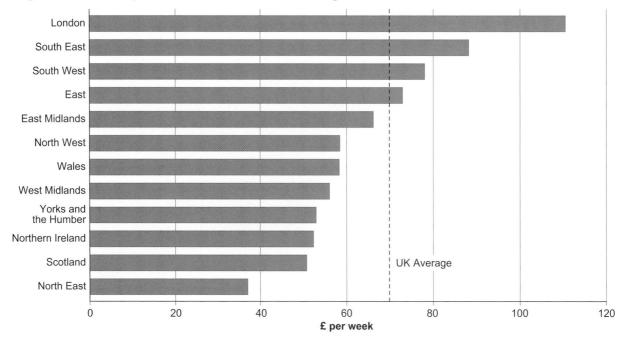

1   Averaged over those households spending on rent.

Figure 2.14 **Expenditure on mortgages[1] by UK Countries and GORs, 2009**

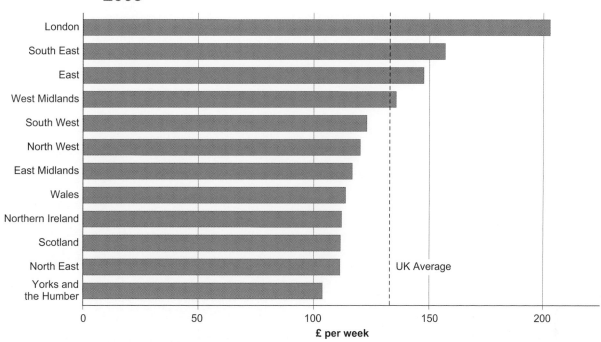

£ per week

1   Averaged over those households spending on mortgages.

Table 2.11 shows the country with the highest average spend on net rent was England, which at £74.10 a week was above the UK average of £70.70. Wales had the next highest average weekly expenditure on net rent at £58.30, followed by Northern Ireland (£52.40) and finally Scotland with the lowest average weekly spend (£50.80).

There were four Government Office regions that had average weekly expenditures on net rent greater than the UK average of £70.70. London spent the most on net rent (£110.50), then the South east (£88.20), followed by the South West (£78.00) and the East (£72.90). All the other regions had average weekly spends lower than the UK average. The region with the lowest average weekly expenditure on net rent was North East (£37.00).

Looking at expenditure on mortgages by country (Table 2.11), England at £137.30 was the only country that had an average weekly expenditure on mortgages greater than the UK average of £133.00 per week. Closely following England was Wales (£113.80), Northern Ireland (£112.00) and finally Scotland (£111.50). The differences between average weekly expenditure by country are much smaller for mortgages compared with net rent.

As with net rent, four regions had a greater average weekly spend on mortgage payments than the UK average (Figure 2.14). London had the highest average spend at £202.80 per week. The next highest regions were the South East (£156.90), the East (£147.60) and the West Midlands (£135.50). The region with the lowest weekly spend was Yorkshire and The Humber at £103.70 per week; roughly £30 a week lower than the UK average.

Table 2.2 **Housing expenditure, 2007 to 2009**

	2007			2008			2009		
	£ per week	% of total expend-iture	% of housing expend-iture	£ per week	% of total expend-iture	% of housing expend-iture	£ per week	% of total expend-iture	% of housing expend-iture
Weighted number of households (thousands)	25,350			25,690			25,980		
Total number of households in sample	6,140			5,850			5,830		
Total number of persons in sample	14,650			13,830			13,740		
Total number of adults in sample	11,220			10,640			10,650		
Weighted average number of persons per household	2.4			2.4			2.3		
Commodity or service	Average weekly household expenditure (£)								
Primary dwelling									
Rent	**31.40**	**5**	**22**	**31.50**	**5**	**22**	**35.40**	**5**	**25**
Gross rent	31.40	5	22	31.50	5	22	35.40	5	25
less housing benefit, rebates and allowances received	11.80	2	8	12.10	2	9	13.70	2	10
Net rent[1]	19.60	3	14	19.40	3	14	21.70	3	16
Mortgage	**53.30**	**8**	**38**	**57.20**	**9**	**40**	**48.70**	**7**	**35**
Mortgage interest payments	35.60	5	25	37.50	6	26	26.70	4	19
Mortgage protection premiums	1.80	0	1	1.90	0	1	1.60	0	1
Capital repayment of mortgage	15.80	2	11	17.80	3	12	20.30	3	15
Outright purchase, including deposits	**[0.20]**	**0**	**0**	**[0.10]**	**0**	**0**	**[4.50]**	**1**	**3**
Secondary dwelling	**6.60**	**1**	**5**	**4.70**	**1**	**3**	**3.60**	**1**	**3**
Rent	[0.00]	0	0	[0.10]	0	0	[0.00]	0	0
Council tax, mortgage, insurance (secondary dwelling)	0.50	0	0	0.50	0	0	1.80	0	1
Purchase of second dwelling	6.10	1	4	4.10	1	3	1.80	0	1
Charges	**25.10**	**4**	**18**	**25.90**	**4**	**18**	**26.50**	**4**	**19**
Council tax, domestic rates	17.90	3	13	18.50	3	13	18.90	3	14
Water charges	6.00	1	4	6.30	1	4	6.50	1	5
Other regular housing payments including service charge for rent	1.20	0	1	1.10	0	1	1.10	0	1
Refuse collection, including skip hire	[0.10]	0	0	[0.10]	0	0	[0.00]	0	0
Moving house	**2.70**	**0**	**2**	**1.80**	**0**	**1**	**1.50**	**0**	**1**
Property transaction – purchase and sale	1.30	0	1	0.90	0	1	0.60	0	0
Property transaction – sale only	0.60	0	0	0.40	0	0	0.40	0	0
Property transaction – purchase only	0.60	0	0	0.30	0	0	0.30	0	0
Property transaction – other payments	0.20	0	0	0.20	0	0	0.20	0	0
Household maintenance and repair	**7.80**	**1**	**6**	**7.20**	**1**	**5**	**6.70**	**1**	**5**
Central heating repairs	1.20	0	1	1.50	0	1	1.30	0	1
House maintenance etc.	4.60	1	3	3.90	1	3	3.70	1	3
Paint, wallpaper, timber	1.20	0	1	0.90	0	1	1.00	0	1
Equipment hire, small materials	0.80	0	1	0.90	0	1	0.70	0	1
Household alterations and improvements	**21.70**	**3**	**15**	**22.10**	**3**	**15**	**21.10**	**3**	**15**
Central heating installation	1.10	0	1	1.20	0	1	0.80	0	1
DIY improvements: double glazing, kitchen units, sheds etc.	1.60	0	1	1.60	0	1	0.90	0	1
Home improvements – contracted out	17.70	3	13	18.10	3	13	18.90	3	14
Bathroom fittings	0.70	0	1	0.50	0	0	0.30	0	0
Purchase of materials for Capital Improvements	0.60	0	0	0.80	0	1	0.30	0	0
Household insurances	**4.90**	**1**	**4**	**5.00**	**1**	**4**	**5.00**	**1**	**4**
Structure	2.40	0	2	2.50	0	2	2.50	0	2
Contents	2.40	0	2	2.50	0	2	2.40	0	2
Household appliances	0.10	0	0	0.10	0	0	0.10	0	0
Housing expenditure	**142.00**	**22**	**100**	**143.40**	**21**	**100**	**139.30**	**21**	**100**
Total expenditure[2]	**656.40**			**674.10**			**653.90**		

Note: Please see page xiii for symbols and conventions used in this report.

1 The figure included in total expenditure is net rent as opposed to gross rent.
2 This total includes all categories recorded in the LCF, including those outside the 'COICOP' total expenditure

ONS, Family Spending 2009, © Crown copyright 2010

Table 2.3 Housing expenditure by gross income decile group, 2009

	Gross income decile group										
	1	2	3	4	5	6	7	8	9	10	All
Weighted number of households (thousands)	2,600	2,600	2,600	2,600	2,600	2,600	2,600	2,600	2,600	2,600	25,980
Total number of households in sample	560	580	600	620	610	600	580	560	560	550	5,830
Total number of persons in sample	700	980	1,210	1,310	1,460	1,440	1,590	1,630	1,680	1,750	13,740
Total number of adults in sample	610	780	930	1,040	1,100	1,140	1,210	1,220	1,280	1,320	10,650
Weighted average number of persons per household	1.3	1.6	2.0	2.1	2.4	2.4	2.7	2.9	3.0	3.1	2.3

Commodity or service	Average weekly household expenditure (£)										
Primary dwelling											
Rent	**66.50**	**54.00**	**46.40**	**40.20**	**33.40**	**27.90**	**21.10**	**22.00**	**21.30**	**21.50**	**35.40**
Gross rent	66.50	54.00	46.40	40.20	33.40	27.90	21.10	22.00	21.30	21.50	35.40
less housing benefit, rebates and allowances received	50.70	36.60	24.50	12.90	8.10	3.30	[0.40]	[0.60]	[0.10]	[0.10]	13.70
Net rent[1]	15.90	17.50	21.90	27.20	25.30	24.60	20.70	21.40	21.10	21.40	21.70
Mortgage	**5.90**	**5.20**	**11.50**	**17.00**	**27.30**	**42.50**	**59.70**	**75.50**	**97.00**	**145.20**	**48.70**
Mortgage interest payments	3.80	2.50	6.40	8.80	14.90	22.50	31.20	41.00	51.10	85.30	26.70
Mortgage protection premiums	[0.10]	[0.10]	0.30	0.70	0.80	1.50	2.30	2.70	3.40	4.10	1.60
Capital repayment of mortgage	1.90	2.60	4.80	7.60	11.60	18.50	26.20	31.90	42.50	55.80	20.30
Outright purchase, including deposits	-	[0.00]	-	-	[40.20]	[0.00]	[0.00]	[4.90]	[0.20]	-	[4.50]
Secondary dwelling	**[0.60]**	-	**[0.10]**	**[0.40]**	**[0.80]**	**[0.20]**	**[1.10]**	**[2.90]**	**6.30**	**23.60**	**3.60**
Rent	-	-	-	-	[0.10]	-	[0.00]	-	[0.00]	[0.20]	[0.00]
Council tax, mortgage, insurance (secondary dwelling)	[0.30]	-	[0.10]	-	[0.40]	[0.20]	[0.60]	[1.30]	[3.40]	[11.70]	1.80
Purchase of second dwelling	[0.30]	-	-	[0.40]	[0.30]	-	[0.50]	[1.60]	[2.80]	11.70	1.80
Charges	**12.10**	**16.60**	**20.70**	**24.40**	**26.00**	**29.00**	**30.10**	**32.20**	**33.70**	**40.10**	**26.50**
Council tax, domestic rates	6.00	9.50	13.50	17.10	18.90	21.20	22.30	23.90	25.50	30.60	18.90
Water charges	5.20	5.60	5.90	6.20	6.30	6.70	6.80	7.30	7.50	7.80	6.50
Other regular housing payments including service charge for rent	0.90	1.50	1.20	1.00	0.80	1.20	0.90	1.00	0.70	1.60	1.10
Refuse collection, including skip hire	-	-	-	[0.10]	[0.00]	-	[0.10]	[0.00]	-	-	[0.00]
Moving house	**[0.30]**	**[0.40]**	**[0.30]**	**[1.60]**	**[0.90]**	**[1.40]**	**[1.20]**	**2.90**	**2.30**	**3.70**	**1.50**
Property transaction – purchase and sale	-	[0.30]	[0.20]	[1.00]	[0.40]	[0.90]	[0.20]	[0.70]	[1.00]	[1.00]	0.60
Property transaction – sale only	[0.20]	-	[0.00]	[0.40]	[0.10]	[0.10]	[0.30]	[0.70]	[0.70]	[1.20]	0.40
Property transaction – purchase only	-	[0.10]	[0.00]	[0.20]	[0.30]	[0.20]	[0.30]	[1.40]	[0.20]	[0.90]	0.30
Property transaction – other payments	[0.10]	[0.00]	[0.00]	[0.10]	[0.10]	[0.20]	[0.40]	[0.20]	[0.40]	[0.60]	0.20
Household maintenance and repair	**1.70**	**3.60**	**4.90**	**5.20**	**5.70**	**6.30**	**6.50**	**8.70**	**8.00**	**16.50**	**6.70**
Central heating repairs	0.20	0.80	1.30	1.10	1.10	1.70	1.30	1.40	1.70	2.50	1.30
House maintenance etc.	1.10	2.10	2.10	2.60	2.80	2.80	2.90	5.60	3.80	10.90	3.70
Paint, wallpaper, timber	0.10	0.40	1.00	1.00	1.00	1.20	1.00	1.00	1.40	2.00	1.00
Equipment hire, small materials	[0.30]	0.30	0.40	0.40	0.80	0.70	1.20	0.70	1.10	1.10	0.70
Household alterations and improvements	**2.00**	**5.60**	**7.60**	**10.50**	**8.30**	**19.20**	**16.30**	**20.90**	**29.70**	**91.30**	**21.10**
Central heating installation	[0.00]	[0.30]	[0.20]	[1.20]	[0.80]	[0.40]	[1.00]	[1.20]	[1.00]	[1.80]	0.80
DIY improvements: double glazing, kitchen units, sheds etc.	[0.10]	[0.30]	[0.10]	[1.30]	[0.20]	[1.30]	[0.60]	[0.40]	[2.50]	[1.80]	0.90
Home improvements – contracted out	[1.80]	4.90	6.30	7.70	6.80	16.20	14.10	18.70	26.00	86.70	18.90
Bathroom fittings	[0.00]	[0.10]	[0.20]	[0.10]	[0.20]	[0.80]	[0.40]	[0.20]	[0.20]	[0.60]	0.30
Purchase of materials for capital improvements	[0.10]	[0.00]	[0.80]	[0.30]	[0.40]	[0.40]	[0.20]	[0.40]	[0.00]	[0.40]	0.30
Household insurances	**1.90**	**2.80**	**3.60**	**3.90**	**4.60**	**5.00**	**5.50**	**6.10**	**6.90**	**9.50**	**5.00**
Structure	0.90	1.30	1.70	1.90	2.20	2.50	2.70	3.10	3.40	5.00	2.50
Contents	1.00	1.50	1.90	1.90	2.30	2.40	2.70	2.80	3.20	4.40	2.40
Household appliances	[0.00]	[0.00]	[0.10]	[0.00]	[0.10]	[0.00]	[0.10]	[0.20]	0.30	[0.10]	0.10
Housing expenditure	**40.40**	**51.60**	**70.40**	**90.20**	**138.90**	**128.30**	**141.20**	**175.60**	**205.20**	**351.30**	**139.30**
Total expenditure[2]	**172.20**	**231.30**	**314.50**	**390.20**	**511.10**	**572.60**	**691.60**	**829.30**	**1028.90**	**1798.10**	**653.90**

Note: Please see page xiii for symbols and conventions used in this report.

1 The figure included in total expenditure is net rent as opposed to gross rent.

2 This total includes all categories recorded in the LCF, including those outside the 'COICOP' total expenditure.

ONS, Family Spending 2009, © Crown copyright 2010

Table 2.4   **Housing expenditure by age of household reference person, 2009**

	Under 30	30 to 49	50 to 64	65 to 74	75 or over	All
Weighted number of households (thousands)	2,770	9,670	6,740	3,310	3,500	25,980
Total number of households in sample	510	2,110	1,640	820	730	5,830
Total number of persons in sample	1,280	6,320	3,590	1,450	1,100	13,740
Total number of adults in sample	920	3,930	3,280	1,420	1,100	10,650
Weighted average number of persons per household	2.4	2.9	2.2	1.8	1.4	2.3
Commodity or service	Average weekly household expenditure (£)					
Primary dwelling						
Rent	**93.90**	**38.90**	**20.60**	**19.90**	**22.90**	**35.40**
Gross rent	93.90	38.90	20.60	19.90	22.90	35.40
less housing benefit, rebates and allowances received	21.90	13.40	10.90	12.00	15.40	13.70
Net rent[1]	72.00	25.50	9.70	7.90	7.50	21.70
Mortgage	**39.30**	**89.30**	**40.50**	**5.30**	**0.40**	**48.70**
Mortgage interest payments	24.10	50.20	19.60	2.90	[0.20]	26.70
Mortgage protection premiums	1.40	3.10	1.10	[0.10]	[0.00]	1.60
Capital repayment of mortgage	13.80	36.00	19.80	2.40	[0.20]	20.30
Outright purchase, including deposits	**[0.00]**	**[0.10]**	**[1.90]**	**-**	**[29.80]**	**[4.50]**
Secondary dwelling	**[1.50]**	**7.30**	**2.60**	**[0.40]**	**[0.00]**	**3.60**
Rent	-	[0.10]	[0.00]	-	[0.00]	[0.00]
Council tax, mortgage, insurance (secondary dwelling)	[0.10]	3.70	1.40	[0.30]	[0.00]	1.80
Purchase of second dwelling	[1.50]	3.40	[1.20]	[0.10]	-	1.80
Charges	**21.70**	**28.00**	**28.40**	**25.90**	**23.00**	**26.50**
Council tax, domestic rates	14.40	20.10	20.60	18.80	15.70	18.90
Water charges	6.20	6.90	6.70	6.10	5.70	6.50
Other regular housing payments including service charge for rent	1.10	0.90	1.00	1.00	1.60	1.10
Refuse collection, including skip hire	-	[0.00]	[0.00]	[0.00]	[0.00]	[0.00]
Moving house	**1.80**	**2.00**	**1.50**	**[0.40]**	**[1.00]**	**1.50**
Property transaction – purchase and sale	[0.90]	0.60	[0.40]	[0.30]	[0.70]	0.60
Property transaction – sale only	-	[0.60]	[0.50]	[0.00]	[0.20]	0.40
Property transaction – purchase only	[0.60]	0.30	[0.50]	[0.00]	[0.10]	0.30
Property transaction – other payments	0.40	0.40	0.10	[0.10]	[0.00]	0.20
Household maintenance and repair	**2.30**	**7.00**	**8.30**	**6.90**	**6.30**	**6.70**
Central heating repairs	0.20	1.10	1.80	1.90	1.30	1.30
House maintenance etc.	1.40	4.00	3.90	3.50	4.20	3.70
Paint, wallpaper, timber	0.50	1.00	1.50	0.90	0.50	1.00
Equipment hire, small materials	0.20	0.80	1.10	0.50	0.30	0.70
Household alterations and improvements	**5.60**	**30.50**	**23.40**	**16.90**	**7.20**	**21.10**
Central heating installation	[0.50]	0.90	0.90	[0.60]	[0.60]	0.80
DIY improvements: double glazing, kitchen units, sheds etc.	[0.10]	0.80	1.50	[1.10]	[0.10]	0.90
Home improvements – contracted out	4.70	28.20	20.00	15.00	6.20	18.90
Bathroom fittings	[0.30]	0.30	0.30	[0.10]	[0.00]	0.30
Purchase of materials for capital improvements	[0.00]	[0.20]	[0.70]	[0.00]	[0.20]	0.30
Household insurances	**2.30**	**5.40**	**5.80**	**4.80**	**4.50**	**5.00**
Structure	1.00	2.70	2.90	2.40	2.20	2.50
Contents	1.30	2.60	2.70	2.40	2.20	2.40
Household appliances	[0.10]	0.10	0.20	[0.00]	[0.10]	0.10
Housing expenditure	**146.60**	**195.00**	**122.10**	**68.60**	**79.80**	**139.30**
Total expenditure[2]	**571.30**	**850.20**	**710.20**	**408.30**	**301.00**	**653.90**

Note: Please see page xiii for symbols and conventions used in this report.

1 The figure included in total expenditure is net rent as opposed to gross rent.

2 This total includes all categories recorded in the LCF, including those outside the 'COICOP' total expenditure.

ONS, Family Spending 2009, © Crown copyright 2010

Table 2.5   **Household expenditure by UK Countries and Government Office Region, 2009**

	North East	North West	Yorks& the Humber	East Midlands	West Midlands	East	London
Grossed number of households (thousands)	1,390	3,230	2,130	2,010	2,180	2,190	3,030
Total number of households in sample	240	580	480	390	530	500	460
Total number of persons in sample	500	1,340	1,120	910	1,310	1,150	1,120
Total number of adults in sample	410	1,050	870	720	1,010	890	840
Weighted average number of persons per household	2.2	2.4	2.2	2.4	2.4	2.2	2.5

Commodity or service	Average weekly household expenditure (£)						
Primary dwelling							
Rent	**30.70**	**33.10**	**27.20**	**28.90**	**29.50**	**29.40**	**75.90**
Gross rent	30.70	33.10	27.20	28.90	29.50	29.40	75.90
less housing benefit, rebates and allowances received	18.20	14.70	12.00	10.00	13.40	10.60	25.40
Net rent[1]	12.50	18.50	15.20	18.90	16.00	18.70	50.60
Mortgage	**41.60**	**40.30**	**39.40**	**44.90**	**46.60**	**62.90**	**59.40**
Mortgage interest payments	19.90	22.00	19.70	23.10	22.90	35.90	37.50
Mortgage protection premiums	1.20	0.90	1.50	1.80	1.80	1.50	2.20
Capital repayment of mortgage	20.50	17.50	18.10	20.00	21.90	25.40	19.70
Outright purchase, including deposits	**[0.10]**	**-**	**[0.00]**	**-**	**-**	**[5.80]**	**-**
Secondary dwelling	**[0.70]**	**[1.50]**	**[0.60]**	**[3.60]**	**[2.30]**	**[2.70]**	**[4.00]**
Rent	-	-	[0.00]	[0.10]	-	-	-
Council tax, mortgage, insurance (secondary dwelling)	[0.70]	[0.90]	[0.30]	-	[0.60]	[1.00]	[1.20]
Purchase of second dwelling	-	[0.60]	[0.30]	[3.60]	[1.70]	[1.70]	[2.70]
Charges	**21.80**	**26.60**	**23.80**	**25.60**	**24.80**	**28.10**	**30.20**
Council tax, domestic rates	15.30	18.10	16.70	18.80	18.00	20.30	20.50
Water charges	6.00	7.50	6.70	6.40	6.20	6.80	6.10
Other regular housing payments including service charge for rent	[0.50]	0.90	0.40	[0.30]	0.40	1.00	3.60
Refuse collection, including skip hire	-	[0.10]	-	-	[0.10]	[0.00]	[0.00]
Moving house	**[0.60]**	**[1.00]**	**[0.30]**	**[1.70]**	**[1.10]**	**[2.30]**	**[3.00]**
Property transaction – purchase and sale	[0.00]	[0.20]	[0.30]	[0.30]	[0.60]	[1.50]	[0.60]
Property transaction – sale only	[0.40]	[0.40]	[0.00]	[0.60]	-	[0.30]	[0.70]
Property transaction – purchase only	[0.10]	[0.30]	[0.00]	[0.70]	[0.30]	[0.10]	[1.20]
Property transaction – other payments	-	[0.10]	[0.00]	[0.10]	[0.10]	[0.40]	[0.60]
Household maintenance and repair	**5.20**	**4.70**	**4.10**	**5.50**	**8.30**	**7.80**	**7.20**
Central heating repairs	0.80	0.90	0.60	1.20	1.80	1.70	1.40
House maintenance etc.	2.60	2.40	2.10	3.00	4.40	3.70	4.40
Paint, wallpaper, timber	[1.20]	0.70	1.10	0.80	1.00	1.20	1.10
Equipment hire, small materials	[0.60]	0.60	0.30	0.50	1.00	1.30	[0.30]
Household alterations and improvements	**12.00**	**16.70**	**12.20**	**14.30**	**25.60**	**23.60**	**39.40**
Central heating installation	[0.60]	[0.40]	[1.00]	[0.90]	[1.00]	[0.50]	[0.90]
DIY improvements: double glazing, kitchen units, sheds etc.	[4.60]	[0.60]	[1.90]	[1.60]	[0.80]	[0.40]	[0.40]
Home improvements – contracted out	6.20	15.20	9.00	11.30	23.20	22.20	37.30
Bathroom fittings	[0.50]	[0.30]	[0.20]	[0.20]	[0.20]	[0.40]	[0.20]
Purchase of materials for Capital Improvements	[0.20]	[0.10]	[0.00]	[0.40]	[0.40]	[0.20]	[0.60]
Household insurances	**4.30**	**4.80**	**4.60**	**4.90**	**5.00**	**5.30**	**5.70**
Structure	2.20	2.40	2.40	2.40	2.50	2.70	2.70
Contents	2.00	2.30	2.20	2.40	2.40	2.30	2.90
Household appliances	[0.00]	[0.10]	[0.00]	[0.10]	[0.10]	[0.20]	[0.10]
Housing expenditure	**98.80**	**114.00**	**100.20**	**119.50**	**129.80**	**157.30**	**199.30**
Total expenditure[2]	**500.10**	**598.40**	**510.80**	**600.50**	**611.60**	**678.90**	**853.10**

Please see page xiii for symbols and conventions used in this report.

1   The figure included in total expenditure is net rent as opposed to gross rent.

2   This total includes all categories recorded in the LCF, including those outside the 'COICOP' total expenditure.

ONS, Family Spending 2009, © Crown copyright 2010

Table 2.5   **Household expenditure by UK Countries and Government Office Region, 2009 (cont.)**

	South East	South West	England	Wales	Scotland	Northern Ireland	United Kingdom
Weighted number of households (thousands)	2,820	2,660	21,640	1,290	2,370	680	25,980
Total number of households in sample	700	520	4,410	270	540	600	5,830
Total number of persons in sample	1,710	1,170	10,330	610	1,230	1,570	13,740
Total number of adults in sample	1,310	920	8,020	500	960	1,170	10,650
Weighted average number of persons per household	2.4	2.3	2.4	2.3	2.2	2.6	2.3

Commodity or service	Average weekly household expenditure (£)						
Primary dwelling							
Rent	**32.30**	**33.60**	**37.20**	**25.60**	**27.00**	**27.80**	**35.40**
Gross rent	32.30	33.60	37.20	25.60	27.00	27.80	35.40
less housing benefit, rebates and allowances received	10.70	11.80	14.30	10.70	11.00	11.10	13.70
Net rent[1]	21.70	21.70	22.90	14.90	16.00	16.70	21.70
Mortgage	**65.00**	**44.00**	**50.00**	**38.10**	**45.30**	**38.80**	**48.70**
Mortgage interest payments	36.40	25.10	27.70	19.20	24.20	20.20	26.70
Mortgage protection premiums	1.80	1.50	1.60	1.00	1.80	2.10	1.60
Capital repayment of mortgage	26.70	17.40	20.70	17.90	19.40	16.40	20.30
Outright purchase, including deposits	**[37.20]**	**-**	**[5.40]**	**[0.10]**	**[0.00]**	**[0.00]**	**[4.50]**
Secondary dwelling	**[3.00]**	**[6.50]**	**2.90**	**[0.30]**	**[11.90]**	**[2.00]**	**3.60**
Rent	[0.20]	[0.10]	[0.00]	-	[0.00]	-	[0.00]
Council tax, mortgage, insurance (secondary dwelling)	[0.80]	[1.70]	0.90	[0.30]	[11.40]	[0.60]	1.80
Purchase of second dwelling	[2.00]	[4.80]	2.00	-	[0.40]	[1.40]	1.80
Charges	**30.60**	**28.70**	**27.20**	**22.90**	**26.40**	**11.10**	**26.50**
Council tax, domestic rates	22.40	20.40	19.20	15.50	19.50	10.70	18.90
Water charges	6.80	7.50	6.70	7.30	6.10	-	6.50
Other regular housing payments including service charge for rent	1.40	0.80	1.20	[0.20]	0.70	0.30	1.10
Refuse collection, including skip hire	-	[0.00]	[0.00]	-	[0.00]	-	[0.00]
Moving house	**2.60**	**[1.30]**	**1.60**	**[0.60]**	**[1.00]**	**[0.10]**	**1.50**
Property transaction - purchase and sale	[1.70]	[0.10]	0.60	[0.20]	[0.40]	-	0.60
Property transaction - sale only	[0.30]	[1.00]	0.40	[0.20]	[0.00]	-	0.40
Property transaction - purchase only	[0.20]	[0.10]	0.40	[0.10]	[0.30]	[0.00]	0.30
Property transaction - other payments	[0.50]	[0.10]	0.20	[0.00]	[0.20]	[0.10]	0.20
Household maintenance and repair	**7.90**	**8.70**	**6.70**	**10.30**	**5.20**	**6.10**	**6.70**
Central heating repairs	2.00	1.20	1.30	1.60	1.20	0.50	1.30
House maintenance etc.	4.00	5.60	3.60	7.00	2.30	3.30	3.70
Paint, wallpaper, timber	1.10	0.80	1.00	[1.10]	1.20	1.60	1.00
Equipment hire, small materials	0.80	1.10	0.70	0.60	0.50	0.60	0.70
Household alterations and improvements	**25.30**	**20.00**	**22.00**	**17.60**	**17.30**	**12.60**	**21.10**
Central heating installation	[1.40]	[0.40]	0.80	[0.60]	[1.10]	[0.20]	0.80
DIY improvements: double glazing, kitchen units, sheds etc.	[0.30]	[0.40]	1.00	[0.20]	[0.30]	[1.00]	0.90
Home improvements - contracted out	22.90	18.80	19.70	16.60	15.70	9.80	18.90
Bathroom fittings	[0.50]	[0.30]	0.30	[0.20]	[0.10]	[0.10]	0.30
Purchase of materials for Capital Improvements	[0.30]	[0.20]	0.30	[0.00]	[0.20]	[1.50]	0.30
Household insurances	**5.30**	**4.90**	**5.00**	**5.00**	**4.80**	**4.00**	**5.00**
Structure	2.70	2.40	2.50	2.50	2.30	1.90	2.50
Contents	2.50	2.40	2.40	2.40	2.40	2.10	2.40
Household appliances	[0.10]	[0.10]	0.10	[0.00]	[0.10]	[0.00]	0.10
Housing expenditure	**198.70**	**135.90**	**143.80**	**109.90**	**127.90**	**91.30**	**139.30**
Total expenditure[2]	**839.40**	**624.60**	**663.40**	**519.00**	**651.20**	**617.30**	**653.90**

Please see page xiii for symbols and conventions used in this report.

1   The figure included in total expenditure is net rent as opposed to gross rent.

2   This total includes all categories recorded in the LCF, including those outside the 'COICOP' total expenditure.

ONS, Family Spending 2009,   © Crown copyright 2010

Table 2.6 Housing expenditure by socio-economic classification of household reference person, 2009

	Large employers & higher managerial	Higher professional	Lower managerial & professional	Intermediate	Small employers	Lower supervisory
Weighted number of households (thousands)	1,200	1,700	4,900	1,520	1,460	1,740
Total number of households in sample	260	370	1,050	360	340	370
Total number of persons in sample	770	990	2,760	860	950	1,010
Total number of adults in sample	540	720	2,060	640	690	760
Weighted average number of persons per household	2.9	2.6	2.6	2.4	2.8	2.7
Commodity or service	Average weekly household expenditure (£)					
Primary dwelling						
Rent	**12.90**	**34.30**	**26.90**	**35.80**	**23.20**	**27.70**
Gross rent	[12.90]	34.30	26.90	35.80	23.20	27.70
less housing benefit, rebates and allowances received	[0.20]	[0.50]	1.80	6.40	3.90	4.70
Net rent[3]	[12.80]	33.90	25.10	29.40	19.40	22.90
Mortgage	**137.50**	**112.00**	**85.80**	**56.00**	**68.50**	**62.90**
Mortgage interest payments	77.90	67.90	46.90	29.60	38.20	30.30
Mortgage protection premiums	4.10	2.40	3.00	1.90	2.60	2.60
Capital repayment of mortgage	55.50	41.70	36.00	24.50	27.70	30.00
Outright purchase, including deposits	**[0.30]**	**-**	**[2.60]**	**-**	**[0.10]**	**[0.10]**
Secondary dwelling	**[31.10]**	**10.90**	**4.60**	**[1.00]**	**[4.00]**	**[0.80]**
Rent	[0.00]	-	[0.10]	-	[0.10]	-
Council tax, mortgage, insurance (secondary dwelling)	[25.20]	[1.90]	[1.10]	[0.20]	[1.90]	[0.50]
Purchase of second dwelling	[5.90]	[9.00]	3.40	[0.80]	[2.00]	[0.30]
Charges	**37.50**	**34.90**	**31.10**	**27.90**	**30.80**	**27.80**
Council tax, domestic rates	27.10	26.70	23.20	20.50	22.40	20.70
Water charges	7.90	7.20	7.00	6.60	6.80	6.70
Other regular housing payments including service charge for rent	2.40	0.90	0.90	0.80	1.70	0.50
Refuse collection, including skip hire	[0.20]	-	[0.00]	-	-	-
Moving house	**[3.00]**	**4.70**	**2.10**	**[0.80]**	**[1.70]**	**[1.80]**
Property transaction – purchase and sale	[1.00]	[1.30]	[0.60]	[0.30]	[0.40]	[1.10]
Property transaction – sale only	[0.60]	[0.60]	[0.60]	[0.10]	[0.80]	[0.30]
Property transaction – purchase only	[0.50]	[2.30]	0.50	[0.20]	[0.10]	[0.30]
Property transaction – other payments	[0.90]	[0.40]	0.40	[0.20]	[0.40]	[0.20]
Household maintenance and repair	**14.10**	**8.70**	**9.50**	**5.70**	**7.00**	**5.70**
Central heating repairs	1.60	1.90	1.70	1.50	1.40	1.00
House maintenance etc.	8.50	5.70	5.20	3.00	3.90	2.00
Paint, wallpaper, timber	2.00	0.90	1.40	0.90	1.00	1.30
Equipment hire, small materials	2.00	[0.20]	1.20	[0.40]	0.70	1.30
Household alterations and improvements	**71.60**	**32.00**	**26.00**	**20.40**	**61.10**	**13.10**
Central heating installation	[1.20]	[1.40]	1.30	[1.50]	[0.70]	[0.80]
DIY improvements: double glazing, kitchen units, sheds etc.	[5.30]	[0.30]	[0.70]	[0.20]	[1.90]	[0.60]
Home improvements – contracted out	64.90	30.10	22.60	18.60	58.10	10.90
Bathroom fittings	[0.10]	[0.20]	0.70	[0.00]	[0.30]	[0.40]
Purchase of materials for capital improvements	[0.20]	[0.00]	[0.70]	[0.10]	[0.10]	[0.40]
Household insurances	**8.20**	**7.50**	**6.10**	**5.10**	**5.80**	**5.20**
Structure	4.30	3.70	3.10	2.60	3.00	2.50
Contents	3.80	3.50	2.90	2.50	2.80	2.60
Household appliances	[0.00]	[0.20]	0.20	[0.10]	[0.10]	[0.10]
Housing expenditure	**316.20**	**244.50**	**193.00**	**146.40**	**198.40**	**140.40**
Total expenditure[4]	**1,580.80**	**1,195.10**	**924.00**	**655.90**	**722.00**	**690.10**

Please see page xiii for symbols and conventions used in this report.

1 Includes those who have never worked.

2 Includes those who are economically inactive.

3 The figure included in total expenditure is net rent as opposed to gross rent.

4 This total includes all categories recorded in the LCF, including those outside the 'COICOP' total expenditure.

ONS, Family Spending 2009, © Crown copyright 2010

Table 2.6 Housing expenditure by socio-economic classification of household reference person, 2009 (cont.)

	Semi-routine	Routine	Long-term unemployed[1]	Students	Occupation not stated[2] & not classifiable	All groups
Weighted number of households (thousands)	1,990	1,470	510	470	9,000	25,980
Total number of households in sample	450	330	120	90	2,100	5,830
Total number of persons in sample	1,190	900	320	210	3,780	13,740
Total number of adults in sample	860	670	170	170	3,380	10,650
Weighted average number of persons per household	2.6	2.7	2.9	2.5	1.8	2.3
Commodity or service	Average weekly household expenditure (£)					
Primary dwelling						
Rent	**47.90**	**43.20**	**108.70**	**105.70**	**34.80**	**35.40**
Gross rent	47.90	43.20	108.70	105.70	34.80	35.40
less housing benefit, rebates and allowances received	13.40	9.10	87.10	15.60	25.70	13.70
Net rent[3]	34.50	34.10	21.60	90.10	9.20	21.70
Mortgage	**34.70**	**41.70**	**3.80**	**37.00**	**4.80**	**48.70**
Mortgage interest payments	17.80	21.60	[3.30]	22.80	2.50	26.70
Mortgage protection premiums	1.10	2.10	[0.10]	[1.60]	0.00	1.60
Capital repayment of mortgage	15.80	18.00	[0.40]	[12.60]	2.30	20.30
Outright purchase, including deposits	**[0.10]**	-	-	-	**[11.60]**	**[4.50]**
Secondary dwelling	**[0.70]**	**[1.10]**	-	**[3.20]**	**[0.20]**	**3.60**
Rent	-	-	-	-	[0.00]	[0.00]
Council tax, mortgage, insurance (secondary dwelling)	[0.60]	[0.00]	-	[1.80]	[0.20]	1.80
Purchase of second dwelling	[0.10]	[1.10]	-	[1.40]	-	1.80
Charges	**25.10**	**25.30**	**9.20**	**15.90**	**21.70**	**26.50**
Council tax, domestic rates	17.40	17.80	2.90	9.20	14.60	18.90
Water charges	6.70	6.30	5.80	5.40	6.00	6.50
Other regular housing payments including service charge for rent	1.00	1.10	[0.40]	[1.20]	1.10	1.10
Refuse collection, including skip hire	[0.00]	-	-	-	[0.00]	[0.00]
Moving house	**[0.80]**	**[0.80]**	**[1.20]**	**[0.10]**	**0.80**	**1.50**
Property transaction – purchase and sale	[0.10]	[0.80]	-	-	[0.40]	0.60
Property transaction – sale only	[0.30]	-	[1.20]	-	[0.20]	0.40
Property transaction – purchase only	[0.30]	[0.00]	-	[0.00]	[0.10]	0.30
Property transaction – other payments	[0.10]	[0.00]	-	[0.10]	[0.00]	0.20
Household maintenance and repair	**3.30**	**3.50**	**3.30**	**[1.20]**	**[5.90]**	**6.70**
Central heating repairs	0.70	0.60	0.00	[0.20]	[1.30]	1.30
House maintenance etc.	1.40	1.20	3.10	[0.30]	[3.30]	3.70
Paint, wallpaper, timber	0.70	1.10	0.20	[0.40]	[0.80]	1.00
Equipment hire, small materials	0.50	0.50	0.00	[0.30]	[0.50]	0.70
Household alterations and improvements	**10.30**	**9.60**	**4.00**	**1.30**	**11.20**	**21.10**
Central heating installation	[0.30]	[0.70]	[0.00]	[0.20]	0.50	0.80
DIY improvements: double glazing, kitchen units, sheds etc.	[0.60]	[1.20]	-	-	0.50	0.90
Home improvements – contracted out	[9.00]	[6.50]	4.00	0.40	10.00	18.90
Bathroom fittings	[0.10]	[0.60]	-	-	0.10	0.30
Purchase of materials for capital improvements	[0.30]	[0.60]	-	[0.70]	[0.10]	0.30
Household insurances	**3.70**	**3.90**	**0.90**	**1.80**	**4.10**	**5.00**
Structure	1.80	1.90	[0.40]	[0.70]	2.00	2.50
Contents	1.90	1.90	0.60	1.10	2.00	2.40
Household appliances	[0.00]	[0.10]	[0.00]	[0.00]	0.00	0.10
Housing expenditure	**113.30**	**119.90**	**44.00**	**150.50**	**69.40**	**139.30**
Total expenditure[4]	**525.20**	**526.90**	**219.30**	**596.30**	**339.50**	**653.90**

Please see page xiii for symbols and conventions used in this report.

1 Includes those who have never worked.

2 Includes those who are economically inactive.

3 The figure included in total expenditure is net rent as opposed to gross rent.

4 This total includes all categories recorded in the LCF, including those outside the 'COICOP' total expenditure.

ONS, Family Spending 2009, © Crown copyright 2010

Table 2.7 Housing expenditure by household composition, 2009

| | Retired households | | Non-retired | | Retired and non-retired households | | | |
| | One Person | Two adults | One Person | Two adults | One adult with children | Two adults with children | Three or more adults | |
							without children	with children
Weighted number of households (thousands)	3,520	2,800	4,000	5,790	1,290	5,140	2,320	1,130
Total number of households in sample	730	730	870	1,270	340	1,190	470	240
Total number of persons in sample	730	1,450	870	2,540	930	4,520	1,560	1,140
Total number of adults in sample	730	1,450	870	2,540	340	2,370	1,560	790
Weighted average number of persons per household	1.0	2.0	1.0	2.0	2.7	3.8	3.4	4.8

Commodity or service	Average weekly household expenditure (£)							
Primary dwelling								
Rent	**31.30**	**13.60**	**44.80**	**33.40**	**84.00**	**33.20**	**34.60**	**36.10**
Gross rent	31.30	13.60	44.80	33.40	84.00	33.20	34.60	36.10
less housing benefit, rebates & allowances received	21.40	8.40	19.80	4.50	52.60	10.50	6.50	14.00
Net rent[1]	9.80	5.20	25.10	28.90	31.40	22.70	28.20	22.10
Mortgage	**1.00**	**3.40**	**37.10**	**58.90**	**32.10**	**99.60**	**49.20**	**83.90**
Mortgage interest payments	0.60	1.40	20.90	32.60	18.60	55.40	24.10	45.80
Mortgage protection premiums	-	[0.00]	1.00	2.00	1.00	3.40	1.70	2.80
Capital repayment of mortgage	[0.40]	2.00	15.20	24.30	12.60	40.80	23.40	35.40
Outright purchase, including deposits	**[29.60]**	**-**	**[0.00]**	**[2.20]**	**-**	**[0.10]**	**[0.10]**	**-**
Secondary dwelling	**0.00**	**0.60**	**8.30**	**5.20**	**0.60**	**3.20**	**4.10**	**1.00**
Rent	-	[0.00]	[0.00]	[0.00]	[0.00]	[0.00]	-	[0.40]
Council tax, mortgage, insurance (secondary dwelling)	-	[0.60]	[7.30]	[1.30]	-	[1.10]	[1.20]	[0.00]
Purchase of second dwelling	-	-	[1.00]	3.90	[0.60]	[2.10]	[2.90]	[0.60]
Charges	**18.70**	**28.70**	**19.60**	**30.20**	**17.40**	**31.50**	**30.80**	**28.90**
Council tax, domestic rates	12.00	21.30	12.70	22.30	10.40	23.00	22.60	21.40
Water charges	5.00	6.70	5.20	6.80	6.80	7.60	7.40	7.50
Other regular housing payments including service charge for rent	1.70	0.70	1.70	1.10	[0.20]	0.80	0.80	[0.10]
Refuse collection, including skip hire	[0.00]	[0.00]	-	[0.00]	-	[0.10]	[0.00]	-
Moving house	**0.70**	**0.40**	**1.20**	**2.40**	**1.50**	**1.90**	**2.30**	**0.10**
Property transaction – purchase and sale	[0.40]	[0.30]	[0.20]	1.00	[0.60]	[0.60]	[0.90]	-
Property transaction – sale only	[0.20]	[0.10]	[0.30]	[0.40]	[0.60]	[0.80]	[0.30]	-
Property transaction – purchase only	[0.00]	[0.00]	[0.20]	0.60	[0.20]	[0.30]	[1.10]	-
Property transaction – other payments	[0.00]	[0.00]	0.50	0.30	[0.10]	0.30	[0.00]	[0.10]
Household maintenance and repair	**5.00**	**9.00**	**4.30**	**7.00**	**2.20**	**8.30**	**8.10**	**8.30**
Central heating repairs	1.10	2.20	0.80	1.50	0.40	1.10	1.80	1.90
House maintenance etc.	3.30	4.90	2.70	3.30	1.10	4.90	3.80	4.10
Paint, wallpaper, timber	0.40	1.30	0.30	1.30	0.30	1.20	1.50	2.10
Equipment hire, small materials	0.20	0.70	0.50	0.90	[0.30]	1.10	1.00	[0.20]
Household alterations and improvements	**6.30**	**14.90**	**8.30**	**22.70**	**4.00**	**35.20**	**24.10**	**69.70**
Central heating installation	[0.60]	[0.60]	[0.40]	1.10	[0.10]	1.10	[0.90]	[1.10]
DIY improvements: double glazing, kitchen units, sheds etc.	[0.10]	[1.30]	[0.40]	1.10	[0.00]	0.50	[2.30]	[2.20]
Home improvements – contracted out	5.50	12.70	6.70	19.50	[3.70]	33.00	20.70	65.30
Bathroom fittings	[0.00]	[0.10]	[0.70]	0.20	[0.10]	[0.20]	[0.20]	[0.90]
Purchase of materials for capital improvements	[0.10]	[0.20]	[0.10]	[0.80]	-	[0.20]	[0.10]	[0.20]
Household insurances	**3.80**	**5.30**	**3.60**	**5.50**	**2.80**	**5.80**	**5.90**	**6.60**
Structure	1.80	2.70	1.70	2.70	1.20	3.00	3.00	3.50
Contents	2.00	2.50	1.80	2.70	1.60	2.80	2.80	3.00
Household appliances	[0.00]	[0.00]	[0.00]	0.20	[0.10]	0.10	[0.10]	[0.00]
Housing expenditure	**74.90**	**67.60**	**107.40**	**163.00**	**92.00**	**208.30**	**152.80**	**220.60**
Total expenditure[2]	**247.40**	**407.20**	**445.70**	**794.00**	**385.70**	**926.40**	**929.10**	**1048.60**

Note: Please see page xiii for symbols and conventions used in this report.

1 The figure included in total expenditure is net rent as opposed to gross rent.

2 This total includes all categories recorded in the LCF, including those outside the 'COICOP' total expenditure.

ONS, Family Spending 2009, © Crown copyright 2010

Table 2.8   Expenditure on rent[1] by renters, 2007 to 2009

	2007		2008		2009	
	£[2]	% of total expenditure	£[2]	% of total expenditure	£[2]	% of total expenditure
Weighted number of households (thousands)	7,660		7,520		7,980	
Total number of households in sample	1,780		1,610		1,680	
Total number of persons in sample	4,050		3,610		3,780	
Total number of adults in sample	2,920		2,570		2,710	
Weighted average number of persons per household	2.3		2.3		2.2	
Total expenditure for renters	**396.50**		**420.90**		**412.20**	
Rent	**103.80**	**26.2**	**107.70**	**25.6**	**115.40**	**28.0**
Gross rent	103.80	26.2	107.70	25.6	115.40	28.0
less housing benefit, rebates and allowances received	38.90	9.8	41.50	9.9	44.70	10.8
Net rent[3]	64.90	16.4	66.30	15.7	70.70	17.2

Note: Please see page xiii for symbols and conventions used in this report.

1   Primary dwelling.

2   Average weekly household expenditure (£).

3   The figure included in total expenditure is net rent as opposed to gross rent.

ONS, Family Spending 2009, © Crown copyright 2010

Table 2.9 **Expenditure on mortgages[1] by mortgage holders, 2007 to 2009**

	2007		2008		2009	
	£[2]	% of total expenditure	£[2]	% of total expenditure	£[2]	% of total expenditure
Weighted number of households (thousands)	9,680		9,830		9,460	
Total number of households in sample	2,330		2,210		2,100	
Total number of persons in sample	6,680		6,330		5,960	
Total number of adults in sample	4,670		4,450		4,210	
Weighted average number of persons per household	2.8		2.8		2.8	
Total expenditure for mortgage payers	**971.60**		**985.30**		**941.30**	
Mortgage	138.80	14.3	148.50	15.1	133.00	14.1
Mortgage interest payments	92.80	9.5	97.40	9.9	73.00	7.8
Mortgage protection premiums	4.80	0.5	4.80	0.5	4.40	0.5
Capital repayment of mortgage	41.20	4.2	46.30	4.7	55.60	5.9

Note: Please see page xiii for symbols and conventions used in this report.

1   Primary dwelling.

2   Average weekly household expenditure (£).

ONS, Family Spending 2009, © Crown copyright 2010

Table 2.10 Expenditure on rent and mortgages[1] by renters and mortgage holders by gross income decile group, 2009

	Gross income decile group										
	1	2	3	4	5	6	7	8	9	10	All
Weighted number of households (thousands)	1,660	1,340	1,090	960	770	640	480	440	370	230	7,980
Total number of households in sample	360	300	240	210	160	140	100	80	70	30	1,680
Total number of persons in sample	470	580	600	520	480	380	260	230	190	100	3,780
Total number of adults in sample	390	400	380	360	310	270	200	170	150	80	2,710
Weighted average number of persons per household	1.3	1.8	2.5	2.5	3.0	2.7	2.6	2.7	2.7	2.9	2.2

Commodity or service	Average weekly household expenditure (£)										
Rent for renters	**104.30**	**105.00**	**110.70**	**108.60**	**113.00**	**113.10**	**113.50**	**130.40**	**150.70**	**240.90**	**115.40**
Gross rent	104.30	105.00	110.70	108.60	112.60	113.10	113.50	130.40	150.70	240.90	115.40
less housing benefit, rebates and allowances received	79.40	71.00	58.50	35.00	27.30	13.40	[2.00]	[3.80]	[0.90]	[0.80]	44.70
Net rent[2]	24.90	33.90	52.30	73.60	85.30	99.80	111.50	126.60	149.80	240.10	70.70

Weighted number of households (thousands)	170	210	320	550	760	1,090	1,360	1,530	1,710	1,760	9,460
Total number of households in sample	40	50	70	140	180	240	300	330	370	380	2,100
Total number of persons in sample	50	90	150	300	460	610	890	1,010	1,170	1,250	5,960
Total number of adults in sample	40	70	110	210	290	440	610	710	840	890	4,210
Weighted average number of persons per household	1.3	1.7	2.0	2.1	2.4	2.5	2.9	3.1	3.1	3.2	2.8

Commodity or service	Average weekly household expenditure (£)										
Mortgage for mortgage holders	**86.30**	**64.10**	**91.20**	**80.40**	**93.10**	**100.80**	**113.30**	**127.50**	**146.00**	**214.10**	**133.00**
Mortgage interest payments	55.70	30.60	51.80	41.50	50.60	53.20	59.20	69.10	76.80	125.70	73.00
Mortgage protection premiums	[2.10]	[1.30]	2.10	3.20	2.70	3.50	4.30	4.50	5.20	6.10	4.40
Capital repayment of mortgage	28.50	32.20	37.20	35.80	39.80	44.10	49.80	53.90	63.90	82.30	55.60

Note: Please see page xiii for symbols and conventions used in this report.

1 Primary dwelling.

2 The figure included in total expenditure is net rent as opposed to gross rent.

ONS, Family Spending 2009, © Crown copyright 2010

Table 2.11 **Expenditure on rent and mortgages[1] by renters and mortgage holders by UK Countries and Government Office Region, 2009**

	North East	North West	Yorks & the Humber	East Midlands	West Midlands	East	London
Weighted number of households (thousands)	470	1,020	610	570	620	560	1,390
Total number of households in sample	80	180	130	100	140	120	210
Total number of persons in sample	160	380	290	210	330	310	480
Total number of adults in sample	120	270	210	160	240	200	340
Weighted average number of persons per household	2.2	2.2	2.1	2.0	2.3	2.3	2.4
Commodity or service	Average weekly household expenditure (£)						
Rent by renters	**90.60**	**104.80**	**94.90**	**101.30**	**103.00**	**114.30**	**165.90**
Gross rent	90.60	104.80	94.90	101.10	103.00	114.30	165.90
less housing benefit, rebates and allowances received	53.60	46.40	41.90	34.90	47.00	41.40	55.40
Net rent[2]	37.00	58.40	53.00	66.20	56.00	72.90	110.50
Weighted number of households (thousands)	520	1,080	800	770	750	930	880
Total number of households in sample	90	190	180	150	190	210	140
Total number of persons in sample	210	540	500	430	580	540	390
Total number of adults in sample	160	370	360	300	400	400	270
Weighted average number of persons per household	2.6	3.0	2.7	2.9	3.0	2.5	3.0
Commodity or service	Average weekly household expenditure (£)						
Mortgage by mortgage holders	**111.40**	**120.10**	**103.70**	**116.60**	**135.50**	**147.60**	**202.80**
Mortgage interest payments	53.40	65.30	52.30	60.00	66.70	84.30	128.00
Mortgage protection premiums	3.20	2.80	4.00	4.50	5.20	3.60	7.60
Capital repayment of mortgage	54.70	52.00	47.40	52.10	63.60	59.70	67.30

	South East	South West	England	Wales	Scotland	Northern Ireland	United Kingdom
Weighted number of households (thousands)	690	740	6,690	330	740	220	7,980
Total number of households in sample	160	140	1,260	70	160	190	1,680
Total number of persons in sample	400	320	2,870	140	350	430	3,780
Total number of adults in sample	270	220	2,040	110	260	310	2,710
Weighted average number of persons per household	2.3	2.3	2.3	2.0	2.0	2.3	2.2
Commodity or service	Average weekly household expenditure (£)						
Rent by renters	**131.70**	**120.50**	**120.40**	**100.10**	**85.70**	**87.30**	**115.40**
Gross rent	131.70	120.40	120.40	100.10	85.70	87.30	115.40
less housing benefit, rebates and allowances received	43.50	42.40	46.30	41.80	34.90	34.90	44.70
Net rent[2]	88.20	78.00	74.10	58.30	50.80	52.40	70.70
Weighted number of households (thousands)	1,160	950	7,830	430	960	230	9,460
Total number of households in sample	290	180	1,600	90	210	200	2,100
Total number of persons in sample	830	490	4,510	260	560	640	5,960
Total number of adults in sample	580	350	3,200	190	410	420	4,210
Weighted average number of persons per household	2.8	2.9	2.8	2.9	2.6	3.2	2.8
Commodity or service	Average weekly household expenditure (£)						
Mortgage by mortgage holders	**156.90**	**122.90**	**137.30**	**113.80**	**111.50**	**112.00**	**133.00**
Mortgage interest payments	88.10	69.90	76.00	57.20	59.50	57.90	73.00
Mortgage protection premiums	4.40	4.10	4.40	3.10	4.30	6.10	4.40
Capital repayment of mortgage	64.40	48.90	56.90	53.40	47.70	48.10	55.60

Note: Please see page xiii for symbols and conventions used in this report.

1 Primary dwelling.

2 The figure included in total expenditure is net rent as opposed to gross rent.

ONS, Family Spending 2009, © Crown copyright 2010

Equivalised income

Background

Equivalisation is a standard methodology that adjusts household income to account for different demands on resources, by considering the household size and composition. The purpose of this chapter is to show the impact of using this methodology on Living Costs and Food Survey (LCF) data. This is the only chapter that presents equivalised income data; other tables included in Family Spending are available on an equivalised income basis on request from the Office for National Statistics (ONS) (see page xvi Introduction).

Equivalisation Methodology

When the incomes of households are compared, income is often adjusted in order to take different demands on resources into account. Household size is an important factor to consider because larger households usually need a higher income than smaller households in order to achieve a comparable standard of living. The composition of a household also affects resource needs, for example living costs for adults are normally higher than those for children.

Equivalisation scales are used to adjust household income in such a way that both household size and composition are taken into account. There are various scales available, which differ in their complexity and methodology. For example, the McClements (1977) equivalence scale was developed for use in the UK: it adjusts household income to reflect the different resource needs of married/cohabiting couples, single adults, and children in various age groups.

The McClements (1977) scale has been used for previous editions of Family Spending, but following consultation with the main users of the LCF data, it has been decided that the Organisation for Economic Cooperation and Development (OECD) modified equivalence scale should be used instead. This scale is more appropriate for use across the world, rather than specifically for the UK, and can therefore be adopted as a universal scale making statistics more comparable across countries.

The OECD-modified equivalence scale is used widely across Europe and it is the standard scale for the Statistical Office of the European Union (EUROSTAT). Several government departments in the UK also use the OECD scale for key household income statistics. For example, the Department for Work and Pensions (DWP) switched from using the McClements (1977) scale to the OECD scale for their 2005/06 Households Below Average Income (HBAI) publication. ONS is also in the process of switching to using the OECD scale for the Effects of Taxes and Benefits on Household Income (ETB) analysis.

For this year's report tables have been created using both the McClements (1977) and the OECD scales, but only the results of the OECD analysis are described in the commentary. From 2011 onwards, only the OECD tables will be published.

To calculate equivalised income using the OECD-modified equivalence scale, each member of the household is first given an equivalence value.

The OECD-modified equivalence values are shown in the table below (The McClements Equivalence Scale is also presented at the end of this section for comparison purposes). Single adult households are taken as the reference group and are given a value of one. For larger households, each additional adult is given a smaller value of 0.5 to reflect the economies of scale achieved when people live together. Economies of scale arise when households share resources such as water and electricity, which reduces the living costs per person. Children under the age of 14 are given a value of 0.3 to take account of their lower living costs while children aged between 14 and 16 are given a value of 0.5 because their living costs are assumed to be the same as those of an adult.

OECD-modified equivalence Scale (Before Housing Costs)	
Type of Household Member	Equivalence value
First adult	1.0
Additional adult	0.5
Child aged: 14–18	0.5
Child aged: 0–13	0.3

In the next stage of the calculation, the equivalence values for each household member are summed to give a total equivalence number for the household. For example, the total equivalence value for a household containing a married couple with two children aged 10 and 14 is calculated as follows:

1 (first adult) + 0.5 (second adult) + 0.5 (14-year-old child) + 0.3 (10-year-old child) = 2.3

The total equivalence value of 2.3 shows that the household needs more than twice the income of a single adult household in order to achieve a comparable standard of living.

In the final step of the calculation the total income for the household is divided by the equivalence value. For example, if the household described in the example above has an annual income of £30,000, their equivalised income is calculated as follows:

£30,000/2.3 = £13,043

For a single adult household with an actual income of £30,000 the equivalised income remains at £30,000, because the equivalence value for this household is equal to one. This demonstrates that a single adult household will have a higher standard of living than a larger household with the same income.

McClements Equivalence Scale (Before Housing Costs)			
Type of household member	Equivalence value	Type of household member	Equivalence value
Cohabiting head of household	0.61	Child aged: 16–18	0.36
Partner/Spouse	0.39	13–15	0.27
1st additional adult	0.42	11–12	0.25
Subsequent adults	0.36	8–10	0.23
Single head of household	0.61	5–7	0.21
1st additional adult	0.46	2–4	0.18
2nd additional adult	0.42	Under 2	0.09
Subsequent adults	0.36		

Results

Equivalised household incomes were calculated for each household using the OECD-modified equivalence scale and the McClements (1977) Equivalence Scale. Household equivalised incomes were then ranked in ascending order and divided into ten equally sized (decile) groups, with households having the lowest equivalised income in the first decile group. Gross (non-equivalised) income data are presented in Tables 3.1 to 3.12; equivalised income data based on the OECD-modified scale are shown in Tables 3.2E to 3.12E; and equivalised income data produced using the McClements (1977) scale are contained in Tables 3.13E to 3.24E.

The income decile groups were as follows:

Income decile	Gross weekly income	Gross weekly equivalised income (OECD-modified scale)	Gross weekly equivalised income (McClements scale)
1	Up to £157	Up to £129	Up to £203
2	£158 to £234	£130 to £174	£204 to £269
3	£235 to £314	£175 to £221	£270 to £340
4	£315 to £409	£222 to £274	£341 to £421
5	£410 to £519	£275 to £334	£422 to £505
6	£520 to £646	£335 to £396	£506 to £598
7	£647 to £795	£397 to £470	£599 to £712
8	£796 to £984	£471 to £585	£713 to £884
9	£985 to £1,347	£586 to £777	£885 to £1,180
10	£1,348 and over	£778 and over	£1,181 and over

Note: the two equivalisation scales appear to give very different results. This is because the modified OECD scale, for any household, always gives equivalised income that is the same or lower than gross income. Conversely, the McClements scale can give equivalised income that is lower or higher than the household's gross income. However, despite these differences, it has been shown that the two scales are relatively similar in terms of interpretation of the impacts of equivalisation.

Household composition by income groups

Table 3.1 shows the household composition of the gross (non-equivalised) income decile groups and the OECD-equivalised income decile groups. Equivalisation had a large impact on households containing one adult without children. The effects of equivalisation were particularly noticeable for households containing one retired adult. These households accounted for just under two-fifths (39 per cent) of households in the lowest gross income decile group but when income was equivalised they accounted for only 11 per cent of the lowest income group. These households tended to move to a higher income decile group after income was equivalised. For example, households containing one retired adult made up 7 per cent of the fifth gross income decile group, but after income was equivalised this group accounted for 15 per cent of the fifth decile group, which was due to households moving up from lower down in the income distribution. Households containing one non-retired adult also moved up the income distribution after income was equivalised. These results demonstrate how equivalisation increases relatively the incomes of one-adult households.

Table 3.1 also shows how equivalisation affected the average household size for each income decile group. As gross income increased the average number of people in each household also increased: the average household size for the highest income group (3.1 people) was almost two and a half times that of the lowest income group (1.3 people). After income was equivalised, the average number of people in each household was similar for each income decile group, with the average varying between 2.0 and 2.6. This pattern of results occurred because the equivalisation process scales up the income of households containing one adult (relative to other households) and scales down the income of households with more people.

Figures 3.1 and 3.1E show the percentage of households with children in each income group before and after income equivalisation. As gross income increased, the proportion of households with children increased: from 12 per cent of households in the bottom gross income decile group to 43 per cent in the top gross income decile group. In contrast, after equivalisation households with children were most likely to be found in the bottom income decile group; just under two-fifths (36 per cent) of households in this group contained at least one child. The proportion of households with children fell to 22 per cent in the second equivalised income decile group before increasing steadily to 34 per cent in the seventh income group. After the seventh decile group, the proportion of households with children fell slightly. These results demonstrate how factoring in living costs for children as part of the equivalisation process can bring about large changes in the income distribution.

Figure 3.1   **Percentage of households with children in each gross income decile group, 2009**

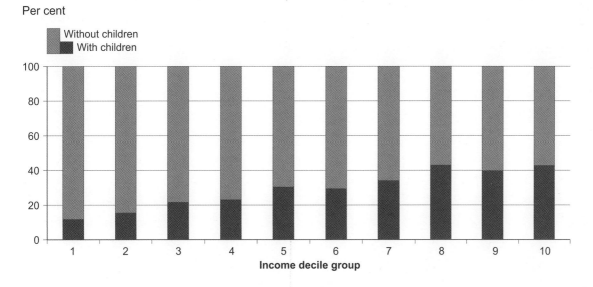

Figure 3.1E **Percentage of households with children in each gross OECD equivalised income decile group, 2009**

Per cent

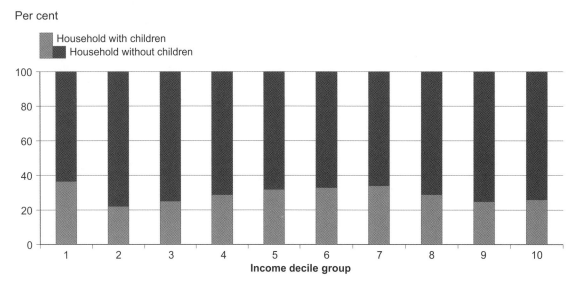

The proportion of households containing at least one retired person in each income group before and after income equivalisation is shown in Figures 3.2 and 3.2E. Equivalisation had a large effect on the proportion of retired households in the lowest income decile group. Retired households accounted for two-fifths (40 per cent) of households in the bottom gross income group but after equivalisation they accounted for only 14 per cent of households in the bottom income group. This result can largely be explained by the fact that a relatively high proportion of retired households contain only one adult and, as explained above, the incomes of single adult households are scaled up (relative to other households) when income is equivalised. The proportion of retired households in the second lowest income decile also decreased after equivalisation, although the effect was much smaller. The opposite was true of the higher income decile groups; the proportion of retired households increased slightly after income was equivalised.

Figure 3.2 **Percentage of retired and non-retired households by gross income decile group, 2009**

Percentage

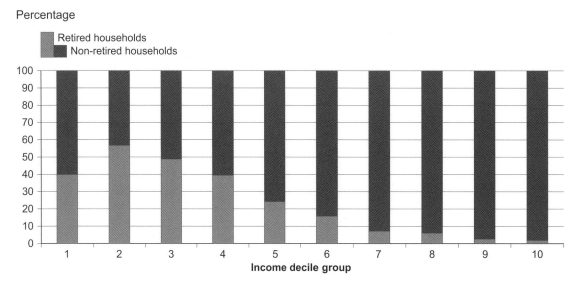

Figure 3.2E **Percentage of retired and non-retired households by OECD equivalised income decile group, 2009**

Percentage

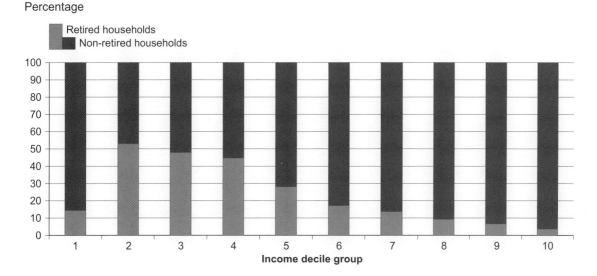

Household expenditure by income

Tables 3.2 and 3.2E show expenditure, in total and for each of the Classification of Individual Consumption According to Purpose (COICOP) categories, by gross and equivalised income decile group respectively. Total expenditure increased with both measures of income, although the gap in spending between the top and the bottom income group was slightly smaller when the equivalised income measure was used. Households in the top gross income decile group spent an average of £992.10 per week; more than six times that of households in the bottom gross income group (£162.70). In comparison, the top equivalised income group spent £898.70 per week, which was just under four times higher than that of the lowest equivalised income group (£228.10). For each COICOP category spending rose consistently with income, although as with total expenditure, the difference in spending between the top and the bottom income groups tended to be smaller when looking at equivalised income.

For most COICOP categories, expenditure in the lower part of the income distribution was lower for the gross income decile groups than for the corresponding equivalised income groups. The opposite was true for the higher income decile groups. Therefore equivalisation flattens the distribution of household expenditure. This pattern of results can be illustrated using the examples of expenditure on food and non-alcoholic drinks, and on clothing and footwear. As shown in Figure 3.3, average weekly expenditure on food and non-alcoholic drinks for the bottom gross income group was £25.90 compared with £35.60 for the bottom equivalised income group. Spending was also higher for the equivalised income groups than for the gross income groups in the next deciles up, from decile two (the second lowest) up to six. From the seventh decile onwards the pattern reversed, and spending was higher in the gross income groups than the equivalised income group. For the top income group, for example, the average weekly spend on food and non-alcoholic drinks was £81.40 per week compared with £68.00 for the top equivalised income group. Figure 3.4 shows that the pattern of results was similar for expenditure on clothing and footwear.

Figure 3.3 **Expenditure on food and non-alcoholic drinks by gross and OECD equivalised income decile group, 2009**

£ per week

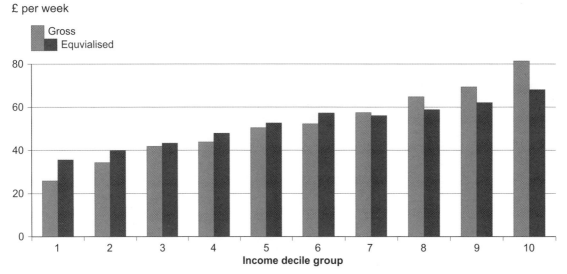

Figure 3.4 **Expenditure on clothing and footwear by gross and OECD equivalised income decile group, 2009**

£ per week

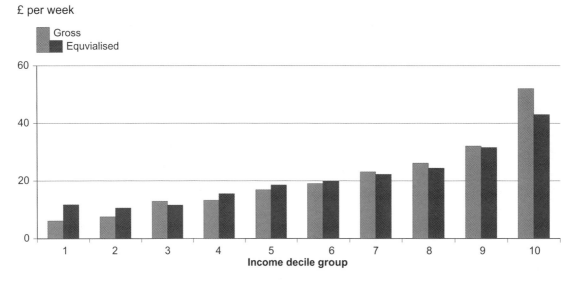

Tables 3.3 and Table 3.3E show the share of total expenditure on each COICOP category, by gross income group and equivalised income group respectively. There was notable variation in spending with income for some COICOP categories. As shown in Figure 3.5, the proportion of total expenditure spent on food and non-alcoholic drinks, and on housing, fuel and power decreased steadily as equivalised income increased. Spending on these categories combined accounted for just under two-fifths (37 per cent) of total expenditure for the bottom equivalised income decile group, compared with just under a fifth (16 per cent) for households in the top equivalised income decile group. In contrast, the proportion of total expenditure spent on transport increased slightly with equivalised income, from 10 per cent for the lowest decile group to 13 per cent in the highest income group. The pattern of results was similar when looking at spending by gross income group.

Figure 3.5   **Percentage of total expenditure on selected items by OECD equivalised income decile group, 2009**

Per cent

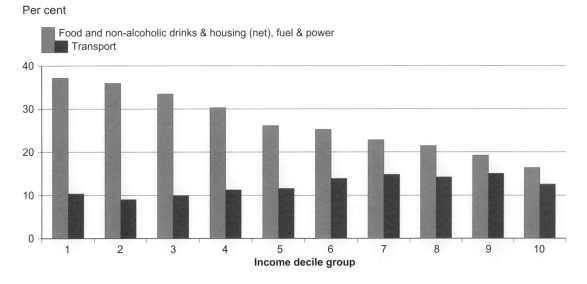

■ Food and non-alcoholic drinks & housing (net), fuel & power
■ Transport

Income decile group

Household expenditure by household composition and income

This section describes the effect that equivalisation has when looking at the expenditure in the income decile groups of different household types (see Tables 3.4 to 3.11 and Tables 3.4E to 3.11E). The analysis focuses on one and two adult households, with and without children. It should be noted that some groups, particularly retired households who are mainly dependent on the state pension, contain a small number of households and the results should therefore be treated with caution.

Equivalisation had a large impact on households containing one adult without children (see Tables 3.4, 3.5, 3.4E, and 3.5E). Expenditure for each income quintile group decreased after equivalisation and the effect was greatest for the highest income groups. This was particularly noticeable for households containing one non-retired adult. Among these households, total expenditure was £157.30 for the bottom gross income but after equivalisation total expenditure fell to £146.00 for the bottom income group. Equivalisation had a much larger impact on households in the higher income quintile groups; total expenditure for households containing one non-retired household in the top gross income decile was £836.10 compared with £532.50 for the top equivalised income group.

Equivalisation had the opposite effect on expenditure for two adult households with children (Table 3.6E). Expenditure for households containing two adults with children increased from £279.60 for the lowest gross income group to £363.10 after income was equivalised. There was a similar increase in expenditure after income was equivalised for each of the remaining quintiles.

Sources of income

Tables 3.12 and 3.12E, and Figures 3.6 and 3.6E show the breakdown of income sources for each income quintile, by gross household income and equivalised household income respectively. Equivalisation mainly affected the distribution of income sources for the lowest income quintile groups. Annuities and pensions made up 9 per cent of the income received by households in the lowest gross income quintile groups, but after income was equivalised this income source accounted for only 4 per cent of total income received by the lowest income group. In contrast, the proportion of total income provided by wages and salaries increased after equivalisation. Among households in the bottom gross income quintile, 8 per cent of income came from salaries and wages compared with 14 per cent for households in the lowest equivalised income quintile. These results largely reflect the fact that after income was equivalised, the lowest quintile groups contained fewer pensioner households and more working households.

Figure 3.6   **Source of income by gross income quintile group, 2009**

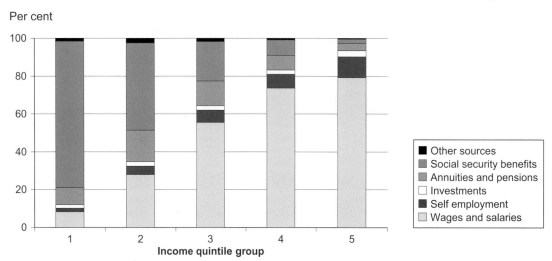

Figure 3.6E **Sources of income by gross OECD equivalised income quintile group, 2009**

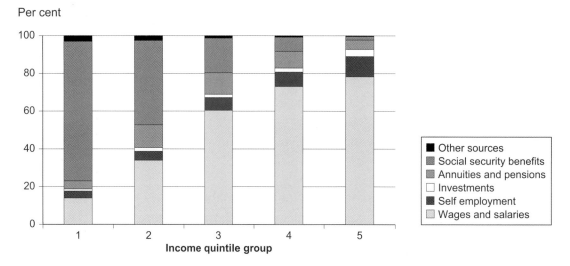

Table 3.1 Percentage of households by composition in each gross and equivalised income decile group (OECD-modified scale) 2009

Percentages

	Income decile group									
	Lowest ten per cent		Second		Third		Fourth		Fifth	
	Gross	Equivalised	Gross	Equivalised	Gross	Equivalised	Gross	Equivalised	Gross	Equivalised
Lower boundary of group (£ per week)			158	130	235	175	315	222	410	275
Average size of household	**1.3**	**2.2**	**1.6**	**2.0**	**2.0**	**2.2**	**2.1**	**2.3**	**2.4**	**2.4**
One adult retired mainly dependent on state pensions[1]	17	5	10	15	[2]	6	-	[3]	-	[1]
One adult, other retired	22	6	35	23	24	21	13	21	7	14
One adult, non-retired	41	34	17	10	14	9	19	10	18	13
One adult, one child	9	10	4	[2]	3	3	3	[2]	[3]	[3]
One adult, two or more children	[1]	8	5	4	6	4	5	3	[3]	[2]
Two adults, retired mainly dependent on state pensions[1]	[1]	[2]	5	6	6	4	3	[2]	[1]	[1]
Two adults, other retired	[0]	[2]	7	9	17	17	24	19	16	13
Two adults, non-retired	7	9	9	9	13	11	14	8	21	15
Two adults, one child	[1]	[3]	[3]	4	[3]	5	5	6	7	10
Two adults, two children	-	3	[2]	4	[2]	6	4	9	8	8
Two adults, three children	[0]	4	[1]	[2]	[3]	3	[2]	3	3	4
Two adults, four or more children	-	[1]	-	[1]	[1]	[1]	[1]	[0]	[1]	[1]
Three adults	[1]	[3]	[2]	[3]	[2]	3	4	4	4	7
Three adults, one or more children	[0]	[4]	[1]	[2]	[2]	[2]	[2]	4	[3]	[3]
All other households without children	-	[3]	[0]	[3]	[0]	4	[1]	4	[2]	4
All other households with children	[1]	[3]	[0]	[2]	[2]	[1]	[1]	[2]	[1]	[2]

	Income decile group									
	Sixth		Seventh		Eighth		Ninth		Highest ten per cent	
	Gross	Equivalised	Gross	Equivalised	Gross	Equivalised	Gross	Equivalised	Gross	Equivalised
Lower boundary of group (£ per week)	520	335	647	397	796	471	985	586	1,348	778
Average size of household	**2.4**	**2.6**	**2.7**	**2.6**	**2.9**	**2.4**	**3.0**	**2.4**	**3.1**	**2.4**
One adult retired mainly dependent on state pensions[1]	-	-	-	-	-	-	-	-	-	-
One adult, other retired	[3]	7	[1]	7	[1]	[3]	[0]	[3]	[1]	[1]
One adult, non-retired	15	12	11	12	8	18	5	15	5	19
One adult, one child	[1]	[2]	[1]	[1]	[1]	[1]	[0]	[1]	[0]	[0]
One adult, two or more children	[2]	[1]	[1]	[1]	[0]	[0]	[1]	[1]	[0]	[0]
Two adults, retired mainly dependent on state pensions[1]	[0]	-	-	[0]	-	-	-	-	-	-
Two adults, other retired	13	10	6	6	5	6	[2]	4	[1]	[2]
Two adults, non-retired	32	22	35	26	29	29	35	37	28	39
Two adults, one child	11	7	11	12	14	12	12	10	14	12
Two adults, two children	8	13	13	12	15	10	13	8	15	8
Two adults, three children	[2]	3	4	[3]	4	[1]	4	[1]	[3]	[2]
Two adults, four or more children	[1]	-	[1]	-	[1]	[1]	[1]	[0]	[1]	[0]
Three adults	6	9	11	8	9	7	12	10	13	8
Three adults, one or more children	[3]	5	3	4	5	[4]	7	4	7	[2]
All other households without children	[2]	7	[2]	6	4	8	6	6	9	4
All other households with children	[2]	[2]	[2]	[2]	[2]	[1]	[2]	[0]	[3]	[1]

Note: Please see page xiii for symbols and conventions used in this report.

1   Mainly dependent on state pension and not economically active – see Appendix B.

ONS, Family Spending 2009, © Crown copyright 2010

Table 3.2 **Household expenditure by gross income decile group, 2009**
based on weighted data and including children's expenditure

	Lowest ten per cent	Second decile group	Third decile group	Fourth decile group	Fifth decile group	Sixth decile group
Lower boundary of group (£ per week)		158	235	315	410	520
Weighted number of households (thousands)	2,600	2,600	2,600	2,600	2,600	2,600
Total number of households in sample	560	580	600	620	610	600
Total number of persons in sample	700	980	1,210	1,310	1,460	1,440
Total number of adults in sample	610	780	930	1,040	1,100	1,140
Weighted average number of persons per household	1.3	1.6	2.0	2.1	2.4	2.4
Commodity or service	Average weekly household expenditure (£)					
1 Food & non-alcoholic drinks	25.90	34.30	41.90	43.90	50.50	52.30
2 Alcoholic drinks, tobacco & narcotics	5.60	7.40	8.20	8.90	11.30	11.70
3 Clothing & footwear	6.10	7.60	12.90	13.30	16.90	19.10
4 Housing (net)[1], fuel & power	37.60	44.40	51.80	59.20	57.80	59.90
5 Household goods & services	9.90	15.10	16.60	20.20	20.40	27.50
6 Health	2.10	3.40	2.70	3.60	6.30	6.30
7 Transport	13.90	16.80	28.30	41.00	46.00	55.90
8 Communication	6.00	6.80	8.90	9.30	10.80	12.40
9 Recreation & culture	15.80	25.50	30.90	38.70	48.30	52.90
10 Education	[4.80]	[1.60]	7.60	6.30	7.10	1.40
11 Restaurants & hotels	9.20	12.50	19.20	22.00	28.80	35.90
12 Miscellaneous goods & services	9.70	15.80	19.50	23.40	29.50	32.90
1–12 All expenditure groups	146.70	191.10	248.50	289.80	333.80	368.30
13 Other expenditure items	16.00	22.50	32.10	43.80	51.10	66.00
Total expenditure	**162.70**	**213.70**	**280.70**	**333.70**	**384.90**	**434.30**
Average weekly expenditure per person (£)						
Total expenditure	**129.60**	**134.60**	**139.00**	**158.10**	**162.10**	**181.20**

Note: The commodity and service categories are not comparable to those in publications before 2001-02

Please see page xiii for symbols and conventions used in this report

1   Excluding mortgage interest payments, council tax and Northern Ireland Rates.

ONS, Family Spending 2009, © Crown copyright 2010

Table 3.2   Household expenditure by gross income decile group, 2009 (cont.)

based on weighted data and including children's expenditure

		Seventh decile group	Eighth decile group	Ninth decile group	Highest ten per cent	All house-holds
Lower boundary of group (£ per week)		647	796	985	1,348	
Weighted number of households (thousands)		2,600	2,600	2,600	2,600	25,980
Total number of households in sample		580	560	560	550	5,830
Total number of persons in sample		1,590	1,630	1,680	1,750	13,740
Total number of adults in sample		1,210	1,220	1,280	1,320	10,650
Weighted average number of persons per household		2.7	2.9	3.0	3.1	2.3
Commodity or service		Average weekly household expenditure (£)				
1	Food & non-alcoholic drinks	57.50	64.80	69.30	81.40	52.20
2	Alcoholic drinks, tobacco & narcotics	12.70	14.50	13.60	17.80	11.20
3	Clothing & footwear	23.10	26.20	32.10	52.10	20.90
4	Housing (net)[1], fuel & power	58.40	63.70	63.00	77.20	57.30
5	Household goods & services	33.80	37.20	34.80	64.10	27.90
6	Health	4.70	6.70	7.40	9.60	5.30
7	Transport	68.80	84.00	99.50	130.20	58.40
8	Communication	13.50	14.90	15.60	18.30	11.70
9	Recreation & culture	66.00	73.40	87.30	139.60	57.90
10	Education	4.90	4.40	8.10	23.60	7.00
11	Restaurants & hotels	42.10	47.60	61.80	104.70	38.40
12	Miscellaneous goods & services	36.60	44.60	57.00	81.40	35.00
1–12	All expenditure groups	422.00	482.20	549.50	799.90	383.10
13	Other expenditure items	78.50	99.00	116.90	192.20	71.80
Total expenditure		**500.50**	**581.20**	**666.40**	**992.10**	**455.00**
Average weekly expenditure per person (£)						
Total expenditure		**188.20**	**200.90**	**224.00**	**316.90**	**194.40**

Note: The commodity and service categories are not comparable to those in publications before 2001–02

Please see page xiii for symbols and conventions used in this report

1   Excluding mortgage interest payments, council tax and Northern Ireland Rates.

ONS, Family Spending 2009, © Crown copyright 2010

Table 3.2E **Household expenditure by gross equivalised income decile group (OECD-modified scale) 2009**
based on weighted data and including children's expenditure

Commodity or service	Lowest ten per cent	Second decile group	Third decile group	Fourth decile group	Fifth decile group	Sixth decile group
Lower boundary of group (£ per week)		130	175	222	275	335
Weighted number of households (thousands)	2,600	2,600	2,590	2,600	2,600	2,600
Total number of households in sample	580	590	590	610	610	590
Total number of persons in sample	1,310	1,220	1,300	1,390	1,490	1,500
Total number of adults in sample	840	910	1,010	1,070	1,140	1,170
Weighted average number of persons per household	2.2	2.0	2.2	2.3	2.4	2.6

Commodity or service	Average weekly household expenditure (£)					
1 Food & non-alcoholic drinks	35.60	39.80	43.40	47.90	52.70	57.30
2 Alcoholic drinks, tobacco & narcotics	8.00	7.90	9.00	8.40	11.30	11.50
3 Clothing & footwear	11.70	10.60	11.60	15.50	18.60	20.00
4 Housing (net)[1], fuel & power	49.20	46.10	54.40	54.10	54.20	57.20
5 Household goods & services	11.40	16.10	16.10	18.90	30.90	26.80
6 Health	2.10	2.10	4.60	3.90	4.90	5.30
7 Transport	23.60	21.60	29.10	38.00	47.40	62.90
8 Communication	7.80	8.40	8.80	9.60	11.60	12.40
9 Recreation & culture	21.70	25.40	37.80	41.80	50.80	55.10
10 Education	7.20	8.90	2.10	6.80	1.00	5.50
11 Restaurants & hotels	15.50	14.30	20.20	24.60	28.90	37.60
12 Miscellaneous goods & services	13.30	15.50	18.80	26.10	35.10	36.20
1–12 All expenditure groups	207.20	216.60	255.90	295.70	347.50	387.70
13 Other expenditure items	20.80	22.40	36.60	41.20	61.80	65.40
Total expenditure	**228.10**	**239.00**	**292.40**	**336.90**	**409.30**	**453.20**
Average weekly expenditure per person (£)						
Total expenditure	**102.80**	**119.50**	**135.70**	**149.40**	**170.60**	**176.90**

Note: The commodity and service categories are not comparable to those in publications before 2001–02.

Please see page xiii for symbols and conventions used in this report.

1 Excluding mortgage interest payments, council tax and Northern Ireland Rates.

ONS, Family Spending 2009, © Crown copyright 2010

Table 3.2E **Household expenditure by gross equivalised income decile group (OECD-modified scale) 2009 (cont.)**
based on weighted data and including children's expenditure

	Seventh decile group	Eighth decile group	Ninth decile group	Highest ten per cent	All house-holds
Lower boundary of group (£ per week)	397	471	586	778	
Weighted number of households (thousands)	2,590	2,600	2,600	2,600	25,980
Total number of households in sample	570	560	570	540	5,830
Total number of persons in sample	1,460	1,380	1,410	1,290	13,740
Total number of adults in sample	1,140	1,130	1,180	1,060	10,650
Weighted average number of persons per household	2.6	2.4	2.4	2.4	2.3
Commodity or service	Average weekly household expenditure (£)				
1 Food & non-alcoholic drinks	56.10	58.80	62.10	68.10	52.20
2 Alcoholic drinks, tobacco & narcotics	13.90	12.30	13.90	15.60	11.20
3 Clothing & footwear	22.30	24.40	31.60	43.00	20.90
4 Housing (net)[1], fuel & power	58.80	58.50	61.60	79.10	57.30
5 Household goods & services	29.30	30.80	39.40	59.70	27.90
6 Health	7.60	5.20	7.80	9.40	5.30
7 Transport	74.40	77.70	96.70	112.80	58.40
8 Communication	13.30	14.40	14.80	15.40	11.70
9 Recreation & culture	64.50	72.90	87.60	121.20	57.90
10 Education	4.70	6.40	7.00	20.10	7.00
11 Restaurants & hotels	43.30	48.30	58.30	92.80	38.40
12 Miscellaneous goods & services	37.90	41.60	50.40	75.60	35.00
1–12 All expenditure groups	426.00	451.30	531.20	712.90	383.10
13 Other expenditure items	76.70	95.40	112.10	185.80	71.80
Total expenditure	**502.70**	**546.60**	**643.30**	**898.70**	**455.00**
Average weekly expenditure per person (£)					
Total expenditure	**195.20**	**223.30**	**264.30**	**382.10**	**194.40**

Note: The commodity and service categories are not comparable to those in publications before 2001–02.

Please see page xiii for symbols and conventions used in this report.

1 Excluding mortgage interest payments, council tax and Northern Ireland Rates.

ONS, Family Spending 2009, © Crown copyright 2010

Table 3.3   **Household expenditure as a percentage of total expenditure by gross income decile group, 2009**

based on weighted data and including children's expenditure

	Lowest ten per cent	Second decile group	Third decile group	Fourth decile group	Fifth decile group	Sixth decile group
Lower boundary of group (£ per week)		158	235	315	410	520
Weighted number of households (thousands)	2,600	2,600	2,600	2,600	2,600	2,600
Total number of households in sample	560	580	600	620	610	600
Total number of persons in sample	700	980	1,210	1,310	1,460	1,440
Total number of adults in sample	610	780	930	1,040	1,100	1,140
Weighted average number of persons per household	1.3	1.6	2.0	2.1	2.4	2.4
Commodity or service	Percentage of total expenditure					
1 Food & non-alcoholic drinks	16	16	15	13	13	12
2 Alcoholic drinks, tobacco & narcotics	3	3	3	3	3	3
3 Clothing & footwear	4	4	5	4	4	4
4 Housing (net)[1], fuel & power	23	21	18	18	15	14
5 Household goods & services	6	7	6	6	5	6
6 Health	1	2	1	1	2	1
7 Transport	9	8	10	12	12	13
8 Communication	4	3	3	3	3	3
9 Recreation & culture	10	12	11	12	13	12
10 Education	[3]	[1]	3	2	2	0
11 Restaurants & hotels	6	6	7	7	7	8
12 Miscellaneous goods & services	6	7	7	7	8	8
1–12 All expenditure groups	90	89	89	87	87	85
13 Other expenditure items	10	11	11	13	13	15
Total expenditure	**100**	**100**	**100**	**100**	**100**	**100**

Note: The commodity and service categories are not comparable to those in publications before 2001–02

Please see page xiii for symbols and conventions used in this report

1   Excluding mortgage interest payments, council tax and Northern Ireland Rates.

ONS, Family Spending 2009, © Crown copyright 2010

Table 3.3   **Household expenditure as a percentage of total expenditure by gross income decile group, 2009 (cont.)**

based on weighted data and including children's expenditure

	Seventh decile group	Eighth decile group	Ninth decile group	Highest ten per cent	All house-holds
Lower boundary of group (£ per week)	647	796	985	1,348	
Weighted number of households (thousands)	2,600	2,600	2,600	2,600	25,980
Total number of households in sample	580	560	560	550	5,830
Total number of persons in sample	1,590	1,630	1,680	1,750	13,740
Total number of adults in sample	1,210	1,220	1,280	1,320	10,650
Weighted average number of persons per household	2.7	2.9	3.0	3.1	2.3
Commodity or service	Percentage of total expenditure				
1 Food & non-alcoholic drinks	11	11	10	8	11
2 Alcoholic drinks, tobacco & narcotics	3	2	2	2	2
3 Clothing & footwear	5	5	5	5	5
4 Housing (net)[1], fuel & power	12	11	9	8	13
5 Household goods & services	7	6	5	6	6
6 Health	1	1	1	1	1
7 Transport	14	14	15	13	13
8 Communication	3	3	2	2	3
9 Recreation & culture	13	13	13	14	13
10 Education	1	1	1	2	2
11 Restaurants & hotels	8	8	9	11	8
12 Miscellaneous goods & services	7	8	9	8	8
1–12 All expenditure groups	84	83	82	81	84
13 Other expenditure items	16	17	18	19	16
Total expenditure	100	100	100	100	100

Note: The commodity and service categories are not comparable to those in publications before 2001–02

Please see page xiii for symbols and conventions used in this report

1   Excluding mortgage interest payments, council tax and Northern Ireland Rates.

ONS, Family Spending 2009, © Crown copyright 2010

Table 3.3E **Household expenditure as a percentage of total expenditure by gross equivalised income decile group (OECD-modified scale) 2009**
based on weighted data and including children's expenditure

	Lowest ten per cent	Second decile group	Third decile group	Fourth decile group	Fifth decile group	Sixth decile group
Lower boundary of group (£ per week)		130	175	222	275	335
Weighted number of households (thousands)	2,600	2,600	2,590	2,600	2,600	2,600
Total number of households in sample	580	590	590	610	610	590
Total number of persons in sample	1,310	1,220	1,300	1,390	1,490	1,500
Total number of adults in sample	840	910	1,010	1,070	1,140	1,170
Weighted average number of persons per household	2.2	2.0	2.2	2.3	2.4	2.6
Commodity or service	Percentage of total expenditure					
1 Food & non-alcoholic drinks	16	17	15	14	13	13
2 Alcoholic drinks, tobacco & narcotics	3	3	3	2	3	3
3 Clothing & footwear	5	4	4	5	5	4
4 Housing (net)[1], fuel & power	22	19	19	16	13	13
5 Household goods & services	5	7	5	6	8	6
6 Health	1	1	2	1	1	1
7 Transport	10	9	10	11	12	14
8 Communication	3	3	3	3	3	3
9 Recreation & culture	10	11	13	12	12	12
10 Education	3	4	1	2	0	1
11 Restaurants & hotels	7	6	7	7	7	8
12 Miscellaneous goods & services	6	6	6	8	9	8
1–12 All expenditure groups	91	91	87	88	85	86
13 Other expenditure items	9	9	13	12	15	14
Total expenditure	100	100	100	100	100	100

Note: The commodity and service categories are not comparable to those in publications before 2001–02.

Please see page xiii for symbols and conventions used in this report.

1 Excluding mortgage interest payments, council tax and Northern Ireland Rates.

ONS, Family Spending 2009, © Crown copyright 2010

Table 3.3E   **Household expenditure as a percentage of total expenditure by gross equivalised income decile group (OECD-modified scale) 2009 (cont.)**
based on weighted data and including children's expenditure

	Seventh decile group	Eighth decile group	Ninth decile group	Highest ten per cent	All house-holds
Lower boundary of group (£ per week)	397	471	586	778	
Weighted number of households (thousands)	2,590	2,600	2,600	2,600	25,980
Total number of households in sample	570	560	570	540	5,830
Total number of persons in sample	1,460	1,380	1,410	1,290	13,740
Total number of adults in sample	1,140	1,130	1,180	1,060	10,650
Weighted average number of persons per household	2.6	2.4	2.4	2.4	2.3
Commodity or service	Percentage of total expenditure				
1 Food & non-alcoholic drinks	11	11	10	8	11
2 Alcoholic drinks, tobacco & narcotics	3	2	2	2	2
3 Clothing & footwear	4	4	5	5	5
4 Housing (net)[1], fuel & power	12	11	10	9	13
5 Household goods & services	6	6	6	7	6
6 Health	2	1	1	1	1
7 Transport	15	14	15	13	13
8 Communication	3	3	2	2	3
9 Recreation & culture	13	13	14	13	13
10 Education	1	1	1	2	2
11 Restaurants & hotels	9	9	9	10	8
12 Miscellaneous goods & services	8	8	8	8	8
1–12 All expenditure groups	85	83	83	79	84
13 Other expenditure items	15	17	17	21	16
Total expenditure	100	100	100	100	100

Note: The commodity and service categories are not comparable to those in publications before 2001–02.

Please see page xiii for symbols and conventions used in this report.

1   Excluding mortgage interest payments, council tax and Northern Ireland Rates.

ONS, Family Spending 2009, © Crown copyright 2010

Table 3.4 **Expenditure of one person non-retired households by gross income quintile group, 2009**
based on weighted data

	Lowest twenty per cent	Second quintile group	Third quintile group	Fourth quintile group	Highest twenty per cent	All house-holds
Lower boundary of group (£ per week)		235	410	647	985	
Weighted number of households (thousands)	1,500	870	880	490	270	4,000
Total number of households in sample	330	200	190	100	50	870
Total number of persons in sample	330	200	190	100	50	870
Total number of adults in sample	330	200	190	100	50	870
Weighted average number of persons per household	1.0	1.0	1.0	1.0	1.0	1.0
Commodity or service	Average weekly household expenditure (£)					
1 Food & non-alcoholic drinks	21.40	26.00	28.80	28.50	27.60	25.30
2 Alcoholic drinks, tobacco & narcotics	7.40	8.00	9.40	10.60	12.40	8.70
3 Clothing & footwear	3.90	8.70	13.10	13.70	15.40	9.00
4 Housing (net)[1], fuel & power	37.50	55.70	51.90	56.20	85.80	50.20
5 Household goods & services	9.00	19.00	14.30	25.80	94.80	20.20
6 Health	1.40	2.70	4.10	4.10	7.10	3.00
7 Transport	15.70	30.40	52.10	54.90	66.30	35.10
8 Communication	5.20	8.20	9.90	11.40	9.70	8.00
9 Recreation & culture	16.90	26.00	35.60	38.20	96.80	31.00
10 Education	[2.50]	[5.10]	[1.40]	[0.90]	[9.40]	3.10
11 Restaurants & hotels	11.00	18.20	27.50	34.20	69.60	23.00
12 Miscellaneous goods & services	8.60	17.80	22.00	27.10	61.10	19.30
1–12 All expenditure groups	140.50	225.90	270.10	305.50	556.10	235.60
13 Other expenditure items	16.80	43.60	62.40	90.40	280.00	59.30
Total expenditure	**157.30**	**269.40**	**332.50**	**395.90**	**836.10**	**294.90**
Average weekly expenditure per person (£)						
Total expenditure	**157.30**	**269.40**	**332.50**	**395.90**	**836.10**	**294.90**

Note: The commodity and service categories are not comparable to those in publications before 2001–02.

Please see page xiii for symbols and conventions used in this report

1   Excluding mortgage interest payments, council tax and Northern Ireland Rates.

ONS, Family Spending 2009, © Crown copyright 2010

Table 3.4E **Expenditure of one adult non-retired households by gross equivalised income quintile group (OECD-modified scale) 2009**
based on weighted data

Commodity or service	Lowest twenty per cent	Second quintile group	Third quintile group	Fourth quintile group	Highest twenty per cent	All house-holds
Lower boundary of group (£ per week)		175	275	397	586	
Weighted number of households (thousands)	1,160	500	670	780	900	4,000
Total number of households in sample	250	120	150	170	180	870
Total number of persons in sample	250	120	150	170	180	870
Total number of adults in sample	250	120	150	170	180	870
Weighted average number of persons per household	1.0	1.0	1.0	1.0	1.0	1.0
Commodity or service	Average weekly household expenditure (£)					
1 Food & non-alcoholic drinks	20.60	24.20	26.60	27.80	28.70	25.30
2 Alcoholic drinks, tobacco & narcotics	7.10	8.50	7.90	9.40	10.90	8.70
3 Clothing & footwear	4.20	5.30	8.20	11.10	15.80	9.00
4 Housing (net)[1], fuel & power	35.60	44.80	58.80	49.40	66.20	50.20
5 Household goods & services	7.30	13.00	22.10	11.80	46.60	20.20
6 Health	0.80	2.90	2.70	4.50	4.60	3.00
7 Transport	14.50	24.20	29.30	45.20	63.10	35.10
8 Communication	5.00	6.40	7.80	10.20	10.70	8.00
9 Recreation & culture	14.40	24.40	25.30	36.70	55.40	31.00
10 Education	[2.90]	[1.10]	[6.30]	[1.50]	[3.30]	3.10
11 Restaurants & hotels	9.60	16.50	18.20	26.50	44.20	23.00
12 Miscellaneous goods & services	7.90	11.50	19.30	20.70	37.30	19.30
1–12 All expenditure groups	130.00	182.70	232.60	254.80	386.90	235.60
13 Other expenditure items	16.00	25.00	42.90	60.30	145.60	59.30
Total expenditure	**146.00**	**207.70**	**275.60**	**315.20**	**532.50**	**294.90**
Average weekly expenditure per person (£)						
Total expenditure	**146.00**	**207.70**	**275.60**	**315.20**	**532.50**	**294.90**

Note: The commodity and service categories are not comparable to those in publications before 2001–02.

Please see page xiii for symbols and conventions used in this report.

1   Excluding mortgage interest payments, council tax and Northern Ireland Rates.

ONS, Family Spending 2009, © Crown copyright 2010

Table 3.5 **Expenditure of one person retired households not mainly dependent on state pensions[1] by gross income quintile group, 2009**

based on weighted data

	Lowest twenty per cent	Second quintile group	Third quintile group	Fourth quintile group	Highest twenty per cent	All house-holds
Lower boundary of group (£ per week)		235	410	647	985	
Weighted number of households (thousands)	1,480	950	250	40	20	2,750
Total number of households in sample	310	200	60	..	..	580
Total number of persons in sample	310	200	60	..	..	580
Total number of adults in sample	310	200	60	..	..	580
Weighted average number of persons per household	1.0	1.0	1.0	1.0	1.0	1.0
Commodity or service	Average weekly household expenditure (£)					
1 Food & non-alcoholic drinks	27.60	30.10	35.00	[40.90]	[29.50]	29.40
2 Alcoholic drinks, tobacco & narcotics	3.70	4.00	7.10	[10.80]	[5.60]	4.30
3 Clothing & footwear	5.20	8.50	8.10	[8.10]	[6.10]	6.70
4 Housing (net)[2], fuel & power	37.40	42.50	43.00	[55.90]	[47.00]	40.00
5 Household goods & services	13.30	15.60	26.70	[37.10]	[46.00]	16.00
6 Health	3.60	3.00	10.60	[7.30]	-	4.00
7 Transport	8.90	22.90	19.90	[37.50]	[33.70]	15.40
8 Communication	6.00	6.80	7.70	[6.80]	[9.90]	6.50
9 Recreation & culture	19.60	26.90	36.50	[56.10]	[62.00]	24.60
10 Education	[0.10]	[1.90]	[0.10]	-	-	[0.70]
11 Restaurants & hotels	8.00	13.10	14.70	[29.30]	[72.50]	11.20
12 Miscellaneous goods & services	15.40	18.60	25.80	[56.30]	[50.20]	18.40
1–12 All expenditure groups	148.80	193.90	235.30	[346.20]	[362.60]	177.20
13 Other expenditure items	15.80	30.90	34.60	[104.60]	[126.70]	25.00
Total expenditure	**164.50**	**224.80**	**269.90**	**[450.80]**	**[489.30]**	**202.20**
Average weekly expenditure per person (£)						
Total expenditure	**164.50**	**224.80**	**269.90**	**[450.80]**	**[489.30]**	**202.20**

Note: The commodity and service categories are not comparable to those in publications before 2001–02.

Please see page xiii for symbols and conventions used in this report

1   Mainly dependent on state pension and not economically active – see Appendix B.

2   Excluding mortgage interest payments, council tax and Northern Ireland Rates.

ONS, Family Spending 2009, © Crown copyright 2010

Table 3.5E **Expenditure of one person retired households not mainly dependent on state pensions[1] by gross equivalised income quintile group (OECD-modified scale) 2009**
based on weighted data

	Lowest twenty per cent	Second quintile group	Third quintile group	Fourth quintile group	Highest twenty per cent	All house-holds
Lower boundary of group (£ per week)		175	275	397	586	
Weighted number of households (thousands)	750	1,090	540	260	110	2,750
Total number of households in sample	160	220	120	60	20	580
Total number of persons in sample	160	220	120	60	20	580
Total number of adults in sample	160	220	120	60	20	580
Weighted average number of persons per household	1.0	1.0	1.0	1.0	1.0	1.0
Commodity or service	Average weekly household expenditure (£)					
1 Food & non-alcoholic drinks	26.30	28.70	31.00	34.30	37.30	29.40
2 Alcoholic drinks, tobacco & narcotics	3.30	4.00	4.50	6.40	[7.40]	4.30
3 Clothing & footwear	4.40	6.80	9.00	8.40	[5.30]	6.70
4 Housing (net)[2], fuel & power	31.90	42.50	44.20	39.30	53.20	40.00
5 Household goods & services	10.70	14.70	16.40	29.70	29.60	16.00
6 Health	4.30	2.60	3.60	10.40	[3.50]	4.00
7 Transport	7.20	11.50	29.80	22.60	[23.30]	15.40
8 Communication	5.90	6.20	7.10	7.60	8.10	6.50
9 Recreation & culture	14.50	26.80	24.80	37.10	41.60	24.60
10 Education	-	[0.10]	[3.40]	[0.10]	-	[0.70]
11 Restaurants & hotels	6.50	10.50	13.70	15.40	[28.90]	11.20
12 Miscellaneous goods & services	9.80	18.90	21.40	23.40	46.50	18.40
1–12 All expenditure groups	125.00	173.30	208.80	234.70	284.70	177.20
13 Other expenditure items	8.70	21.90	37.80	34.80	84.00	25.00
Total expenditure	**133.70**	**195.10**	**246.60**	**269.50**	**368.60**	**202.20**
Average weekly expenditure per person (£)						
Total expenditure	**133.70**	**195.10**	**246.60**	**269.50**	**368.60**	**202.20**

Note: The commodity and service categories are not comparable to those in publications before 2001–02.

Please see page xiii for symbols and conventions used in this report.

1   Mainly dependent on state pension and not economically active – see Appendix B.

2   Excluding mortgage interest payments, council tax and Northern Ireland Rates.

ONS, Family Spending 2009, © Crown copyright 2010

Table 3.6 **Expenditure of two adult households with children by gross income quintile group, 2009**

based on weighted data and including children's expenditure

	Lowest twenty per cent	Second quintile group	Third quintile group	Fourth quintile group	Highest twenty per cent	All house-holds
Lower boundary of group (£ per week)		235	410	647	985	
Weighted number of households (thousands)	170	590	1,110	1,650	1,620	5,140
Total number of households in sample	40	130	260	380	380	1,190
Total number of persons in sample	140	530	1,010	1,430	1,410	4,520
Total number of adults in sample	80	270	520	760	750	2,370
Weighted average number of persons per household	3.6	3.9	3.8	3.8	3.7	3.8
Commodity or service	Average weekly household expenditure (£)					
1 Food & non-alcoholic drinks	54.00	58.60	60.70	71.70	87.90	72.30
2 Alcoholic drinks, tobacco & narcotics	13.40	12.00	11.40	12.40	15.00	13.00
3 Clothing & footwear	13.80	20.90	22.40	28.80	43.60	30.70
4 Housing (net)[1], fuel & power	66.80	75.90	70.10	60.10	61.00	64.60
5 Household goods & services	12.00	18.30	21.90	32.70	52.50	34.30
6 Health	[1.50]	1.40	3.00	6.00	7.90	5.30
7 Transport	29.80	44.40	49.20	83.50	115.80	80.00
8 Communication	9.50	11.70	12.80	14.90	16.50	14.40
9 Recreation & culture	19.50	38.80	57.00	66.20	129.00	79.30
10 Education	[6.20]	11.90	1.90	3.80	29.50	12.50
11 Restaurants & hotels	17.10	31.90	32.60	45.50	76.30	49.90
12 Miscellaneous goods & services	17.70	29.60	32.70	48.20	78.30	51.20
1–12 All expenditure groups	261.30	355.60	375.70	473.90	713.30	507.50
13 Other expenditure items	18.30	52.20	71.00	99.20	171.50	107.80
Total expenditure	**279.60**	**407.70**	**446.70**	**573.10**	**884.80**	**615.30**
Average weekly expenditure per person (£)						
Total expenditure	**78.10**	**104.40**	**118.00**	**151.60**	**236.70**	**163.00**

Note: The commodity and service categories are not comparable to those in publications before 2001–02.

Please see page xiii for symbols and conventions used in this report

1   Excluding mortgage interest payments, council tax and Northern Ireland Rates.

ONS, Family Spending 2009, © Crown copyright 2010

Table 3.6E **Expenditure of two adult households with children by gross equivalised income quintile group (OECD-modified scale) 2009**
based on weighted data and including children's expenditure

	Lowest twenty per cent	Second quintile group	Third quintile group	Fourth quintile group	Highest twenty per cent	All house-holds
Lower boundary of group (£ per week)		175	275	397	586	
Weighted number of households (thousands)	640	870	1,230	1,330	1,080	5,140
Total number of households in sample	160	200	290	290	260	1,190
Total number of persons in sample	660	800	1,090	1,060	910	4,520
Total number of adults in sample	310	400	570	580	510	2,370
Weighted average number of persons per household	4.2	3.9	3.8	3.6	3.5	3.8
Commodity or service	Average weekly household expenditure (£)					
1 Food & non-alcoholic drinks	60.70	62.20	69.60	72.00	90.90	72.30
2 Alcoholic drinks, tobacco & narcotics	12.80	11.10	12.90	12.20	15.80	13.00
3 Clothing & footwear	20.70	21.20	26.80	29.80	49.60	30.70
4 Housing (net)[1], fuel & power	70.00	73.30	62.50	60.20	62.10	64.60
5 Household goods & services	17.80	19.10	29.10	36.30	59.50	34.30
6 Health	1.20	2.60	4.60	5.70	10.00	5.30
7 Transport	39.80	47.30	71.60	88.70	128.90	80.00
8 Communication	11.60	12.70	14.00	15.90	16.10	14.40
9 Recreation & culture	34.50	53.00	62.50	80.20	144.70	79.30
10 Education	11.10	2.80	3.80	8.30	36.20	12.50
11 Restaurants & hotels	24.60	38.80	40.00	49.70	85.20	49.90
12 Miscellaneous goods & services	25.70	30.50	43.20	50.90	92.30	51.20
1–12 All expenditure groups	330.60	374.50	440.70	510.00	791.30	507.50
13 Other expenditure items	32.40	65.50	94.50	117.70	189.30	107.80
Total expenditure	**363.10**	**440.10**	**535.20**	**627.70**	**980.60**	**615.30**
Average weekly expenditure per person (£)						
Total expenditure	**86.80**	**112.20**	**140.00**	**173.30**	**276.50**	**163.00**

Note: The commodity and service categories are not comparable to those in publications before 2001–02.

Please see page xiii for symbols and conventions used in this report.

1 Excluding mortgage interest payments, council tax and Northern Ireland Rates.

ONS, Family Spending 2009, © Crown copyright 2010

Table 3.7   **Expenditure of one adult households with children by gross income quintile group, 2009**

based on weighted data and including children's expenditure

	Lowest twenty per cent	Second quintile group	Third quintile group	Fourth quintile group	Highest twenty per cent	All house-holds
Lower boundary of group (£ per week)		235	410	647	985	
Weighted number of households (thousands)	490	450	250	60	30	1,290
Total number of households in sample	140	120	60	20	..	340
Total number of persons in sample	340	360	170	40	20	930
Total number of adults in sample	140	120	60	20	..	340
Weighted average number of persons per household	2.4	3.0	2.7	2.5	2.7	2.7
Commodity or service	Average weekly household expenditure (£)					
1 Food & non-alcoholic drinks	38.10	47.80	51.00	[51.70]	[61.60]	45.20
2 Alcoholic drinks, tobacco & narcotics	9.30	7.00	9.20	[7.70]	[7.60]	8.40
3 Clothing & footwear	15.80	16.50	17.80	[26.70]	[51.40]	17.80
4 Housing (net)[1], fuel & power	51.50	60.60	65.50	[81.70]	[69.80]	59.30
5 Household goods & services	13.30	17.80	29.60	[29.50]	[25.10]	19.10
6 Health	1.10	1.30	2.10	[1.60]	[2.10]	1.40
7 Transport	18.20	30.30	38.80	[59.70]	[100.10]	30.50
8 Communication	7.20	11.40	14.60	[15.20]	[14.60]	10.70
9 Recreation & culture	23.50	33.70	47.80	[73.20]	[103.10]	36.20
10 Education	[6.30]	[2.20]	[1.20]	[21.50]	[22.50]	5.00
11 Restaurants & hotels	12.60	23.40	35.00	[58.50]	[71.40]	24.40
12 Miscellaneous goods & services	13.00	27.00	47.60	[39.80]	[89.10]	27.90
1–12 All expenditure groups	209.90	279.20	360.20	[466.80]	[618.60]	286.00
13 Other expenditure items	21.10	37.10	64.90	[86.10]	[166.30]	42.00
Total expenditure	**231.00**	**316.30**	**425.00**	**[553.00]**	**[784.90]**	**328.00**
Average weekly expenditure per person (£)						
Total expenditure	**95.70**	**104.20**	**157.60**	**[219.00]**	**[291.30]**	**121.60**

Note: The commodity and service categories are not comparable to those in publications before 2001–02.

Please see page xiii for symbols and conventions used in this report

1   Excluding mortgage interest payments, council tax and Northern Ireland Rates.

ONS, Family Spending 2009, © Crown copyright 2010

Table 3.7E   **Expenditure of one adult households with children by gross equivalised income quintile group (OECD-modified scale) 2009**
based on weighted data and including children's expenditure

	Lowest twenty per cent	Second quintile group	Third quintile group	Fourth quintile group	Highest twenty per cent	All house-holds
Lower boundary of group (£ per week)		175	275	397	586	
Weighted number of households (thousands)	650	320	200	60	50	1,290
Total number of households in sample	180	90	50	20	10	340
Total number of persons in sample	510	230	120	40	30	930
Total number of adults in sample	180	90	50	20	10	340
Weighted average number of persons per household	2.8	2.7	2.4	2.4	2.5	2.7
Commodity or service	Average weekly household expenditure (£)					
1 Food & non-alcoholic drinks	43.40	45.50	46.30	[46.10]	[63.10]	45.20
2 Alcoholic drinks, tobacco & narcotics	9.20	6.50	7.00	[16.00]	[5.40]	8.40
3 Clothing & footwear	15.90	18.60	16.50	[21.80]	[40.30]	17.80
4 Housing (net)[1], fuel & power	49.70	73.00	57.60	[59.70]	[107.20]	59.30
5 Household goods & services	15.60	17.20	19.40	[54.00]	[32.70]	19.10
6 Health	1.50	0.60	2.70	[0.30]	[2.80]	1.40
7 Transport	18.50	33.30	43.60	[49.00]	[98.00]	30.50
8 Communication	8.60	11.90	13.10	[15.20]	[14.20]	10.70
9 Recreation & culture	25.90	36.70	47.70	[56.10]	[101.20]	36.20
10 Education	[5.10]	[2.70]	[1.20]	[1.50]	[42.70]	5.00
11 Restaurants & hotels	16.90	21.30	35.80	[47.30]	[71.00]	24.40
12 Miscellaneous goods & services	14.60	30.70	49.90	[49.10]	[70.90]	27.90
1–12 All expenditure groups	224.80	298.20	340.70	[416.10]	[649.50]	286.00
13 Other expenditure items	23.10	44.70	61.20	[97.10]	[130.60]	42.00
Total expenditure	**247.80**	**342.90**	**402.00**	**[513.20]**	**[780.10]**	**328.00**
Average weekly expenditure per person (£)						
Total expenditure	**88.00**	**126.20**	**166.20**	**[212.50]**	**[313.80]**	**121.60**

Note: The commodity and service categories are not comparable to those in publications before 2001–02.

Please see page xiii for symbols and conventions used in this report.

1   Excluding mortgage interest payments, council tax and Northern Ireland Rates.

ONS, Family Spending 2009, © Crown copyright 2010

Table 3.8   **Expenditure of two adult non-retired households by gross income quintile group, 2009**
based on weighted data

Commodity or service	Lowest twenty per cent	Second quintile group	Third quintile group	Fourth quintile group	Highest twenty per cent	All house-holds
Lower boundary of group (£ per week)		235	410	647	985	
Weighted number of households (thousands)	400	690	1,380	1,680	1,640	5,790
Total number of households in sample	90	160	320	360	350	1,270
Total number of persons in sample	170	320	650	710	690	2,540
Total number of adults in sample	170	320	650	710	690	2,540
Weighted average number of persons per household	2.0	2.0	2.0	2.0	2.0	2.0
Commodity or service	Average weekly household expenditure (£)					
1 Food & non-alcoholic drinks	38.80	45.60	52.00	50.30	59.80	52.00
2 Alcoholic drinks, tobacco & narcotics	11.90	10.60	12.50	13.50	15.00	13.20
3 Clothing & footwear	12.00	13.50	17.00	20.90	35.30	22.60
4 Housing (net)[1], fuel & power	57.60	62.80	58.80	64.20	74.60	65.20
5 Household goods & services	17.80	20.20	30.40	29.20	43.50	31.70
6 Health	3.60	4.60	5.20	5.20	10.50	6.50
7 Transport	29.00	47.40	60.30	73.70	107.10	73.80
8 Communication	9.00	10.00	11.80	12.40	14.50	12.30
9 Recreation & culture	30.50	42.20	49.80	71.30	104.60	69.30
10 Education	[12.00]	[10.30]	[1.40]	[5.60]	4.50	5.30
11 Restaurants & hotels	19.40	20.40	35.40	43.40	82.90	48.30
12 Miscellaneous goods & services	15.80	21.90	36.10	34.10	61.20	39.50
1–12 All expenditure groups	257.20	309.70	370.70	423.80	613.40	439.80
13 Other expenditure items	42.70	38.70	62.40	89.00	146.30	89.70
Total expenditure	**299.90**	**348.30**	**433.20**	**512.80**	**759.70**	**529.50**
Average weekly expenditure per person (£)						
Total expenditure	**150.00**	**174.20**	**216.60**	**256.40**	**379.80**	**264.70**

Note: The commodity and service categories are not comparable to those in publications before 2001–02.

Please see page xiii for symbols and conventions used in this report

1   Excluding mortgage interest payments, council tax and Northern Ireland Rates.

ONS, Family Spending 2009, © Crown copyright 2010

Table 3.8E **Expenditure of two adult non-retired households by gross equivalised income quintile group (OECD-modified scale) 2009**
based on weighted data

Commodity or service	Lowest twenty per cent	Second quintile group	Third quintile group	Fourth quintile group	Highest twenty per cent	All house-holds
Lower boundary of group (£ per week)		175	275	397	586	
Weighted number of households (thousands)	530	570	1,080	1,560	2,050	5,790
Total number of households in sample	110	130	250	340	430	1,270
Total number of persons in sample	230	270	510	670	860	2,540
Total number of adults in sample	230	270	510	670	860	2,540
Weighted average number of persons per household	2.0	2.0	2.0	2.0	2.0	2.0

Commodity or service	Average weekly household expenditure (£)					
1 Food & non-alcoholic drinks	40.80	44.90	51.80	50.50	58.10	52.00
2 Alcoholic drinks, tobacco & narcotics	11.20	11.20	12.50	12.80	15.00	13.20
3 Clothing & footwear	12.70	13.00	16.70	20.10	32.70	22.60
4 Housing (net)[1], fuel & power	66.80	55.70	58.20	63.20	72.80	65.20
5 Household goods & services	21.60	17.10	31.60	26.40	42.50	31.70
6 Health	3.00	5.40	5.20	5.10	9.50	6.50
7 Transport	28.50	51.10	58.80	68.80	103.40	73.80
8 Communication	9.00	10.20	11.70	11.90	14.40	12.30
9 Recreation & culture	30.60	44.10	48.10	65.50	100.30	69.30
10 Education	[18.30]	[3.90]	[1.30]	[5.60]	4.20	5.30
11 Restaurants & hotels	18.70	21.20	34.40	39.70	77.20	48.30
12 Miscellaneous goods & services	16.50	22.30	37.10	33.00	56.50	39.50
1–12 All expenditure groups	277.70	300.10	367.60	402.70	586.60	439.80
13 Other expenditure items	**37.80**	**42.50**	**58.40**	**80.00**	**140.10**	**89.70**
Total expenditure	**315.50**	**342.60**	**426.00**	**482.70**	**726.70**	**529.50**
Average weekly expenditure per person (£)						
Total expenditure	**157.80**	**171.30**	**213.00**	**241.30**	**363.40**	**264.70**

Note: The commodity and service categories are not comparable to those in publications before 2001–02.

Please see page xiii for symbols and conventions used in this report.

1 Excluding mortgage interest payments, council tax and Northern Ireland Rates.

ONS, Family Spending 2009, © Crown copyright 2010

Table 3.9   **Expenditure of one person retired households mainly dependent on state pensions[1] by gross income quintile group, 2009**
based on weighted data

	Lowest twenty per cent	Second quintile group	Third quintile group	Fourth quintile group	Highest twenty per cent	All house-holds
Lower boundary of group (£ per week)		235	410	647	985	
Weighted number of households (thousands)	710	60	0	0	0	770
Total number of households in sample	140	10	0	0	0	150
Total number of persons in sample	140	10	0	0	0	150
Total number of adults in sample	140	10	0	0	0	150
Weighted average number of persons per household	1.0	1.0	0	0	0	1.0
Commodity or service	Average weekly household expenditure (£)					
1 Food & non-alcoholic drinks	26.70	[23.40]	-	-	-	26.40
2 Alcoholic drinks, tobacco & narcotics	2.40	[2.30]	-	-	-	2.40
3 Clothing & footwear	5.30	[10.50]	-	-	-	5.70
4 Housing (net)[2], fuel & power	33.00	[28.90]	-	-	-	32.70
5 Household goods & services	11.80	[9.50]	-	-	-	11.60
6 Health	4.90	[0.60]	-	-	-	4.50
7 Transport	6.80	[12.60]	-	-	-	7.30
8 Communication	5.40	[6.30]	-	-	-	5.40
9 Recreation & culture	16.80	[19.00]	-	-	-	17.00
10 Education	[0.00]	-	-	-	-	[0.00]
11 Restaurants & hotels	6.80	[13.30]	-	-	-	7.30
12 Miscellaneous goods & services	11.80	[11.20]	-	-	-	11.80
1–12 All expenditure groups	131.70	[137.60]	-	-	-	132.10
13 Other expenditure items	16.50	[20.20]	-	-	-	16.80
Total expenditure	**148.10**	**[157.80]**	-	-	-	**148.90**
Average weekly expenditure per person (£)					-	
Total expenditure	**148.10**	**[157.80]**	-	-	-	**148.90**

Note: The commodity and service categories are not comparable to those in publications before 2001–02.

Please see page xiii for symbols and conventions used in this report

1   Mainly dependent on state pension and not economically active – see Appendix B.

2   Excluding mortgage interest payments, council tax and Northern Ireland Rates.

ONS, Family Spending 2009, © Crown copyright 2010

Table 3.9E **Expenditure of one person retired households mainly dependent on state pensions[1] by gross equivalised income quintile group (OECD-modified scale) 2009**
based on weighted data

	Lowest twenty per cent	Second quintile group	Third quintile group	Fourth quintile group	Highest twenty per cent	All house- holds
Lower boundary of group (£ per week)		175	275	397	586	
Weighted number of households (thousands)	530	220	20	0	0	770
Total number of households in sample	110	40	..	0	0	150
Total number of persons in sample	110	40	..	0	0	150
Total number of adults in sample	110	40	..	0	0	150
Weighted average number of persons per household	1.0	1.0	1.0	0	0	1.0
Commodity or service	Average weekly household expenditure (£)					
1 Food & non-alcoholic drinks	25.30	29.80	[14.70]	-	-	26.40
2 Alcoholic drinks, tobacco & narcotics	1.50	[4.70]	-	-	-	2.40
3 Clothing & footwear	4.40	[8.70]	[5.20]	-	-	5.70
4 Housing (net)[2], fuel & power	30.70	35.80	[52.20]	-	-	32.70
5 Household goods & services	11.90	10.70	[15.00]	-	-	11.60
6 Health	1.30	12.50	[0.10]	-	-	4.50
7 Transport	6.00	9.80	[13.10]	-	-	7.30
8 Communication	5.30	5.40	[9.00]	-	-	5.40
9 Recreation & culture	11.80	28.50	[23.40]	-	-	17.00
10 Education	[0.00]	-	-	-	-	[0.00]
11 Restaurants & hotels	6.40	7.30	[35.70]	-	-	7.30
12 Miscellaneous goods & services	10.30	15.40	[9.50]	-	-	11.80
1–12 All expenditure groups	115.10	168.70	[177.90]	-	-	132.10
13 Other expenditure items	17.20	13.30	[50.30]	-	-	16.80
Total expenditure	**132.30**	**182.00**	**[228.30]**	**-**	**-**	**148.90**
Average weekly expenditure per person (£)						
Total expenditure	**132.30**	**182.00**	**[228.30]**	**-**	**-**	**148.90**

Note: The commodity and service categories are not comparable to those in publications before 2001–02.

Please see page xiii for symbols and conventions used in this report.

1   Mainly dependent on state pension and not economically active – see Appendix B.

2   Excluding mortgage interest payments, council tax and Northern Ireland Rates.

ONS, Family Spending 2009, © Crown copyright 2010

Table 3.10   **Expenditure of two adult retired households mainly dependent on state pensions[1] by gross income quintile group, 2009**
based on weighted data

Commodity or service	Lowest twenty per cent	Second quintile group	Third quintile group	Fourth quintile group	Highest twenty per cent	All house-holds
Lower boundary of group (£ per week)		235	410	647	985	
Weighted number of households (thousands)	150	220	30	0	0	400
Total number of households in sample	40	60	..	0	0	120
Total number of persons in sample	90	130	10	0	0	230
Total number of adults in sample	90	130	10	0	0	230
Weighted average number of persons per household	2.0	2.0	2.0	0	0	2.0

Commodity or service	Average weekly household expenditure (£)					
1 Food & non-alcoholic drinks	45.90	47.40	[55.60]	-	-	47.40
2 Alcoholic drinks, tobacco & narcotics	[4.20]	7.80	[3.20]	-	-	6.10
3 Clothing & footwear	[5.30]	9.90	[5.20]	-	-	7.80
4 Housing (net)[2], fuel & power	30.50	40.50	[43.80]	-	-	36.90
5 Household goods & services	17.70	21.10	[17.60]	-	-	19.60
6 Health	[1.30]	3.10	[3.80]	-	-	2.50
7 Transport	36.50	24.80	[58.40]	-	-	31.80
8 Communication	5.10	7.00	[8.70]	-	-	6.40
9 Recreation & culture	32.80	43.50	[70.00]	-	-	41.30
10 Education	-	-	-	-	-	-
11 Restaurants & hotels	7.40	12.80	[30.40]	-	-	12.00
12 Miscellaneous goods & services	16.20	16.70	[19.60]	-	-	16.70
1–12 All expenditure groups	202.90	234.70	[316.30]	-	-	228.40
13 Other expenditure items	34.00	35.80	[13.50]	-	-	33.50
Total expenditure	**236.90**	**270.40**	**[329.80]**	**-**	**-**	**261.90**
Average weekly expenditure per person (£)						
Total expenditure	**118.50**	**135.20**	**[164.90]**	**-**	**-**	**131.00**

Note: The commodity and service categories are not comparable to those in publications before 2001–02.

Please see page xiii for symbols and conventions used in this report

1   Mainly dependent on state pension and not economically active – see Appendix B.

2   Excluding mortgage interest payments, council tax and Northern Ireland Rates.

ONS, Family Spending 2009, © Crown copyright 2010

Table 3.10E **Expenditure of two adult retired households mainly dependent on state pensions[1] by gross equivalised income quintile group (OECD-modified scale) 2009**
based on weighted data

Commodity or service	Lowest twenty per cent	Second quintile group	Third quintile group	Fourth quintile group	Highest twenty per cent	All house-holds
Lower boundary of group (£ per week)		175	275	397	586	
Weighted number of households (thousands)	210	160	20	..	0	400
Total number of households in sample	60	50	..	..	0	120
Total number of persons in sample	120	90	10	..	0	230
Total number of adults in sample	120	90	10	..	0	230
Weighted average number of persons per household	2.0	2.0	2.0	2.0	0	2.0
Commodity or service	Average weekly household expenditure (£)					
1 Food & non-alcoholic drinks	46.30	47.40	[52.40]	[73.30]	-	47.40
2 Alcoholic drinks, tobacco & narcotics	5.60	7.20	[3.80]	-	-	6.10
3 Clothing & footwear	5.70	10.90	[5.30]	[4.60]	-	7.80
4 Housing (net)[2], fuel & power	34.20	39.10	[41.50]	[56.60]	-	36.90
5 Household goods & services	15.90	24.60	[15.10]	[31.10]	-	19.60
6 Health	1.70	3.20	[4.40]	-	-	2.50
7 Transport	32.30	26.30	[66.20]	[16.20]	-	31.80
8 Communication	5.70	7.00	[7.90]	[12.90]	-	6.40
9 Recreation & culture	29.50	51.30	[75.70]	[39.00]	-	41.30
10 Education	-	-	-	-	-	-
11 Restaurants & hotels	8.10	13.80	[33.00]	[15.90]	-	12.00
12 Miscellaneous goods & services	16.90	16.00	[20.30]	[15.90]	-	16.70
1–12 All expenditure groups	201.80	246.80	[325.80]	[265.50]	-	228.40
13 Other expenditure items	36.50	33.20	[16.00]	-	-	33.50
Total expenditure	**238.30**	**280.00**	**[341.70]**	**[265.50]**	**-**	**261.90**
Average weekly expenditure per person (£)						
Total expenditure	**119.20**	**140.00**	**[170.90]**	**[132.80]**	**-**	**131.00**

Note: The commodity and service categories are not comparable to those in publications before 2001–02.

Please see page xiii for symbols and conventions used in this report.

1 Mainly dependent on state pension and not economically active – see Appendix B.

2 Excluding mortgage interest payments, council tax and Northern Ireland Rates.

ONS, Family Spending 2009, © Crown copyright 2010

Table 3.11 **Expenditure of two adult retired households not mainly dependent on state pensions[1] by gross income quintile group, 2009**
based on weighted data

	Lowest twenty per cent	Second quintile group	Third quintile group	Fourth quintile group	Highest twenty per cent	All house- holds
Lower boundary of group (£ per week)		235	410	647	985	
Weighted number of households (thousands)	180	1,070	760	300	100	2,400
Total number of households in sample	40	280	200	80	30	610
Total number of persons in sample	70	550	390	150	50	1,220
Total number of adults in sample	70	550	390	150	50	1,220
Weighted average number of persons per household	2.0	2.0	2.0	2.0	2.0	2.0
Commodity or service	Average weekly household expenditure (£)					
1 Food & non-alcoholic drinks	43.70	51.30	56.10	61.70	68.70	54.30
2 Alcoholic drinks, tobacco & narcotics	10.10	9.90	11.60	14.00	19.40	11.40
3 Clothing & footwear	7.70	9.30	15.40	20.00	[20.50]	12.90
4 Housing (net)[2], fuel & power	37.60	43.00	41.90	58.80	72.00	45.50
5 Household goods & services	12.70	19.80	21.40	55.10	126.00	28.60
6 Health	[5.40]	4.60	14.90	8.40	[9.90]	8.60
7 Transport	19.20	30.40	41.10	73.40	71.60	40.00
8 Communication	9.20	7.70	8.80	11.30	12.50	8.80
9 Recreation & culture	29.00	41.90	56.90	80.90	69.30	51.70
10 Education	-	[0.10]	[0.60]	[1.10]	[1.20]	[0.40]
11 Restaurants & hotels	15.80	19.00	30.50	53.40	60.10	28.40
12 Miscellaneous goods & services	12.20	20.00	26.10	40.20	90.50	26.80
1–12 All expenditure groups	202.50	257.00	325.30	478.40	621.60	317.30
13 Other expenditure items	12.10	36.00	46.40	78.10	89.40	45.00
Total expenditure	**214.70**	**293.10**	**371.70**	**556.40**	**711.10**	**362.30**
Average weekly expenditure per person (£)						
Total expenditure	**107.30**	**146.50**	**185.90**	**278.20**	**355.50**	**181.20**

Note: The commodity and service categories are not comparable to those in publications before 2001–02.

Please see page xiii for symbols and conventions used in this report.

1   Mainly dependent on state pension and not economically active – see Appendix B.

2   Excluding mortgage interest payments, council tax and Northern Ireland Rates.

ONS, Family Spending 2009, © Crown copyright 2010

Table 3.11E **Expenditure of two adult retired households not mainly dependent on state pensions[1] by gross equivalised income quintile group (OECD-modified scale) 2009**
based on weighted data

	Lowest twenty per cent	Second quintile group	Third quintile group	Fourth quintile group	Highest twenty per cent	All house-holds
Lower boundary of group (£ per week)		175	275	397	586	
Weighted number of households (thousands)	300	960	630	350	160	2,400
Total number of households in sample	70	250	170	90	40	610
Total number of persons in sample	140	490	330	170	80	1,220
Total number of adults in sample	140	490	330	170	80	1,220
Weighted average number of persons per household	2.0	2.0	2.0	2.0	2.0	2.0
Commodity or service	Average weekly household expenditure (£)					
1 Food & non-alcoholic drinks	47.10	51.60	54.60	59.50	70.70	54.30
2 Alcoholic drinks, tobacco & narcotics	10.90	9.70	11.00	13.80	18.20	11.40
3 Clothing & footwear	9.20	9.10	14.80	16.60	26.80	12.90
4 Housing (net)[2], fuel & power	36.70	43.80	41.90	49.60	76.30	45.50
5 Household goods & services	16.90	19.30	18.80	42.30	114.20	28.60
6 Health	4.10	4.90	8.70	21.90	9.40	8.60
7 Transport	31.20	28.60	41.30	58.50	79.40	40.00
8 Communication	8.70	7.70	8.30	11.20	12.20	8.80
9 Recreation & culture	32.00	42.60	49.80	90.80	64.30	51.70
10 Education	-	[0.10]	[0.20]	[1.80]	[1.10]	[0.40]
11 Restaurants & hotels	17.00	19.00	27.10	50.80	61.30	28.40
12 Miscellaneous goods & services	14.40	20.30	26.50	33.70	74.30	26.80
1–12 All expenditure groups	228.30	256.70	302.90	450.70	608.10	317.30
13 Other expenditure items	16.30	37.70	46.40	65.70	90.80	45.00
Total expenditure	**244.50**	**294.40**	**349.30**	**516.40**	**699.00**	**362.30**
Average weekly expenditure per person (£)						
Total expenditure	**122.30**	**147.20**	**174.70**	**258.20**	**349.50**	**181.20**

Note: The commodity and service categories are not comparable to those in publications before 2001–02.

Please see page xiii for symbols and conventions used in this report.

1   Mainly dependent on state pension and not economically active – see Appendix B.

2   Excluding mortgage interest payments, council tax and Northern Ireland Rates.

ONS, Family Spending 2009, © Crown copyright 2010

Table 3.12   **Income and source of income by gross income quintile group, 2009**

based on weighted data

Gross equivalised income quintile group	Weighted number of house- holds	Number of house- holds in the sample	Weekly house- hold income Dispo- sable	Gross	Source of income Wages and salaries	Self employ- ment	Invest- ments	Annuities and pensions[1]	Social security benefits[2]	Other sources
	(000s)	Number	£	£	Percentage of gross weekly household income					
Lowest twenty per cent	5,200	1,140	150	153	8	2	2	9	77	2
Second quintile group	5,200	1,220	295	317	28	4	2	17	46	3
Third quintile group	5,190	1,210	453	523	55	6	2	13	21	2
Fourth quintile group	5,200	1,140	660	801	74	7	2	8	8	1
Highest twenty per cent	5,200	1,120	1,233	1,619	79	11	3	4	2	0

Please see page xiii for symbols and conventions used in this report.

1   Other than social security benefits.

2   Excluding housing benefit and council tax benefit (rates rebate in Northern Ireland) – see Appendix B.

ONS, Family Spending 2009, © Crown copyright 2010

Table 3.12E **Income and source of income by gross equivalised income quintile group (OECD-modified scale) 2009**
based on weighted data

| | Weighted number of house-holds | Number of house-holds in the sample | Weekly house-hold income | | Source of income | | | | | |
			Dispo-sable	Gross	Wages and salaries	Self employ-ment	Invest-ments	Annuities and pensions[1]	Social security benefits[2]	Other sources
Gross equivalised income quintile group	(000s)	Number	£	£	Percentage of gross weekly household income					
Lowest twenty per cent	5,200	1,170	174	178	14	4	1	4	74	3
Second quintile group	5,190	1,200	318	342	34	5	2	12	45	3
Third quintile group	5,200	1,200	478	556	60	7	2	12	18	1
Fourth quintile group	5,190	1,140	656	800	73	8	2	9	7	1
Highest twenty per cent	5,190	1,120	1,165	1,538	78	11	4	5	2	0

Please see page xiii for symbols and conventions used in this report.

1   Other than social security benefits.

2   Excluding housing benefit and council tax benefit (rates rebate in Northern Ireland) – see Appendix B.

ONS, Family Spending 2009, © Crown copyright 2010

Table 3.13E Percentage of households by composition in each gross and equivalised income decile group (McClements-modified scale) 2009

Percentages

	Income decile group									
	Lowest ten per cent		Second		Third		Fourth		Fifth	
	Gross	Equivalised	Gross	Equivalised	Gross	Equivalised	Gross	Equivalised	Gross	Equivalised
Lower boundary of group (£ per week)			158	204	235	270	315	341	410	422
Average size of household	**1.3**	**2.3**	**1.6**	**2.0**	**2.0**	**2.2**	**2.1**	**2.3**	**2.4**	**2.5**
One adult retired mainly dependent on state pensions[1]	17	4	10	14	[2]	6	[0]	4	-	[1]
One adult, other retired	22	[3]	35	22	24	21	13	20	7	15
One adult, non-retired	41	32	17	11	14	9	19	10	18	9
One adult, one child	9	9	4	3	3	3	3	[2]	[3]	[2]
One adult, two or more children	[1]	8	5	5	6	3	5	5	[3]	[2]
Two adults, retired mainly dependent on state pensions[1]	[1]	3	5	6	6	4	3	[2]	[3]	[1]
Two adults, other retired	[0]	[3]	7	11	17	18	24	18	17	12
Two adults, non-retired	7	11	9	8	13	11	14	9	22	16
Two adults, one child	[1]	[4]	[3]	[4]	[3]	5	5	5	7	9
Two adults, two children	-	3	[2]	4	[2]	6	4	9	8	9
Two adults, three children	[0]	4	[1]	[2]	[3]	3	[2]	3	3	[3]
Two adults, four or more children	-	[1]	-	[2]	[1]	[1]	[1]	[1]	[1]	[1]
Three adults	[1]	4	[2]	[3]	[2]	3	4	6	4	8
Three adults, one or more children	-	4	[1]	[2]	[2]	[3]	[2]	[3]	[3]	[3]
All other households without children	-	[3]	[0]	[4]	[0]	4	[0]	[3]	[2]	6
All other households with children	[1]	[3]	[0]	[2]	[0]	[2]	[1]	[1]	[1]	[2]
	100	100	100	100	100	100	100	100	100	100

	Income decile group									
	Sixth		Seventh		Eighth		Ninth		Highest ten per cent	
	Gross	Equivalised	Gross	Equivalised	Gross	Equivalised	Gross	Equivalised	Gross	Equivalised
Lower boundary of group (£ per week)	520	506	647	599	796	713	985	885	1,348	1,181
Average size of household	**2.4**	**2.5**	**2.7**	**2.5**	**2.9**	**2.4**	**3.0**	**2.4**	**3.1**	**2.2**
One adult retired mainly dependent on state pensions[1]	-	[0]	-	-	-	-	-	-	-	-
One adult, other retired	[3]	9	[1]	8	[1]	4	[0]	[3]	[1]	[2]
One adult, non-retired	15	12	11	13	8	17	5	17	5	24
One adult, one child	[1]	[3]	[1]	[1]	[1]	[1]	[0]	[1]	[0]	[0]
One adult, two or more children	[2]	[1]	[1]	[1]	[0]	[0]	[1]	[1]	[0]	[0]
Two adults, retired mainly dependent on state pensions[1]	[0]	-	-	[0]	-	-	-	-	-	-
Two adults, other retired	13	10	6	6	6	7	[2]	4	[1]	[2]
Two adults, non-retired	32	21	35	26	29	29	35	37	28	38
Two adults, one child	11	9	11	11	14	12	12	10	14	13
Two adults, two children	8	11	13	11	15	10	13	9	15	7
Two adults, three children	[2]	4	4	[2]	4	[1]	4	[1]	[3]	[2]
Two adults, four or more children	[1]	-	[1]	[0]	[1]	[0]	[1]	[0]	[1]	[0]
Three adults	6	8	11	7	10	8	12	10	13	5
Three adults, one or more children	[3]	6	3	[4]	5	[3]	7	3	7	[2]
All other households without children	[2]	5	[2]	7	4	7	6	4	9	[3]
All other households with children	[2]	[2]	[2]	[2]	[2]	[1]	[2]	[0]	[3]	[1]
	100	100	100	100	100	100	100	100	100	100

Note: Please see page xiii for symbols and conventions used in this report.

1 Mainly dependent on state pension and not economically active – see Appendix B.

ONS, Family Spending 2009, © Crown copyright 2010

Table 3.14E **Household expenditure by gross equivalised income decile group (McClements-modified scale) 2009**

based on weighted data and including children's expenditure

	Lowest ten per cent	Second decile group	Third decile group	Fourth decile group	Fifth decile group	Sixth decile group
Lower boundary of group (£ per week)		204	270	341	422	506
Weighted number of households (thousands)	2,600	2,600	2,600	2,600	2,600	2,600
Total number of households in sample	580	600	590	610	590	600
Total number of persons in sample	1,360	1,260	1,310	1,390	1,470	1,520
Total number of adults in sample	890	940	1,040	1,070	1,140	1,170
Weighted average number of persons per household	2.3	2.0	2.2	2.3	2.5	2.5
Commodity or service	Average weekly household expenditure (£)					
1 Food & non-alcoholic drinks	37.50	39.70	44.50	48.70	53.90	56.10
2 Alcoholic drinks, tobacco & narcotics	8.40	8.00	9.70	8.40	11.20	11.50
3 Clothing & footwear	13.20	10.50	11.20	16.20	19.00	19.80
4 Housing (net)[1], fuel & power	50.10	47.40	52.30	54.80	50.30	60.70
5 Household goods & services	11.20	17.10	15.90	21.20	26.50	31.20
6 Health	2.10	2.40	4.20	4.10	5.10	5.20
7 Transport	25.90	22.00	30.50	38.60	52.20	58.80
8 Communication	8.30	8.40	8.70	10.00	11.90	12.50
9 Recreation & culture	22.60	27.30	36.00	42.50	53.80	56.20
10 Education	7.80	9.10	1.50	6.70	1.80	4.60
11 Restaurants & hotels	16.80	16.20	19.20	24.30	31.50	38.00
12 Miscellaneous goods & services	14.00	15.90	18.70	27.10	35.00	35.70
1–12 All expenditure groups	217.80	223.80	252.50	302.70	352.30	390.10
13 Other expenditure items	21.80	25.80	35.10	40.70	62.30	68.60
Total expenditure	**239.60**	**249.50**	**287.60**	**343.40**	**414.50**	**458.80**
Average weekly expenditure per person (£)						
Total expenditure	**102.20**	**124.60**	**131.30**	**152.30**	**166.30**	**181.90**

Note: The commodity and service categories are not comparable to those in publications before 2001–02.

Please see page xiii for symbols and conventions used in this report

1   Excluding mortgage interest payments, council tax and Northern Ireland Rates.

ONS, Family Spending 2009, © Crown copyright 2010

Table 3.14E Household expenditure by gross equivalised income decile group (McClements-modified scale) 2009 (cont.)

based on weighted data and including children's expenditure

	Seventh decile group	Eighth decile group	Ninth decile group	Highest ten per cent	All house-holds
Lower boundary of group (£ per week)	599	713	885	1,181	
Weighted number of households (thousands)	2,600	2,600	2,590	2,600	25,980
Total number of households in sample	570	570	570	540	5,830
Total number of persons in sample	1,430	1,390	1,360	1,240	13,740
Total number of adults in sample	1,130	1,130	1,130	1,010	10,650
Weighted average number of persons per household	2.5	2.4	2.4	2.2	2.3
Commodity or service	Average weekly household expenditure (£)				
1 Food & non-alcoholic drinks	56.00	59.50	60.70	65.00	52.20
2 Alcoholic drinks, tobacco & narcotics	13.20	12.50	13.70	15.10	11.20
3 Clothing & footwear	22.90	25.40	30.20	41.00	20.90
4 Housing (net)[1], fuel & power	60.40	58.60	62.90	75.60	57.30
5 Household goods & services	28.10	33.70	36.00	58.60	27.90
6 Health	7.00	6.10	7.30	9.40	5.30
7 Transport	72.90	80.10	93.30	110.10	58.40
8 Communication	13.20	13.80	14.70	15.10	11.70
9 Recreation & culture	62.40	72.60	88.50	116.80	57.90
10 Education	5.10	8.10	5.90	19.30	7.00
11 Restaurants & hotels	42.80	48.40	57.30	89.40	38.40
12 Miscellaneous goods & services	38.10	43.10	48.20	74.80	35.00
1–12 All expenditure groups	422.00	462.00	518.70	690.20	383.10
13 Other expenditure items	74.80	94.70	109.30	185.10	71.80
Total expenditure	**496.80**	**556.60**	**627.90**	**875.30**	**455.00**
Average weekly expenditure per person (£)					
Total expenditure	**195.50**	**227.60**	**265.10**	**391.30**	**194.40**

Note: The commodity and service categories are not comparable to those in publications before 2001–02.

Please see page xiii for symbols and conventions used in this report

1   Excluding mortgage interest payments, council tax and Northern Ireland Rates.

ONS, Family Spending 2009, © Crown copyright 2010

Table 3.15E **Household expenditure as a percentage of total expenditure by gross equivalised income decile group (McClements-modified scale) 2009**

based on weighted data and including children's expenditure

	Lowest ten per cent	Second decile group	Third decile group	Fourth decile group	Fifth decile group	Sixth decile group
Lower boundary of group (£ per week)		204	270	341	422	506
Weighted number of households (thousands)	2,600	2,600	2,600	2,600	2,600	2,600
Total number of households in sample	580	600	590	610	590	600
Total number of persons in sample	1,360	1,260	1,310	1,390	1,470	1,520
Total number of adults in sample	890	940	1,040	1,070	1,140	1,170
Weighted average number of persons per household	2.3	2.0	2.2	2.3	2.5	2.5
Commodity or service	Percentage of total expenditure					
1 Food & non-alcoholic drinks	16	16	15	14	13	12
2 Alcoholic drinks, tobacco & narcotics	4	3	3	2	3	3
3 Clothing & footwear	6	4	4	5	5	4
4 Housing (net)[1], fuel & power	21	19	18	16	12	13
5 Household goods & services	5	7	6	6	6	7
6 Health	1	1	1	1	1	1
7 Transport	11	9	11	11	13	13
8 Communication	3	3	3	3	3	3
9 Recreation & culture	9	11	13	12	13	12
10 Education	3	4	1	2	0	1
11 Restaurants & hotels	7	6	7	7	8	8
12 Miscellaneous goods & services	6	6	6	8	8	8
1–12 All expenditure groups	91	90	88	88	85	85
13 Other expenditure items	9	10	12	12	15	15
Total expenditure	100	100	100	100	100	100

Note: The commodity and service categories are not comparable to those in publications before 2001–02

Please see page xiii for symbols and conventions used in this report

1 Excluding mortgage interest payments, council tax and Northern Ireland Rates.

ONS, Family Spending 2009, © Crown copyright 2010

Table 3.15E **Household expenditure as a percentage of total expenditure by gross equivalised income decile group (McClements-modified scale) 2009 (cont.)**
based on weighted data and including children's expenditure

	Seventh decile group	Eighth decile group	Ninth decile group	Highest ten per cent	All house- holds
Lower boundary of group (£ per week)	599	713	885	1,181	
Weighted number of households (thousands)	2,600	2,600	2,590	2,600	25,980
Total number of households in sample	570	570	570	540	5,830
Total number of persons in sample	1,430	1,390	1,360	1,240	13,740
Total number of adults in sample	1,130	1,130	1,130	1,010	10,650
Weighted average number of persons per household	2.5	2.4	2.4	2.2	2.3
Commodity or service	Percentage of total expenditure				
1 Food & non-alcoholic drinks	11	11	10	7	11
2 Alcoholic drinks, tobacco & narcotics	3	2	2	2	2
3 Clothing & footwear	5	5	5	5	5
4 Housing (net)[1], fuel & power	12	11	10	9	13
5 Household goods & services	6	6	6	7	6
6 Health	1	1	1	1	1
7 Transport	15	14	15	13	13
8 Communication	3	2	2	2	3
9 Recreation & culture	13	13	14	13	13
10 Education	1	1	1	2	2
11 Restaurants & hotels	9	9	9	10	8
12 Miscellaneous goods & services	8	8	8	9	8
1–12 All expenditure groups	85	83	83	79	84
13 Other expenditure items	15	17	17	21	16
Total expenditure	100	100	100	100	100

Note: The commodity and service categories are not comparable to those in publications before 2001–02

Please see page xiii for symbols and conventions used in this report

1   Excluding mortgage interest payments, council tax and Northern Ireland Rates.

ONS, Family Spending 2009, © Crown copyright 2010

Table 3.16E **Expenditure of one person non-retired households by gross equivalised income quintile group (McClements-modified scale) 2009**
based on weighted data

Commodity or service	Lowest twenty per cent	Second quintile group	Third quintile group	Fourth quintile group	Highest twenty per cent	All house- holds
Lower boundary of group (£ per week)		270	422	599	885	
Weighted number of households (thousands)	1,120	480	560	770	1,070	4,000
Total number of households in sample	240	110	130	170	220	870
Total number of persons in sample	240	110	130	170	220	870
Total number of adults in sample	240	110	130	170	220	870
Weighted average number of persons per household	1.0	1.0	1.0	1.0	1.0	1.0
Commodity or service	Average weekly household expenditure (£)					
1 Food & non-alcoholic drinks	20.30	24.40	25.60	27.80	28.90	25.30
2 Alcoholic drinks, tobacco & narcotics	7.00	8.50	7.30	10.30	10.10	8.70
3 Clothing & footwear	3.70	5.80	8.30	10.00	15.40	9.00
4 Housing (net)[1], fuel & power	34.50	48.40	54.20	53.90	62.50	50.20
5 Household goods & services	7.30	12.90	22.80	12.50	40.90	20.20
6 Health	0.90	2.90	3.00	4.70	4.00	3.00
7 Transport	14.50	24.30	30.70	39.60	60.50	35.10
8 Communication	4.90	6.50	7.50	9.20	11.10	8.00
9 Recreation & culture	14.40	23.40	25.20	31.20	54.60	31.00
10 Education	[3.00]	[1.10]	[6.50]	[1.80]	[3.10]	3.10
11 Restaurants & hotels	9.40	16.00	18.60	21.50	43.60	23.00
12 Miscellaneous goods & services	7.70	11.30	19.40	19.10	35.20	19.30
1–12 All expenditure groups	127.70	185.70	229.10	241.80	370.10	235.60
13 Other expenditure items	15.90	22.10	46.00	51.70	134.00	59.30
Total expenditure	**143.60**	**207.80**	**275.10**	**293.50**	**504.10**	**294.90**
Average weekly expenditure per person (£)						
Total expenditure	**143.60**	**207.80**	**275.10**	**293.50**	**504.10**	**294.90**

Note: The commodity and service categories are not comparable to those in publications before 2001–02.

Please see page xiii for symbols and conventions used in this report

1 Excluding mortgage interest payments, council tax and Northern Ireland Rates.

ONS, Family Spending 2009, © Crown copyright 2010

Table 3.17E **Expenditure of one person retired households not mainly dependent on state pensions[1] by gross equivalised income quintile group (McClements-modified scale) 2009**
based on weighted data

	Lowest twenty per cent	Second quintile group	Third quintile group	Fourth quintile group	Highest twenty per cent	All house-holds
Lower boundary of group (£ per week)		270	422	599	885	
Weighted number of households (thousands)	630	1,060	620	310	120	2,750
Total number of households in sample	140	210	130	70	30	580
Total number of persons in sample	140	210	130	70	30	580
Total number of adults in sample	140	210	130	70	30	580
Weighted average number of persons per household	1.0	1.0	1.0	1.0	1.0	1.0
Commodity or service	Average weekly household expenditure (£)					
1 Food & non-alcoholic drinks	26.10	28.90	30.00	32.90	38.80	29.40
2 Alcoholic drinks, tobacco & narcotics	3.20	3.70	4.70	5.80	[7.90]	4.30
3 Clothing & footwear	5.10	6.00	9.00	8.10	[4.90]	6.70
4 Housing (net)[2], fuel & power	31.10	42.40	44.40	37.50	50.00	40.00
5 Household goods & services	12.00	13.50	15.70	27.20	30.40	16.00
6 Health	4.80	2.60	2.60	10.50	[3.50]	4.00
7 Transport	7.50	10.70	23.10	29.00	23.30	15.40
8 Communication	6.00	6.00	7.40	6.90	7.90	6.50
9 Recreation & culture	15.30	23.00	28.10	37.00	37.40	24.60
10 Education	[0.00]	[0.10]	[2.90]	[0.10]	-	[0.70]
11 Restaurants & hotels	6.40	9.80	13.90	14.70	[26.30]	11.20
12 Miscellaneous goods & services	9.80	18.30	19.20	24.90	42.90	18.40
1–12 All expenditure groups	127.10	165.00	200.90	234.80	273.20	177.20
13 Other expenditure items	8.10	21.40	33.40	34.40	77.00	25.00
Total expenditure	**135.20**	**186.40**	**234.30**	**269.10**	**350.20**	**202.20**
Average weekly expenditure per person (£)						
Total expenditure	**135.20**	**186.40**	**234.30**	**269.10**	**350.20**	**202.20**

Note: The commodity and service categories are not comparable to those in publications before 2001–02.

Please see page xiii for symbols and conventions used in this report

1   Mainly dependent on state pension and not economically active – see Appendix B.

2   Excluding mortgage interest payments, council tax and Northern Ireland Rates.

ONS, Family Spending 2009, © Crown copyright 2010

Table 3.18E Expenditure of two adult households with children by gross equivalised income quintile group (McClements-modified scale) 2009

based on weighted data and including children's expenditure

	Lowest twenty per cent	Second quintile group	Third quintile group	Fourth quintile group	Highest twenty per cent	All house-holds
Lower boundary of group (£ per week)		270	422	599	885	
Weighted number of households (thousands)	650	860	1,260	1,280	1,100	5,140
Total number of households in sample	160	200	290	280	260	1,190
Total number of persons in sample	690	780	1,120	1,030	910	4,520
Total number of adults in sample	320	390	590	570	510	2,370
Weighted average number of persons per household	4.2	3.9	3.8	3.6	3.5	3.8
Commodity or service	Average weekly household expenditure (£)					
1 Food & non-alcoholic drinks	62.30	61.90	68.50	73.20	89.90	72.30
2 Alcoholic drinks, tobacco & narcotics	12.50	11.70	12.50	12.70	15.30	13.00
3 Clothing & footwear	21.10	22.20	26.60	29.90	48.70	30.70
4 Housing (net)[1], fuel & power	68.40	72.40	63.30	60.40	62.60	64.60
5 Household goods & services	18.20	19.60	28.90	37.20	58.10	34.30
6 Health	1.30	2.20	4.70	5.80	10.10	5.30
7 Transport	40.40	51.30	68.40	92.40	124.80	80.00
8 Communication	11.70	13.00	14.10	15.60	16.10	14.40
9 Recreation & culture	36.00	54.80	64.50	77.50	143.40	79.30
10 Education	11.80	2.20	3.70	10.00	34.10	12.50
11 Restaurants & hotels	31.10	34.80	40.30	50.00	84.00	49.90
12 Miscellaneous goods & services	26.40	30.50	41.80	52.50	91.50	51.20
1–12 All expenditure groups	341.30	376.50	437.30	517.10	778.70	507.50
13 Other expenditure items	44.70	58.90	95.90	117.90	185.50	107.80
Total expenditure	**386.00**	**435.40**	**533.20**	**635.00**	**964.20**	**615.30**
Average weekly expenditure per person (£)						
Total expenditure	**92.10**	**110.30**	**140.20**	**174.90**	**273.20**	**163.00**

Note: The commodity and service categories are not comparable to those in publications before 2001–02.

Please see page xiii for symbols and conventions used in this report

1   Excluding mortgage interest payments, council tax and Northern Ireland Rates.

ONS, Family Spending 2009, © Crown copyright 2010

Table 3.19E Expenditure of one adult households with children by gross equivalised income quintile group (McClements-modified scale) 2009

based on weighted data and including children's expenditure

	Lowest twenty per cent	Second quintile group	Third quintile group	Fourth quintile group	Highest twenty per cent	All house-holds
Lower boundary of group (£ per week)		270	422	599	885	
Weighted number of households (thousands)	640	330	180	80	50	1,290
Total number of households in sample	180	90	50	20	10	340
Total number of persons in sample	510	230	110	50	30	930
Total number of adults in sample	180	90	50	20	10	340
Weighted average number of persons per household	2.8	2.7	2.4	2.3	2.5	2.7

Commodity or service	Average weekly household expenditure (£)					
1 Food & non-alcoholic drinks	43.00	48.90	42.60	43.30	[63.10]	45.20
2 Alcoholic drinks, tobacco & narcotics	8.90	7.10	7.20	[13.80]	[5.40]	8.40
3 Clothing & footwear	15.90	18.30	18.70	[16.70]	[40.30]	17.80
4 Housing (net)[1], fuel & power	49.70	70.00	62.00	58.60	[107.20]	59.30
5 Household goods & services	14.90	18.50	20.60	[43.20]	[32.70]	19.10
6 Health	1.50	0.70	2.90	[0.20]	[2.80]	1.40
7 Transport	18.70	31.10	49.70	[41.40]	[98.00]	30.50
8 Communication	8.50	12.30	12.10	15.20	[14.20]	10.70
9 Recreation & culture	25.70	37.90	48.70	47.60	[101.20]	36.20
10 Education	[5.10]	[2.60]	[1.30]	[1.20]	[42.70]	5.00
11 Restaurants & hotels	16.90	22.40	36.20	39.80	[71.00]	24.40
12 Miscellaneous goods & services	14.10	31.10	50.30	49.60	[70.90]	27.90
1–12 All expenditure groups	223.10	300.90	352.30	370.50	[649.50]	286.00
13 Other expenditure items	23.50	46.30	57.20	86.10	[130.60]	42.00
Total expenditure	**246.60**	**347.20**	**409.50**	**456.60**	**[780.10]**	**328.00**
Average weekly expenditure per person (£)						
Total expenditure	**87.10**	**127.40**	**170.40**	**197.90**	**[313.80]**	**121.60**

Note: The commodity and service categories are not comparable to those in publications before 2001–02.

Please see page xiii for symbols and conventions used in this report

1   Excluding mortgage interest payments, council tax and Northern Ireland Rates.

ONS, Family Spending 2009, © Crown copyright 2010

Table 3.20E **Expenditure of two adult non-retired households by gross equivalised income quintile group (McClements-modified scale) 2009**

based on weighted data

	Lowest twenty per cent	Second quintile group	Third quintile group	Fourth quintile group	Highest twenty per cent	All house- holds
Lower boundary of group (£ per week)		270	422	599	885	
Weighted number of households (thousands)	580	570	1,060	1,550	2,030	5,790
Total number of households in sample	120	140	250	340	430	1,270
Total number of persons in sample	250	270	500	670	850	2,540
Total number of adults in sample	250	270	500	670	850	2,540
Weighted average number of persons per household	2.0	2.0	2.0	2.0	2.0	2.0
Commodity or service	Average weekly household expenditure (£)					
1 Food & non-alcoholic drinks	40.70	45.70	52.10	50.40	58.10	52.00
2 Alcoholic drinks, tobacco & narcotics	11.60	12.20	11.70	12.90	15.10	13.20
3 Clothing & footwear	12.90	12.30	17.00	20.50	32.70	22.60
4 Housing (net)[1], fuel & power	65.70	55.90	57.70	63.30	73.20	65.20
5 Household goods & services	21.70	16.20	32.20	26.20	42.80	31.70
6 Health	3.10	5.30	5.70	4.80	9.60	6.50
7 Transport	28.50	52.30	60.00	68.30	104.10	73.80
8 Communication	9.40	9.80	11.90	11.90	14.40	12.30
9 Recreation & culture	30.60	43.90	48.90	65.70	100.90	69.30
10 Education	[18.80]	[1.80]	[1.30]	[5.70]	4.20	5.30
11 Restaurants & hotels	19.50	20.70	35.50	39.90	77.30	48.30
12 Miscellaneous goods & services	16.60	22.30	38.70	32.50	56.70	39.50
1–12 All expenditure groups	279.10	298.40	372.80	401.90	589.10	439.80
13 Other expenditure items	**36.50**	**44.70**	**62.80**	**77.40**	**141.00**	**89.70**
Total expenditure	**315.60**	**343.10**	**435.50**	**479.30**	**730.10**	**529.50**
Average weekly expenditure per person (£)						
Total expenditure	**157.80**	**171.60**	**217.80**	**239.60**	**365.10**	**264.70**

Note: The commodity and service categories are not comparable to those in publications before 2001–02.

Please see page xiii for symbols and conventions used in this report

1   Excluding mortgage interest payments, council tax and Northern Ireland Rates.

ONS, Family Spending 2009, © Crown copyright 2010

Table 3.21E **Expenditure of one person retired households mainly dependent on state pensions[1] by gross equivalised income quintile group (McClements-modified scale) 2009**
based on weighted data

	Lowest twenty per cent	Second quintile group	Third quintile group	Fourth quintile group	Highest twenty per cent	All house-holds
Lower boundary of group (£ per week)		270	422	599	885	
Weighted number of households (thousands)	480	260	30	0	0	770
Total number of households in sample	100	50	..	0	0	150
Total number of persons in sample	100	50	..	0	0	150
Total number of adults in sample	100	50	..	0	0	150
Weighted average number of persons per household	1.0	1.0	1.0	0	0	1.0
Commodity or service	Average weekly household expenditure (£)					
1 Food & non-alcoholic drinks	25.00	29.50	[22.40]	-	-	26.40
2 Alcoholic drinks, tobacco & narcotics	1.60	[4.10]	[0.60]	-	-	2.40
3 Clothing & footwear	4.60	7.60	[5.70]	-	-	5.70
4 Housing (net)[2], fuel & power	30.40	36.10	[40.20]	-	-	32.70
5 Household goods & services	12.70	9.60	[11.90]	-	-	11.60
6 Health	1.40	10.90	[0.60]	-	-	4.50
7 Transport	6.30	7.50	[23.50]	-	-	7.30
8 Communication	5.20	5.70	[6.70]	-	-	5.40
9 Recreation & culture	11.10	27.10	[24.30]	-	-	17.00
10 Education	[0.10]	-	-	-	-	[0.00]
11 Restaurants & hotels	6.70	6.90	[21.00]	-	-	7.30
12 Miscellaneous goods & services	10.10	14.90	[11.90]	-	-	11.80
1–12 All expenditure groups	115.20	159.70	[168.50]	-	-	132.10
13 Other expenditure items	16.20	15.60	[37.60]	-	-	16.80
Total expenditure	**131.40**	**175.20**	**[206.20]**	**-**	**-**	**148.90**
Average weekly expenditure per person (£)						
Total expenditure	**131.40**	**175.20**	**[206.20]**	**-**	**-**	**148.90**

Note: The commodity and service categories are not comparable to those in publications before 2001–02.

Please see page xiii for symbols and conventions used in this report

1   Mainly dependent on state pension and not economically active – see Appendix B.

2   Excluding mortgage interest payments, council tax and Northern Ireland Rates.

ONS, Family Spending 2009, © Crown copyright 2010

Table 3.22E **Expenditure of two adult retired households mainly dependent on state pensions[1] by gross equivalised income quintile group (McClements-modified scale) 2009**
based on weighted data

	Lowest twenty per cent	Second quintile group	Third quintile group	Fourth quintile group	Highest twenty per cent	All house-holds
Lower boundary of group (£ per week)		270	422	599	885	
Weighted number of households (thousands)	230	150	20	..	0	400
Total number of households in sample	70	40	..	..	0	120
Total number of persons in sample	140	80	10	..	0	230
Total number of adults in sample	140	80	10	..	0	230
Weighted average number of persons per household	2.0	2.0	2.0	2.0	0	2.0
Commodity or service	Average weekly household expenditure (£)					
1 Food & non-alcoholic drinks	46.70	47.40	[49.40]	[73.30]	-	47.40
2 Alcoholic drinks, tobacco & narcotics	5.90	[6.90]	[4.60]	-	-	6.10
3 Clothing & footwear	5.30	12.20	[4.30]	[4.60]	-	7.80
4 Housing (net)[2], fuel & power	33.90	40.60	[39.20]	[56.60]	-	36.90
5 Household goods & services	16.00	26.10	[10.70]	[31.10]	-	19.60
6 Health	2.00	[3.40]	[1.50]	-	-	2.50
7 Transport	31.10	29.00	[62.50]	[16.20]	-	31.80
8 Communication	5.60	7.50	[6.40]	[12.90]	-	6.40
9 Recreation & culture	30.50	53.50	[74.90]	[39.00]	-	41.30
10 Education	-	-	-	-	-	-
11 Restaurants & hotels	8.80	15.80	[19.60]	[15.90]	-	12.00
12 Miscellaneous goods & services	16.50	16.40	[20.90]	[15.90]	-	16.70
1–12 All expenditure groups	202.40	258.80	[293.90]	[265.50]	-	228.40
13 Other expenditure items	34.90	35.10	[13.80]	-	-	33.50
Total expenditure	**237.30**	**293.90**	**[307.70]**	**[265.50]**	**-**	**261.90**
Average weekly expenditure per person (£)						
Total expenditure	**118.70**	**147.00**	**[153.90]**	**[132.80]**	**-**	**131.00**

Note: The commodity and service categories are not comparable to those in publications before 2001–02.

Please see page xiii for symbols and conventions used in this report

1   Mainly dependent on state pension and not economically active – see Appendix B.

2   Excluding mortgage interest payments, council tax and Northern Ireland Rates.

ONS, Family Spending 2009, © Crown copyright 2010

Table 3.23E **Expenditure of two adult retired households not mainly dependent on state pensions[1] by gross equivalised income quintile group (McClements-modified scale) 2009**
based on weighted data

	Lowest twenty per cent	Second quintile group	Third quintile group	Fourth quintile group	Highest twenty per cent	All house-holds
Lower boundary of group (£ per week)		270	422	599	885	
Weighted number of households (thousands)	360	940	590	350	150	2,400
Total number of households in sample	90	250	150	90	40	610
Total number of persons in sample	170	490	310	170	80	1,220
Total number of adults in sample	170	490	310	170	80	1,220
Weighted average number of persons per household	2.0	2.0	2.0	2.0	2.0	2.0
Commodity or service	Average weekly household expenditure (£)					
1 Food & non-alcoholic drinks	47.20	52.30	53.90	61.30	68.30	54.30
2 Alcoholic drinks, tobacco & narcotics	9.90	10.10	10.80	14.40	17.60	11.40
3 Clothing & footwear	9.20	9.50	14.70	21.00	17.30	12.90
4 Housing (net)[2], fuel & power	37.10	44.10	42.20	54.90	65.30	45.50
5 Household goods & services	15.40	20.80	17.60	51.40	99.70	28.60
6 Health	4.40	4.60	9.20	22.40	8.90	8.60
7 Transport	27.30	29.40	43.10	61.90	74.80	40.00
8 Communication	9.80	7.20	8.40	11.20	12.50	8.80
9 Recreation & culture	32.70	42.10	52.70	89.70	65.20	51.70
10 Education	-	[0.10]	[0.20]	[1.80]	[1.20]	[0.40]
11 Restaurants & hotels	17.10	19.00	29.10	49.80	62.10	28.40
12 Miscellaneous goods & services	17.40	19.60	26.70	35.60	74.60	26.80
1–12 All expenditure groups	227.40	259.00	308.70	475.30	567.50	317.30
13 Other expenditure items	17.60	38.60	47.20	70.60	83.30	45.00
Total expenditure	**245.00**	**297.60**	**355.90**	**545.90**	**650.70**	**362.30**
Average weekly expenditure per person (£)						
Total expenditure	**122.50**	**148.80**	**177.90**	**273.00**	**325.40**	**181.20**

Note: The commodity and service categories are not comparable to those in publications before 2001–02.

Please see page xiii for symbols and conventions used in this report.

1   Mainly dependent on state pension and not economically active – see Appendix B.

2   Excluding mortgage interest payments, council tax and Northern Ireland Rates.

ONS, Family Spending 2009, © Crown copyright 2010

Table 3.24E Income and source of income by gross equivalised income quintile group (McClements-modified scale) 2009
based on weighted data

	Weighted number of house- holds	Number of house- holds in the sample	Weekly house- hold income		Source of income					
			Dispo- sable	Gross	Wages and salaries	Self employ- ment	Invest- ments	Annuities and pensions[1]	Social security benefits[2]	Other sources
Gross equivalised income quintile group	(000s)	Number	£	£	Percentage of gross weekly household income					
Lowest twenty per cent	5,200	1,180	180	184	15	4	1	4	72	4
Second quintile group	5,200	1,200	323	349	36	5	2	12	43	2
Third quintile group	5,200	1,190	486	567	61	7	2	11	18	1
Fourth quintile group	5,200	1,140	662	806	72	8	2	9	7	1
Highest twenty per cent	5,190	1,110	1,140	1,509	79	11	4	5	2	0

Please see page xiii for symbols and conventions used in this report.

1   Other than social security benefits.

2   Excluding housing benefit and council tax benefit (rates rebate in Northern Ireland) – see Appendix B.

ONS, Family Spending 2009, © Crown copyright 2010

Trends in household expenditure over time

Background

This chapter presents household expenditure data over time using two different classifications:

1. Classification Of Individual COnsumption by Purpose (COICOP). COICOP is the internationally agreed standard classification for reporting household consumption expenditure, and has been used since 2001/02, first in the Expenditure and Food Survey (EFS), and subsequently in the Living Costs and Food survey (LCF)

2. The Family Expenditure Survey (FES) classification. This was the main classification prior to 2001/02. Although it is has now been superseded, its use here enables a longer time series to be presented.

The figures and tables in this chapter (except Table 4.5) present figures that have been deflated using the All Items Retail Prices Index (RPI) data. This allows a comparison of expenditure in real terms to be made between the survey years. The commentary refers to the time series produced using these deflated figures. In addition, expenditure over time using COICOP in real terms is shown in Table 4.5, but no commentary is given on this table.

Interpreting EFS/LCF time series data

Before the introduction of the Expenditure and Food Survey (EFS) in 2001/02, expenditure data were collected via the Family Expenditure Survey (FES) and classified using the FES method of classification. These data have been retained and published alongside the COICOP time series and are presented in Tables 4.1 and 4.2.

Time series data based on the FES classification from 2001/02 (Tables 4.1 and 4.2) have been constructed by mapping COICOP data onto the FES classification. As such, the 'all expenditure groups' totals in Table 4.1 may not equal the sum of the component commodities or services as the mapping process is not exact. Due to the differences in the definitions of the classification headings, it is not possible to directly compare the FES data with the COICOP data. For example, 'Motoring' in the FES classification includes vehicle insurance, whereas the 'Transport' heading under COICOP excludes this expenditure.

As mentioned above, Tables 4.1 to 4.4 contain data that have been deflated to 2009 prices. To produce these data, each year's expenditure figures have been adjusted using the 'All items RPI' to account for price inflation that has occurred since that year. This results in a table of figures displayed in 'real terms' (that is at prices relative to 2009 prices), which allows comparisons to be made between different survey years. (The 'All Items RPI' can be downloaded from the Office for National Statistics website at: www.statistics.gov.uk/cci/nugget.asp?ID=21). Data in Table 4.5 have not been deflated to 2009 prices and therefore show the actual expenditure figures for each survey year.

Each year the Living Costs and Food Survey (LCF), previously the EFS, is reviewed and changes are made to keep it up to date. As such, year-on-year changes should be interpreted with caution. A detailed explanation of the items that feed into each COICOP heading can be found in Appendix A, while details of definition changes can be found in Appendix B.

Trends for the categories with lower levels of spending need to be treated with a degree of caution as the standard errors for these categories tend to be higher (standard errors are discussed in more detail in Appendix B). It should also be noted that there may be underreporting on certain items (notably tobacco and alcohol).

COICOP time series data in this publication are not directly comparable with UK National Accounts household expenditure data, which are published in *Consumer Trends*. (This publication can be downloaded from the Office for National Statistics website at www.statistics.gov.uk/statbase/Product.asp?vlnk=242). National Accounts figures draw on a number of sources in addition to the LCF (please refer to Appendix B of *Consumer Trends* for details) and may be more appropriate for deriving long term trends on expenditure.

Household expenditure over time

Figure 4.1 and Table 4.3 show total household expenditure at 2009 prices, broken down by COICOP, over the period 2003/04 to 2009. In 2003/04 the average total weekly expenditure was £489.70. It grew to a peak of £493.40 in 2004/05 before falling to its lowest value of £455.00 in 2009.

Figure 4.1 **Total household expenditure based on COICOP classification, 2003–04 to 2009, at 2009 prices[1]**

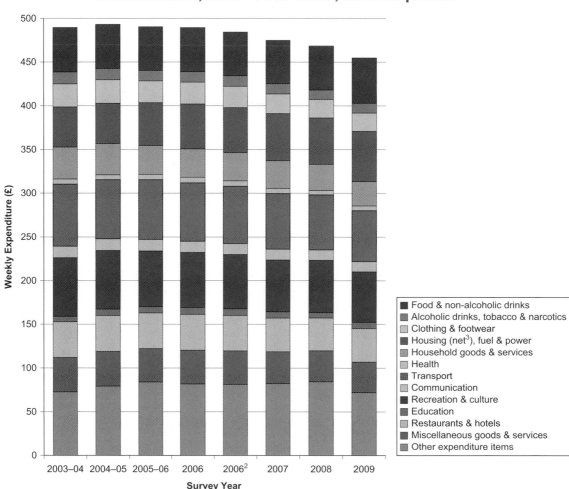

1 Figures have been deflated to 2009 prices using the RPI all items index.

2 Figures from 2006 onwards are based on weighted data using updated weights, with non-response weights and population figs based on 2001 census.

3 Excluding mortgage interest payments, council tax and Northern Ireland rates.

Excluding the other items category, 'Transport' consistently had the highest average weekly spend throughout the time series. Spending levels were greatest at the start of the time series, with households spending £71.10 per week in 2003/04; this subsequently fell every year to reach the lowest level of £58.40 in 2009. The next highest expenditure was on 'Recreation and culture', which followed a similar trend to expenditure on 'Transport'. 'Recreation and culture' had a weekly spending level of £67.10 in 2003/04 before steadily declining to its lowest amount of £57.90 in 2009. 'Recreation and culture', and 'Transport' each accounted for between 12 and 15 per cent of overall spending throughout the time series.

Among the twelve COICOP headings, 'Food and non–alcoholic drink', and 'Education' had the most consistent expenditure over the time series. 'Food and non-alcoholic drink' expenditure varied between £50.10 and £52.20 per week (between 10 and 11 per cent of total expenditure for each year); education expenditure varied between £6.10 and £7.80 per week (between 1 and 2 per cent of total expenditure for each year). These two categories were the only headline groups, apart from 'Housing, fuel and power', that did not experience a noticeable decline in expenditure between 2003/04 and 2009.

As a proportion of total weekly expenditure, spending on each of the following categories remained relatively stable across the time series: 'Restaurants and hotels' (8 per cent),'Household goods and services' (between 6 and 7 per cent) and 'Clothing and footwear' (5 per cent). Of these three categories, clothing and footwear experienced the greatest variation in average weekly spending throughout the time series, from a highest level of £27.10 per week in 2004/05 to a lowest of £20.90 per week in 2009. 'Household goods and services' experienced a similar decline in average weekly expenditure, from £36.60 in 2003/04 to £27.90 in 2009. Expenditure on 'Restaurants and hotels' was relatively stable over the time series; its highest value was £41.00 per week in 2004/05 and its lowest was £37.50 in 2008. It increased slightly in 2009 to £38.40.

Table 4.1   **Household expenditure based on the FES classification, 1994–95 to 2009 at 2009 prices[1]**

Year	1994 –95	1995[2] –96	1995[3] –96	1996 –97	1997 –98	1998 –99	1999 –2000	2000 –01	2001[4] –02
Weighted number of households (thousands)			24,130	24,310	24,560	24,660	25,330	25,030	24,450
Total number of households in sample	6,850	6,800	6,800	6,420	6,410	6,630	7,100	6,640	7,470
Total number of persons	16,620	16,590	16,590	15,730	15,430	16,220	16,790	15,930	18,120
Weighted average number of persons per household	2.4	2.4	2.4	2.5	2.4	2.4	2.3	2.4	2.4

Commodity or service	Average weekly household expenditure (£)								
1 Housing (Net)[7]	68.20	68.70	69.30	68.10	69.30	74.60	73.30	79.70	81.00
2 Fuel and power	19.00	18.40	18.30	18.40	16.90	15.30	14.60	14.80	14.40
3 Food and non-alcoholic drinks	74.10	75.30	77.00	78.00	76.80	76.90	76.60	77.20	76.10
4 Alcoholic drink	18.10	16.20	17.40	18.20	19.10	18.20	19.70	18.70	17.60
5 Tobacco	8.20	8.30	8.40	8.60	8.50	7.60	7.70	7.60	6.70
6 Clothing and footwear	25.20	24.40	25.30	26.00	27.30	28.30	26.90	27.40	27.50
7 Household goods	33.30	33.40	34.00	37.00	36.30	38.70	39.50	40.70	40.60
8 Household services	22.20	21.50	21.60	22.50	23.80	24.70	24.30	27.40	29.00
9 Personal goods and services	15.80	16.40	16.70	16.40	17.10	17.40	17.80	18.30	18.40
10 Motoring	53.20	52.70	54.40	58.60	63.60	67.50	67.50	68.70	71.20
11 Fares and other travel costs	9.80	8.80	9.50	10.70	11.60	10.80	11.80	11.80	11.50
12 Leisure goods	20.40	19.50	20.60	22.00	23.40	23.20	23.80	24.60	24.10
13 Leisure services	45.90	45.60	46.60	48.60	53.10	54.70	56.50	63.10	63.80
14 Miscellaneous	3.40	3.40	1.70	1.40	1.40	1.60	1.80	0.90	2.30
1–14 All expenditure groups	416.90	412.70	420.70	434.70	448.10	459.70	461.70	481.10	484.00

Average weekly expenditure per person (£)									
All expenditure groups	173.70	172.00	175.80	173.90	186.70	191.50	200.70	204.40	204.60

	Average weekly household income (£)[8]								
Gross income (£)	543	542	555	562	578	596	617	627	664
Disposable income (£)	439	437	446	459	471	484	502	510	544

Note: The commodity and service categories are not comparable to the COICOP categories used in Tables 4.3 and 4.4.

Figures are based on FES data between 1984 and 2000–01, EFS data between 2000–01 and 2007, and LCF thereafter.

1   Figures have been deflated to 2009 prices using the RPI all items index. 1994–95 to 2005–06 figures have been adjusted using financial year index numbers downloaded at http://www.statistics.gov.uk/STATBASE/tsdataset.asp?vlnk=7173&More=N&All=Y. 1992 and 2006 to 2007 figures have been adjusted using calendar year index numbers downloaded at http://www.statistics.gov.uk/STATBASE/tsdataset.asp?vlnk=7172&More=N&All=Y.

2   From 1992 to this version of 1995–96, figures shown are based on unweighted, adult only data.

3   From this version of 1995–96, figures are shown based on weighted data, including children's expenditure. Weighting is based on the population figures from the 1991 and 2001 Censuses

4   From 2001–02 onwards, commodities and services are based on COICOP codes broadly mapped to FES.

5   From 1995–96 to this version of 2006, figures shown are based on weighted data using non-response weights based on the 1991 Census and population figures from the 1991 and 2001 Censuses.

6   From this version of 2006, figures shown are based on weighted data using updated weights, with non-response weights and population figures based on the 2001 Census.

7   An improvement to the imputation of mortgage interest payments has been implemented for 2006 data onwards which should lead to a slight discontinuity. An error was discovered in the derivation of mortgage capital repayments which was leading to double counting. This has been amended for 2006 data onwards.

8   Does not include imputed income from owner-occupied and rent-free households.

ONS, Family Spending 2009, © Crown copyright 2010

Table 4.1   **Household expenditure based on the FES classification, 1994–95 to 2009 at 2009 prices[1] (cont.)**

Year	2002 –03	2003 –04	2004 –05	2005 –06	2006[5]	2006[6]	2007	2008	2009
Weighted number of households (thousands)	24,350	24,670	24,430	24,800	24,790	25,440	25,350	25,690	25,980
Total number of households in sample	6,930	7,050	6,800	6,790	6,650	6,650	6,140	5,850	5,830
Total number of persons	16,590	16,970	16,260	16,090	15,850	15,850	14,650	13,830	13,740
Weighted average number of persons per household	2.4	2.4	2.4	2.4	2.4	2.3	2.4	2.4	2.3

Commodity or service	Average weekly household expenditure (£)								
1 Housing (Net)[7]	80.30	81.90	87.20	89.50	90.00	89.70	95.20	93.50	85.20
2 Fuel and power	14.10	14.00	14.20	15.40	17.10	17.00	17.70	18.80	21.30
3 Food and non-alcoholic drinks	77.50	76.00	76.50	75.20	75.90	75.10	73.80	74.10	75.60
4 Alcoholic drink	17.80	17.30	16.80	16.40	16.00	15.90	15.20	13.30	14.00
5 Tobacco	6.50	6.40	5.70	5.00	5.00	5.00	4.70	4.60	4.40
6 Clothing and footwear	26.40	26.20	26.70	24.80	24.70	24.40	22.40	21.10	20.60
7 Household goods	40.70	41.10	40.40	37.10	37.20	36.70	35.80	33.80	31.80
8 Household services	28.10	29.10	29.90	30.00	28.70	28.50	27.40	27.20	26.70
9 Personal goods and services	18.30	18.90	18.20	18.70	19.00	18.90	18.40	17.10	17.70
10 Motoring	74.20	73.00	71.10	70.60	67.30	65.90	64.20	63.30	60.00
11 Fares and other travel costs	11.70	11.30	10.70	12.20	12.00	11.90	11.20	14.10	11.00
12 Leisure goods	24.70	25.10	24.40	21.50	21.20	20.90	20.80	18.90	18.50
13 Leisure services	64.50	64.40	67.60	69.70	71.50	70.40	63.80	65.60	63.40
14 Miscellaneous	2.40	2.20	2.30	2.40	2.30	2.20	2.00	2.00	2.00
1–14 All expenditure groups	487.30	487.00	491.70	488.50	487.90	482.60	472.50	467.30	452.20

Average weekly expenditure per person (£)									
All expenditure groups	**204.60**	**206.60**	**206.00**	**206.10**	**206.40**	**206.40**	**200.50**	**198.20**	**193.20**

	Average weekly household income (£)[8]								
Gross income (£)	**665**	**668**	**682**	**682**	**692**	**685**	**682**	**709**	**683**
Disposable income (£)	**546**	**544**	**556**	**554**	**562**	**556**	**552**	**579**	**558**

Note: The commodity and service categories are not comparable to the COICOP categories used in Tables 4.3 and 4.4.

Figures are based on FES data between 1984 and 2000–01 and EFS data thereafter.

1   Figures have been deflated to 2009 prices using the RPI all items index. 1994–95 to 2005–06 figures have been adjusted using financial year index numbers downloaded at http://www.statistics.gov.uk/STATBASE/tsdataset.asp?vlnk=7173&More=N&All=Y. 1992 and 2006 to 2007 figures have been adjusted using calendar year index numbers downloaded at http://www.statistics.gov.uk/STATBASE/tsdataset.asp?vlnk=7172&More=N&All=Y.

2   From 1992 to this version of 1995–96, figures shown are based on unweighted, adult only data.

3   From this version of 1995–96, figures are shown based on weighted data, including children's expenditure. Weighting is based on the population figures from the 1991 and 2001 Censuses

4   From 2001–02 onwards, commodities and services are based on COICOP codes broadly mapped to FES.

5   From 1995–96 to this version of 2006, figures shown are based on weighted data using non-response weights based on the 1991 Census and population figures from the 1991 and 2001 Censuses.

6   From this version of 2006, figures shown are based on weighted data using updated weights, with non-response weights and population figures based on the 2001 Census.

7   An improvement to the imputation of mortgage interest payments has been implemented for 2006 data onwards which should lead to a slight discontinuity. An error was discovered in the derivation of mortgage capital repayments which was leading to double counting. This has been amended for 2006 data onwards.

8   Does not include imputed income from owner-occupied and rent-free households.

ONS, Family Spending 2009, © Crown copyright 2010

Table 4.2 **FES household expenditure as a percentage of total expenditure, 1994–95 to 2009**

based on the FES classification at 2009 prices[1]

Year	1994 –95	1995[2] –96	1995[3] –96	1996 –97	1997 –98	1998 –99	1999– 2000	2000 –01	2001[4] –02
Weighted number of households (thousands)			24,130	24,310	24,560	24,660	25,330	25,030	24,450
Total number of households in sample	6,850	6,800	6,800	6,420	6,410	6,630	7,100	6,640	7,470
Total number of persons	16,620	16,590	16,590	15,730	15,430	16,220	16,790	15,930	18,120
Weighted average number of persons per household	2.4	2.4	2.4	2.5	2.4	2.4	2.3	2.4	2.4

Commodity or service	Percentage of total expenditure								
1 Housing (Net)[7]	16	17	16	16	15	16	16	17	17
2 Fuel and power	5	4	4	4	4	3	3	3	3
3 Food and non-alcoholic drinks	18	18	18	18	17	17	17	16	16
4 Alcoholic drink	4	4	4	4	4	4	4	4	4
5 Tobacco	2	2	2	2	2	2	2	2	1
6 Clothing and footwear	6	6	6	6	6	6	6	6	6
7 Household goods	8	8	8	9	8	8	9	8	8
8 Household services	5	5	5	5	5	5	5	6	6
9 Personal goods and services	4	4	4	4	4	4	4	4	4
10 Motoring	13	13	13	13	14	15	15	14	15
11 Fares and other travel costs	2	2	2	2	3	2	3	2	2
12 Leisure goods	5	5	5	5	5	5	5	5	5
13 Leisure services	11	11	11	11	12	12	12	13	13
14 Miscellaneous	1	1	0	0	0	0	0	0	0
1–14 All expenditure groups	100	100	100	100	100	100	100	100	100

1 Figures have been deflated to 2009 prices using the RPI all items index. 1994–95 to 2005–06 figures have been adjusted using financial year index numbers downloaded at http://www.statistics.gov.uk/STATBASE/tsdataset.asp?vlnk=7173&More=N&All=Y. 1992 and 2006 to 2007 figures have been adjusted using calendar year index numbers downloaded at http://www.statistics.gov.uk/STATBASE/tsdataset.asp?vlnk=7172&More=N&All=Y.

2 From 1992 to this version of 1995–96, figures shown are based on unweighted, adult only data.

3 From this version of 1995–96, figures are shown based on weighted data, including children's expenditure. Weighting is based on the population figures from the 1991 and 2001 Censuses.

4 From 2001–02 onwards, commodities and services are based on COICOP codes broadly mapped to FES.

5 From 1995–96 to this version of 2006, figures shown are based on weighted data using non–response weights based on the 1991 Census and population figures from the 1991 and 2001 Censuses.

6 From this version of 2006, figures shown are based on weighted data using updated weights, with non-response weights and population figures based on the 2001 Census.

7 An improvement to the imputation of mortgage interest payments has been implemented for 2006 data onwards which should lead to a slight discontinuity. An error was discovered in the derivation of mortgage capital repayments which was leading to double counting. This has been amended for 2006 data onwards.

ONS, Family Spending 2009, © Crown copyright 2010

Table 4.2 **FES household expenditure as a percentage of total expenditure, 1994–95 to 2009 (cont.)**
based on the FES classification at 2009 prices[1]

Year	2002 –03	2003 –04	2004 –05	2005 –06	2006[5]	2006[6]	2007	2008	2009
Weighted number of households (thousands)	24,350	24,670	24,430	24,800	24,790	25,440	25,350	25,690	25,980
Total number of households in sample	6,930	7,050	6,800	6,790	6,650	6,650	6,140	5,850	5,830
Total number of persons	16,590	16,970	16,260	16,090	15,850	15,850	14,650	13,830	13,740
Weighted average number of persons per household	2.4	2.4	2.4	2.4	2.4	2.3	2.4	2.4	2.3

Commodity or service	Percentage of total expenditure								
1 Housing (Net)[7]	16	17	18	18	18	19	20	20	19
2 Fuel and power	3	3	3	3	4	4	4	4	5
3 Food and non-alcoholic drinks	16	16	16	15	16	16	16	16	17
4 Alcoholic drink	4	4	3	3	3	3	3	3	3
5 Tobacco	1	1	1	1	1	1	1	1	1
6 Clothing and footwear	5	5	5	5	5	5	5	5	5
7 Household goods	8	8	8	8	8	8	8	7	7
8 Household services	6	6	6	6	6	6	6	6	6
9 Personal goods and services	4	4	4	4	4	4	4	4	4
10 Motoring	15	15	14	14	14	14	14	14	13
11 Fares and other travel costs	2	2	2	3	2	2	2	3	2
12 Leisure goods	5	5	5	4	4	4	4	4	4
13 Leisure services	13	13	14	14	15	15	13	14	14
14 Miscellaneous	0	0	0	0	0	0	0	0	0
1–14 All expenditure groups	100	100	100	100	100	100	100	100	100

1 Figures have been deflated to 2009 prices using the RPI all items index. 1994–95 to 2005–06 figures have been adjusted using financial year index numbers downloaded at http://www.statistics.gov.uk/STATBASE/tsdataset.asp?vlnk=7173&More=N&All=Y. 1992 and 2006 to 2007 figures have been adjusted using calendar year index numbers downloaded at http://www.statistics.gov.uk/STATBASE/tsdataset.asp?vlnk=7172&More=N&All=Y.

2 From 1992 to this version of 1995–96, figures shown are based on unweighted, adult only data.

3 From this version of 1995–96, figures are shown based on weighted data, including children's expenditure. Weighting is based on the population figures from the 1991 and 2001 Censuses.

4 From 2001–02 onwards, commodities and services are based on COICOP codes broadly mapped to FES.

5 From 1995–96 to this version of 2006, figures shown are based on weighted data using non–response weights based on the 1991 Census and population figures from the 1991 and 2001 Censuses.

6 From this version of 2006, figures shown are based on weighted data using updated weights, with non-response weights and population figures based on the 2001 Census.

7 An improvement to the imputation of mortgage interest payments has been implemented for 2006 data onwards which should lead to a slight discontinuity. An error was discovered in the derivation of mortgage capital repayments which was leading to double counting. This has been amended for 2006 data onwards.

ONS, Family Spending 2009, © Crown copyright 2010

Table 4.3   **Household expenditure based on COICOP classification, 2003–04 to 2009 at 2009 prices[1]**

based on weighted data and including children's expenditure

Year	2003 –04	2004 –05	2005 –06	2006[2]	2006[3]	2007	2008	2009
Weighted number of households (thousands)	24,670	24,430	24,800	24,790	25,440	25,350	25,690	25,980
Total number of households in sample	7,050	6,800	6,790	6,650	6,650	6,140	5,850	5,830
Total number of persons in sample	16,970	16,260	16,090	15,850	15,850	14,650	13,830	13,740
Total number of adults in sample	12,620	12,260	12,170	12,000	12,000	11,220	10,640	10,650
Weighted average number of persons per household	2.4	2.4	2.4	2.4	2.3	2.4	2.4	2.3

Commodity or service	Average weekly household expenditure (£)							
1 Food & non-alcoholic drinks	51.00	50.80	50.10	50.60	49.90	49.80	50.40	52.20
2 Alcoholic drinks, tobacco & narcotics	13.70	12.90	11.90	12.00	12.00	11.60	10.70	11.20
3 Clothing & footwear	26.60	27.10	25.20	25.10	24.80	22.80	21.50	20.90
4 Housing(net)[4], fuel & power	45.70	45.90	48.90	51.30	51.30	53.60	52.80	57.30
5 Household goods & services	36.60	35.90	33.20	32.60	32.30	31.80	30.00	27.90
6 Health	5.90	5.60	6.10	6.30	6.30	5.90	5.10	5.30
7 Transport	71.10	67.60	68.30	66.90	65.60	63.80	63.10	58.40
8 Communication	13.10	13.30	13.20	12.70	12.60	12.30	11.90	11.70
9 Recreation & culture	67.10	67.00	63.70	63.10	62.10	59.40	59.80	57.90
10 Education	6.10	7.40	7.30	7.80	7.50	7.00	6.20	7.00
11 Restaurants & hotels	40.90	41.00	40.60	40.90	40.50	38.50	37.50	38.40
12 Miscellaneous goods & services	39.40	39.60	38.30	38.80	38.50	36.50	35.50	35.00
1–12 All expenditure groups	417.30	414.20	406.80	408.00	403.20	392.90	384.40	383.10
13 Other expenditure items[5]	72.50	79.20	83.90	81.60	81.00	82.10	84.20	71.80
Total expenditure	**489.70**	**493.40**	**490.60**	**489.60**	**484.20**	**474.90**	**468.60**	**455.00**

Average weekly expenditure per person (£)								
Total expenditure	**207.80**	**206.70**	**208.10**	**207.10**	**207.10**	**201.50**	**198.80**	**194.40**

	Average weekly household income (£)							
Gross income (£)	**668**	**682**	**682**	**692**	**685**	**682**	**709**	**683**
Disposable income (£)	**544**	**556**	**554**	**562**	**556**	**552**	**579**	**558**

Note: The commodity and service categories are not comparable to the FES categories used in Tables 4.2 and 4.3

1   Figures have been deflated to 2009 prices using the RPI all items index. 2002–03 to 2005–06 figures have been adjusted using financial year index numbers downloaded at http://www.statistics.gov.uk/STATBASE/tsdataset.asp?vlnk=7173&More=N&All=Y. 2006 to 2007 figures have been adjusted using calendar year index numbers downloaded at http://www.statistics.gov.uk/STATBASE/tsdataset.asp?vlnk=7172&More=N&All=Y.

2   From 2002–03 to this version of 2006, figures shown are based on weighted data using non-response weights based on the 1991 Census and population figures from the 1991 and 2001 Censuses.

3   From this version of 2006, figures shown are based on weighted data using updated weights, with non-response weights and population figures based on the 2001 Census.

4   Excluding mortgage interest payments, council tax and Northern Ireland rates.

5   An error was discovered in the derivation of mortgage capital repayments which was leading to double counting. This has been amended for the 2006 data onwards.

ONS, Family Spending 2009, © Crown copyright 2010

Table 4.4

Household expenditure as a percentage of total expenditure based on COICOP classification, 2003–04 to 2009 at 2009 prices[1]

based on weighted data and including children's expenditure

Year	2003 –04	2004 –05	2005 –06	2006[2]	2006[3]	2007	2008	2009
Weighted number of households (thousands)	24,670	24,430	24,800	24,790	25,440	25,350	25,690	25,980
Total number of households in sample	7,050	6,800	6,790	6,650	6,650	6,140	5,850	5,830
Total number of persons in sample	16,970	16,260	16,090	15,850	15,850	14,650	13,830	13,740
Total number of adults in sample	12,620	12,260	12,170	12,000	12,000	11,220	10,640	10,650
Weighted average number of persons per household	2.4	2.4	2.4	2.4	2.3	2.4	2.4	2.3

Commodity or service	Percentage of total expenditure							
1 Food & non-alcoholic drinks	10	10	10	10	10	10	11	11
2 Alcoholic drinks, tobacco & narcotics	3	3	2	2	2	2	2	2
3 Clothing & footwear	5	5	5	5	5	5	5	5
4 Housing(net)[4], fuel & power	9	9	10	10	11	11	11	13
5 Household goods & services	7	7	7	7	7	7	6	6
6 Health	1	1	1	1	1	1	1	1
7 Transport	15	14	14	14	14	13	13	13
8 Communication	3	3	3	3	3	3	3	3
9 Recreation & culture	14	14	13	13	13	12	13	13
10 Education	1	1	1	2	2	1	1	2
11 Restaurants & hotels	8	8	8	8	8	8	8	8
12 Miscellaneous goods & services	8	8	8	8	8	8	8	8
1–12 All expenditure groups	**85**	**84**	**83**	**83**	**83**	**83**	**82**	**84**
13 Other expenditure items[5]	**15**	**16**	**17**	**17**	**17**	**17**	**18**	**16**
Total expenditure	**100**	**100**	**100**	**100**	**100**	**100**	**100**	**100**

Note: The commodity and service categories are not comparable to the FES categories used in Tables 4.2 and 4.3.

1 Figures have been deflated to 2009 prices using the RPI all items index. 2002–03 to 2005–06 figures have been adjusted using financial year index numbers downloaded at http://www.statistics.gov.uk/STATBASE/tsdataset.asp?vlnk=7173&More=N&All=Y. 2006 to 2007 figures have been adjusted using calendar year index numbers downloaded at http://www.statistics.gov.uk/STATBASE/tsdataset.asp?vlnk=7172&More=N&All=Y.

2 From 1995–96 to this version of 2006, figures shown are based on weighted data using non-response weights based on the 1991 Census and population figures from the 1991 and 2001 Censuses.

3 From this version of 2006, figures shown are based on weighted data using updated weights, with non-response weights and population figures based on the 2001 Census.

4 Excluding mortgage interest payments, council tax and Northern Ireland rates.

5 An error was discovered in the derivation of mortgage capital repayments which was leading to double counting. This has been amended for the 2006 data onwards.

ONS, Family Spending 2009, © Crown copyright 2010

Table 4.5   **Household expenditure 2003–04 to 2009 COICOP based current[1] prices**

based on weighted data and including children's expenditure

Year	2003 –04	2004 –05	2005 –06	2006[2]	2006[3]	2007	2008	2009
Weighted number of households (thousands)	24,670	24,430	24,800	24,790	25,440	25,350	25,690	25,980
Total number of households in sample	7,050	6,800	6,790	6,650	6,650	6,140	5,850	5,830
Total number of persons in sample	16,970	16,260	16,090	15,850	15,850	14,650	13,830	13,740
Total number of adults in sample	12,620	12,260	12,170	12,000	12,000	11,220	10,640	10,650
Weighted average number of persons per household	2.4	2.4	2.4	2.4	2.3	2.4	2.4	2.3

Commodity or service	Average weekly household expenditure (£)							
1 Food & non-alcoholic drinks	43.50	44.70	45.30	46.90	46.30	48.10	50.70	52.20
2 Alcoholic drinks, tobacco & narcotics	11.70	11.30	10.80	11.10	11.10	11.20	10.80	11.20
3 Clothing & footwear	22.70	23.90	22.70	23.20	23.00	22.00	21.60	20.90
4 Housing(net)[4], fuel & power	39.00	40.40	44.20	47.60	47.50	51.80	53.00	57.30
5 Household goods & services	31.30	31.60	30.00	30.30	29.90	30.70	30.10	27.90
6 Health	5.00	4.90	5.50	5.90	5.80	5.70	5.10	5.30
7 Transport	60.70	59.60	61.70	62.00	60.80	61.70	63.40	58.40
8 Communication	11.20	11.70	11.90	11.70	11.60	11.90	12.00	11.70
9 Recreation & culture	57.30	59.00	57.50	58.50	57.60	57.40	60.10	57.90
10 Education	5.20	6.50	6.60	7.20	7.00	6.80	6.20	7.00
11 Restaurants & hotels	34.90	36.10	36.70	37.90	37.60	37.20	37.70	38.40
12 Miscellaneous goods & services	33.60	34.90	34.60	36.00	35.70	35.30	35.60	35.00
1–12 All expenditure groups	356.20	364.70	367.60	378.30	373.80	379.80	386.30	383.10
13 Other expenditure items[5]	61.90	69.70	75.80	75.60	75.10	79.30	84.60	71.80
Total expenditure	**418.10**	**434.40**	**443.40**	**453.90**	**449.00**	**459.20**	**471.00**	**455.00**

Average weekly expenditure per person (£)								
Total expenditure	**177.40**	**182.00**	**188.00**	**192.00**	**192.00**	**194.80**	**199.80**	**194.40**

	Average weekly household income (£)							
Gross income (£)	**570**	**601**	**616**	**642**	**635**	**659**	**713**	**683**
Disposable income (£)	**464**	**489**	**500**	**521**	**515**	**534**	**582**	**558**

Note: The commodity and service categories are not comparable to those in publications before 2001–02

1   Data in Table 4.5 have not been deflated to 2009 prices and therefore show the actual expenditure for the year they were collected. Because inflation is not taken into account, comparisons between the years should be made with caution.

2   From 2002–03 to this version of 2006, figures shown are based on weighted data using non-response weights based on the 1991 Census and population figures from the 1991 and 2001 Censuses.

3   From this version of 2006, figures shown are based on weighted data using updated weights, with non-response weights and population figures based on the 2001 Census.

4   Excluding mortgage interest payments, council tax and Northern Ireland rates.

5   An error was discovered in the derivation of mortgage capital repayments which was leading to double counting. This has been amended for the 2006 data onwards.

ONS, Family Spending 2009, © Crown copyright 2010

Household expenditure by Output Area Classification

Background

This chapter presents income and expenditure by Output Area Classification (OAC). The classification is designed to group together geographic areas based on a series of characteristics which are shared by these groupings. Hence areas sharing an OAC classification have characteristics in common, but may be distributed over different parts of the UK.

The aim is to provide an overview that highlights key findings from the 2009 Living Costs and Food Survey (LCF) by OAC but not a comprehensive analysis of income and expenditure. A similar chapter was included in the 2008 edition of Family Spending. The analysis was well received, so the theme is revisited in this edition. Tables showing expenditure and income by OAC groupings have been included since the 2008 edition.

There are seven categories in the highest OAC 'supergroup' classification, these are subdivided into 21 OAC groups. Most of the tables and figures in this chapter present LCF data aggregated at the OAC supergroup level, considered to be the most appropriate level at which to present the data for the purposes of an overview. In addition, presentation of some results by the lower-level OA classification provides further detail while illustrating how the characteristics of the higher groups sometimes mask differences in the lower groups.

Introducing OAC

Output Areas are the smallest geographical units used to release data from the 2001 Census. Each census agency was responsible for the creation of the OAs in their countries and there are some slight differences in the methodology employed by the different agencies. The Office for National Statistics (ONS) and Northern Ireland Statistics and Research Agency (NISRA) both adopted the ONS methodology, based upon a minimum OA size of 40 households and 100 residents. This differed somewhat from the design methodology used in Scotland, where OAs were matched more closely to the 1991 Census OAs and thus maintained a smaller minimum size of 20 households and 50 residents.

Table 5.1   Average size of OAs by census agency[1]

Country	OAs	Population	Households	Average Population per OA	Average Households per OA
UK	223,060	58,789,154	24,479,439	264	110
England and Wales	175,434	52,041,916	21,660,475	297	124
Scotland	42,604	5,062,011	2,192,246	119	52
Northern Ireland	5,022	1,685,267	626,718	336	125

As Table 5.1 shows, 223,060 different output areas were produced from the 2001 Census data. Due to the high number of individual OAs, it was hoped that clustering groups of areas based on shared characteristics would enhance understanding of the areas and enable a clearer identification of patterns in their distribution.

Fundamentally, the classification is used to group together geographic areas based upon a series of characteristics which are shared by the populations in these groupings. The 2001 Census was the first in which this type of classification was formulated to enhance the publication of results.

Developing the Classification

In order to be considered an official census-based National Statistic, the variables chosen to formulate the OA classification were drawn solely from the 2001 Census. As noted in the official technical report, 'the goal of the variable choice for this classification was to select the minimum possible number of variables that satisfactorily represent the main dimensions of the 2001 Census' (Vickers and Rees 2005)[2]. After several revisions, an eventual list of 41 variables was drawn from the 2001 Census outputs. These variables were together deemed representative of five main domains within the census outputs; Demographic Structure, Household Composition, Housing, Socio-Economic status and Employment.

To develop the classification itself, the output areas were then placed in groups which were considered sufficiently similar according to the values recorded for particular census variables. This was achieved using the statistical method of cluster analysis; specifically involving the use of the k-means clustering algorithm in the SPSS statistical package. The k-means algorithm is a very commonly used method in the geodemographics sector and is principally used to reduce the level of within-cluster variability. Initially, the whole data set of 223,060 OAs was input into the k-means algorithm to produce the first level of the cluster hierarchy, the supergroups. Subsequently, the seven clustered data sets produced for the supergroups were then each re-clustered separately to produce the middle-tier of the hierarchy, the groups. The files produced for the groups were themselves then re-clustered to produce the lowest tier of the classification, the subgroups. Table 5.2 shows the way in which the OAC groups can be mapped to the highest tier of the hierarchy, the supergroups.

Table 5.2[3] Relationship of OAC supergroups to OAC groups

OAC Supergroup Label	OAC Group	OAC Group Label
1 – Blue collar communities	1A	Terraced blue collar
	1B	Younger blue collar
	1C	Older blue collar
2 – City living	2A	Transient communities
	2B	Settled in the city
3 – Countryside	3A	Village life
	3B	Agricultural
	3C	Accessible countryside
4 – Prospering suburbs	4A	Prospering younger families
	4B	Prospering older families
	4C	Prospering semis
	4D	Thriving suburbs
5 – Constrained by circumstances	5A	Senior communities
	5B	Older workers
	5C	Public housing
6 – Typical traits	6A	Settled households
	6B	Least divergent
	6C	Young families in terraced homes
	6D	Aspiring households
7 – Multicultural	7A	Asian communities
	7B	Afro-Caribbean communities

Cluster Profiling and Naming

To complete the classification, cluster profiles were created and then given names which would clearly distinguish them from those used in other classifications. The fundamental aim of the cluster profiles was 'to create a short description, using text and visuals which expands on the cluster names but only takes a few seconds to read but which significantly expands the user's understanding of the group' (Vickers and Rees 2006)[4]. Table 5.3 summarises the cluster profiles. It indicates the distinctive variables which set each cluster apart from the remaining clusters, based on how far their cluster values deviate from the overall mean for those variables.

Much time was taken in producing names for the clusters and all were 'reviewed, developed and approved by a group of ONS Neighbourhood Statistics and geography specialists' (Vickers and Rees 2006)[5]. This was in order to ensure that the resultant labels were concise, inoffensive and reflected accurately what kinds of areas were represented by each cluster.

It is important to note that the cluster names, while carefully chosen, cannot represent all the complexity of the groups. The names should therefore be treated with caution, and not used independently of the cluster profiles.

A considerable amount of detail on the OA classification is available on the ONS website:
www.statistics.gov.uk/about/methodology_by_theme/area_classification/oa

This includes a full technical report[6] which provides a detailed explanation of the methodology underpinning the classification, as well as a significant amount of information relating to the cluster profiles.

Household Expenditure by OAC

Figure 5.1 and table 5.4 show expenditure by OAC supergroup, in total and for each of the Classification of Individual Consumption by Purpose (COICOP) categories. As might be expected, there are considerable differences in total expenditure. The supergroups with the highest expenditure are supergroups 2 (city living) and 4 (prospering suburbs), spending an average of £457.90 and £454.10 per week, respectively, followed by supergroup 3 (countryside), with expenditure of £433.70. Supergroup 5 (constrained by circumstances) showed the lowest expenditure at £269.20 followed by supergroup 1 (blue collar communities).

Figure 5.1 **Average weekly household expenditure by OAC supergroup 2009**

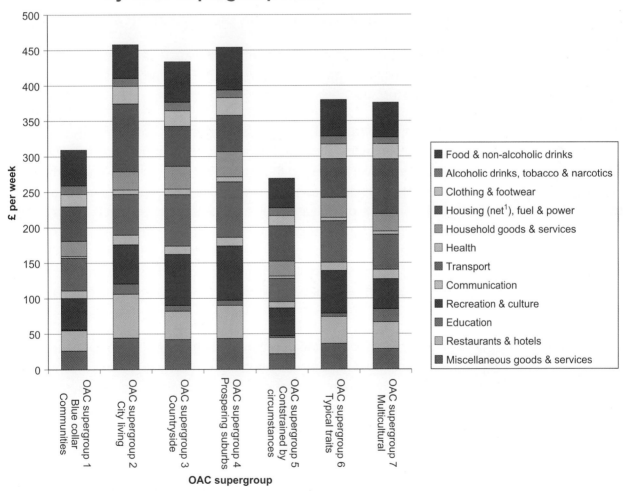

1   Excluding mortgage interest payments,council tax and Northern Ireland rates.

The pattern of total expenditures observed for 2009 is similar to 2007, when the analysis was first conducted. Since 2007 supergroup 2 (city living) total average weekly household expenditure has gradually risen to exhibit the largest expenditure of all OAC supergroups. Supergroup 4 (prospering suburbs) and 3 (countryside) continue to be in the top three. All other supergroups have maintained the same rank for the three-year period, with supergroup 5 (constrained by circumstances) remaining consistently the lowest.

The differences in total expenditure between supergroups can be considered in more detail by COICOP categories. High expenditure by supergroup 2, 'city living', was partially attributable to expenditure on housing, fuel and power (£95.60), which was higher than for any other group. Expenditure on housing fuel and power showed high variability between supergroups; after 'city living' the next highest expenditure in this category was by supergroup 7 'multicultural' (£77.00). All other supergroups spent considerably less, with supergroup 1 (blue collar communities) spending the least at £48.40 per week.

Other categories also showed a high level of variability between supergroups. For example, transport expenditure was highest for supergroup 4 'prospering suburbs' (£77.90) and supergroup 3 'countryside' (£72.20), and lowest for supergroup 5 'constrained by circumstances' (£32.70). Spending on restaurants and hotels was almost three times as much in the highest-spending category, 'city living' (£62.20) than the lowest, 'constrained by circumstances' (£22.80).

By contrast, average weekly household expenditure for alcoholic drinks, tobacco and narcotics, health and communication showed minimal differences between OAC supergroups. This pattern is consistent with the results obtained for 2007.

When looking at data at the supergroup level (Table 5.5), it is important to note that the supergroups are high-level clusters containing thousands of individual output areas. As such, when the expenditure estimates are broken down further, to the middle tier of the cluster hierarchy (OAC groups), the supergroups can exhibit considerable internal variability for certain expenditure categories. For example, high expenditure on housing fuel and power by supergroup 2 'city living' (noted in the previous paragraph), differs for the supergroup's individual group levels. The high expenditure for this supergroup is largely driven by group 2A 'transient communities' with an average weekly expenditure of £120.10, considerably higher than group 2B 'settled in the city' at £82.00. This latter figure is lower than 'Affro-Carribean communities' within the 'multicultural' supergroup (£90.00).

Expenditure on transport revealed interesting variation within supergroups. High expenditure on transport within supergroup 4 (prospering suburbs) was attributably mainly to group 4a 'prospering younger families', at £97.80. Within supergroup 5 'constrained by circumstances', which showed the lowest expenditure on transport overall, expenditure was notably low among group 5a 'senior communities', at £19.00. 'Prospering younger families' also spent highly on recreation and culture (£88.60), but the second highest-spending group on this category was group 3a 'village life'(£82.10), within the 'countryside' supergroup.

Household Income by OAC

Table 5.6 and Figure 5.2 show average gross weekly household income by OAC supergroup. The clustering process used to create the classification did not include a direct income indicator, though it did include correlated variables such as the ownership of two or more cars, so it is interesting to see that expenditure and income follow broadly the same pattern at the supergroup level, as was the case in 2007. However, it should be noted that the survey is not designed to produce a balance sheet of income and expenditure for individual households or groups of households and as such, this comparison is only intended to provide an approximate indication of the broad similarities between the two.

Figure 5.2   Average gross normal household income by OAC supergroup, 2009

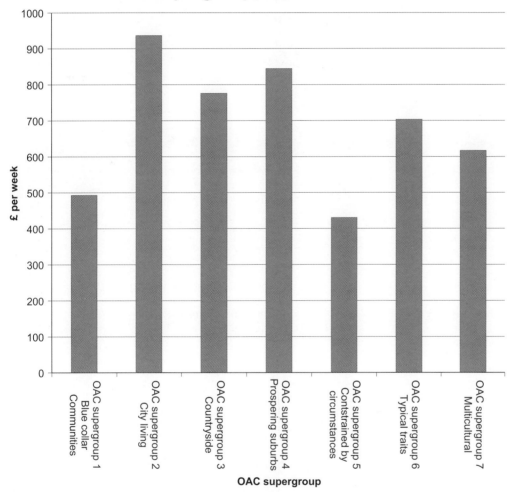

Notes

1, 3, 4 & 5: See Vickers, D. & Rees, P. (2006) *Creating the UK National Statistics 2001 output area classification*.

2 & 6: See Vickers, D., Rees, P. & Birkin, M. (2005) *Creating the national classification of Census output areas: data, methods and results.*

Table 5.3   OAC cluster profiles, supergroup level[1]

OAC Supergroup	Variables with proportions above the national average	Variables with proportions below the national average
1 **Blue collar communities**	Age 5-14 Lone parent households Households with non-dependent children Terraced Housing Routine/Semi-routine Employment Mining/Quarrying/Construction employment Manufacturing Employment Retail Trade Employment Lone parent households	Indian, Pakistani and Bangladeshi Black Born Outside the UK Rent (Private) Flats HE Qualification Financial Intermediation Employment
2 **City living**	Age 25-44 Born Outside UK Population Density Single person household Rent (Private) Flats No Central Heating HE Qualification Students Financial Intermediation Employment	Ages 0-4, 5-14, 25-44 and 65+ Single Parent Household Households with non-dependent children Rooms per household Provide unpaid care Economically inactive looking after family General employment
3 **Countryside**	Ages 45-64 and 65+ Detached Housing Rooms per Household 2+ Car Households Work from Home Provide Unpaid Care Agricultural Employment	Indian, Pakistani and Bangladeshi Black Population Density Single Person Household Flats People Per Room Public Transport to Work Unemployment

Table 5.3   OAC cluster profiles, supergroup level[1]

4 **Prospering suburbs**	Age 45-64 Two adults no children Households with non-dependent children Detached housing Rooms per household 2+ Car households Provide unpaid care	Indian, Pakistani and Bangladeshi Black Divorced/Separated Single Person Household Single Pensioner Households Renting Public and Private Terraced Housing Flats No Central Heating LLTI Unemployment
5 **Constrained by circumstances**	Age 65+ Divorced/separated Single Pensioner Households Lone Parent Households Rent (Public) Flats People per Room Routine/Semi-routine employment LLTI Unemployment	Two adults no children Rent (Private) Detached Housing Rooms per household HE Qualifications 2+ Car Households Work From Home
6 **Typical traits**	Work Part Time Terraced Housing	Age 65+ Rent (Public)
7 **Muliticultural**	Ages 0-4 and 5-15 Indian, Pakistani and Bangladeshi Black Born Outside UK Population Density No Central Heating	Ages 45-64 and 65+ Single Pensioner Households Two adults No Children Economically inactive/ looking after family/home

Table 5.3   OAC cluster profiles, supergroup level[1]

People per Room

Public transport to work

Students

Unemployment

Note: Please see page xii for symbols and conventions used in this report.

1 Adapted from Vickers, D.,Rees,P. & Birkin,M (2005) Creating the national classification of Census output areas: data, methods and results.

Table 5.4 **Average weekly household expenditure by OAC supergroup, 2009**

based on weighted data and including children's expenditure

	Blue collar Communities	City living	Countryside	Prospering suburbs	Constrained by circumstances	Typical traits	Multicultural	
	OAC Super-group 1	OAC Super-group 2	OAC Super-group 3	OAC Super-group 4	OAC Super-group 5	OAC Super-group 6	OAC Super-group 7	All house-holds
Weighted number of households (thousands)	4,330	1,600	3,330	5,720	2,980	5,240	2,790	25,980
Total number of households in sample	1030	290	850	1,360	670	1,130	490	5,830
Total number of persons in sample	2,560	580	2,060	3,350	1,340	2,620	1,240	13,740
Total number of adults in sample	1,860	480	1,670	2,660	1,060	2,030	880	10,650
Weighted average number of persons per household	2.5	2.0	2.4	2.4	2.0	2.3	2.6	2.3

Commodity or service	Average weekly household expenditure (£)							
1 Food & non-alcoholic drinks	50.20	47.40	56.80	60.10	41.50	51.50	49.00	52.20
2 Alcoholic drinks, tobacco & narcotics	12.30	11.00	12.30	10.70	11.10	11.10	9.40	11.20
3 Clothing & footwear	17.40	24.80	21.90	25.20	14.40	20.90	21.40	20.90
4 Housing (net)[1], fuel & power	48.40	95.60	56.10	50.90	49.90	54.50	77.00	57.30
5 Household goods & services	21.80	25.90	32.40	35.50	21.00	28.30	24.60	27.90
6 Health	2.50	6.20	7.90	7.50	3.40	4.70	4.50	5.30
7 Transport	45.60	57.30	72.20	77.90	32.70	58.60	49.70	58.40
8 Communication	10.90	13.60	12.00	12.20	8.80	11.70	13.20	11.70
9 Recreation & culture	44.40	55.20	71.80	76.40	39.40	59.70	41.90	57.90
10 Education	1.10	14.40	8.00	7.30	2.30	5.00	18.70	7.00
11 Restaurants & hotels	28.50	62.20	40.10	47.00	22.80	37.90	37.70	38.40
12 Miscellaneous goods & services	26.50	44.30	42.20	43.50	22.00	36.20	29.00	35.00
1–12 All expenditure groups	309.60	457.90	433.70	454.10	269.20	380.00	376.10	383.10

Note: Please see page xiii for Symbols and conventions used in this report.

1 Excluding mortgage interest payments, council tax and Northern Ireland rates.

ONS, Family Spending 2009, © Crown copyright 2010

Table 5.5 **Average weekly household expenditure by OAC group, 2009**
based on weighted data and including children's expenditure

	Terraced blue collar	Younger blue collar	Older blue collar	Transient communities	Settled in the city	Village life	Agricultural	Accessible countryside	Propsering younger families	Prospering older families	Prospering semis
	OAC group 1A	OAC group 1B	OAC group 1C	OAC group 2A	OAC group 2B	OAC group 3A	OAC group 3B	OAC group 3C	OAC group 4A	OAC group 4B	OAC group 4C
Weighted number of households (thousands)	1,230	1,580	1,520	570	1,030	1,230	1,010	1,080	1,230	1,470	1,910
Total number of households in sample	280	380	370	90	200	310	310	240	310	370	430
Total number of persons in sample	690	970	910	180	400	740	770	550	810	900	1,020
Total number of adults in sample	500	680	690	160	320	600	610	450	610	730	820
Weighted average number of persons per household	2.4	2.5	2.4	1.9	2.0	2.4	2.4	2.3	2.6	2.4	2.4

Commodity or service	Average weekly household expenditure (£)										
1 Food & non-alcoholic drinks	48.90	50.00	51.40	42.50	50.10	54.80	57.00	58.80	62.00	61.20	57.30
2 Alcoholic drinks, tobacco & narcotics	12.30	12.20	12.30	8.80	12.30	12.60	10.50	13.50	10.20	11.20	10.20
3 Clothing & footwear	16.30	17.10	18.40	21.40	26.80	21.70	23.70	20.60	28.40	26.20	23.50
4 Housing (net)[1], fuel & power	44.60	51.70	48.10	120.10	82.00	54.00	52.60	61.80	52.80	49.00	50.80
5 Household goods & services	21.80	20.90	22.60	14.10	32.40	34.60	27.90	34.00	33.60	37.90	34.80
6 Health	1.70	2.40	3.30	3.90	7.40	7.40	6.20	10.20	5.50	6.90	6.60
7 Transport	44.10	43.30	49.10	49.80	61.50	67.10	76.60	73.80	97.80	73.30	68.40
8 Communication	10.90	10.90	11.00	11.90	14.50	12.30	11.60	12.00	12.50	12.10	11.60
9 Recreation & culture	44.50	40.60	48.30	44.00	61.40	82.10	60.60	70.60	88.60	73.40	69.70
10 Education	0.40	2.10	0.70	14.60	14.20	8.10	3.00	12.60	7.20	6.00	5.40
11 Restaurants & hotels	26.40	30.00	28.80	67.10	59.50	39.90	36.50	43.80	45.90	50.50	44.70
12 Miscellaneous goods & services	27.70	24.30	27.80	39.50	47.00	40.30	36.00	50.10	50.10	42.60	38.90
1–12 All expenditure groups	299.60	305.50	321.80	437.70	469.00	434.90	402.20	461.80	494.50	450.30	422.00

Note: Please see page xiii for Symbols and conventions used in this report.

1 Excluding mortgage interest payments, council tax and Northern Ireland rates.

ONS, Family Spending 2009, © Crown copyright 2010

Table 5.5 **Average weekly household expenditure by OAC group, 2009 (cont.)**

based on weighted data and including children's expenditure

	Thriving suburbs	Senior communities	Older workers	Public housing	Settled households	Least divergent	Young families in terraced homes	Aspiring households	Asian communities	Afro-Caribbean communities	
	OAC group 4D	OAC group 5A	OAC group 5B	OAC group 5C	OAC group 6A	OAC group 6B	OAC group 6C	OAC group 6D	OAC group 7A	OAC group 7B	All house-holds
Weighted number of households (thousands)	1,130	390	1,920	660	1,480	1,390	1,340	1,030	1,640	1,140	25,980
Total number of households in sample	260	80	440	150	310	320	280	230	300	180	5,830
Total number of persons in sample	620	130	890	320	740	700	650	520	830	410	13,740
Total number of adults in sample	500	110	710	250	590	550	500	390	580	310	10,650
Weighted average number of persons per household	2.3	1.5	2.0	2.1	2.4	2.2	2.3	2.3	2.8	2.3	2.3

Commodity or service	Average weekly household expenditure (£)										
1 Food & non-alcoholic drinks	61.20	33.60	42.40	43.20	55.10	51.40	45.60	54.00	49.70	48.10	52.20
2 Alcoholic drinks, tobacco & narcotics	11.50	7.00	11.40	12.50	11.20	10.20	12.10	10.90	9.60	9.20	11.20
3 Clothing & footwear	23.30	9.00	14.50	17.20	20.70	18.30	20.30	25.20	21.80	20.90	20.90
4 Housing (net)[1], fuel & power	51.40	45.20	52.20	45.70	51.20	51.60	53.80	64.00	67.90	90.00	57.30
5 Household goods & services	35.60	14.40	24.70	14.20	26.80	32.40	25.00	29.10	30.00	16.90	27.90
6 Health	12.00	2.50	4.10	2.00	3.90	6.30	2.60	6.60	4.00	5.20	5.30
7 Transport	78.10	19.00	33.10	39.70	66.30	58.60	47.00	62.80	54.40	43.00	58.40
8 Communication	12.80	7.10	8.90	9.60	12.10	11.60	10.80	12.70	13.60	12.50	11.70
9 Recreation & culture	78.30	27.80	42.40	37.50	64.60	57.00	50.00	68.70	52.40	26.80	57.90
10 Education	12.10	2.40	2.60	1.50	2.90	3.10	3.10	12.80	17.50	20.60	7.00
11 Restaurants & hotels	47.70	22.60	23.30	21.40	41.50	34.20	35.00	41.50	43.40	29.40	38.40
12 Miscellaneous goods & services	45.30	16.50	23.30	21.40	40.70	34.60	28.60	41.70	33.10	23.10	35.00
1–12 All expenditure groups	469.20	207.20	282.90	265.80	397.00	369.20	333.90	429.90	397.20	345.80	383.10

Note: Please see page xiii for Symbols and conventions used in this report.

1   Excluding mortgage interest payments, council tax and Northern Ireland Rates.

ONS, Family Spending 2009, © Crown copyright 2010

Table 5.6   **Average gross normal weekly household income by OAC supergroup, 2009**
based on weighted data

	Blue collar Communities	City living	Countryside	Prospering suburbs	Contstrained by circumstances	Typical traits	Multicultural	
	OAC Super-group 1	OAC Super-group 2	OAC Super-group 3	OAC Super-group 4	OAC Super-group 5	OAC Super-group 6	OAC Super-group 7	All house-holds
Weighted number of households (thousands)	4,330	1,600	3,330	5,720	2,980	5,240	2,790	25,980
Total number of households in sample	1,030	290	850	1,360	670	1,130	490	5,830
Total number of persons in sample	2,560	580	2,060	3,350	1,340	2,620	1,240	13,740
Total number of adults in sample	1,860	480	1,670	2,660	1,060	2,030	880	10,650
Weighted average number of persons per household	2.5	2.0	2.4	2.4	2.0	2.3	2.6	2.3
Gross normal weekly household income	**493.00**	**936.70**	**775.90**	**844.80**	**430.70**	**703.00**	**616.90**	**682.60**

Note: Please see page xiii for Symbols and conventions used in this report.

ONS, Family Spending 2009, © Crown copyright 2010

Appendix A

Table A1 **Components of household expenditure, 2009**
based on weighted data and including children's expenditure

Commodity or service	Average weekly expenditure all house-holds (£)	Total weekly expenditure (£ million)	Recording house-holds in sample	Percentage standard error (full method)
Total number of households			5,830	
1 Food & non-alcoholic drinks	**52.20**	**1,355**	**5,800**	**0.8**
1.1 Food	48.00	1248	5,800	0.8
1.1.1 Bread, rice and cereals	5.00	129	5,690	1.0
1.1.1.1 Rice	0.40	9	1,390	5.3
1.1.1.2 Bread	2.60	68	5,560	1.0
1.1.1.3 Other breads and cereals	2.00	52	4,690	1.4
1.1.2 Pasta products	0.40	11	2,410	2.6
1.1.3 Buns, cakes, biscuits etc.	3.20	84	5,170	1.3
1.1.3.1 Buns, crispbread and biscuits	1.80	48	4,770	1.4
1.1.3.2 Cakes and puddings	1.40	36	3,790	2.1
1.1.4 Pastry (savoury)	0.70	19	2,100	2.6
1.1.5 Beef (fresh, chilled or frozen)	1.70	43	2,740	2.5
1.1.6 Pork (fresh, chilled or frozen)	0.70	17	1,420	4.0
1.1.7 Lamb (fresh, chilled or frozen)	0.60	17	1,000	4.8
1.1.8 Poultry (fresh, chilled or frozen)	2.00	52	3,040	2.2
1.1.9 Bacon and ham	1.00	26	2,700	2.6
1.1.10 Other meats and meat preparations	5.40	139	5,200	1.4
1.1.10.1 Sausages	0.70	19	2,620	2.2
1.1.10.2 Offal, pate etc.	0.10	3	800	4.9
1.1.10.3 Other preserved or processed meat and meat preparations	4.50	117	5,020	1.5
1.1.10.4 Other fresh, chilled or frozen edible meat	[0.00]	[0]	20	30.7
1.1.11 Fish and fish products	2.30	59	3,830	2.1
1.1.11.1 Fish (fresh, chilled or frozen)	0.70	19	1,450	3.8
1.1.11.2 Seafood, dried, smoked or salted fish	0.50	14	1,320	4.1
1.1.11.3 Other preserved or processed fish and seafood	1.00	26	2,990	2.2
1.1.12 Milk	2.80	73	5,400	1.3
1.1.12.1 Whole milk	0.70	17	1,720	3.4
1.1.12.2 Low fat milk	1.90	49	4,430	1.7
1.1.12.3 Preserved milk	0.20	6	490	7.3
1.1.13 Cheese and curd	1.80	46	4,230	1.6
1.1.14 Eggs	0.60	16	3,250	1.8
1.1.15 Other milk products	2.00	51	4,500	1.6
1.1.15.1 Other milk products	0.90	24	3,410	2.1
1.1.15.2 Yoghurt	1.00	27	3,290	2.0
1.1.16 Butter	0.30	9	1,780	2.6
1.1.17 Margarine, other vegetable fats and peanut butter	0.50	13	2,830	2.1
1.1.18 Cooking oils and fats	0.30	8	1,360	3.9
1.1.18.1 Olive oil	0.10	3	490	6.3
1.1.18.2 Edible oils and other edible animal fats	0.20	4	960	4.9
1.1.19 Fresh fruit	2.90	77	4,830	1.6
1.1.19.1 Citrus fruits (fresh)	0.50	12	2,440	2.5
1.1.19.2 Bananas (fresh)	0.50	12	3,590	1.7
1.1.19.3 Apples (fresh)	0.50	14	2,860	2.4
1.1.19.4 Pears (fresh)	0.10	4	1,080	3.3
1.1.19.5 Stone fruits (fresh)	0.40	9	1,640	3.6
1.1.19.6 Berries (fresh)	1.00	25	2,650	2.5
1.1.20 Other fresh, chilled or frozen fruits	0.30	8	1,570	3.4
1.1.21 Dried fruit and nuts	0.50	14	1,910	3.2
1.1.22 Preserved fruit and fruit based products	0.10	3	1,030	4.5
1.1.23 Fresh vegetables	3.80	98	5,250	1.4
1.1.23.1 Leaf and stem vegetables (fresh or chilled)	0.80	20	3,440	2.1
1.1.23.2 Cabbages (fresh or chilled)	0.40	10	2,740	2.0
1.1.23.3 Vegetables grown for their fruit (fresh, chilled or frozen)	1.30	34	4,320	1.8
1.1.23.4 Root crops, non-starchy bulbs and mushrooms (fresh, chilled or frozen)	1.30	34	4,700	1.4

Note: The commodity and service categories are not comparable with those in publications before 2001–02.
The numbering is sequential, it does not use actual COICOP codes.
Please see page xiii for symbols and conventions used in this report.

ONS, Family Spending 2009,   © Crown copyright 2010

Table A1 **Components of household expenditure, 2009 (cont.)**
based on weighted data and including children's expenditure

		Average weekly expenditure all house- holds (£)	Total weekly expenditure (£ million)	Recording house- holds in sample	Percentage standard error (full method)
Commodity or service					
1	**Food & non-alcoholic drinks (continued)**				
1.1.24	Dried vegetables	0.00	1	260	9.7
1.1.25	Other preserved or processed vegetables	1.30	33	4,290	1.8
1.1.26	Potatoes	0.90	22	3,970	1.5
1.1.27	Other tubers and products of tuber vegetables	1.30	34	4,000	1.4
1.1.28	Sugar and sugar products	0.30	9	2,170	2.4
1.1.28.1	Sugar	0.20	6	1,880	2.6
1.1.28.2	Other sugar products	0.10	2	570	5.4
1.1.29	Jams, marmalades	0.30	7	1,710	3.1
1.1.30	Chocolate	1.60	41	3,570	2.5
1.1.31	Confectionery products	0.60	15	2,770	2.7
1.1.32	Edible ices and ice cream	0.50	13	1,870	2.8
1.1.33	Other food products	2.40	63	4,790	2.0
1.1.33.1	Sauces, condiments	1.20	31	3,800	1.8
1.1.33.2	Baker's yeast, dessert preparations, soups	0.90	24	3,250	4.1
1.1.33.3	Salt, spices, culinary herbs and other food products	0.30	8	1,520	5.6
1.2	Non-alcoholic drinks	4.10	107	5,300	1.4
1.2.1	Coffee	0.60	16	1,860	3.0
1.2.2	Tea	0.50	12	2,020	2.6
1.2.3	Cocoa and powdered chocolate	0.10	2	510	5.6
1.2.4	Fruit and vegetable juices	1.10	28	3,380	2.1
1.2.5	Mineral or spring waters	0.20	6	1,210	4.6
1.2.6	Soft drinks (inc. fizzy and ready to drink fruit drinks)	1.70	43	3,800	2.1
2	**Alcoholic drink, tobacco & narcotics**	**11.20**	**290**	**3,650**	**2.0**
2.1	Alcoholic drinks	6.80	176	3,010	2.4
2.1.1	Spirits and liqueurs (brought home)	1.30	34	830	4.2
2.1.2	Wines, fortified wines (brought home)	3.50	91	2,060	3.8
2.1.2.1	Wine from grape or other fruit (brought home)	3.20	82	1,900	4.0
2.1.2.2	Fortified wine (brought home)	0.20	4	210	8.8
2.1.2.3	Champagne and sparkling wines (brought home)	0.20	5	180	13.5
2.1.3	Beer, lager, ciders and perry (brought home)	1.90	50	1,600	3.4
2.1.3.1	Beer and lager (brought home)	1.60	42	1,370	3.6
2.1.3.2	Ciders and perry (brought home)	0.30	8	430	7.6
2.1.4	Alcopops (brought home)	0.10	1	120	10.6
2.2	Tobacco and narcotics	4.40	114	1,420	3.7
2.2.1	Cigarettes	3.80	99	1,300	4.1
2.2.2	Cigars, other tobacco products and narcotics	0.60	16	380	6.0
2.2.2.1	Cigars	0.00	1	20	32.1
2.2.2.2	Other tobacco	0.60	15	360	6.1
2.2.2.3	Narcotics	[0.00]	[0]	-	90.1
3	**Clothing & footwear**	**20.90**	**544**	**3,910**	**2.4**
3.1	Clothing	17.00	443	3,720	2.6
3.1.1	Men's outer garments	4.00	103	1,170	5.1
3.1.2	Men's under garments	0.40	9	450	6.6
3.1.3	Women's outer garments	7.90	206	2,180	3.4
3.1.4	Women's under garments	1.00	26	1,090	4.8
3.1.5	Boys' outer garments (5-15)	0.70	17	400	7.0
3.1.6	Girls' outer garments (5-15)	1.00	25	520	7.0
3.1.7	Infants' outer garments (under 5)	0.70	18	500	6.5
3.1.8	Children's under garments (under 16)	0.40	10	530	6.0

Note: The commodity and service categories are not comparable with those in publications before 2001–02.
The numbering is sequential, it does not use actual COICOP codes.
Please see page xiii for symbols and conventions used in this report.

ONS, Family Spending 2009, © *Crown copyright 2010*

Table A1 **Components of household expenditure, 2009 (cont.)**
based on weighted data and including children's expenditure

Commodity or service			Average weekly expenditure all house- holds (£)	Total weekly expenditure (£ million)	Recording house- holds in sample	Percentage standard error (full method)
3	**Clothing & footwear (continued)**					
	3.1.9	Accessories	0.70	18	860	5.1
		3.1.9.1 Men's accessories	0.20	6	260	8.9
		3.1.9.2 Women's accessories	0.30	9	460	7.3
		3.1.9.3 Children's accessories	0.10	3	230	9.4
		3.1.9.4 Protective head gear (crash helmets)	0.00	1	20	30.1
	3.1.10	Haberdashery, clothing materials and clothing hire	0.20	4	240	14.4
	3.1.11	Dry cleaners, laundry and dyeing	0.30	7	190	10.5
		3.1.11.1 Dry cleaners and dyeing	0.20	5	150	12.0
		3.1.11.2 Laundry, launderettes	0.10	1	50	22.5
3.2	Footwear		3.90	101	1,580	3.8
	3.2.1	Footwear for men	1.00	27	420	8.1
	3.2.2	Footwear for women	2.10	53	930	4.8
	3.2.3	Footwear for children (5 to 15 years) and infants (under 5)	0.70	19	490	6.0
	3.2.4	Repair and hire of footwear	0.10	2	60	16.0
4	**Housing(net)[1], fuel & power**		**57.30**	**1,489**	**5,800**	**1.5**
4.1	Actual rentals for housing		35.50	921	1,680	2.8
	4.1.1	Gross rent	35.40	921	1,670	2.8
	4.1.2	less housing benefit, rebates and allowances received	13.70	357	1,120	3.4
	4.1.3	Net rent[2]	21.70	564	1,260	3.8
	4.1.4	Second dwelling - rent	[0.00]	0	..	67.8
4.2	Maintenance and repair of dwelling		6.70	174	2,510	4.9
	4.2.1	Central heating repairs	1.30	34	1,530	5.5
	4.2.2	House maintenance etc.	3.70	96	1,030	8.2
	4.2.3	Paint, wallpaper, timber	1.00	27	480	8.2
	4.2.4	Equipment hire, small materials	0.70	18	420	10.3
4.3	Water supply and miscellaneous services relating to the dwelling		7.60	198	4,850	1.4
	4.3.1	Water charges	6.50	170	4,630	0.8
	4.3.2	Other regular housing payments including service charge for rent	1.10	28	630	8.8
	4.3.3	Refuse collection, including skip hire	[0.00]	0	..	51.8
4.4	Electricity, gas and other fuels		21.30	552	5,530	0.9
	4.4.1	Electricity	10.20	265	5,390	1.0
	4.4.2	Gas	9.70	252	4,290	1.4
	4.4.3	Other fuels	1.30	35	610	7.5
		4.4.3.1 Coal and coke	0.20	4	120	21.5
		4.4.3.2 Oil for central heating	1.10	29	480	8.2
		4.4.3.3 Paraffin, wood, peat, hot water etc.	0.10	2	60	23.2
5	**Household goods & services**		**27.90**	**726**	**5,360**	**4.1**
5.1	Furniture and furnishings, carpets and other floor coverings		14.40	373	2,110	6.6
	5.1.1	Furniture and furnishings	11.10	289	1,750	7.8
		5.1.1.1 Furniture	10.30	267	1,220	8.3
		5.1.1.2 Fancy, decorative goods	0.70	17	700	7.0
		5.1.1.3 Garden furniture	0.20	5	50	23.1
	5.1.2	Floor coverings	3.20	84	780	7.9
		5.1.2.1 Soft floor coverings	2.90	76	730	8.4
		5.1.2.2 Hard floor coverings	0.30	8	60	25.0
5.2	Household textiles		1.50	40	1,020	6.1
	5.2.1	Bedroom textiles, including duvets and pillows	0.70	19	410	8.8
	5.2.2	Other household textiles, including cushions, towels, curtains	0.80	21	730	8.9

Note: The commodity and service categories are not comparable with those in publications before 2001–02.
The numbering is sequential, it does not use actual COICOP codes.
Please see page xiii for symbols and conventions used in this report.

1 Excluding mortgage interest payments, council tax and NI rates.
2 The figure included in total expenditure is net rent as opposed to gross rent

ONS, Family Spending 2009, © *Crown copyright 2010*

Table A1 **Components of household expenditure, 2009 (cont.)**
based on weighted data and including children's expenditure

	Commodity or service	Average weekly expenditure all house-holds (£)	Total weekly expenditure (£ million)	Recording house-holds in sample	Percentage standard error (full method)
5	**Household goods & services (continued)**				
5.3	Household appliances	3.10	80	530	14.4
	5.3.1 Gas cookers	[0.10]	[2]	..	58.7
	5.3.2 Electric cookers, combined gas/electric cookers	0.20	5	40	37.5
	5.3.3 Clothes washing machines and drying machines	0.70	17	90	18.9
	5.3.4 Refrigerators, freezers and fridge-freezers	0.20	6	50	26.5
	5.3.5 Other major electrical appliances, dishwashers, micro-waves vacuum cleaners, heaters etc.	1.40	36	140	26.2
	5.3.6 Fire extinguisher, water softener, safes etc	[0.00]	[0]	..	82.8
	5.3.7 Small electric household appliances, excluding hairdryers	0.30	9	220	9.5
	5.3.8 Repairs to gas and electrical appliances and spare parts	0.20	5	50	22.0
	5.3.9 Rental/hire of major household appliances	[0.00]	[0]	..	40.9
5.4	Glassware, tableware and household utensils	1.40	35	1,640	4.5
	5.4.1 Glassware, china, pottery, cutlery and silverware	0.40	10	660	8.0
	5.4.2 Kitchen and domestic utensils	0.60	14	940	5.8
	5.4.3 Repair of glassware, tableware and household utensils	[0.00]	[0]	..	-
	5.4.4 Storage and other durable household articles	0.40	10	520	8.5
5.5	Tools and equipment for house and garden	2.20	58	1,810	6.7
	5.5.1 Electrical tools	0.30	7	60	19.5
	5.5.2 Garden tools, equipment and accessories e.g. lawn mowers etc.	0.40	11	290	12.7
	5.5.3 Small tools	0.30	8	360	9.6
	5.5.4 Door, electrical and other fittings	0.70	18	440	16.1
	5.5.5 Electrical consumables	0.50	14	1,180	5.4
5.6	Goods and services for routine household maintenance	5.40	140	4,940	4.3
	5.6.1 Cleaning materials	2.30	59	4,080	1.8
	5.6.1.1 Detergents, washing-up liquid, washing powder	1.10	28	2,780	2.2
	5.6.1.2 Disinfectants, polishes, other cleaning materials etc.	1.20	32	3,320	2.5
	5.6.2 Household goods and hardware	1.30	33	3,710	2.9
	5.6.2.1 Kitchen disposables	0.70	19	3,150	2.5
	5.6.2.2 Household hardware and appliances, matches	0.20	6	760	7.1
	5.6.2.3 Kitchen gloves, cloths etc.	0.10	3	930	5.4
	5.6.2.4 Pins, needles, tape measures, nails, nuts and bolts etc.	0.20	5	410	10.7
	5.6.3 Domestic services, carpet cleaning, hire/repair of furniture/furnishings	1.80	47	880	11.7
	5.6.3.1 Domestic services, including cleaners, gardeners, au pairs	1.30	33	300	16.3
	5.6.3.2 Carpet cleaning, ironing service, window cleaner	0.50	12	650	6.8
	5.6.3.3 Hire/repair of household furniture and furnishings	[0.10]	[3]	10	56.5
6	**Health**	**5.30**	**137**	**2,960**	**6.5**
6.1	Medical products, appliances and equipment	3.30	85	2,790	7.8
	6.1.1 Medicines, prescriptions and healthcare products	2.00	52	2,660	10.8
	6.1.1.1 NHS prescription charges and payments	0.20	5	220	8.4
	6.1.1.2 Medicines and medical goods (not NHS)	1.20	31	2,420	3.7
	6.1.1.3 Other medical products (e.g. plasters, condoms, hot water bottle etc.)	0.20	4	390	9.5
	6.1.1.4 Non-optical appliances and equipment (e.g. wheelchairs, batteries for hearing aids, shoe build-up)	0.40	11	40	47.5
	6.1.2 Spectacles, lenses, accessories and repairs	1.30	33	290	11.1
	6.1.2.1 Purchase of spectacles, lenses, prescription sunglasses	1.20	32	250	11.3
	6.1.2.2 Accessories/repairs to spectacles/lenses	0.00	1	50	17.8
6.2	Hospital services	2.00	53	430	10.2
	6.2.1 Out patient services	2.00	52	430	10.3
	6.2.1.1 NHS medical, optical, dental and medical auxiliary services	0.70	19	210	12.7
	6.2.1.2 Private medical, optical, dental and medical auxiliary services	1.30	33	230	14.6
	6.2.1.3 Other services	-	-	0	-
	6.2.2 In-patient hospital services	[0.00]	[0]	..	68.4

Note: The commodity and service categories are not comparable with those in publications before 2001–02.
   The numbering is sequential, it does not use actual COICOP codes.
   Please see page xiii for symbols and conventions used in this report.

ONS, Family Spending 2009, © *Crown copyright 2010*

Table A1   **Components of household expenditure, 2009 (cont.)**
based on weighted data and including children's expenditure

Commodity or service			Average weekly expenditure all house-holds (£)	Total weekly expenditure (£ million)	Recording house-holds in sample	Percentage standard error (full method)
7	**Transport**		**58.40**	**1,518**	**4,950**	**1.9**
7.1	Purchase of vehicles		19.50	505	1,400	4.4
	7.1.1	Purchase of new cars and vans	6.50	170	340	9.2
	7.1.1.1	Outright purchases	3.50	92	110	11.7
	7.1.1.2	Loan/Hire Purchase of new car/van	3.00	77	230	13.6
	7.1.2	Purchase of second hand cars or vans	12.40	321	1,080	4.6
	7.1.2.1	Outright purchases	8.00	207	620	6.1
	7.1.2.2	Loan/Hire Purchase of second hand car/van	4.40	115	520	6.3
	7.1.3	Purchase of motorcycles	0.60	15	60	16.5
	7.1.3.1	Outright purchases of new or second hand motorcycles	0.30	7	20	26.3
	7.1.3.2	Loan/Hire Purchase of new or second hand motorcycles	[0.10]	[3]	20	25.2
	7.1.3.3	Purchase of bicycles and other vehicles	0.20	5	30	29.9
7.2	Operation of personal transport		29.30	762	4,290	1.7
	7.2.1	Spares and accessories	2.00	52	470	9.0
	7.2.1.1	Car/van accessories and fittings	0.20	4	110	16.1
	7.2.1.2	Car/van spare parts	1.50	39	280	10.1
	7.2.1.3	Motorcycle accessories and spare parts	0.10	4	30	32.5
	7.2.1.4	Bicycle accessories, repairs and other costs	0.20	5	90	20.1
	7.2.2	Petrol, diesel and other motor oils	19.20	500	3,810	1.7
	7.2.2.1	Petrol	14.70	381	3,180	1.9
	7.2.2.2	Diesel oil	4.50	116	1,060	3.5
	7.2.2.3	Other motor oils	0.10	2	80	15.8
	7.2.3	Repairs and servicing	5.90	155	1,780	3.6
	7.2.3.1	Car or van repairs, servicing and other work	5.90	153	1,760	3.6
	7.2.3.2	Motorcycle repairs and servicing	0.10	1	30	24.8
	7.2.4	Other motoring costs	2.20	56	2,140	4.2
	7.2.4.1	Motoring organisation subscription (e.g. AA and RAC)	0.40	10	900	6.1
	7.2.4.2	Garage rent, other costs (excluding fines), car washing etc.	0.60	17	330	9.4
	7.2.4.3	Parking fees, tolls, and permits (excluding motoring fines)	0.80	20	1,220	5.5
	7.2.4.4	Driving lessons	0.30	7	60	16.8
	7.2.4.5	Anti-freeze, battery water, cleaning materials	0.10	3	290	12.2
7.3	Transport services		9.60	250	2,300	4.0
	7.3.1	Rail and tube fares	2.50	64	690	6.9
	7.3.1.1	Season tickets	0.80	22	140	11.5
	7.3.1.2	Other than season tickets	1.60	42	610	7.5
	7.3.2	Bus and coach fares	1.30	33	930	5.7
	7.3.2.1	Season tickets	0.40	10	160	9.3
	7.3.2.2	Other than season tickets	0.90	23	840	6.0
	7.3.3	Combined fares	1.10	29	190	10.4
	7.3.3.1	Combined fares other than season tickets	0.30	7	80	14.9
	7.3.3.2	Combined fares season tickets	0.90	23	120	13.0
	7.3.4	Other travel and transport	4.80	125	1,350	6.5
	7.3.4.1	Air fares (within UK)	[0.10]	[4]	20	30.5
	7.3.4.2	Air fares (international)	1.10	30	50	21.1
	7.3.4.3	School travel	0.00	1	20	25.8
	7.3.4.4	Taxis and hired cars with drivers	1.20	30	840	5.2
	7.3.4.5	Other personal travel and transport services	0.30	7	300	13.7
	7.3.4.6	Hire of self-drive cars, vans, bicycles	0.20	5	30	27.5
	7.3.4.7	Car leasing	1.70	43	200	8.7
	7.3.4.8	Water travel, ferries and season tickets	0.20	5	60	30.9

Note: The commodity and service categories are not comparable with those in publications before 2001–02.
The numbering is sequential, it does not use actual COICOP codes.
Please see page xiii for symbols and conventions used in this report.

ONS, Family Spending 2009,   © *Crown copyright 2010*

Table A1   **Components of household expenditure, 2009 (cont.)**
based on weighted data and including children's expenditure

Commodity or service			Average weekly expenditure all house-holds (£)	Total weekly expenditure (£ million)	Recording house-holds in sample	Percentage standard error (full method)
8	**Communication**		**11.70**	**303**	**5,490**	**1.3**
8.1	Postal services		0.40	11	910	6.3
8.2	Telephone and telefax equipment		0.50	12	160	11.8
	8.2.1	Telephone purchase	0.10	2	30	23.8
	8.2.2	Mobile phone purchase	0.40	10	130	13.1
	8.2.3	Answering machine, fax machine, modem purchase	[0.00]	[0]	..	80.7
8.3	Telephone and telefax services		10.80	280	5,460	1.2
	8.3.1	Telephone account	5.70	149	5,030	1.2
	8.3.2	Telephone coin and other payments	0.10	1	60	25.6
	8.3.3	Mobile phone account	3.90	103	2,320	2.4
	8.3.4	Mobile phone - other payments	1.00	27	860	4.4
9	**Recreation & culture**		**57.90**	**1,503**	**5,770**	**2.8**
9.1	Audio-visual, photographic and information processing equipment		7.00	182	1,690	6.7
	9.1.1	Audio equipment and accessories, CD players	1.50	38	690	7.8
		9.1.1.1 Audio equipment, CD players including in car	0.80	20	120	13.6
		9.1.1.2 Audio accessories e.g. tapes, headphones etc.	0.70	18	610	5.7
	9.1.2	TV, video and computers	4.80	124	1,220	8.3
		9.1.2.1 Purchase of TV and digital decoder	1.50	40	120	15.1
		9.1.2.2 Satellite dish purchase and installation	[0.10]	[3]	10	35.6
		9.1.2.3 Cable TV connection	[0.00]	[0]	..	104.4
		9.1.2.4 Video recorder	[0.00]	[1]	..	50.2
		9.1.2.5 DVD player/recorder	0.10	2	20	35.3
		9.1.2.6 Blank, pre-recorded video cassettes, DVDs	0.90	23	750	5.7
		9.1.2.7 Personal computers, printers and calculators	1.80	48	370	15.1
		9.1.2.8 Spare parts for TV, video, audio	0.10	3	70	22.0
		9.1.2.9 Repair of audio-visual, photographic and information processing	0.20	4	30	26.3
	9.1.3	Photographic, cine and optical equipment	0.70	19	130	23.2
		9.1.3.1 Photographic and cine equipment	0.70	18	110	23.7
		9.1.3.2 Camera films	[0.00]	[0]	20	37.9
		9.1.3.3 Optical instruments, binoculars, telescopes, microscopes	[0.00]	[0]	10	40.8
9.2	Other major durables for recreation and culture		2.50	66	120	24.0
	9.2.1	Purchase of boats, trailers and horses	[0.60]	0	..	74.2
	9.2.2	Purchase of caravans, mobile homes (including decoration)	0.90	24	30	32.6
	9.2.3	Accessories for boats, horses, caravans and motor caravans	[0.20]	[5]	20	54.5
	9.2.4	Musical instruments (purchase and hire)	0.20	6	40	41.5
	9.2.5	Major durables for indoor recreation	[0.00]	[0]	..	108.0
	9.2.6	Maintenance and repair of other major durables	0.20	6	30	51.9
	9.2.7	Purchase of motor caravan (new and second–hand) – outright purchase	[0.30]	[7]	..	55.7
	9.2.8	Purchase of motor caravan (new and second–hand) – loan/HP	[0.10]	[2]	..	42.0
9.3	Other recreational items and equipment, gardens and pets		10.50	273	3,950	3.2
	9.3.1	Games, toys and hobbies	2.20	56	1,430	5.2
	9.3.2	Computer software and games	1.50	39	380	8.1
		9.3.2.1 Computer software and game cartridges	0.90	24	330	7.2
		9.3.2.2 Computer games consoles	0.60	16	70	15.6
	9.3.3	Equipment for sport, camping and open-air recreation	0.80	20	420	10.7
	9.3.4	Horticultural goods, garden equipment and plants etc.	2.60	67	2,060	7.7
		9.3.4.1 BBQ and swings	0.10	2	50	55.7
		9.3.4.2 Plants, flowers, seeds, fertilisers, insecticides	2.40	62	1,980	8.1
		9.3.4.3 Garden decorative	0.10	2	50	21.6
		9.3.4.4 Artificial flowers, pot pourri	0.00	1	70	16.0
	9.3.5	Pets and pet food	3.50	91	2,180	4.3
		9.3.5.1 Pet food	1.90	49	2,040	3.6
		9.3.5.2 Pet purchase and accessories	0.60	17	600	7.9
		9.3.5.3 Veterinary and other services for pets identified separately	1.00	26	190	11.1

Note: The commodity and service categories are not comparable with those in publications before 2001–02.
The numbering is sequential, it does not use actual COICOP codes.
Please see page xiii for symbols and conventions used in this report.

ONS, Family Spending 2009,   © Crown copyright 2010

Table A1   **Components of household expenditure, 2009 (cont.)**
based on weighted data and including children's expenditure

			Average weekly expenditure all house-holds (£)	Total weekly expenditure (£ million)	Recording house-holds in sample	Percentage standard error (full method)
Commodity or service						
9	**Recreation & culture (continued)**					
9.4	Recreational and cultural services		18.70	487	5,510	6.2
	9.4.1	Sports admissions, subscriptions, leisure class fees and equipment hire	5.00	131	2,010	4.4
		9.4.1.1 Spectator sports: admission charges	0.60	15	150	20.6
		9.4.1.2 Participant sports (excluding subscriptions)	1.00	27	890	5.9
		9.4.1.3 Subscriptions to sports and social clubs	1.40	37	800	7.8
		9.4.1.4 Leisure class fees	1.90	51	880	6.4
		9.4.1.5 Hire of equipment for sport and open air recreation	0.00	1	30	44.2
	9.4.2	Cinema, theatre and museums etc.	2.30	59	970	5.9
		9.4.2.1 Cinemas	0.60	15	540	5.3
		9.4.2.2 Live entertainment: theatre, concerts, shows	1.30	33	330	9.8
		9.4.2.3 Museums, zoological gardens, theme parks, houses and gardens	0.40	11	230	9.4
	9.4.3	TV, video, satellite rental, cable subscriptions, TV licences and Internet	5.90	154	5,140	1.2
		9.4.3.1 TV licences	2.30	59	4,900	0.5
		9.4.3.2 Satellite subscriptions	2.40	63	1,740	2.5
		9.4.3.3 Rent for TV/Satellite/VCR	0.20	6	170	10.1
		9.4.3.4 Cable subscriptions	0.60	17	650	6.0
		9.4.3.5 TV slot meter payments	[0.00]	[0]	10	37.8
		9.4.3.6 Video, cassette and CD hire	0.10	2	120	12.9
		9.4.3.7 Internet subscription fees	0.30	8	290	10.0
	9.4.4	Miscellaneous entertainments	1.10	30	1,140	6.2
		9.4.4.1 Admissions to clubs, dances, discos, bingo	0.50	13	500	8.4
		9.4.4.2 Social events and gatherings	0.20	5	260	12.1
		9.4.4.3 Subscriptions for leisure activities and other subscriptions	0.40	11	530	11.3
	9.4.5	Development of film, deposit for film development, passport photos, holiday and school photos	0.30	7	210	21.0
	9.4.6	Gambling payments	4.10	106	2,750	27.5
		9.4.6.1 Football pools stakes	0.00	1	40	23.2
		9.4.6.2 Bingo stakes excluding admission	0.30	9	150	17.6
		9.4.6.3 Lottery	1.80	48	2,480	3.0
		9.4.6.4 Bookmaker, tote, other betting stakes	1.80	48	600	61.0
9.5	Newspapers, books and stationery		5.90	152	5,080	1.9
	9.5.1	Books	1.30	35	1,250	5.0
	9.5.2	Stationery, diaries, address books, art materials	0.60	16	1,380	5.1
	9.5.3	Cards, calendars, posters and other printed matter	1.20	31	2,620	2.9
	9.5.4	Newspapers	1.80	47	3,620	2.0
	9.5.5	Magazines and periodicals	0.90	23	2,630	3.0
9.6	Package holidays		13.20	344	810	5.1
	9.6.1	Package holidays – UK	0.90	24	160	11.7
	9.6.2	Package holidays – abroad	12.30	319	680	5.4
10	**Education**		**7.00**	**181**	**460**	**11.8**
10.1	Education fees		6.70	173	340	12.4
	10.1.1	Nursery and primary education	0.60	14	50	25.5
	10.1.2	Secondary education	1.50	39	60	21.1
	10.1.3	Sixth form college/college education	0.50	12	50	45.1
	10.1.4	University education	3.50	92	120	19.7
	10.1.5	Other education	0.60	16	90	22.6
10.2	Payments for school trips, other ad-hoc expenditure		0.30	9	140	15.0
	10.2.1	Nursery and primary education	0.20	4	80	18.8
	10.2.2	Secondary education	0.10	4	50	26.6
	10.2.3	Sixth form college/college education	[0.00]	[0]	..	74.5
	10.2.4	University education	[0.00]	[0]	..	62.5
	10.2.5	Other education	[0.00]	[0]	..	88.7

Note: The commodity and service categories are not comparable with those in publications before 2001–02.
The numbering is sequential, it does not use actual COICOP codes.
Please see page xiii for symbols and conventions used in this report.

ONS, Family Spending 2009,   © Crown copyright 2010

Table A1 **Components of household expenditure, 2009 (cont.)**
based on weighted data and including children's expenditure

Commodity or service	Average weekly expenditure all house- holds (£)	Total weekly expenditure (£ million)	Recording house- holds in sample	Percentage standard error (full method)
11	**Restaurants & hotels**	**38.40**	**997**	**5,100**	**2.7**
11.1	Catering services	31.30	812	5,060	2.6
11.1.1	Restaurant and café meals	13.30	346	4,100	2.3
11.1.2	Alcoholic drinks (away from home)	7.20	187	2,560	3.0
11.1.3	Take away meals eaten at home	3.80	99	2,500	2.4
11.1.4	Other take-away and snack food	4.20	108	3,300	2.3
11.1.4.1	Hot and cold food	2.90	75	2,830	2.6
11.1.4.2	Confectionery	0.30	9	1,710	3.4
11.1.4.3	Ice cream	0.10	4	610	5.5
11.1.4.4	Soft drinks	0.80	20	2,170	2.7
11.1.5	Contract catering (food)	0.80	22	40	69.0
11.1.6	Canteens	1.90	51	1,700	4.5
11.1.6.1	School meals	0.70	18	590	10.4
11.1.6.2	Meals bought and eaten at the workplace	1.30	33	1,330	4.2
11.2	Accommodation services	7.10	185	1,010	7.0
11.2.1	Holiday in the UK	3.00	77	700	5.3
11.2.2	Holiday abroad	4.10	106	380	11.4
11.2.3	Room hire	[0.10]	[1]	20	45.3
12	**Miscellaneous goods and services**	**35.00**	**911**	**5,690**	**2.3**
12.1	Personal care	10.50	273	5,050	2.5
12.1.1	Hairdressing, beauty treatment	3.40	87	1,410	4.8
12.1.2	Toilet paper	0.80	20	2,650	2.1
12.1.3	Toiletries and soap	2.20	56	4,010	2.3
12.1.3.1	Toiletries (disposable including tampons, lipsyl, toothpaste etc.)	1.30	34	3,380	3.0
12.1.3.2	Bar of soap, liquid soap, shower gel etc.	0.40	9	1,730	3.8
12.1.3.3	Toilet requisites (durable including razors, hairbrushes, toothbrushes etc.)	0.50	13	1,390	4.1
12.1.4	Baby toiletries and accessories (disposable)	0.70	17	990	5.0
12.1.5	Hair products, cosmetics and electrical appliances for personal care	3.50	92	3,130	3.6
12.1.5.1	Hair products	0.80	20	1,790	3.7
12.1.5.2	Cosmetics and related accessories	2.50	66	2,370	4.5
12.1.5.3	Electrical appliances for personal care, including hairdryers, shavers etc.	0.20	6	120	13.5
12.2	Personal effects	3.10	80	1,460	11.4
12.2.1	Jewellery, clocks and watches and other personal effects	1.90	50	1,020	17.8
12.2.2	Leather and travel goods (excluding baby items)	0.80	21	540	6.8
12.2.3	Sunglasses (non-prescription)	0.10	2	70	29.5
12.2.4	Baby equipment (excluding prams and pushchairs)	0.10	3	50	30.3
12.2.5	Prams, pram accessories and pushchairs	0.10	4	20	34.8
12.2.6	Repairs to personal goods	0.00	1	30	26.5
12.3	Social protection	3.30	85	270	13.4
12.3.1	Residential homes	[0.40]	[10]	..	70.9
12.3.2	Home help	0.50	13	40	46.3
12.3.3	Nursery, crèche, playschools	0.60	16	90	16.9
12.3.4	Child care payments	1.80	46	160	12.4

Note: The commodity and service categories are not comparable with those in publications before 2001–02.
The numbering is sequential, it does not use actual COICOP codes.
Please see page xiii for symbols and conventions used in this report.

ONS, Family Spending 2009, © Crown copyright 2010

Table A1   **Components of household expenditure, 2009 (cont.)**
based on weighted data and including children's expenditure

		Average weekly expenditure all house-holds (£)	Total weekly expenditure (£ million)	Recording house-holds in sample	Percentage standard error (full method)
Commodity or service					
12	**Miscellaneous goods and services (continued)**				
12.4	Insurance	14.70	383	5,140	2.5
	12.4.1 Household insurances	5.00	129	4,590	1.5
	12.4.1.1 Structure insurance	2.50	64	3,730	1.7
	12.4.1.2 Contents insurance	2.40	63	4,420	1.5
	12.4.1.3 Insurance for household appliances	0.10	2	110	22.8
	12.4.2 Medical insurance premiums	1.40	37	580	7.5
	12.4.3 Vehicle insurance including boat insurance	8.30	214	4,360	3.8
	12.4.3.1 Vehicle insurance	8.30	214	4,360	3.8
	12.4.3.2 Boat insurance (not home)	-	-	0	-
	12.4.4 Non-package holiday, other travel insurance	0.10	2	30	36.6
12.5	Other services	3.40	90	1,930	6.4
	12.5.1 Moving house	1.80	46	320	10.1
	12.5.1.1 Moving and storage of furniture	0.30	7	160	14.4
	12.5.1.2 Property transaction – purchase and sale	0.60	15	50	17.7
	12.5.1.3 Property transaction – sale only	0.40	10	30	22.2
	12.5.1.4 Property transaction – purchase only	0.30	9	70	25.1
	12.5.1.5 Property transaction – other payments	0.20	6	100	22.9
	12.5.2 Bank, building society, post office, credit card charges	0.50	13	980	6.7
	12.5.2.1 Bank and building society charges	0.50	12	860	7.0
	12.5.2.2 Bank and Post Office counter charges	[0.00]	[0]	..	53.3
	12.5.2.3 Annual standing charge for credit cards	0.10	1	150	17.5
	12.5.2.4 Commission travellers' cheques and currency	[0.00]	[0]	..	79.6
	12.5.3 Other services and professional fees	1.20	30	980	10.3
	12.5.3.1 Other professional fees including court fines	0.20	6	30	24.2
	12.5.3.2 Legal fees	0.20	6	20	40.0
	12.5.3.3 Funeral expenses	[0.00]	[1]	..	54.5
	12.5.3.4 TU and professional organisations	0.60	15	790	7.6
	12.5.3.5 Other payments for services e.g. photocopying	0.10	2	170	21.8
1–12	**All expenditure groups**	**383.10**	**9,954**	**5,830**	**1.1**
13	**Other expenditure items**	**71.80**	**1,866**	**5,460**	**2.4**
13.1	Housing: mortgage interest payments, council tax etc.	49.00	1273	4,990	2.7
	13.1.1 Mortgage interest payments	26.70	695	2,120	2.9
	13.1.2 Mortgage protection premiums	1.60	41	990	4.4
	13.1.3 Council tax, domestic rates	18.90	490	4,930	0.8
	13.1.5 Council tax, mortgage (second dwelling)	1.80	47	50	54.8
13.2	Licences, fines and transfers	3.40	87	4,280	3.4
	13.2.1 Stamp duty, licences and fines (excluding motoring fines)	0.40	11	130	24.7
	13.2.2 Motoring fines	[0.10]	[1]	20	29.5
	13.2.3 Motor vehicle road taxation payments less refunds	2.90	75	4,250	1.2
13.3	Holiday spending	8.50	221	270	9.6
	13.3.1 Money spent abroad	8.50	220	270	9.5
	13.3.2 Duty free goods bought in UK	[0.00]	[0]	..	82.9

Note: The commodity and service categories are not comparable with those in publications before 2001–02.
The numbering is sequential, it does not use actual COICOP codes.
Please see page xiii for symbols and conventions used in this report.

ONS, Family Spending 2009, © Crown copyright 2010

Table A1 **Components of household expenditure, 2009 (cont.)**
based on weighted data and including children's expenditure

	Average weekly expenditure all house-holds (£)	Total weekly expenditure (£ million)	Recording house-holds in sample	Percentage standard error (full method)
Commodity or service				
13 Other expenditure items (continued)				
13.4 Money transfers and credit	11.00	285	3,020	4.8
13.4.1 Money, cash gifts given to children	0.10	3	110	17.0
13.4.1.1 Money given to children for specific purposes	0.10	2	110	15.0
13.4.1.2 Cash gifts to children (no specific purpose)	[0.00]	[0]	..	75.4
13.4.2 Cash gifts and donations	9.20	240	2,470	5.5
13.4.2.1 Money/presents given to those outside the household	3.40	87	1,010	8.2
13.4.2.2 Charitable donations and subscriptions	2.20	57	1,670	10.1
13.4.2.3 Money sent abroad	1.70	43	300	17.2
13.4.2.4 Maintenance allowance expenditure	2.00	52	160	10.5
13.4.3 Club instalment payments (child) and interest on credit cards	1.60	42	930	6.2
13.4.3.1 Club instalment payment	-	-	0	-
13.4.3.2 Interest on credit cards	1.60	42	930	6.2
Total expenditure	**455.00**	**11,820**	**5,830**	**1.1**
14 Other items recorded				
14.1 Life assurance, contributions to pension funds	19.80	515	2,940	2.9
14.1.1 Life assurance premiums eg mortgage endowment policies	4.10	107	1,870	4.9
14.1.2 Contributions to pension and superannuation funds etc.	11.30	294	1,700	2.8
14.1.3 Personal pensions	4.40	114	670	8.7
14.2 Other insurance including friendly societies	1.30	34	1,220	5.0
14.3 Income tax, payments less refunds	91.80	2,384	4,530	4.4
14.3.1 Income tax paid by employees under PAYE	69.70	1,811	3,100	2.5
14.3.2 Income tax paid direct eg by retired or unoccupied persons	4.60	121	150	61.2
14.3.3 Income tax paid direct by self-employed	5.90	152	290	13.4
14.3.4 Income tax deducted at source from income under covenant from investments or from annuities and pensions	9.90	257	2,610	3.7
14.3.5 Income tax on bonus earnings	2.60	69	820	11.0
14.3.6 Income tax refunds under PAYE	0.10	2	30	37.9
14.3.7 Income tax refunds other than PAYE	0.90	23	250	27.2
14.4 National insurance contribution	27.90	725	3,060	1.6
14.4.1 NI contributions paid by employees	27.80	721	3,030	1.6
14.4.2 NI contributions paid by non-employees	0.10	4	60	29.5
14.5 Purchase or alteration of dwellings (contracted out), mortgages	47.80	1,241	2,370	25.8
14.5.1 Outright purchase of houses, flats etc. including deposits	[4.50]	[118]	10	86.9
14.5.2 Capital repayment of mortgage	20.30	529	1,730	2.7
14.5.3 Central heating installation	0.80	21	110	12.9
14.5.4 DIY improvements: Double glazing, kitchen units, sheds etc.	0.90	22	80	26.4
14.5.5 Home improvements - contracted out	18.90	491	850	12.3
14.5.6 Bathroom fittings	0.30	7	80	22.0
14.5.7 Purchase of materials for Capital Improvements	0.30	7	50	30.0
14.5.8 Purchase of second dwelling	1.80	46	60	22.3
14.6 Savings and investments	5.70	148	830	7.7
14.6.1 Savings, investments (excluding AVCs)	5.00	129	650	8.4
14.6.2 Additional Voluntary Contributions	0.60	14	100	16.0
14.6.3 Food stamps, other food related expenditure	0.20	4	170	16.9
14.7 Pay off loan to clear other debt	2.30	60	280	8.2
14.8 Windfall receipts from gambling etc.[3]	2.30	61	530	36.0

Note: The commodity and service categories are not comparable with those in publications before 2001–02.
The numbering is sequential, it does not use actual COICOP codes.
Please see page xiii for symbols and conventions used in this report.

3 Expressed as an income figure as opposed to an expenditure figure.

ONS, Family Spending 2009, © *Crown copyright 2010*

Table A2   **Expenditure on alcoholic drink by place of purchase, 2009**

based on weighted data including children's expenditure

		Average weekly expenditure all house-holds (£)	Total weekly expenditure (£ million)	Recording households in sample
By type of premises				
11	**Bought and consumed on licenced premises:**			
11.1.2	Alcoholic drinks (away from home)	7.20	187	2,560
11.1.2.1	Spirits and liqueurs (away from home)	1.00	25	760
11.1.2.2	Wine from grape or other fruit (away from home)	1.30	34	1,010
11.1.2.3	Fortified wine (away from home)	0.00	0	20
11.1.2.4	Champagne and sparkling wines (away from home)	0.10	2	70
11.1.2.5	Ciders and perry (away from home)	0.30	9	330
11.1.2.6	Beer and lager (away from home)	3.70	97	1,940
11.1.2.7	Alcopops (away from home)	0.10	3	130
11.1.2.8	Round of drinks (away from home)	0.70	18	270
2	**Bought at off-licences (including large supermarket chains):**			
2.1	Alcoholic drinks	6.80	176	3,010
2.1.1	Spirits and liqueurs (brought home)	1.30	34	830
2.1.2	Wines, fortified wines (brought home)	3.50	91	2,060
2.1.2.1	Wine from grape or other fruit (brought home)	3.20	82	1,900
2.1.2.2	Fortified wine (brought home)	0.20	4	210
2.1.2.3	Champagne and sparkling wines (brought home)	0.20	5	180
2.1.3	Beer, lager, ciders and perry (brought home)	1.90	50	1,600
2.1.3.1	Beer and lager (brought home)	1.60	42	1,370
2.1.3.2	Ciders and perry (brought home)	0.30	8	430
2.1.4	Alcopops (brought home)	0.10	1	120
2A	**Bought from large supermarket chains:**			
2.1A	Alcoholic drinks	4.60	120	2,500
2.1.1A	Spirits and liqueurs (brought home)	1.00	26	690
2.1.2A	Wines, fortified wines (brought home)	2.30	60	1,690
2.1.2.1A	Wine from grape or other fruit (brought home)	2.10	54	1,550
2.1.2.2A	Fortified wine (brought home)	0.10	3	180
2.1.2.3A	Champagne and sparkling wines (brought home)	0.10	3	140
2.1.3A	Beer, lager, ciders and perry (brought home)	1.30	33	1,220
2.1.3.1A	Beer and lager (brought home)	1.10	27	1,030
2.1.3.2A	Ciders and perry (brought home)	0.20	5	330
2.1.4A	Alcopops (brought home)	0.00	1	80
2B	**Bought from other off-licence outlets:**			
2.1B	Alcoholic drinks	2.20	56	1,240
2.1.1B	Spirits and liqueurs (brought home)	0.30	7	220
2.1.2B	Wines, fortified wines (brought home)	1.20	31	740
2.1.2.1B	Wine from grape or other fruit (brought home)	1.10	28	690
2.1.2.2B	Fortified wine (brought home)	0.00	1	40
2.1.2.3B	Champagne and sparkling wines (brought home)	0.10	2	50
2.1.3B	Beer, lager, ciders and perry (brought home)	0.70	17	590
2.1.3.1B	Beer and lager (brought home)	0.60	14	510
2.1.3.2B	Ciders and perry (brought home)	0.10	3	130
2.1.4B	Alcopops (brought home)	0.00	0	40

Note: The commodity and service categories are not comparable with those in publications before 2001–02.
The numbering is sequential, it does not use actual COICOP codes.
Please see page xiii for symbols and conventions used in this report.

ONS, Family Spending 2009, © Crown copyright 2010

Table A3　Expenditure on food and non-alcoholic drinks by place of purchase, 2009

based on weighted data and including children's expenditure

		Large supermarket chains			Other outlets		
		Average weekly expenditure all house-holds (£)	Total weekly expenditure (£ million)	Recording house-holds in sample	Average weekly expenditure all house-holds (£)	Total weekly expenditure (£ million)	Recording house-holds in sample
1	Food and non-alcoholic drinks	37.70	980	5,460	14.50	376	5,320
1.1	Food	34.70	902	5,460	13.30	347	5,260
1.1.1	Bread, rice and cereals	3.60	93	5,150	1.40	36	3,380
1.1.1.1	Rice	0.20	6	1,130	0.10	3	330
1.1.1.2	Bread	1.80	46	4,850	0.80	21	3,040
1.1.1.3	Other breads and cereals	1.60	41	4,080	0.40	11	1,580
1.1.2	Pasta products	0.30	8	2,070	0.10	2	530
1.1.3	Buns, cakes, biscuits etc.	2.40	63	4,600	0.80	21	2,480
1.1.3.1	Buns, crispbread and biscuits	1.40	37	4,120	0.40	11	1,950
1.1.3.2	Cakes and puddings	1.00	27	3,190	0.40	9	1,430
1.1.4	Pastry (savoury)	0.60	15	1,720	0.10	4	540
1.1.5	Beef (fresh, chilled or frozen)	1.10	28	2,000	0.60	16	990
1.1.6	Pork (fresh, chilled or frozen)	0.40	11	1,020	0.20	6	470
1.1.7	Lamb (fresh, chilled or frozen)	0.30	9	680	0.30	8	360
1.1.8	Poultry (fresh, chilled or frozen)	1.40	36	2,370	0.60	15	990
1.1.9	Bacon and ham	0.70	18	2,050	0.30	8	940
1.1.10	Other meats and meat preparations	4.00	104	4,550	1.40	35	2,510
1.1.10.1	Sausages	0.50	13	1,960	0.20	6	950
1.1.10.2	Offal, pate etc.	0.10	2	630	0.00	1	190
1.1.10.3	Other preserved or processed meat and meat preparations	3.40	89	4,360	1.10	28	2,240
1.1.10.4	Other fresh, chilled or frozen meat	[0.00]	[0]	..	[0.00]	[0]	..
1.1.11	Fish and fish products	1.70	44	3,250	0.60	16	1,160
1.1.11.1	Fish (fresh, chilled or frozen)	0.50	13	1,110	0.30	7	410
1.1.11.2	Seafood, dried, smoked or salted fish	0.40	10	1,100	0.10	4	290
1.1.11.3	Other preserved or processed fish and seafood	0.00 0.80	21	2,520	0.20	5	750
1.1.12	Milk	1.60	42	4,270	1.20	31	3,170
1.1.12.1	Whole milk	0.30	9	1,240	0.30	8	960
1.1.12.2	Low fat milk	1.10	29	3,450	0.80	21	2,470
1.1.12.3	Preserved milk	0.20	4	400	0.10	2	120
1.1.13	Cheese and curd	1.40	36	3,630	0.40	10	1,200
1.1.14	Eggs	0.40	12	2,330	0.20	5	1,170
1.1.15	Other milk products	1.60	43	4,040	0.30	8	1,280
1.1.15.1	Other milk products	0.80	20	2,980	0.20	4	870
1.1.15.2	Yoghurt	0.90	23	2,900	0.20	4	710
1.1.16	Butter	0.30	7	1,500	0.10	2	390
1.1.17	Margarine, other vegetable fats and peanut butter	0.40	10	2,370	0.10	3	660
1.1.18	Cooking oils and fats	0.20	6	1,140	0.10	2	270
1.1.18.1	Olive oil	0.10	3	410	0.00	1	80
1.1.18.2	Edible oils and other edible animal fats	0.10	3	790	0.00	1	200
1.1.19	Fresh fruit	2.30	61	4,320	0.60	16	1,750
1.1.19.1	Citrus fruits (fresh)	0.40	10	2,050	0.10	2	620
1.1.19.2	Bananas (fresh)	0.40	9	3,070	0.10	3	990
1.1.19.3	Apples (fresh)	0.40	11	2,380	0.10	3	730
1.1.19.4	Pears (fresh)	0.10	3	900	0.00	1	230
1.1.19.5	Stone fruits (fresh)	0.30	7	1,370	0.10	2	420
1.1.19.6	Berries (fresh)	0.80	20	2,250	0.20	5	700

Note:　The commodity and service categories are not comparable with those in publications before 2001–02.
　　　　The numbering is sequential, it does not use actual COICOP codes.
　　　　Please see page xiii for symbols and conventions used in this report.

ONS, Family Spending 2009,　© Crown copyright 2010

Table A3 **Expenditure on food and non-alcoholic drinks by place of purchase, 2009 (cont.)**

based on weighted data and including children's expenditure

		Large supermarket chains			Other outlets		
		Average weekly expenditure all house-holds (£)	Total weekly expenditure (£ million)	Recording house-holds in sample	Average weekly expenditure all house-holds (£)	Total weekly expenditure (£ million)	Recording house-holds in sample
1	**Food and non-alcoholic drinks (continued)**						
1.1.20	Other fresh, chilled or frozen fruits	0.20	6	1,340	0.10	1	310
1.1.21	Dried fruit and nuts	0.40	10	1,560	0.20	4	520
1.1.22	Preserved fruit and fruit based products	0.10	3	860	0.00	1	210
1.1.23	Fresh vegetables	3.00	77	4,710	0.80	21	2,300
1.1.23.1	Leaf and stem vegetables (fresh or chilled)	0.60	16	3,030	0.10	4	900
1.1.23.2	Cabbages (fresh or chilled)	0.30	8	2,240	0.10	3	780
1.1.23.3	Vegetables grown for their fruit (fresh, chilled or frozen)	1.00	27	3,750	0.30	7	1,360
1.1.23.4	Root crops, non-starchy bulbs and mushrooms (fresh, chilled or frozen)	1.00	26	4,070	0.30	8	1,680
1.1.24	Dried vegetables and other preserved and processed vegetable	0.60	16	3,130	0.70	17	2,900
1.1.25	Potatoes	0.60	17	3,220	0.20	6	1,280
1.1.26	Other tubers and products of tuber vegetables	1.00	26	3,340	0.30	8	1,580
1.1.27	Sugar and sugar products	0.30	7	1,680	0.10	2	640
1.1.28.1	Sugar	0.20	5	1,410	0.10	2	560
1.1.28.2	Other sugar products	0.10	2	460	0.00	1	120
1.1.28	Jams, marmalades	0.20	5	1,410	0.10	2	390
1.1.29	Chocolate	1.00	26	2,720	0.60	14	1,810
1.1.30	Confectionery products	0.30	8	1,900	0.30	7	1,500
1.1.31	Edible ices and ice cream	0.40	10	1,420	0.10	4	640
1.1.32	Other food products	1.80	46	4,200	0.60	17	1,760
1.1.32.1	Sauces, condiments	1.00	25	3,310	0.20	6	1,020
1.1.32.2	Baker's yeast, dessert preparations, soups	0.70	17	2,740	0.30	7	930
1.1.32.3	Salt, spices, culinary herbs and other food products	0.20	4	1,160	0.10	4	460
1.2	**Non-alcoholic drinks**	3.00	78	4,640	1.10	29	2,700
1.2.1	Coffee	0.50	12	1,470	0.10	4	490
1.2.2	Tea	0.30	9	1,520	0.10	3	600
1.2.3	Cocoa and powdered chocolate	0.10	2	410	0.00	1	110
1.2.4	Fruit and vegetable juices (inc. fruit squash)	0.90	22	2,900	0.20	6	920
1.2.5	Mineral or spring waters	0.20	4	960	0.10	2	370
1.2.6	Soft drinks	1.10	29	3,090	0.60	14	1,840

Note: The commodity and service categories are not comparable with those in publications before 2001–02.
The numbering is sequential, it does not use actual COICOP codes.
Please see page xiii for symbols and conventions used in this report.

ONS, Family Spending 2009, © Crown copyright 2010

Table A4   **Expenditure on selected items by place of purchase, 2009**
based on weighted data and including children's expenditure

		Large supermarket chains			Other outlets		
		Average weekly expenditure all house-holds (£)	Total weekly expenditure (£ million)	Recording house-holds in sample	Average weekly expenditure all house-holds (£)	Total weekly expenditure (£ million)	Recording house-holds in sample
2	**Alcoholic drink and tobacco**						
2.2	Tobacco	1.30	33	690	3.10	81	1,220
2.2.1	Cigarettes	1.10	29	630	2.70	70	1,110
2.2.2	Cigars and other tobacco products	0.20	4	130	0.40	11	310
2.2.2.1	Cigars	[0.00]	[0]	..	0.00	1	20
2.2.2.2	Other tobacco	0.20	4	120	0.40	11	290
5	**Household goods and services**						
5.5.5	Electrical consumable	0.20	5	580	0.40	9	690
5.6.1	Cleaning materials	1.60	41	3,290	0.70	18	1,690
7	**Transport**						
7.2.2	Petrol, diesel & other motor oils	8.20	212	2,110	11.10	287	2,650
7.2.2.1	Petrol	6.40	166	1,750	8.30	216	2,140
7.2.2.2	Diesel oil	1.80	46	490	2.70	70	730
7.2.2.3	Other motor oils	0.00	0	20	0.10	2	60
8	**Communication**						
8.1	Postal services	-	-	0	0.40	11	910
9	**Recreation and culture**						
9.3.5.1	Pet food	0.90	24	1,440	0.90	25	1,110
9.5.2	Stationery, diaries, address books, & art materials						
9.5.3	Cards, calendars, posters and other printed matter	0.50	12	1,480	1.30	35	2,470
9.5.4	Newspapers	0.30	7	1,620	1.50	40	3,230
9.5.5	Magazines and periodicals	0.30	8	1,310	0.60	15	1,850
12	**Miscellaneous goods and services**						
12.1.2	Toilet paper	0.60	15	1,970	0.20	5	830
12.1.3.1	Toiletries and other toilet requisites - & toothpaste, deodorant, tampons,						
12.1.3.3	razors, hairbrushes, toothbrushes	1.00	25	2,640	0.90	22	1,910
12.1.3.2	Bar of soap, liquid soap, shower gel etc	0.20	6	1,240	0.10	4	600
12.1.5.2	Cosmetics and related accessories	0.50	13	1,230	2.10	54	1,510

Note: The commodity and service categories are not comparable with those in publications before 2001–02.
The numbering is sequential, it does not use actual COICOP codes.
Please see page xiii for symbols and conventions used in this report.

ONS, Family Spending 2009, © Crown copyright 2010

Table A5 **Expenditure on clothing and footwear by place of purchase, 2009**
based on weighted data and including children's expenditure

		Large supermarket chains				Clothing chains				Other outlets			
		Average weekly expenditure all households (£)	Total weekly expenditure (£ million)	Recording households in sample		Average weekly expenditure all households (£)	Total weekly expenditure (£ million)	Recording households in sample		Average weekly expenditure all households (£)	Total weekly expenditure (£ million)	Recording households in sample	
3	**Clothing and footwear**	**1.70**	**45**	**1,430**		**8.10**	**210**	**2,050**		**10.80**	**281**	**2,750**	
3.1	Clothing	1.60	41	1,390		7.20	187	1,970		8.00	207	2,400	
3.1.1	Men's outer garments	0.20	6	210		1.50	38	500		2.20	58	640	
3.1.2	Men's under garments	0.10	2	140		0.20	5	210		0.10	3	140	
3.1.3	Women's outer garments	0.60	16	520		3.80	100	1,200		3.50	90	1,100	
3.1.4	Women's under garments	0.10	4	370		0.60	14	540		0.30	8	340	
3.1.5	Boys' outer garments	0.10	2	140		0.20	5	110		0.40	10	220	
3.1.6	Girls' outer garments	0.10	3	140		0.30	8	190		0.50	14	290	
3.1.7	Infants' outer garments	0.20	4	190		0.30	7	210		0.30	7	200	
3.1.8	Children's under garments	0.10	3	230		0.10	4	190		0.10	3	200	
3.1.9	Accessories	0.10	1	190		0.20	6	280		0.40	10	480	
3.1.9.1	Men's accessories	0.00	0	40		0.10	2	80		0.20	4	150	
3.1.9.2	Women's accessories	0.00	1	100		0.10	4	170		0.20	4	220	
3.1.9.3	Children's accessories	0.00	0	60		0.00	1	50		0.10	2	150	
3.1.10	Haberdashery and clothing hire	0.00	0	40		[0.00]	[1]	10		0.10	3	200	
3.2	Footwear	0.10	4	210		0.90	23	500		2.80	73	1,060	
3.2.1	Men's	0.00	0	30		0.20	5	90		0.80	22	310	
3.2.2	Women's	0.10	2	110		0.60	15	360		1.40	36	550	
3.2.3	Children's	0.00	1	90		0.10	2	90		0.60	15	350	

Note: The commodity and service categories are not comparable with those in publications before 2001–02.
'The numbering system is sequential, it does not use actual COICOP codes.
Please see page xiii for symbols and conventions used in this report.

ONS, Family Spending 2009, © *Crown copyright 2010*

Table A6   **Household expenditure by gross income decile group, 2009**

based on weighted data and including children's expenditure

Commodity or service	Lowest ten per cent	Second decile group	Third decile group	Fourth decile group	Fifth decile group	Sixth decile group
Lower boundary of group (£ per week)		158	235	315	410	520
Weighted number of households (thousands)	2,600	2,600	2,600	2,600	2,600	2,600
Total number of households in sample	560	580	600	620	610	600
Total number of persons in sample	700	980	1,210	1,310	1,460	1,440
Total number of adults in sample	610	780	930	1,040	1,100	1,140
Weighted average number of persons per household	1.3	1.6	2.0	2.1	2.4	2.4
Commodity or service	Average weekly household expenditure (£)					
1 Food & non-alcoholic drinks	25.90	34.30	41.90	43.90	50.50	52.30
2 Alcoholic drinks, tobacco & narcotics	5.60	7.40	8.20	8.90	11.30	11.70
3 Clothing & footwear	6.10	7.60	12.90	13.30	16.90	19.10
4 Housing(net)[1], fuel & power	37.60	44.40	51.80	59.20	57.80	59.90
5 Household goods & services	9.90	15.10	16.60	20.20	20.40	27.50
6 Health	2.10	3.40	2.70	3.60	6.30	6.30
7 Transport	13.90	16.80	28.30	41.00	46.00	55.90
8 Communication	6.00	6.80	8.90	9.30	10.80	12.40
9 Recreation & culture	15.80	25.50	30.90	38.70	48.30	52.90
10 Education	[4.80]	[1.60]	7.60	6.30	7.10	1.40
11 Restaurants & hotels	9.20	12.50	19.20	22.00	28.80	35.90
12 Miscellaneous goods & services	9.70	15.80	19.50	23.40	29.50	32.90
1–12 All expenditure groups	146.70	191.10	248.50	289.80	333.80	368.30
13 Other expenditure items	16.00	22.50	32.10	43.80	51.10	66.00
Total expenditure	**162.70**	**213.70**	**280.70**	**333.70**	**384.90**	**434.30**
Average weekly expenditure per person (£) **Total expenditure**	**129.60**	**134.60**	**139.00**	**158.10**	**162.10**	**181.20**

Note: The commodity and service categories are not comparable to those in publications before 2001–02.
Please see page xiii for symbols and conventions used in this report.

1 Excluding mortgage interest payments, council tax and Northern Ireland rates.

ONS, Family Spending 2009, © *Crown copyright 2010*

Table A6   **Household expenditure by gross income decile group, 2009 (cont.)**

based on weighted data and including children's expenditure

	Seventh decile group	Eighth decile group	Ninth decile group	Highest ten per cent	All house-holds
Lower boundary of group (£ per week)	647	796	985	1,348	
Weighted number of households (thousands)	2,600	2,600	2,600	2,600	25,980
Total number of households in sample	580	560	560	550	5830
Total number of persons in sample	1590	1630	1680	1750	13740
Total number of adults in sample	1210	1220	1280	1320	10650
Weighted average number of persons per household	2.7	2.9	3.0	3.1	2.3
Commodity or service	Average weekly household expenditure (£)				
1 Food & non-alcoholic drinks	57.50	64.80	69.30	81.40	52.20
2 Alcoholic drinks, tobacco & narcotics	12.70	14.50	13.60	17.80	11.20
3 Clothing & footwear	23.10	26.20	32.10	52.10	20.90
4 Housing(net)[1], fuel & power	58.40	63.70	63.00	77.20	57.30
5 Household goods & services	33.80	37.20	34.80	64.10	27.90
6 Health	4.70	6.70	7.40	9.60	5.30
7 Transport	68.80	84.00	99.50	130.20	58.40
8 Communication	13.50	14.90	15.60	18.30	11.70
9 Recreation & culture	66.00	73.40	87.30	139.60	57.90
10 Education	4.90	4.40	8.10	23.60	7.00
11 Restaurants & hotels	42.10	47.60	61.80	104.70	38.40
12 Miscellaneous goods & services	36.60	44.60	57.00	81.40	35.00
1–12 All expenditure groups	422.00	482.20	549.50	799.90	383.10
13 Other expenditure items	78.50	99.00	116.90	192.20	71.80
Total expenditure	**500.50**	**581.20**	**666.40**	**992.10**	**455.00**
Average weekly expenditure per person (£)					
Total expenditure	**188.20**	**200.90**	**224.00**	**316.90**	**194.40**

Note: The commodity and service categories are not comparable to those in publications before 2001–02.
Please see page xiii for symbols and conventions used in this report.

1 Excluding mortgage interest payments, council tax and Northern Ireland rates.

ONS, Family Spending 2009, © Crown copyright 2010

Table A7   **Household expenditure as a percentage of total expenditure by gross income decile group, 2009**

		Seventh decile group	Eighth decile group	Ninth decile group	Highest ten per cent	All house-holds
Lower boundary of group (£ per week)		647	796	985	1,348	
Weighted number of households (thousands)		2,600	2,600	2,600	2,600	25,980
Total number of households in sample		580	560	560	550	5,830
Total number of persons in sample		1,590	1,630	1,680	1,750	13,740
Total number of adults in sample		1,210	1,220	1,280	1,320	10,650
Weighted average number of persons per household		2.7	2.9	3.0	3.1	2.3
Commodity or service		Percentage of total expenditure				
1	Food & non-alcoholic drinks	11	11	10	8	11
2	Alcoholic drinks, tobacco & narcotics	3	3	2	2	2
3	Clothing & footwear	5	5	5	5	5
4	Housing(net)[1], fuel & power	12	11	9	8	13
5	Household goods & services	7	6	5	6	6
6	Health	1	1	1	1	1
7	Transport	14	14	15	13	13
8	Communication	3	3	2	2	3
9	Recreation & culture	13	13	13	14	13
10	Education	1	1	1	2	2
11	Restaurants & hotels	8	8	9	11	8
12	Miscellaneous goods & services	7	8	9	8	8
1–12	All expenditure groups	84	83	82	81	84
13	**Other expenditure items**	**16**	**17**	**18**	**19**	**16**
	Total expenditure	**100**	**100**	**100**	**100**	**100**

Note: The commodity and service categories are not comparable to those in publications before 2001–02.
Please see page xiii for symbols and conventions used in this report.

1 Excluding mortgage interest payments, council tax and Northern Ireland rates.

ONS, Family Spending 2009,   © Crown copyright 2010

Table A8 **Detailed household expenditure by gross income decile group, 2009**
based on weighted data and including children's expenditure

	Lowest ten per cent	Second decile group	Third decile group	Fourth decile group	Fifth decile group	Sixth decile group
Lower boundary of group (£ per week)		158	235	315	410	520
Weighted number of households (thousands)	2,600	2,600	2,600	2,600	2,600	2,600
Total number of households in sample	560	580	600	620	610	600
Total number of persons in sample	700	980	1210	1310	1460	1440
Total number of adults in sample	610	780	930	1040	1100	1140
Weighted average number of persons per household	1.3	1.6	2.0	2.1	2.4	2.4

Commodity or service	Average weekly household expenditure (£)					
1 **Food & non-alcoholic drinks**	**25.90**	**34.30**	**41.90**	**43.90**	**50.50**	**52.30**
1.1 Food	24.00	31.70	38.50	40.40	46.50	48.10
1.1.1 Bread, rice and cereals	2.60	3.40	4.10	4.10	4.70	4.90
1.1.2 Pasta products	0.20	0.20	0.30	0.30	0.40	0.40
1.1.3 Buns, cakes, biscuits etc.	1.60	2.30	2.80	3.00	3.30	3.30
1.1.4 Pastry (savoury)	0.30	0.30	0.40	0.50	0.60	0.80
1.1.5 Beef (fresh, chilled or frozen)	0.60	1.10	1.10	1.50	1.60	1.70
1.1.6 Pork (fresh, chilled or frozen)	0.30	0.40	0.60	0.60	0.70	0.70
1.1.7 Lamb (fresh, chilled or frozen)	0.40	0.50	0.80	0.60	0.70	0.50
1.1.8 Poultry (fresh, chilled or frozen)	0.80	1.20	1.50	1.50	1.70	1.90
1.1.9 Bacon and ham	0.50	0.70	0.80	0.90	1.00	1.10
1.1.10 Other meat and meat preparations	3.00	3.90	4.30	4.60	5.50	5.60
1.1.11 Fish and fish products	1.10	1.50	2.10	1.80	2.30	2.40
1.1.12 Milk	1.70	2.30	2.50	2.50	3.00	2.80
1.1.13 Cheese and curd	0.80	1.00	1.30	1.30	1.70	1.80
1.1.14 Eggs	0.30	0.50	0.50	0.60	0.70	0.70
1.1.15 Other milk products	0.90	1.30	1.60	1.60	1.80	2.00
1.1.16 Butter	0.20	0.30	0.30	0.30	0.30	0.30
1.1.17 Margarine, other vegetable fats and peanut butter	0.30	0.40	0.50	0.50	0.50	0.50
1.1.18 Cooking oils and fats	0.20	0.20	0.20	0.30	0.30	0.30
1.1.19 Fresh fruit	1.40	1.80	2.30	2.40	2.70	2.80
1.1.20 Other fresh, chilled or frozen fruits	0.10	0.20	0.20	0.30	0.20	0.30
1.1.21 Dried fruit and nuts	0.30	0.30	0.30	0.50	0.50	0.50
1.1.22 Preserved fruit and fruit based products	0.10	0.10	0.20	0.10	0.10	0.10
1.1.23 Fresh vegetables	1.80	2.20	2.70	3.00	3.40	3.50
1.1.24 Dried vegetables	0.00	0.00	0.00	0.00	0.10	0.00
1.1.25 Other preserved or processed vegetables	0.50	0.70	0.90	0.90	1.10	1.30
1.1.26 Potatoes	0.50	0.60	0.80	0.80	0.90	0.90
1.1.27 Other tubers and products of tuber vegetables	0.70	0.80	1.10	1.20	1.30	1.50
1.1.28 Sugar and sugar products	0.20	0.30	0.30	0.30	0.40	0.30
1.1.29 Jams, marmalades	0.10	0.20	0.20	0.20	0.30	0.30
1.1.30 Chocolate	0.80	1.00	1.20	1.20	1.60	1.70
1.1.31 Confectionery products	0.30	0.40	0.50	0.60	0.60	0.60
1.1.32 Edible ices and ice cream	0.20	0.30	0.40	0.40	0.60	0.50
1.1.33 Other food products	1.20	1.40	1.70	1.90	2.10	2.40
1.2 Non-alcoholic drinks	1.90	2.60	3.40	3.50	4.00	4.20
1.2.1 Coffee	0.30	0.40	0.60	0.60	0.60	0.60
1.2.2 Tea	0.30	0.40	0.40	0.40	0.40	0.50
1.2.3 Cocoa and powdered chocolate	0.00	0.10	0.10	0.10	0.10	0.10
1.2.4 Fruit and vegetable juices (inc. fruit squash)	0.40	0.60	0.80	0.80	0.90	1.10
1.2.5 Mineral or spring waters	0.10	0.10	0.20	0.10	0.20	0.20
1.2.6 Soft drinks (inc. fizzy and ready to drink fruit drinks)	0.80	1.00	1.30	1.50	1.70	1.80

Note: The commodity and service categories are not comparable to those in publications before 2001–02.
The numbering system is sequential, it does not use actual COICOP codes.
Please see page xiii for symbols and conventions used in this report.

ONS, Family Spending 2009, © Crown copyright 2010

Table A8   **Detailed household expenditure by gross income decile group, 2009 (cont.)**

based on weighted data and including children's expenditure

		Seventh decile group	Eighth decile group	Ninth decile group	Highest ten per cent	All house-holds
Lower boundary of group (£ per week)		647	796	985	1348	
Weighted number of households (thousands)		2600	2600	2600	2600	25980
Total number of households in sample		580	560	560	550	5830
Total number of persons in sample		1590	1630	1680	1750	13740
Total number of adults in sample		1210	1220	1280	1320	10650
Weighted average number of persons per household		2.7	2.9	3	3.1	2.3
Commodity or service		Average weekly household expenditure (£)				
1	**Food & non-alcoholic drinks**	**57.5**	**64.8**	**69.3**	**81.4**	**52.2**
1.1	Food	52.8	59.7	64.1	74.8	48.0
1.1.1	Bread, rice and cereals	5.6	6.3	6.5	7.3	5.0
1.1.2	Pasta products	0.4	0.6	0.6	0.7	0.4
1.1.3	Buns, cakes, biscuits etc.	3.5	4.1	4.0	4.6	3.2
1.1.4	Pastry (savoury)	1.0	0.9	1.1	1.3	0.7
1.1.5	Beef (fresh, chilled or frozen)	1.9	2.2	2.4	2.7	1.7
1.1.6	Pork (fresh, chilled or frozen)	0.8	0.9	0.8	0.7	0.7
1.1.7	Lamb (fresh, chilled or frozen)	0.5	0.7	0.9	0.9	0.6
1.1.8	Poultry (fresh, chilled or frozen)	2.2	2.5	2.9	3.7	2.0
1.1.9	Bacon and ham	1.2	1.1	1.2	1.4	1.0
1.1.10	Other meat and meat preparations	6.0	6.5	6.9	7.4	5.4
1.1.11	Fish and fish products	2.2	2.7	2.9	3.8	2.3
1.1.12	Milk	3.2	3.4	3.4	3.3	2.8
1.1.13	Cheese and curd	2.1	2.1	2.6	2.9	1.8
1.1.14	Eggs	0.7	0.8	0.8	0.9	0.6
1.1.15	Other milk products	2.1	2.5	2.8	3.2	2.0
1.1.16	Butter	0.4	0.4	0.4	0.5	0.3
1.1.17	Margarine, other vegetable fats and peanut butter	0.6	0.6	0.5	0.5	0.5
1.1.18	Cooking oils and fats	0.3	0.3	0.3	0.5	0.3
1.1.19	Fresh fruit	3.1	3.4	4.1	5.5	2.9
1.1.20	Other fresh, chilled or frozen fruits	0.3	0.3	0.4	0.6	0.3
1.1.21	Dried fruit and nuts	0.6	0.6	0.7	1.1	0.5
1.1.22	Preserved fruit and fruit based products	0.1	0.2	0.1	0.2	0.1
1.1.23	Fresh vegetables	4.1	4.7	5.4	6.9	3.8
1.1.24	Dried vegetables	0.0	0.0	0.0	0.1	0.0
1.1.25	Other preserved or processed vegetables	1.4	1.6	1.9	2.3	1.3
1.1.26	Potatoes	1.0	1.0	1.0	1.1	0.9
1.1.27	Other tubers and products of tuber vegetables	1.6	1.7	1.7	1.5	1.3
1.1.28	Sugar and sugar products	0.4	0.4	0.4	0.4	0.3
1.1.29	Jams, marmalades	0.2	0.3	0.3	0.4	0.3
1.1.30	Chocolate	1.7	2.1	2.1	2.4	1.6
1.1.31	Confectionery products	0.7	0.7	0.7	0.8	0.6
1.1.32	Edible ices and ice cream	0.6	0.6	0.6	0.8	0.5
1.1.33	Other food products	2.5	3.3	3.5	4.4	2.4
1.2	Non-alcoholic drinks	4.6	5.1	5.3	6.6	4.1
1.2.1	Coffee	0.7	0.7	0.6	1.0	0.6
1.2.2	Tea	0.4	0.5	0.4	0.7	0.5
1.2.3	Cocoa and powdered chocolate	0.1	0.1	0.1	0.1	0.1
1.2.4	Fruit and vegetable juices, mineral waters	1.1	1.3	1.5	2.3	1.1
1.2.5	Mineral or spring waters	0.2	0.2	0.4	0.4	0.2
1.2.6	Soft drinks (inc. fizzy and ready to drink fruit drinks)	2.1	2.2	2.2	2.2	1.7

Note: The commodity and service categories are not comparable to those in publications before 2001–02.
The numbering system is sequential, it does not use actual COICOP codes.
Please see page xiii for symbols and conventions used in this report.

ONS, Family Spending 2009, © Crown copyright 2010

Table A8   **Detailed household expenditure by gross income decile group, 2009 (cont.)**
based on weighted data and including children's expenditure

Commodity or service		Lowest ten per cent	Second decile group	Third decile group	Fourth decile group	Fifth decile group	Sixth decile group
		Average weekly household expenditure (£)					
2	**Alcoholic drink, tobacco & narcotics**	**5.60**	**7.40**	**8.20**	**8.90**	**11.30**	**11.70**
2.1	Alcoholic drinks	2.20	3.20	4.30	4.60	6.10	6.90
2.1.1	Spirits and liqueurs (brought home)	0.60	0.90	1.40	1.30	1.70	1.50
2.1.2	Wines, fortified wines (brought home)	0.70	1.10	1.70	2.00	2.60	3.20
2.1.3	Beer, lager, ciders and perry (brought home)	0.90	1.20	1.10	1.30	1.70	2.20
2.1.4	Alcopops (brought home)	[0.00]	[0.00]	[0.00]	[0.00]	[0.10]	[0.10]
2.2	Tobacco and narcotics	3.40	4.10	3.90	4.30	5.20	4.80
2.2.1	Cigarettes	2.60	3.60	3.30	3.40	4.70	4.20
2.2.2	Cigars, other tobacco products and narcotics	0.80	0.60	0.60	0.90	0.50	0.70
3	**Clothing & footwear**	**6.10**	**7.60**	**12.90**	**13.30**	**16.90**	**19.10**
3.1	Clothing	4.70	6.10	10.20	10.70	13.70	15.80
3.1.1	Men's outer garments	0.80	1.00	1.70	2.50	2.70	4.90
3.1.2	Men's under garments	0.10	0.20	0.20	0.20	0.30	0.40
3.1.3	Women's outer garments	2.20	2.80	4.90	4.90	6.30	6.60
3.1.4	Women's under garments	0.30	0.60	0.70	0.70	0.90	0.90
3.1.5	Boys' outer garments (5-15)	[0.20]	0.30	0.50	0.40	0.60	0.60
3.1.6	Girls' outer garments (5-15)	[0.60]	0.30	0.70	0.70	1.20	0.60
3.1.7	Infants' outer garments (under 5)	0.20	0.30	0.30	0.50	0.70	0.80
3.1.8	Children's under garments (under 16)	0.10	0.20	0.40	0.30	0.30	0.30
3.1.9	Accessories	0.10	0.20	0.50	0.40	0.50	0.50
3.1.10	Haberdashery and clothing hire	[0.10]	0.10	0.10	[0.10]	0.10	0.20
3.1.11	Dry cleaners, laundry and dyeing	[0.10]	[0.20]	[0.10]	[0.00]	[0.10]	[0.10]
3.2	Footwear	1.40	1.50	2.80	2.60	3.20	3.20
4	**Housing (net)[1], fuel & power**	**37.60**	**44.40**	**51.80**	**59.20**	**57.80**	**59.90**
4.1	Actual rentals for housing	66.50	54.00	46.40	40.20	33.50	27.90
4.1.1	Gross rent	66.50	54.00	46.40	40.20	33.40	27.90
4.1.2	less housing benefit, rebates & allowances rec'd	50.70	36.60	24.50	12.90	8.10	3.30
4.1.3	Net rent[2]	15.90	17.50	21.90	27.20	25.30	24.60
4.1.4	Second dwelling rent	-	-	-	-	[0.10]	-
4.2	Maintenance and repair of dwelling	1.70	3.60	4.90	5.20	5.70	6.30
4.3	Water supply and miscellaneous services relating to the dwelling	6.10	7.00	7.10	7.30	7.10	7.80
4.4	Electricity, gas and other fuels	13.90	16.30	17.90	19.50	19.70	21.10
4.4.1	Electricity	6.90	7.90	8.80	9.40	9.50	10.20
4.4.2	Gas	6.30	7.40	8.10	9.00	9.00	9.70
4.4.3	Other fuels	0.70	1.00	1.00	1.10	1.20	1.20

Note: The commodity and service categories are not comparable to those in publications before 2001–02.
The numbering system is sequential, it does not use actual COICOP codes.
Please see page xiii for symbols and conventions used in this report.

1 Excluding mortgage interest payments, council tax and Northern Ireland rates

2 The figure included in total expenditure is net rent as opposed to gross rent

ONS, Family Spending 2009, © Crown copyright 2010

Table A8   **Detailed household expenditure by gross income decile group, 2009 (cont.)**
based on weighted data and including children's expenditure

Commodity or service		Seventh decile group	Eighth decile group	Ninth decile group	Highest ten per cent	All house- holds
		Average weekly household expenditure (£)				
2	**Alcoholic drink, tobacco & narcotics**	**12.7**	**14.5**	**13.6**	**17.8**	**11.2**
2.1	Alcoholic drinks	7.4	9.2	9.4	14.4	6.8
2.1.1	Spirits and liqueurs (brought home)	1.2	1.4	1.1	1.9	1.3
2.1.2	Wines, fortified wines (brought home)	3.6	4.9	5.6	9.6	3.5
2.1.3	Beer, lager, ciders and perry (brought home)	2.5	2.8	2.6	2.8	1.9
2.1.4	Alcopops (brought home)	0.1	0.1	0.1	0.1	0.1
2.2	Tobacco and narcotics	5.3	5.3	4.3	3.4	4.4
2.2.1	Cigarettes	4.5	4.8	3.8	3.2	3.8
2.2.2	Cigars, other tobacco products and narcotics	0.8	0.5	0.4	0.2	0.6
3	**Clothing & footwear**	**23.1**	**26.2**	**32.1**	**52.1**	**20.9**
3.1	Clothing	18.6	21.0	26.4	43.1	17.0
3.1.1	Men's outer garments	4.8	4.7	6.6	10.0	4.0
3.1.2	Men's under garments	0.5	0.4	0.6	0.8	0.4
3.1.3	Women's outer garments	8.1	10.0	12.4	21.0	7.9
3.1.4	Women's under garments	1.1	1.2	1.7	1.9	1.0
3.1.5	Boys' outer garments (5-15)	0.8	1.1	1.0	1.2	0.7
3.1.6	Girls' outer garments (5-15)	1.2	1.1	1.0	2.2	1.0
3.1.7	Infants' outer garments (under 5)	0.7	1.0	1.0	1.5	0.7
3.1.8	Children's under garments (under 16)	0.4	0.4	0.6	0.7	0.4
3.1.9	Accessories	0.8	0.7	1.1	2.2	0.7
3.1.10	Haberdashery and clothing hire	0.1	0.1	0.2	0.5	0.2
3.1.11	Dry cleaners, laundry and dyeing	0.1	0.3	0.4	1.2	0.3
3.2	Footwear	4.5	5.2	5.7	8.9	3.9
4	**Housing (net)¹, fuel & power**	**58.4**	**63.7**	**63.0**	**77.2**	**57.3**
4.1	Actual rentals for housing	21.1	22.0	21.3	21.7	35.5
4.1.1	Gross rent	21.1	22.0	21.3	21.5	35.4
4.1.2	less housing benefit, rebates & allowances rec'd	0.4	0.6	0.1	0.1	13.7
4.1.3	Net rent²	20.7	21.4	21.1	21.4	21.7
4.1.4	Second dwelling rent	0.0	-	0.0	0.2	0.0
4.2	Maintenance and repair of dwelling	6.5	8.7	8.0	16.5	6.7
4.3	Water supply and miscellaneous services relating to the dwelling	7.8	8.3	8.2	9.4	7.6
4.4	Electricity, gas and other fuels	23.4	25.2	25.7	29.7	21.3
4.4.1	Electricity	11.6	11.8	12.3	13.8	10.2
4.4.2	Gas	10.2	11.9	11.7	13.7	9.7
4.4.3	Other fuels	1.6	1.6	1.7	2.2	1.3

Note: The commodity and service categories are not comparable to those in publications before 2001–02.
The numbering system is sequential, it does not use actual COICOP codes.
Please see page xiii for symbols and conventions used in this report.

1 Excluding mortgage interest payments, council tax and Northern Ireland rates.

2 The figure included in total expenditure is net rent as opposed to gross rent.

ONS, Family Spending 2009, © Crown copyright 2010

Table A8   **Detailed household expenditure by gross income decile group, 2009 (cont.)**

based on weighted data and including children's expenditure

Commodity or service	Lowest ten per cent	Second decile group	Third decile group	Fourth decile group	Fifth decile group	Sixth decile group
	Average weekly household expenditure (£)					
5 Household goods & services	**9.9**	**15.1**	**16.6**	**20.2**	**20.4**	**27.5**
5.1 Furniture and furnishings, carpets and other floor coverings	4.6	8.4	7.6	8.7	9.0	14.5
5.1.1 Furniture and furnishings	3.9	5.3	6.2	7.0	6.3	12.2
5.1.2 Floor coverings	0.7	3.1	1.4	1.7	2.7	2.2
5.2 Household textiles	0.3	0.5	1.3	1.0	1.4	1.4
5.3 Household appliances	1.9	1.7	1.6	4.0	2.2	3.6
5.4 Glassware, tableware and household utensils	0.4	0.5	0.9	1.0	1.3	1.1
5.5 Tools and equipment for house and garden	0.3	0.7	1.6	1.3	1.5	2.3
5.6 Goods and services for routine household maintenance	2.4	3.3	3.5	4.2	5.0	4.6
5.6.1 Cleaning materials	1.0	1.3	1.8	2.0	2.2	2.1
5.6.2 Household goods and hardware	0.5	0.7	0.8	1.1	1.0	1.1
5.6.3 Domestic services, carpet cleaning, hire of furniture/furnishings	0.9	1.3	0.9	1.2	1.8	1.3
6 Health	**2.1**	**3.4**	**2.7**	**3.6**	**6.3**	**6.3**
6.1 Medical products, appliances and equipment	1.4	2.4	1.9	2.7	3.3	4.9
6.1.1 Medicines, prescriptions, healthcare products etc.	1.0	1.1	1.3	1.4	1.6	3.6
6.1.2 Spectacles, lenses, accessories and repairs	0.4	1.3	0.6	1.4	1.7	1.3
6.2 Hospital services	0.7	1.0	0.8	0.9	3.0	1.4
7 Transport	**13.9**	**16.8**	**28.3**	**41.0**	**46.0**	**55.9**
7.1 Purchase of vehicles	3.7	4.2	7.3	14.8	15.5	16.3
7.1.1 Purchase of new cars and vans	1.1	1.4	2.4	4.5	4.8	6.5
7.1.2 Purchase of second hand cars or vans	2.0	2.8	4.9	9.9	10.1	9.3
7.1.3 Purchase of motorcycles and other vehicles	0.5	0.0	0.0	0.3	0.6	0.6
7.2 Operation of personal transport	6.6	8.6	15.3	20.2	24.2	30.0
7.2.1 Spares and accessories	0.5	0.4	1.3	0.9	1.8	1.9
7.2.2 Petrol, diesel and other motor oils	4.7	5.6	9.9	13.4	16.1	20.2
7.2.3 Repairs and servicing	1.0	1.7	3.1	4.4	4.7	5.7
7.2.4 Other motoring costs	0.4	0.9	1.0	1.5	1.7	2.2
7.3 Transport services	3.6	4.0	5.6	6.0	6.3	9.5
7.3.1 Rail and tube fares	1.5	1.0	0.5	0.7	1.2	1.6
7.3.2 Bus and coach fares	0.8	0.6	1.2	1.2	1.8	1.3
7.3.3 Combined fares	0.1	0.0	0.2	0.1	0.6	1.0
7.3.4 Other travel and transport	1.3	2.4	3.7	4.0	2.8	5.6
8 Communication	**6.0**	**6.8**	**8.9**	**9.3**	**10.8**	**12.4**
8.1 Postal services	0.3	0.3	0.4	0.3	0.3	0.6
8.2 Telephone and telefax equipment	0.1	0.2	0.6	0.2	0.5	0.5
8.3 Telephone and telefax services	5.6	6.4	7.9	8.8	10.0	11.3

Note: The commodity and service categories are not comparable to those in publications before 2001–02.
The numbering system is sequential, it does not use actual COICOP codes.
Please see page xiii for symbols and conventions used in this report.

ONS, Family Spending 2009,   © Crown copyright 2010

Table A8   **Detailed household expenditure by gross income decile group, 2009 (cont.)**
based on weighted data and including children's expenditure

		Seventh decile group	Eighth decile group	Ninth decile group	Highest ten per cent	All house-holds
Commodity or service		Average weekly household expenditure (£)				
5	**Household goods & services**	**33.8**	**37.2**	**34.8**	**64.1**	**27.9**
5.1	Furniture and furnishings, carpets and other floor coverings	16.7	19.1	19.7	35.6	14.4
5.1.1	Furniture and furnishings	13.6	14.7	15.4	26.8	11.1
5.1.2	Floor coverings	3.1	4.3	4.4	8.9	3.2
5.2	Household textiles	1.4	2.5	1.8	3.6	1.5
5.3	Household appliances	6.5	4.8	1.6	2.8	3.1
5.4	Glassware, tableware and household utensils	1.5	1.7	1.7	3.4	1.4
5.5	Tools and equipment for house and garden	2.6	3.2	3.4	5.4	2.2
5.6	Goods and services for routine household maintenance	5.1	6	6.4	13.2	5.4
5.6.1	Cleaning materials	2.5	2.9	3.2	3.8	2.3
5.6.2	Household goods and hardware	1.6	1.8	1.7	2.4	1.3
5.6.3	Domestic services, carpet cleaning, hire/repair of furniture/furnishings	1.1	1.3	1.5	7	1.8
6	**Health**	**4.7**	**6.7**	**7.4**	**9.6**	**5.3**
6.1	Medical products, appliances and equipment	2.9	4	3.6	5.5	3.3
6.1.1	Medicines, prescriptions, healthcare products etc.	1.7	2.8	2.1	3.5	2
6.1.2	Spectacles, lenses, accessories and repairs	1.2	1.2	1.4	2	1.3
6.2	Hospital services	1.8	2.7	3.8	4.1	2
7	**Transport**	**68.8**	**84**	**99.5**	**130.2**	**58.4**
7.1	Purchase of vehicles	23.4	27.7	33.5	48.2	19.5
7.1.1	Purchase of new cars and vans	8.9	7.6	6.1	21.9	6.5
7.1.2	Purchase of second hand cars or vans	14.1	19.3	26.9	24.3	12.4
7.1.3	Purchase of motorcycles and other vehicles	0.4	0.8	0.4	1.9	0.6
7.2	Operation of personal transport	35.1	44.7	50.8	57.9	29.3
7.2.1	Spares and accessories	1.9	3.8	3.9	3.4	2
7.2.2	Petrol, diesel and other motor oils	22.9	29.9	34.2	35.6	19.2
7.2.3	Repairs and servicing	7.6	8.1	9.4	13.8	5.9
7.2.4	Other motoring costs	2.6	3	3.3	5.1	2.2
7.3	Transport services	10.3	11.6	15.2	24.1	9.6
7.3.1	Rail and tube fares	1.7	3	4.8	8.8	2.5
7.3.2	Bus and coach fares	1.7	1.1	1.3	1.4	1.3
7.3.3	Combined fares	1.7	0.8	2.8	4	1.1
7.3.4	Other travel and transport	5.3	6.7	6.3	9.9	4.8
8	**Communication**	**13.5**	**14.9**	**15.6**	**18.3**	**11.7**
8.1	Postal services	0.5	0.4	0.5	0.7	0.4
8.2	Telephone and telefax equipment	0.5	0.9	0.5	0.7	0.5
8.3	Telephone and telefax services	12.6	13.6	14.6	16.9	10.8

Note: The commodity and service categories are not comparable to those in publications before 2001–02.
The numbering system is sequential, it does not use actual COICOP codes.
Please see page xiii for symbols and conventions used in this report.

ONS, Family Spending 2009,   © Crown copyright 2010

Table A8   **Detailed household expenditure by gross income decile group, 2009 (cont.)**
based on weighted data and including children's expenditure

Commodity or service			Lowest ten per cent	Second decile group	Third decile group	Fourth decile group	Fifth decile group	Sixth decile group
			Average weekly household expenditure (£)					
9	**Recreation & culture**		**15.8**	**25.5**	**30.9**	**38.7**	**48.3**	**52.9**
9.1	Audio-visual, photographic and information processing equipment		1.9	4.7	3.6	3.2	5.2	5.1
	9.1.1	Audio equipment and accessories, CD players	0.3	1.3	0.7	0.6	1.1	2.0
	9.1.2	TV, video and computers	1.6	3.2	2.5	2.4	3.9	2.9
	9.1.3	Photographic, cine and optical equipment	0.0	0.2	0.3	0.2	0.2	0.3
9.2	Other major durables for recreation and culture		0.0	0.1	0.2	1.1	4.9	1.1
9.3	Other recreational items and equipment, gardens and pets		3.2	4.6	5.9	8.2	9.8	11.2
	9.3.1	Games, toys and hobbies	0.4	0.7	1.3	1.7	1.8	2.9
	9.3.2	Computer software and games	0.2	0.6	0.6	0.9	2.0	1.9
	9.3.3	Equipment for sport, camping and open-air recreation	0.1	0.2	0.4	0.4	0.3	1.0
	9.3.4	Horticultural goods, garden equipment and plants	0.7	1.3	1.6	2.3	1.8	2.1
	9.3.5	Pets and pet food	1.8	1.7	2.0	3.0	3.9	3.4
9.4	Recreational and cultural services		6.8	7.4	10.3	11.7	15.5	16.6
	9.4.1	Sports admissions, subscriptions, leisure class fees and equipment hire	1.1	0.7	1.5	1.7	2.5	4.9
	9.4.2	Cinema, theatre and museums etc.	0.2	0.5	1.0	1.5	2.3	1.5
	9.4.3	TV, video, satellite rental, cable subscriptions, TV licences and the Internet	3.5	3.6	4.4	5.0	6.0	5.9
	9.4.4	Miscellaneous entertainments	0.5	0.4	0.5	0.9	1.1	1.0
	9.4.5	Development of film, deposit for film development, passport photos, holiday and school photos	0.0	0.1	0.2	0.1	0.2	0.2
	9.4.6	Gambling payments	1.6	2.1	2.8	2.6	3.4	3.1
9.5	Newspapers, books and stationery		2.7	3.5	4.7	4.7	5.0	5.7
	9.5.1	Books	0.3	0.5	0.9	0.9	0.8	1.2
	9.5.2	Diaries, address books, cards etc.	0.7	0.8	1.4	1.4	1.6	1.5
	9.5.3	Newspapers	1.3	1.8	1.8	1.9	1.8	2.0
	9.5.4	Magazines and periodicals	0.5	0.5	0.7	0.6	0.8	1.0
9.6	Package holidays		1.1	5.1	6.2	9.7	7.8	13.2
	9.6.1	Package holidays – UK	0.4	0.8	1.4	1.0	0.7	1.7
	9.6.2	Package holidays – abroad	0.7	4.3	4.9	8.7	7.1	11.4
10	**Education**		**4.8**	**1.6**	**7.6**	**6.3**	**7.1**	**1.4**
10.1	Education fees		4.8	1.5	7.4	6.2	6.8	1.3
10.2	Payments for school trips, other ad-hoc expenditure		0.0	0.1	0.1	0.1	0.3	0.2
11	**Restaurants & hotels**		**9.2**	**12.5**	**19.2**	**22.0**	**28.8**	**35.9**
11.1	Catering services		8.4	11.3	16.5	18.7	24.9	30.3
	11.1.1	Restaurant and café meals	3.6	4.8	7.3	8.5	10.3	12.6
	11.1.2	Alcoholic drinks (away from home)	2.3	2.9	3.5	3.8	6.1	7.9
	11.1.3	Take away meals eaten at home	1.4	2.2	2.4	2.8	3.5	4.0
	11.1.4	Other take-away and snack food	0.9	1.2	2.5	2.6	3.3	3.9
	11.1.5	Contract catering (food) and canteens	0.3	0.3	0.8	0.9	1.7	2.0
11.2	Accommodation services		0.8	1.2	2.7	3.4	3.9	5.6
	11.2.1	Holiday in the UK	0.2	0.7	1.4	1.8	2.7	2.9
	11.2.2	Holiday abroad	0.7	0.4	1.3	1.5	1.2	2.6
	11.2.3	Room hire	-	-	0.0	0.0	0.0	0.0

Note: The commodity and service categories are not comparable to those in publications before 2001–02.
The numbering system is sequential, it does not use actual COICOP codes.
Please see page xiii for symbols and conventions used in this report.

ONS, Family Spending 2009, © Crown copyright 2010

Table A8   **Detailed household expenditure by gross income decile group, 2009 (cont.)**
based on weighted data and including children's expenditure

		Seventh decile group	Eighth decile group	Ninth decile group	Highest ten per cent	All house-holds
Commodity or service		Average weekly household expenditure (£)				
9	**Recreation & culture**	**66.00**	**73.40**	**87.30**	**139.60**	**57.90**
9.1	Audio-visual, photographic and information processing equipment	10.10	10.50	11.80	13.80	7.00
9.1.1	Audio equipment and accessories, CD players	1.20	2.00	2.10	3.40	1.50
9.1.2	TV, video and computers	7.10	7.90	7.50	8.90	4.80
9.1.3	Photographic, cine and optical equipment	[1.80]	[0.60]	[2.30]	1.40	0.70
9.2	Other major durables for recreation and culture	[3.00]	[1.80]	4.10	8.90	2.50
9.3	Other recreational items and equipment, gardens and pets	12.50	14.10	15.30	20.20	10.50
9.3.1	Games, toys and hobbies	3.00	2.90	3.20	3.50	2.20
9.3.2	Computer software and games	1.90	2.90	2.30	1.90	1.50
9.3.3	Equipment for sport, camping and open-air recreation	0.60	1.40	1.10	2.20	0.80
9.3.4	Horticultural goods, garden equipment and plants	2.80	3.00	4.00	6.10	2.60
9.3.5	Pets and pet food	4.20	3.90	4.70	6.50	3.50
9.4	Recreational and cultural services	20.40	22.10	26.90	49.60	18.70
9.4.1	Sports admissions, subscriptions, leisure class fees and equipment hire	5.90	6.30	9.30	16.50	5.00
9.4.2	Cinema, theatre and museums etc.	2.40	2.60	3.50	7.00	2.30
9.4.3	TV, video, satellite rental, cable subscriptions, TV licences and the Internet	7.10	7.30	8.50	8.20	5.90
9.4.4	Miscellaneous entertainments	1.30	1.90	1.50	2.40	1.10
9.4.5	Development of film, deposit for film development, passport photos, holiday and school photos	0.20	0.60	0.80	0.50	0.30
9.4.6	Gambling payments	3.50	3.30	3.30	14.90	4.10
9.5	Newspapers, books and stationery	6.60	7.40	7.70	10.50	5.90
9.5.1	Books	1.60	2.00	1.80	3.60	1.30
9.5.2	Diaries, address books, cards etc.	2.00	2.50	2.80	3.50	1.80
9.5.3	Newspapers	1.90	1.80	1.80	2.00	1.80
9.5.4	Magazines and periodicals	1.10	1.10	1.20	1.40	0.90
9.6	Package holidays	13.50	17.60	21.50	36.60	13.20
9.6.1	Package holidays – UK	[0.60]	[0.80]	[0.60]	[1.40]	0.90
9.6.2	Package holidays – abroad	12.90	16.80	20.90	35.20	12.30
10	**Education**	**4.90**	**4.40**	**8.10**	**23.60**	**7.00**
10.1	Education fees	4.60	4.00	7.60	22.30	6.70
10.2	Payments for school trips, other ad-hoc expenditure	[0.30]	0.40	[0.40]	1.30	0.30
11	**Restaurants & hotels**	**42.10**	**47.60**	**61.80**	**104.70**	**38.40**
11.1	Catering services	36.40	39.00	51.40	76.00	31.30
11.1.1	Restaurant and café meals	14.00	16.20	22.10	33.90	13.30
11.1.2	Alcoholic drinks (away from home)	9.60	8.50	13.00	14.70	7.20
11.1.3	Take away meals eaten at home	4.70	5.50	5.40	6.00	3.80
11.1.4	Other take-away and snack food	5.00	6.00	7.00	9.10	4.20
11.1.5	Contract catering (food) and canteens	3.10	2.70	3.80	12.30	2.80
11.2	Accommodation services	5.70	8.60	10.50	28.70	7.10
11.2.1	Holiday in the UK	2.80	3.90	5.30	7.80	3.00
11.2.2	Holiday abroad	2.70	4.70	5.10	20.70	4.10
11.2.3	Room hire	[0.10]	[0.00]	[0.10]	[0.30]	[0.10]

Note: The commodity and service categories are not comparable to those in publications before 2001–02.
The numbering system is sequential, it does not use actual COICOP codes.
Please see page xiii for symbols and conventions used in this report.

ONS, Family Spending 2009,   © Crown copyright 2010

Table A8   **Detailed household expenditure by gross income decile group, 2009 (cont.)**
based on weighted data and including children's expenditure

		Lowest ten per cent	Second decile group	Third decile group	Fourth decile group	Fifth decile group	Sixth decile group
Commodity or service		Average weekly household expenditure (£)					
12	**Miscellaneous goods & services**	**9.70**	**15.80**	**19.50**	**23.40**	**29.50**	**32.90**
12.1	Personal care	3.70	5.00	6.40	7.30	9.10	8.80
12.1.1	Hairdressing, beauty treatment	1.20	1.80	2.00	2.60	2.60	2.40
12.1.2	Toilet paper	0.40	0.50	0.60	0.70	0.70	0.80
12.1.3	Toiletries and soap	1.00	1.10	1.40	1.50	2.00	2.00
12.1.4	Baby toiletries and accessories (disposable)	0.20	0.40	0.50	0.50	0.60	0.70
12.1.5	Hair products, cosmetics and related electrical appliances	0.90	1.20	1.90	2.00	3.20	3.00
12.2	Personal effects	0.40	1.10	1.50	1.50	1.70	3.20
12.3	Social protection	[0.20]	[2.60]	[0.60]	[1.00]	3.80	2.20
12.4	Insurance	4.50	5.90	9.90	10.80	12.80	14.50
12.4.1	Household insurances – structural, contents and appliances	1.90	2.80	3.60	3.90	4.60	5.00
12.4.2	Medical insurance premiums	[0.30]	[0.20]	0.50	0.70	1.30	1.50
12.4.3	Vehicle insurance including boat insurance	2.30	2.90	5.80	6.20	6.80	8.00
12.4.4	Non-package holiday, other travel insurance	-	-	-	-	[0.10]	[0.00]
12.5	Other services n.e.c	0.90	1.20	1.20	2.80	2.10	4.30
12.5.1	Moving house	[0.50]	0.60	[0.40]	1.80	1.00	1.80
12.5.2	Bank, building society, post office, credit card charges	0.20	0.20	0.30	0.30	0.40	0.60
12.5.3	Other services and professional fees	[0.20]	0.40	0.50	0.70	0.70	1.80
1-12	**All expenditure groups**	**146.70**	**191.10**	**248.50**	**289.80**	**333.80**	**368.30**
13	**Other expenditure items**	**16.00**	**22.50**	**32.10**	**43.80**	**51.10**	**66.00**
13.1	Housing: mortgage interest payments, council tax etc.	10.30	12.10	20.30	26.50	34.90	45.30
13.2	Licences, fines and transfers	1.00	2.00	2.00	2.40	2.80	3.30
13.3	Holiday spending	[1.00]	[4.80]	[2.50]	[7.00]	[3.70]	7.50
13.4	Money transfers and credit	3.70	3.60	7.30	7.80	9.60	9.90
13.4.1	Money, cash gifts given to children	[0.00]	[0.00]	[0.00]	[0.10]	[0.10]	[0.10]
13.4.2	Cash gifts and donations	3.20	3.20	6.60	6.60	8.40	8.10
13.4.3	Club instalment payments (child) and interest on credit cards	0.60	0.30	0.70	1.20	1.10	1.70
Total expenditure		**162.70**	**213.70**	**280.70**	**333.70**	**384.90**	**434.30**
14	**Other items recorded**						
14.1	Life assurance and contributions to pension funds	1.20	1.10	3.40	4.40	7.90	12.20
14.2	Other insurance inc. friendly societies	0.30	0.30	0.60	0.70	0.80	1.20
14.3	Income tax, payments *less* refunds	1.50	4.90	11.10	22.50	38.50	58.60
14.4	National insurance contributions	[0.60]	0.80	2.70	6.40	13.10	21.40
14.5	Purchase or alteration of dwellings, mortgages	4.20	8.20	12.40	18.50	60.50	37.70
14.6	Savings and investments	0.20	0.40	1.50	1.80	2.20	2.50
14.7	Pay off loan to clear other debt	[0.40]	[0.60]	[0.40]	[0.80]	1.70	3.70
14.8	Windfall receipts from gambling etc[3]	1.20	1.30	1.60	1.30	1.50	1.00

Note: The commodity and service categories are not comparable to those in publications before 2001–02.
The numbering system is sequential, it does not use actual COICOP codes.
Please see page xiii for symbols and conventions used in this report.

3 Expressed as an income figure as opposed to an expenditure figure.

ONS, Family Spending 2009, © Crown copyright 2010

Table A8   **Detailed household expenditure by gross income decile group, 2009 (cont.)**
based on weighted data and including children's expenditure

		Seventh decile group	Eighth decile group	Ninth decile group	Highest ten per cent	All house-holds
Commodity or service				Average weekly household expenditure (£)		
12	**Miscellaneous goods & services**	**36.60**	**44.60**	**57.00**	**81.40**	**35.00**
12.1	Personal care	11.30	13.40	15.80	24.20	10.50
	12.1.1 Hairdressing, beauty treatment	3.40	4.20	4.80	8.40	3.40
	12.1.2 Toilet paper	0.90	1.00	1.10	1.10	0.80
	12.1.3 Toiletries and soap	2.30	2.60	3.20	4.70	2.20
	12.1.4 Baby toiletries and accessories (disposable)	0.70	0.80	1.50	1.00	0.70
	12.1.5 Hair products, cosmetics and related electrical appliances	4.10	4.80	5.30	9.10	3.50
12.2	Personal effects	2.30	3.60	7.90	7.80	3.10
12.3	Social protection	3.30	2.90	6.20	9.70	3.30
12.4	Insurance	16.70	19.50	22.40	30.50	14.70
	12.4.1 Household insurances - structural, contents and appliances	5.50	6.10	6.90	9.50	5.00
	12.4.2 Medical insurance premiums	1.40	1.60	2.20	4.70	1.40
	12.4.3 Vehicle insurance including boat insurance	9.70	11.70	12.80	16.20	8.30
	12.4.4 Non-package holiday, other travel insurance	[0.10]	[0.00]	[0.40]	[0.10]	0.10
12.5	Other services n.e.c	2.90	5.20	4.80	9.10	3.40
	12.5.1 Moving house	1.30	3.20	2.60	4.50	1.80
	12.5.2 Bank, building society, post office, credit card charges	0.60	0.70	0.60	1.30	0.50
	12.5.3 Other services and professional fees	1.10	1.30	1.60	3.30	1.20
1-12	**All expenditure groups**	**422.00**	**482.20**	**549.50**	**799.90**	**383.10**
13	**Other expenditure items**	**78.50**	**99.00**	**116.90**	**192.20**	**71.80**
13.1	Housing: mortgage interest payments, council tax etc.	56.40	68.80	83.50	131.80	49.00
13.2	Licences, fines and transfers	3.90	5.30	5.10	5.90	3.40
13.3	Holiday spending	6.20	10.20	13.80	28.20	8.50
13.4	Money transfers and credit	12.00	14.80	14.50	26.30	11.00
	13.4.1 Money, cash gifts given to children	[0.20]	[0.30]	[0.20]	[0.10]	0.10
	13.4.2 Cash gifts and donations	10.20	11.90	11.40	22.60	9.20
	13.4.3 Club instalment payments (child) & interest on credit cards	1.60	2.60	2.90	3.60	1.60
Total expenditure		**500.50**	**581.20**	**666.40**	**992.10**	**455.00**
14	**Other items recorded**					
14.1	Contributions to pension funds	18.90	25.00	39.70	84.50	19.80
14.2	Other insurance inc. friendly societies	1.50	1.60	2.10	4.00	1.30
14.3	Income tax, payments *less* refunds	84.50	105.70	162.80	427.70	91.80
14.4	National insurance contributions	33.50	44.20	64.60	91.90	27.90
14.5	Purchase or alteration of dwellings, mortgages	43.20	59.30	75.20	158.80	47.80
14.6	Savings and investments	4.80	6.40	11.30	25.90	5.70
14.7	Pay off loan to clear other debt	3.20	4.20	5.10	3.20	2.30
14.8	Windfall receipts from gambling etc[3]	1.80	1.80	1.70	10.10	2.30

Note: The commodity and service categories are not comparable to those in publications before 2001–02.
The numbering system is sequential, it does not use actual COICOP codes.
Please see page xiii for symbols and conventions used in this report.

3 Expressed as an income figure as opposed to an expenditure figure.

ONS, Family Spending 2009, © *Crown copyright 2010*

Table A9   **Household expenditure by disposable income decile group 2009**

based on weighted data and including children's expenditure

	Lowest ten per cent	Second decile group	Third decile group	Fourth decile group	Fifth decile group	Sixth decile group
Lower boundary of group (£ per week)		154	226	289	368	450
Weighted number of households (thousands)	2,600	2,600	2,600	2,600	2,590	2,600
Total number of households in sample	550	580	600	620	610	590
Total number of persons in sample	700	940	1140	1300	1440	1480
Total number of adults in sample	620	770	890	1030	1100	1150
Weighted average number of persons per household	1.3	1.6	1.9	2.1	2.3	2.5
Commodity or service	Average weekly household expenditure (£)					
1 Food & non-alcoholic drinks	26.00	33.80	39.90	43.60	49.10	53.10
2 Alcoholic drinks, tobacco & narcotics	5.90	7.30	7.60	9.60	11.30	12.00
3 Clothing & footwear	6.20	8.20	11.50	13.20	17.00	20.00
4 Housing(net)[1], fuel & power	38.90	44.30	52.10	55.00	61.10	61.10
5 Household goods & services	17.60	15.30	18.50	18.10	20.60	26.50
6 Health	2.10	3.40	2.60	4.40	4.80	5.30
7 Transport	14.40	18.60	27.70	38.60	45.00	57.50
8 Communication	6.00	7.10	8.50	9.00	11.30	12.30
9 Recreation & culture	21.00	25.30	28.90	40.40	43.90	54.60
10 Education	4.80	1.60	6.20	4.10	5.10	7.10
11 Restaurants & hotels	11.70	12.70	18.70	21.20	30.60	34.70
12 Miscellaneous goods & services	11.20	15.50	20.10	22.30	28.20	33.20
1-12 All expenditure groups	165.80	193.00	242.20	279.50	328.10	377.40
13 Other expenditure items	16.80	24.90	31.10	43.50	51.10	66.80
Total expenditure	**182.60**	**218.00**	**273.30**	**323.00**	**379.20**	**444.20**
Average weekly expenditure per person (£)						
Total expenditure	**144.40**	**140.10**	**147.50**	**154.20**	**162.20**	**176.50**

Note: The commodity and service categories are not comparable to those in publications before 2001-02.
      Please see page xiii for symbols and conventions used in this report.

1 Excluding mortgage interest payments, council tax and Northern Ireland rates

ONS, Family Spending 2009, © Crown copyright 2010

Table A9 **Household expenditure by disposable income decile group, 2009 (cont.)**

based on weighted data and including children's expenditure

	Seventh decile group	Eighth decile group	Ninth decile group	Highest ten per cent	All house-holds
Lower boundary of group (£ per week)	544	650	796	1,066	
Weighted number of households (thousands)	2,600	2,600	2,600	2,600	25,980
Total number of households in sample	580	570	570	550	5,830
Total number of persons in sample	1,560	1,680	1,740	1,760	13,740
Total number of adults in sample	1,180	1,240	1,330	1,340	10,650
Weighted average number of persons per household	2.6	2.9	3.1	3.2	2.3
Commodity or service	Average weekly household expenditure (£)				
1 Food & non-alcoholic drinks	57.10	66.10	71.20	81.80	52.20
2 Alcoholic drinks, tobacco & narcotics	12.30	14.30	13.50	17.90	11.20
3 Clothing & footwear	22.20	26.60	32.60	51.90	20.90
4 Housing(net)[1], fuel & power	59.50	61.50	61.70	77.80	57.30
5 Household goods & services	34.40	33.60	36.50	58.20	27.90
6 Health	6.20	6.80	7.40	9.90	5.30
7 Transport	68.40	81.50	99.70	133.00	58.40
8 Communication	13.50	14.50	15.80	18.60	11.70
9 Recreation & culture	67.10	74.20	89.40	134.00	57.90
10 Education	4.50	4.20	7.10	25.20	7.00
11 Restaurants & hotels	41.10	48.90	61.50	102.70	38.40
12 Miscellaneous goods & services	37.10	44.20	54.70	84.10	35.00
1–12 All expenditure groups	423.50	476.50	551.20	795.10	383.10
13 Other expenditure items	77.80	98.10	118.40	189.80	71.80
Total expenditure	**501.30**	**574.50**	**669.60**	**984.80**	**455.00**
Average weekly expenditure per person (£)					
Total expenditure	**189.20**	**197.20**	**219.20**	**311.30**	**194.40**

Note: The commodity and service categories are not comparable to those in publications before 2001–02.
   Please see page xiii for symbols and conventions used in this report.

1 Excluding mortgage interest payments, council tax and Northern Ireland rates.

ONS, Family Spending 2009, © *Crown copyright 2010*

Table A10   **Household expenditure as a percentage of total expenditure by disposable income decile group, 2009**

based on weighted data and including children's expenditure

	Lowest ten per cent	Second decile group	Third decile group	Fourth decile group	Fifth decile group	Sixth decile group
Lower boundary of group (£ per week)		154	226	289	368	450
Weighted number of households (thousands)	2,600	2,600	2,600	2,600	2,590	2,600
Total number of households in sample	550	580	600	620	610	590
Total number of persons in sample	700	940	1,140	1,300	1,440	1,480
Total number of adults in sample	620	770	890	1,030	1,100	1,150
Weighted average number of persons per household	1.3	1.6	1.9	2.1	2.3	2.5
Commodity or service	Percentage of total expenditure					
1 Food & non-alcoholic drinks	14	16	15	14	13	12
2 Alcoholic drinks, tobacco & narcotics	3	3	3	3	3	3
3 Clothing & footwear	3	4	4	4	4	5
4 Housing(net)[1], fuel & power	21	20	19	17	16	14
5 Household goods & services	10	7	7	6	5	6
6 Health	1	2	1	1	1	1
7 Transport	8	9	10	12	12	13
8 Communication	3	3	3	3	3	3
9 Recreation & culture	11	12	11	13	12	12
10 Education	3	1	2	1	1	2
11 Restaurants & hotels	6	6	7	7	8	8
12 Miscellaneous goods & services	6	7	7	7	7	7
1–12 All expenditure groups	91	89	89	87	87	85
13 Other expenditure items	9	11	11	13	13	15
Total expenditure	100	100	100	100	100	100

Note: The commodity and service categories are not comparable to those in publications before 2001–02.
Please see page xiii for symbols and conventions used in this report.

1 Excluding mortgage interest payments, council tax and Northern Ireland rates.

ONS, Family Spending 2009, © Crown copyright 2010

Table A10   **Household expenditure as a percentage of total expenditure by disposable income decile group, 2009 (cont.)**

based on weighted data and including children's expenditure

	Seventh decile group	Eighth decile group	Ninth decile group	Highest ten per cent	All house-holds
Lower boundary of group (£ per week)	544	650	796	1,066	
Weighted number of households (thousands)	2,600	2,600	2,600	2,600	25,980
Total number of households in sample	580	570	570	550	5,830
Total number of persons in sample	1,560	1,680	1,740	1,760	13,740
Total number of adults in sample	1,180	1,240	1,330	1,340	10,650
Weighted average number of persons per household	2.6	2.9	3.1	3.2	2.3
Commodity or service	Percentage of total expenditure				
1 Food & non-alcoholic drinks	11	12	11	8	11
2 Alcoholic drinks, tobacco & narcotics	2	2	2	2	2
3 Clothing & footwear	4	5	5	5	5
4 Housing(net)[1], fuel & power	12	11	9	8	13
5 Household goods & services	7	6	5	6	6
6 Health	1	1	1	1	1
7 Transport	14	14	15	14	13
8 Communication	3	3	2	2	3
9 Recreation & culture	13	13	13	14	13
10 Education	1	1	1	3	2
11 Restaurants & hotels	8	9	9	10	8
12 Miscellaneous goods & services	7	8	8	9	8
1–12 All expenditure groups	84	83	82	81	84
13 Other expenditure items	16	17	18	19	16
Total expenditure	100	100	100	100	100

Note: The commodity and service categories are not comparable to those in publications before 2001–02.
Please see page xiii for symbols and conventions used in this report.

1 Excluding mortgage interest payments, council tax and Northern Ireland rates.

ONS, Family Spending 2009, © *Crown copyright 2010*

Table A11   **Household expenditure by age of household reference person, 2009**

based on weighted data and including children's expenditure

		Less than 30	30 to 49	50 to 64	65 to 74	75 or over	All house-holds
Weighted number of households (thousands)		2,770	9,670	6,740	3,310	3,500	25,980
Total number of households in sample		510	2,110	1,640	820	730	5,830
Total number of persons in sample		1,280	6,320	3,590	1,450	1,100	13,740
Total number of adults in sample		920	3,930	3,280	1,420	1,100	10,650
Weighted average number of persons per household		2.4	2.9	2.2	1.8	1.4	2.3
Commodity or service		Average weekly household expenditure (£)					
1	Food & non-alcoholic drinks	39.40	58.70	56.50	50.10	37.70	52.20
2	Alcoholic drinks, tobacco & narcotics	9.50	12.80	13.50	9.50	5.20	11.20
3	Clothing & footwear	18.60	28.00	23.20	12.60	7.00	20.90
4	Housing(net)[1], fuel & power	97.30	62.50	48.90	43.10	40.80	57.30
5	Household goods & services	18.90	32.40	31.40	23.60	20.20	27.90
6	Health	3.70	4.50	6.30	5.20	6.80	5.30
7	Transport	52.40	72.70	68.10	43.50	19.10	58.40
8	Communication	11.60	13.90	12.20	9.50	6.50	11.70
9	Recreation & culture	38.90	68.90	69.40	49.50	28.00	57.90
10	Education	19.40	8.10	6.50	1.40	[0.30]	7.00
11	Restaurants & hotels	34.40	49.70	43.10	25.90	13.10	38.40
12	Miscellaneous goods & services	30.40	43.30	37.20	24.80	21.50	35.00
1-12	All expenditure groups	374.40	455.40	416.30	298.80	206.40	383.10
13	Other expenditure items	56.00	103.30	69.00	42.90	30.00	71.80
Total expenditure		**430.40**	**558.80**	**485.40**	**341.70**	**236.40**	**455.00**
Average weekly expenditure per person (£)							
Total expenditure		**177.60**	**191.40**	**219.20**	**191.30**	**164.20**	**194.40**

Note: The commodity and service categories are not comparable to those in publications before 2001-02.
Please see page xiii for symbols and conventions used in this report.

1 Excluding mortgage interest payments, council tax and Northern Ireland rates.

ONS, Family Spending 2009, © Crown copyright 2010

Table A12   **Household expenditure as a percentage of total expenditure by age of household reference person, 2009**

based on weighted data and including children's expenditure

Commodity or service	Less than 30	30 to 49	50 to 64	65 to 74	75 or over	All house-holds
Weighted number of households (thousands)	2,770	9,670	6,740	3,310	3,500	25,980
Total number of households in sample	510	2,110	1,640	820	730	5,830
Total number of persons in sample	1,280	6,320	3,590	1,450	1,100	13,740
Total number of adults in sample	920	3,930	3,280	1,420	1,100	10,650
Weighted average number of persons per household	2.4	2.9	2.2	1.8	1.4	2.3

Commodity or service	Percentage of total expenditure					
1 Food & non-alcoholic drinks	9	11	12	15	16	11
2 Alcoholic drinks, tobacco & narcotics	2	2	3	3	2	2
3 Clothing & footwear	4	5	5	4	3	5
4 Housing(net)¹, fuel & power	23	11	10	13	17	13
5 Household goods & services	4	6	6	7	9	6
6 Health	1	1	1	2	3	1
7 Transport	12	13	14	13	8	13
8 Communication	3	2	3	3	3	3
9 Recreation & culture	9	12	14	14	12	13
10 Education	5	1	1	0	[0]	2
11 Restaurants & hotels	8	9	9	8	6	8
12 Miscellaneous goods & services	7	8	8	7	9	8
1-12 All expenditure groups	87	82	86	87	87	84
13 Other expenditure items	13	18	14	13	13	16
Total expenditure	**100**	**100**	**100**	**100**	**100**	**100**

Note: The commodity and service categories are not comparable to those in publications before 2001-02.
Please see page xiii for symbols and conventions used in this report.

1 Excluding mortgage interest payments, council tax and Northern Ireland rates.

ONS, Family Spending 2009, © Crown copyright 2010

Table A13   **Detailed household expenditure by age of household reference person, 2009**
based on weighted data and including children's expenditure

		Less than 30	30 to 49	50 to 64	65 to 74	75 or over	All house-holds
Weighted number of households (thousands)		2770	9670	6740	3310	3500	25980
Total number of households in sample		510	2110	1640	820	730	5830
Total number of persons in sample		1280	6320	3590	1450	1100	13740
Total number of adults in sample		920	3930	3280	1420	1100	10650
Weighted average number of persons per household		2.4	2.9	2.2	1.8	1.4	2.3

Commodity or service		Average weekly household expenditure (£)					
1	**Food & non-alcoholic drinks**	**39.40**	**58.70**	**56.50**	**50.10**	**37.70**	**52.20**
1.1	Food	35.90	53.70	52.30	46.50	35.40	48.00
1.1.1	Bread, rice and cereals	4.20	5.90	5.10	4.30	3.30	5.00
1.1.2	Pasta products	0.60	0.60	0.40	0.20	0.10	0.40
1.1.3	Buns, cakes, biscuits etc.	2.10	3.50	3.50	3.30	2.90	3.20
1.1.4	Pastry (savoury)	0.80	1.00	0.70	0.40	0.30	0.70
1.1.5	Beef (fresh, chilled or frozen)	1.10	1.80	2.10	1.70	1.00	1.70
1.1.6	Pork (fresh, chilled or frozen)	0.40	0.60	0.80	0.80	0.50	0.70
1.1.7	Lamb (fresh, chilled or frozen)	0.30	0.60	0.70	0.80	0.60	0.60
1.1.8	Poultry (fresh, chilled or frozen)	1.60	2.40	2.20	1.60	1.10	2.00
1.1.9	Bacon and ham	0.50	1.00	1.20	1.20	0.80	1.00
1.1.10	Other meat and meat preparations	4.00	5.80	5.70	5.60	4.10	5.40
1.1.11	Fish and fish products	1.30	2.30	2.70	2.40	2.20	2.30
1.1.12	Milk	2.40	3.20	2.70	2.70	2.40	2.80
1.1.13	Cheese and curd	1.40	2.00	1.90	1.60	1.10	1.80
1.1.14	Eggs	0.50	0.70	0.70	0.60	0.50	0.60
1.1.15	Other milk products	1.40	2.20	2.00	1.90	1.60	2.00
1.1.16	Butter	0.10	0.30	0.40	0.50	0.40	0.30
1.1.17	Margarine, other vegetable fats and peanut butter	0.30	0.50	0.50	0.60	0.50	0.50
1.1.18	Cooking oils and fats	0.20	0.30	0.30	0.20	0.20	0.30
1.1.19	Fresh fruit	1.80	3.10	3.40	3.10	2.40	2.90
1.1.20	Other fresh, chilled or frozen fruits	0.20	0.30	0.40	0.30	0.20	0.30
1.1.21	Dried fruit and nuts	0.30	0.60	0.60	0.60	0.40	0.50
1.1.22	Preserved fruit and fruit based products	0.10	0.10	0.10	0.20	0.20	0.10
1.1.23	Fresh vegetables	2.70	4.10	4.30	3.70	2.70	3.80
1.1.24	Dried vegetables	[0.00]	0.10	0.00	0.00	0.00	0.00
1.1.25	Other preserved or processed vegetables	1.10	1.50	1.40	1.00	0.60	1.30
1.1.26	Potatoes	0.60	0.80	1.00	1.00	0.70	0.90
1.1.27	Other tubers and products of tuber vegetables	1.20	1.70	1.30	1.00	0.60	1.30
1.1.28	Sugar and sugar products	0.20	0.40	0.40	0.40	0.30	0.30
1.1.29	Jams, marmalades	0.10	0.20	0.30	0.30	0.30	0.30
1.1.30	Chocolate	1.20	1.80	1.60	1.50	1.10	1.60
1.1.31	Confectionery products	0.50	0.70	0.60	0.50	0.40	0.60
1.1.32	Edible ices and ice cream	0.40	0.60	0.50	0.40	0.30	0.50
1.1.33	Other food products	2.30	3.00	2.50	1.90	1.30	2.40
1.2	Non-alcoholic drinks	3.50	5.00	4.30	3.60	2.40	4.10
1.2.1	Coffee	0.30	0.60	0.80	0.70	0.50	0.60
1.2.2	Tea	0.30	0.40	0.50	0.60	0.50	0.50
1.2.3	Cocoa and powdered chocolate	0.00	0.10	0.10	0.10	0.10	0.10
1.2.4	Fruit and vegetable juices (inc. fruit squash)	1.00	1.40	1.10	0.80	0.50	1.10
1.2.5	Mineral or spring waters	0.10	0.30	0.20	0.10	0.10	0.20
1.2.6	Soft drinks (inc. fizzy and ready to drink fruit drinks)	1.70	2.20	1.60	1.30	0.60	1.70

Note: The commodity and service categories are not comparable to those in publications before 2001–02.
The numbering system is sequential, it does not use actual COICOP codes.
Please see page xiii for symbols and conventions used in this report.

ONS, Family Spending 2009, © Crown copyright 2010

Table A13 Detailed household expenditure by age of household reference person, 2009 (cont.)

based on weighted data and including children's expenditure

		Less than 30	30 to 49	50 to 64	65 to 74	75 or over	All house-holds
Commodity or service		Average weekly household expenditure (£)					
2	**Alcoholic drink, tobacco & narcotics**	**9.50**	**12.80**	**13.50**	**9.50**	**5.20**	**11.20**
2.1	Alcoholic drinks	4.20	7.60	8.60	5.70	4.00	6.80
2.1.1	Spirits and liqueurs (brought home)	0.60	1.10	1.50	1.80	1.50	1.30
2.1.2	Wines, fortified wines (brought home)	1.50	4.00	4.80	2.90	1.90	3.50
2.1.3	Beer, lager, ciders and perry (brought home)	2.10	2.50	2.20	1.10	0.50	1.90
2.1.4	Alcopops (brought home)	0.10	0.10	0.10	[0.00]	[0.00]	0.10
2.2	Tobacco and narcotics	5.30	5.10	4.90	3.80	1.20	4.40
2.2.1	Cigarettes	4.40	4.40	4.30	3.40	1.10	3.80
2.2.2	Cigars, other tobacco products and narcotics	0.90	0.70	0.60	0.40	[0.10]	0.60
3	**Clothing & footwear**	**18.60**	**28.00**	**23.20**	**12.60**	**7.00**	**20.90**
3.1	Clothing	14.90	22.50	19.10	10.40	6.00	17.00
3.1.1	Men's outer garments	4.30	5.30	4.20	2.30	1.00	4.00
3.1.2	Men's under garments	0.20	0.40	0.50	0.30	0.20	0.40
3.1.3	Women's outer garments	6.60	9.20	10.20	5.30	3.50	7.90
3.1.4	Women's under garments	0.70	1.10	1.30	0.80	0.60	1.00
3.1.5	Boys' outer garments (5-15)	0.20	1.40	0.40	0.30	[0.00]	0.70
3.1.6	Girls' outer garments (5-15)	0.30	2.00	0.50	0.20	[0.10]	1.00
3.1.7	Infants' outer garments (under 5)	1.20	1.10	0.40	0.30	[0.10]	0.70
3.1.8	Children's under garments (under 16)	0.40	0.60	0.20	0.20	[0.10]	0.40
3.1.9	Accessories	0.60	0.90	0.90	0.30	0.20	0.70
3.1.10	Haberdashery, clothing materials and clothing hire	[0.20]	0.20	0.20	0.10	0.10	0.20
3.1.11	Dry cleaners, laundry and dyeing	[0.10]	0.40	0.30	0.20	0.20	0.30
3.2	Footwear	3.60	5.50	4.10	2.20	1.00	3.90
4	**Housing (net)[1], fuel & power**	**97.30**	**62.50**	**48.90**	**43.10**	**40.80**	**57.30**
4.1	Actual rentals for housing	93.90	39.00	20.60	19.90	23.00	35.50
4.1.1	Gross rent	93.90	38.90	20.60	19.90	22.90	35.40
4.1.2	*less* housing benefit, rebates & allowances rec'd	21.90	13.40	10.90	12.00	15.40	13.70
4.1.3	Net rent[2]	72.00	25.50	9.70	7.90	7.50	21.70
4.1.4	Second dwelling rent	-	[0.10]	[0.00]	-	[0.00]	[0.00]
4.2	Maintenance and repair of dwelling	2.30	7.00	8.30	6.90	6.30	6.70
4.3	Water supply and miscellaneous services relating to the dwelling	7.30	7.90	7.80	7.10	7.30	7.60
4.4	Electricity, gas and other fuels	15.70	22.10	23.10	21.30	19.60	21.30
4.4.1	Electricity	8.10	10.80	11.00	10.20	9.00	10.20
4.4.2	Gas	7.30	10.20	10.50	9.50	9.10	9.70
4.4.3	Other fuels	0.40	1.20	1.70	1.60	1.50	1.30

Note: The commodity and service categories are not comparable to those in publications before 2001-02.
  The numbering system is sequential, it does not use actual COICOP codes.
  Please see page xiii for symbols and conventions used in this report.

1 Excluding mortgage interest payments, council tax and Northern Ireland rates.

2 The figure included in total expenditure is net rent as opposed to gross rent.

ONS, Family Spending 2009, © Crown copyright 2010

Table A13 **Detailed household expenditure by age of household reference person, 2009 (cont.)**

based on weighted data and including children's expenditure

		Less than 30	30 to 49	50 to 64	65 to 74	75 or over	All house-holds
Commodity or service		Average weekly household expenditure (£)					
5	**Household goods & services**	**18.90**	**32.40**	**31.40**	**23.60**	**20.20**	**27.90**
5.1	Furniture and furnishings and floor coverings	11.30	17.90	15.40	11.60	7.80	14.40
5.1.1	Furniture and furnishings	9.00	14.10	11.80	8.60	5.70	11.10
5.1.2	Floor coverings	2.30	3.80	3.50	3.00	2.10	3.20
5.2	Household textiles	1.10	1.60	1.80	1.40	1.20	1.50
5.3	Household appliances	1.30	3.60	4.20	2.00	2.00	3.10
5.4	Glassware, tableware and household utensils	1.10	1.40	1.70	1.30	0.80	1.40
5.5	Tools and equipment for house and garden	1.50	2.60	2.70	2.20	0.90	2.20
5.6	Goods and services for routine household maintenance	2.60	5.30	5.70	5.10	7.50	5.40
5.6.1	Cleaning materials	1.60	2.60	2.50	2.30	1.50	2.30
5.6.2	Household goods and hardware	0.90	1.40	1.50	1.30	0.80	1.30
5.6.3	Domestic services, carpet cleaning, hire of furniture/furnishings	0.20	1.20	1.70	1.60	5.30	1.80
6	**Health**	**3.70**	**4.50**	**6.30**	**5.20**	**6.80**	**5.30**
6.1	Medical products, appliances and equipment	2.20	2.60	3.80	3.50	4.50	3.30
6.1.1	Medicines, prescriptions and healthcare products	1.20	1.90	2.10	1.60	3.00	2.00
6.1.2	Spectacles, lenses, accessories and repairs	0.90	0.70	1.80	1.80	1.50	1.30
6.2	Hospital services	1.60	1.80	2.50	1.70	2.30	2.00
7	**Transport**	**52.40**	**72.70**	**68.10**	**43.50**	**19.10**	**58.40**
7.1	Purchase of vehicles	15.60	24.40	23.50	14.00	6.40	19.50
7.1.1	Purchase of new cars and vans	5.70	6.20	9.20	6.30	3.20	6.50
7.1.2	Purchase of second hand cars or vans	9.00	17.20	14.00	7.70	3.20	12.40
7.1.3	Purchase of motorcycles and other vehicles	[0.90]	1.00	[0.40]	[0.00]	[0.00]	0.60
7.2	Operation of personal transport	24.40	35.40	35.00	24.30	10.40	29.30
7.2.1	Spares and accessories	2.70	2.20	2.10	2.00	0.70	2.00
7.2.2	Petrol, diesel and other motor oils	15.40	23.70	23.20	15.00	6.30	19.20
7.2.3	Repairs and servicing	4.20	7.00	7.10	5.50	2.60	5.90
7.2.4	Other motoring costs	2.10	2.50	2.60	1.80	0.70	2.20
7.3	Transport services	12.50	13.00	9.60	5.20	2.30	9.60
7.3.1	Rail and tube fares	3.00	3.80	2.30	0.90	0.20	2.50
7.3.2	Bus and coach fares	2.20	1.70	1.30	0.20	0.20	1.30
7.3.4	Combined fares	2.60	1.70	0.70	[0.20]	[0.10]	1.10
7.3.5	Other travel and transport	4.70	5.90	5.30	3.90	1.90	4.80
8	**Communication**	**11.60**	**13.90**	**12.20**	**9.50**	**6.50**	**11.70**
8.1	Postal services	0.20	0.40	0.60	0.60	0.50	0.40
8.2	Telephone and telefax equipment	[0.50]	0.60	0.30	0.60	[0.20]	0.50
8.3	Telephone and telefax services	10.90	13.00	11.30	8.30	5.80	10.80

Note: The commodity and service categories are not comparable to those in publications before 2001–02.

The numbering system is sequential, it does not use actual COICOP codes.

Please see page xiii for symbols and conventions used in this report.

ONS, Family Spending 2009, © Crown copyright 2010

Table A13   **Detailed household expenditure by age of household reference person, 2009 (cont.)**
based on weighted data and including children's expenditure

Commodity or service	Less than 30	30 to 49	50 to 64	65 to 74	75 or over	All house-holds
	Average weekly household expenditure (£)					
9 Recreation & culture	**38.90**	**68.90**	**69.40**	**49.50**	**28.00**	**57.90**
9.1 Audio-visual, photographic and information processing equipment	6.50	7.70	9.40	3.60	3.90	7.00
9.1.1 Audio equipment and accessories, CD players	1.40	2.00	1.70	0.70	0.40	1.50
9.1.2 TV, video and computers	4.80	4.80	6.60	2.70	3.30	4.80
9.1.3 Photographic, cine and optical equipment	[0.20]	0.90	1.20	[0.20]	[0.20]	0.70
9.2 Other major durables for recreation and culture	[0.30]	3.00	3.70	[3.50]	[0.00]	2.50
9.3 Other recreational items and equipment, gardens and pets	7.10	13.00	12.20	8.60	4.70	10.50
9.3.1 Games, toys and hobbies	2.10	3.20	1.70	1.80	0.50	2.20
9.3.2 Computer software and games	1.50	2.20	1.80	0.50	[0.10]	1.50
9.3.3 Equipment for sport, camping and open-air recreation	0.50	1.10	0.70	0.80	[0.20]	0.80
9.3.4 Horticultural goods, garden equipment and plants	1.00	2.20	3.70	2.90	2.10	2.60
9.3.5 Pets and pet food	2.00	4.20	4.30	2.70	1.80	3.50
9.4 Recreational and cultural services	14.30	25.20	19.80	14.80	6.10	18.70
9.4.1 Sports admissions, subscriptions, leisure class fees and equipment hire	3.90	7.70	5.40	1.90	0.70	5.00
9.4.2 Cinema, theatre and museums etc.	1.60	2.90	2.50	2.10	0.70	2.30
9.4.3 TV, video, satellite rental, cable subscriptions, TV licences and the Internet	6.10	7.20	6.40	5.70	1.60	5.90
9.4.4 Miscellaneous entertainments	1.20	1.40	1.20	0.70	0.90	1.10
9.4.5 Development of film, deposit for film development, passport photos, holiday and school photos	[0.20]	0.50	0.20	0.20	0.10	0.30
9.4.6 Gambling payments	1.40	5.50	4.00	4.20	2.20	4.10
9.5 Newspapers, books and stationery	3.00	5.90	6.80	6.70	5.60	5.90
9.5.1 Books	1.00	1.60	1.50	0.90	0.90	1.30
9.5.2 Diaries, address books, cards etc.	1.10	2.10	2.10	1.70	1.10	1.80
9.5.3 Newspapers	0.40	1.10	2.20	3.20	2.80	1.80
9.5.4 Magazines and periodicals	0.60	1.00	1.00	0.90	0.70	0.90
9.6 Package holidays	7.80	14.20	17.50	12.20	7.70	13.20
9.6.1 Package holidays – UK	[0.40]	0.70	0.90	1.30	1.90	0.90
9.6.2 Package holidays – abroad	7.40	13.50	16.60	10.90	5.80	12.30
10 Education	**19.40**	**8.10**	**6.50**	**1.40**	**[0.30]**	**7.00**
10.1 Education fees	19.30	7.40	6.20	[1.30]	[0.30]	6.70
10.2 Payments for school trips, other ad-hoc expenditure	[0.10]	0.60	[0.30]	[0.10]	[0.00]	0.30
11 Restaurants & hotels	**34.40**	**49.70**	**43.10**	**25.90**	**13.10**	**38.40**
11.1 Catering services	31.50	40.90	34.10	19.40	10.40	31.30
11.1.1 Restaurant and café meals	10.70	15.10	16.20	11.30	6.80	13.30
11.1.2 Alcoholic drinks (away from home)	8.90	8.60	8.60	4.80	1.70	7.20
11.1.3 Take away meals eaten at home	5.00	5.30	3.30	2.00	1.30	3.80
11.1.4 Other take-away and snack food	4.80	6.40	4.10	1.10	0.50	4.20
11.1.5 Contract catering (food) and canteens	2.10	5.50	1.90	0.20	0.00	2.80
11.2 Accommodation services	2.90	8.80	9.00	6.50	2.70	7.10
11.2.1 Holiday in the UK	1.30	3.40	3.60	2.80	2.00	3.00
11.2.2 Holiday abroad	1.50	5.30	5.40	3.70	[0.80]	4.10
11.2.3 Room hire	[0.10]	[0.10]	[0.00]	[0.00]	[0.00]	[0.10]

Note: The commodity and service categories are not comparable to those in publications before 2001–02.
The numbering system is sequential, it does not use actual COICOP codes.
Please see page xiii for symbols and conventions used in this report.

ONS, Family Spending 2009, © Crown copyright 2010

Table A13 **Detailed household expenditure by age of household reference person, 2009 (cont.)**

based on weighted data and including children's expenditure

		Less than 30	30 to 49	50 to 64	65 to 74	75 or over	All house-holds
Commodity or service				Average weekly household expenditure (£)			
12	**Miscellaneous goods & services**	**30.40**	**43.30**	**37.20**	**24.80**	**21.50**	**35.00**
12.1	Personal care	9.00	12.50	11.70	8.20	6.10	10.50
12.1.1	Hairdressing, beauty treatment	1.90	3.60	3.90	3.00	3.00	3.40
12.1.2	Toilet paper	0.50	0.90	0.80	0.80	0.50	0.80
12.1.3	Toiletries and soap	1.70	2.60	2.50	1.70	1.10	2.20
12.1.4	Baby toiletries and accessories (disposable)	1.70	1.00	0.30	0.10	0.10	0.70
12.1.5	Hair products, cosmetics and related electrical appliances	3.10	4.40	4.10	2.50	1.30	3.50
12.2	Personal effects	3.00	4.20	3.20	1.70	1.00	3.10
12.3	Social protection	2.10	5.70	[1.20]	[1.20]	3.40	3.30
12.4	Insurance	11.60	16.30	17.70	12.10	9.80	14.70
12.4.1	Household insurances – structural, contents and appliances	2.30	5.40	5.80	4.80	4.50	5.00
12.4.2	Medical insurance premiums	0.40	1.10	2.10	1.80	1.70	1.40
12.4.3	Vehicle insurance including boat insurance	8.80	9.80	9.70	5.40	3.70	8.30
12.4.4	Non-package holiday, other travel insurance	[0.10]	[0.00]	[0.20]	[0.10]	[0.00]	0.10
12.5	Other services	4.60	4.50	3.50	1.60	1.40	3.40
12.5.1	Moving house	2.10	2.30	1.70	[0.60]	[1.30]	1.80
12.5.2	Bank, building society, post office, credit card charges	0.60	0.80	0.50	0.30	0.10	0.50
12.5.3	Other services and professional fees	1.90	1.40	1.30	0.70	[0.00]	1.20
1–12	**All expenditure groups**	**374.40**	**455.40**	**416.30**	**298.80**	**206.40**	**383.10**
13	**Other expenditure items**	**56.00**	**103.30**	**69.00**	**42.90**	**30.00**	**71.80**
13.1	Housing: mortgage interest payments, council tax etc.	39.90	77.20	42.70	22.20	15.90	49.00
13.2	Licences, fines and transfers	2.20	4.10	3.90	2.80	1.70	3.40
13.3	Holiday spending	6.00	9.90	11.90	7.00	[1.30]	8.50
13.4	Money transfers and credit	7.80	12.10	10.60	10.90	11.10	11.00
13.4.1	Money, cash gifts given to children	[0.00]	0.20	[0.10]	[0.00]	0.00	0.10
13.4.2	Cash gifts and donations	6.70	9.10	9.10	10.30	10.70	9.20
13.4.3	Club instalment payments (child) and interest on credit cards	1.00	2.80	1.40	0.60	0.30	1.60
Total expenditure		**430.40**	**558.80**	**485.40**	**341.70**	**236.40**	**455.00**
14	**Other items recorded**						
14.1	Life assurance & contributions to pension funds	11.10	29.50	26.70	3.80	2.00	19.80
14.2	Other insurance inc. friendly societies	0.70	1.80	1.50	0.60	0.70	1.30
14.3	Income tax, payments *less* refunds	69.20	132.20	107.20	34.90	22.20	91.80
14.4	National insurance contributions	31.20	42.70	31.30	3.10	1.30	27.90
14.5	Purchase or alteration of dwellings, mortgages	21.00	70.00	46.40	19.30	37.20	47.80
14.6	Savings and investments	4.30	7.40	8.30	2.00	0.70	5.70
14.7	Pay off loan to clear other debt	2.20	4.10	1.70	[0.80]	[0.10]	2.30
14.8	Windfall receipts from gambling etc[3]	1.30	3.70	1.90	2.10	0.50	2.30

Note: The commodity and service categories are not comparable to those in publications before 2001–02.

The numbering system is sequential, it does not use actual COICOP codes.

Please see page xiii for symbols and conventions used in this report.

3 Expressed as an income figure as opposed to an expenditure figure.

ONS, Family Spending 2009, © *Crown copyright 2010*

Table A14 **Household expenditure by gross income quintile group where the household reference person is aged under 30, 2007–2009**

based on weighted data and including children's expenditure

	Lowest twenty per cent	Second quintile group	Third quintile group	Fourth quintile group	Highest twenty per cent	All house-holds
Lower boundary of group (£ per week)[1]		235	410	647	985	
Average weighted number of households (thousands)	550	460	660	610	360	2,640
Total number of households in sample (over 3 years)	340	300	400	330	190	1,560
Total number of persons in sample (over 3 years)	750	790	1,000	850	480	3,880
Total number of adults in sample (over 3 years)	440	460	740	700	440	2,790
Weighted average number of persons per household	2.1	2.5	2.5	2.5	2.5	2.4
Commodity or service	Average weekly household expenditure (£)					
1 Food & non-alcoholic drinks	27.70	33.40	41.90	43.00	49.40	38.80
2 Alcoholic drinks, tobacco & narcotics	9.00	8.70	10.60	12.50	9.90	10.20
3 Clothing & footwear	11.10	16.20	21.00	25.20	37.20	21.40
4 Housing(net)[2], fuel & power	56.60	84.20	97.20	87.70	110.00	86.00
5 Household goods & services	13.70	15.90	20.60	27.20	35.70	22.00
6 Health	0.80	2.00	2.90	4.50	7.20	3.30
7 Transport	14.30	34.60	49.50	77.00	114.30	54.90
8 Communication	6.90	10.20	14.40	16.10	18.60	13.10
9 Recreation & culture	17.90	29.30	43.20	55.40	67.00	41.70
10 Education	11.10	17.00	13.90	9.00	[3.60]	11.50
11 Restaurants & hotels	14.60	21.90	36.30	49.90	72.90	37.50
12 Miscellaneous goods & services	10.20	21.80	36.90	40.10	52.10	31.60
1–12 All expenditure groups	193.90	295.30	388.50	447.80	578.00	371.90
13 Other expenditure items	7.70	37.20	63.60	107.00	165.90	71.90
Total expenditure	**201.60**	**332.50**	**452.10**	**554.70**	**744.00**	**443.80**
Average weekly expenditure per person (£) **Total expenditure**	**94.30**	**132.50**	**177.70**	**221.60**	**297.90**	**182.00**

Note: The commodity and service categories are not comparable to those in publications before 2001–02.
Please see page xiii for symbols and conventions used in this report.
This table is based on a three year average.

1 Lower boundary of 2009 gross income quintile groups (£ per week).

2 Excluding mortgage interest payments, council tax and Northern Ireland rates.

ONS, Family Spending 2009,   © Crown copyright 2010

Table A15   **Household expenditure by gross income quintile group where the household
reference person is aged 30 to 49, 2007–2009**

based on weighted data and including children's expenditure

	Lowest twenty per cent	Second quintile group	Third quintile group	Fourth quintile group	Highest twenty per cent	All house-holds
Lower boundary of group (£ per week)[1]		235	410	647	985	
Average weighted number of households (thousands)	1,020	1,280	1,950	2,540	2,940	9,720
Total number of households in sample (over 3 years)	710	920	1,370	1,730	1,930	6,660
Total number of persons in sample (over 3 years)	1,420	2,610	4,070	5,540	6,410	20,040
Total number of adults in sample (over 3 years)	870	1,410	2,450	3,500	4,230	12,460
Weighted average number of persons per household	1.9	2.8	2.8	3.1	3.3	2.9
Commodity or service	Average weekly household expenditure (£)					
1 Food & non-alcoholic drinks	32.20	44.10	50.40	60.20	71.50	56.60
2 Alcoholic drinks, tobacco & narcotics	8.30	10.40	11.70	12.60	15.50	12.50
3 Clothing & footwear	9.80	19.90	20.60	28.00	42.80	28.00
4 Housing(net)[2], fuel & power	47.00	60.60	58.00	58.30	65.00	59.40
5 Household goods & services	13.20	19.00	22.70	38.00	54.80	34.90
6 Health	1.60	1.90	3.90	3.90	7.50	4.50
7 Transport	21.10	37.90	54.80	76.00	125.30	75.80
8 Communication	7.90	11.20	13.80	14.50	17.20	14.10
9 Recreation & culture	20.90	34.20	50.20	68.80	108.20	67.40
10 Education	3.10	3.00	2.40	4.40	21.80	8.90
11 Restaurants & hotels	14.10	23.80	33.10	48.00	79.20	47.70
12 Miscellaneous goods & services	15.10	22.60	32.00	44.50	71.10	44.10
1–12 All expenditure groups	194.30	288.60	353.50	457.30	680.00	453.90
13 Other expenditure items	24.10	48.80	78.80	112.90	197.20	113.70
Total expenditure	**218.30**	**337.40**	**432.30**	**570.10**	**877.10**	**567.50**
Average weekly expenditure per person (£) **Total expenditure**	**114.00**	**121.30**	**151.80**	**182.20**	**269.50**	**193.30**

Note: The commodity and service categories are not comparable to those in publications before 2001–02.
Please see page xiii for symbols and conventions used in this report.
This table is based on a three year average.

1 Lower boundary of 2009 gross income quintile groups (£ per week).

2 Excluding mortgage interest payments, council tax and Northern Ireland rates.

ONS, Family Spending 2009, © *Crown copyright 2010*

Table A16   **Household expenditure by gross income quintile group where the household reference person is aged 50 to 64, 2007–2009**

based on weighted data and including children's expenditure

	Lowest twenty per cent	Second quintile group	Third quintile group	Fourth quintile group	Highest twenty per cent	All house-holds
Lower boundary of group (£ per week)[1]		235	410	647	985	
Weighted number of households (thousands)	1,100	1,110	1,400	1,440	1,600	6,650
Total number of households in sample (over 3 years)	820	830	1,050	1,070	1,110	4,880
Total number of persons in sample (over 3 years)	1,120	1,440	2,240	2,630	3,240	10,670
Total number of adults in sample (over 3 years)	1,060	1,330	2,040	2,380	2,900	9,710
Weighted average number of persons per household	1.4	1.8	2.1	2.4	3.0	2.2
Commodity or service	Average weekly household expenditure (£)					
1 Food & non-alcoholic drinks	30.30	41.40	52.60	61.40	78.20	55.10
2 Alcoholic drinks, tobacco & narcotics	8.60	10.70	12.70	15.30	16.90	13.30
3 Clothing & footwear	8.10	12.80	18.90	24.50	45.40	23.60
4 Housing(net)[2], fuel & power	35.50	47.40	48.90	49.40	57.80	48.60
5 Household goods & services	12.90	23.20	30.50	36.50	52.80	33.00
6 Health	2.40	3.90	5.80	7.70	14.40	7.40
7 Transport	22.00	40.70	61.50	80.80	139.10	74.30
8 Communication	7.20	9.70	11.50	14.10	17.80	12.60
9 Recreation & culture	24.40	41.60	55.10	77.40	124.40	69.30
10 Education	[0.90]	2.30	2.80	9.10	16.90	7.20
11 Restaurants & hotels	11.50	22.80	33.10	47.80	82.00	42.80
12 Miscellaneous goods & services	13.60	21.70	31.20	40.60	65.90	37.00
1–12 All expenditure groups	177.40	278.10	364.50	464.70	711.60	424.10
13 Other expenditure items	21.30	44.90	58.90	82.20	133.00	73.20
Total expenditure	**198.70**	**323.00**	**423.40**	**546.90**	**844.60**	**497.30**
Average weekly expenditure per person (£)						
Total expenditure	**144.60**	**183.80**	**197.00**	**223.80**	**280.60**	**223.40**

Note: The commodity and service categories are not comparable to those in publications before 2001–02.
Please see page xiii for symbols and conventions used in this report.
This table is based on a three year average.

1 Lower boundary of 2009 gross income quintile groups (£ per week).

2 Excluding mortgage interest payments, council tax and Northern Ireland rates.

ONS, Family Spending 2009, © Crown copyright 2010

Table A17   **Household expenditure by gross income quintile group where the household reference person is aged 65 to 74, 2007–2009**

based on weighted data and including children's expenditure

	Lowest twenty per cent	Second quintile group	Third quintile group	Fourth quintile group	Highest twenty per cent	All house-holds
Lower boundary of group (£ per week)[1]		235	410	647	985	
Average weighted number of households (thousands)	890	1,070	680	370	180	3,200
Total number of households in sample (over 3 years)	680	870	540	270	130	2,480
Total number of persons in sample (over 3 years)	830	1,500	1,070	630	300	4,320
Total number of adults in sample (over 3 years)	830	1,490	1,050	600	290	4,260
Weighted average number of persons per household	1.2	1.7	2.0	2.5	2.4	1.8
Commodity or service	Average weekly household expenditure (£)					
1 Food & non-alcoholic drinks	31.10	44.90	53.30	70.90	69.80	47.30
2 Alcoholic drinks, tobacco & narcotics	5.90	8.80	10.60	14.40	15.70	9.40
3 Clothing & footwear	5.60	10.00	16.70	24.40	25.90	12.80
4 Housing(net)[2], fuel & power	33.80	38.80	43.70	50.40	52.00	40.50
5 Household goods & services	12.20	21.00	29.90	44.50	55.80	25.10
6 Health	2.30	4.10	8.70	7.90	12.00	5.40
7 Transport	14.80	34.50	53.00	73.30	97.50	41.00
8 Communication	6.00	7.90	9.70	13.00	14.60	8.70
9 Recreation & culture	23.20	45.70	79.20	91.60	109.60	55.00
10 Education	[0.00]	[1.10]	[0.40]	[3.00]	[6.00]	1.10
11 Restaurants & hotels	10.00	19.60	30.00	44.30	67.10	24.60
12 Miscellaneous goods & services	12.10	21.10	27.10	37.50	66.90	24.20
1–12 All expenditure groups	157.00	257.50	362.30	475.30	592.90	295.10
13 Other expenditure items	18.30	41.30	43.40	95.80	83.60	43.60
Total expenditure	**175.40**	**298.80**	**405.70**	**571.10**	**676.50**	**338.70**
Average weekly expenditure per person (£) **Total expenditure**	**144.00**	**174.80**	**203.00**	**230.90**	**277.90**	**192.20**

Note: The commodity and service categories are not comparable to those in publications before 2001–02.
Please see page xiii for symbols and conventions used in this report.
This table is based on a three year average.

1 Lower boundary of 2009 gross income quintile groups (£ per week).

2 Excluding mortgage interest payments, council tax and Northern Ireland rates.

ONS, Family Spending 2009, © Crown copyright 2010

Table A18 **Household expenditure by gross income quintile group where the household reference person is aged 75 or over, 2007–2009**

based on weighted data and including children's expenditure

Commodity or service	Lowest twenty per cent	Second quintile group	Third quintile group	Fourth quintile group	Highest twenty per cent	All house-holds
Lower boundary of group (£ per week)[1]		235	410	647	985	
Average weighted number of households (thousands)	1,570	1,210	450	180	70	3,470
Total number of households in sample (over 3 years)	930	820	310	120	40	2,230
Total number of persons in sample (over 3 years)	1,070	1,300	580	260	110	3,310
Total number of adults in sample (over 3 years)	1,060	1,300	570	250	110	3,290
Weighted average number of persons per household	1.1	1.5	1.8	2.1	2.8	1.4

Commodity or service	Average weekly household expenditure (£)					
1 Food & non-alcoholic drinks	26.50	36.50	48.00	58.00	77.20	35.30
2 Alcoholic drinks, tobacco & narcotics	2.90	5.10	8.10	8.30	13.50	4.80
3 Clothing & footwear	4.90	7.70	10.00	14.70	28.50	7.40
4 Housing (net)[2], fuel & power	32.50	39.40	41.30	46.10	73.60	37.50
5 Household goods & services	12.30	16.20	25.20	39.30	85.00	18.20
6 Health	3.50	5.40	10.20	9.90	10.30	5.60
7 Transport	7.00	19.80	34.10	39.40	88.80	18.20
8 Communication	5.10	5.90	7.40	10.30	13.20	6.10
9 Recreation & culture	16.10	26.10	51.60	75.00	99.20	28.60
10 Education	[0.00]	[0.10]	[2.40]	[2.40]	[0.10]	0.50
11 Restaurants & hotels	7.00	12.10	21.40	34.00	50.00	12.80
12 Miscellaneous goods & services	13.00	17.50	32.80	54.90	90.80	20.60
1–12 All expenditure groups	130.70	191.70	292.60	392.30	630.10	195.70
13 Other expenditure items	15.60	28.30	42.10	81.10	98.50	28.10
Total expenditure	**146.30**	**220.00**	**334.70**	**473.40**	**728.60**	**223.70**
Average weekly expenditure per person (£) **Total expenditure**	**131.30**	**144.80**	**185.70**	**222.80**	**257.20**	**156.60**

Note: The commodity and service categories are not comparable to those in publications before 2001–02.
  Please see page xiii for symbols and conventions used in this report.
  This table is based on a three year average.

1 Lower boundary of 2009 gross income quintile groups (£ per week).

2 Excluding mortgage interest payments, council tax and Northern Ireland rates.

ONS, Family Spending 2009, © *Crown copyright 2010*

Table A19   **Household expenditure by economic activity status of the household reference person, 2009**

based on weighted data and including children's expenditure

	Employees			Self-employed	All in employ-ment[1]
	Full-time	Part-time	All		
Weighted number of households (thousands)	11,380	2,260	13,640	2,010	15,680
Total number of households in sample	2,450	530	2,980	460	3,450
Total number of persons in sample	6,560	1,400	7,960	1,290	9,270
Total number of adults in sample	4,910	970	5,870	940	6,820
Weighted average number of persons per household	2.6	2.7	2.6	2.8	2.7
Commodity or service	Average weekly household expenditure (£)				
1 Food & non-alcoholic drinks	58.80	56.10	58.30	63.00	58.90
2 Alcoholic drinks, tobacco & narcotics	13.10	11.50	12.90	13.90	13.00
3 Clothing & footwear	28.60	21.60	27.40	25.50	27.10
4 Housing (net)[2], fuel & power	66.30	66.10	66.30	63.10	65.90
5 Household goods & services	33.70	27.60	32.70	37.60	33.30
6 Health	5.50	5.40	5.50	4.60	5.40
7 Transport	80.50	56.40	76.50	80.50	77.00
8 Communication	13.80	12.00	13.50	16.40	13.90
9 Recreation & culture	75.80	59.30	73.00	67.90	72.30
10 Education	9.20	6.10	8.70	13.60	9.30
11 Restaurants & hotels	53.10	32.60	49.70	55.30	50.40
12 Miscellaneous goods & services	45.60	33.60	43.60	46.00	43.90
1-12 All expenditure groups	484.00	388.50	468.20	487.50	470.20
13 Other expenditure items	102.60	61.50	95.80	116.10	98.30
Total expenditure	**586.60**	**450.00**	**564.00**	**603.60**	**568.50**
Average weekly expenditure per person (£) **Total expenditure**	**222.40**	**168.10**	**213.30**	**215.20**	**213.30**

Note: The commodity and service categories are not comparable to those in publications before 2001-02.
Please see page xiii for symbols and conventions used in this report.

1 Includes households where household reference person was on a Government supported training scheme.

2 Excluding mortgage interest payments, council tax and Northern Ireland rates.

ONS, Family Spending 2009, © *Crown copyright 2010*

Table A19   **Household expenditure by economic activity status of the household reference person, 2009 (cont.)**

based on weighted data and including children's expenditure

	Unem-ployed	All economically active[1]	Economically inactive Retired	Other	All	All house-holds
Weighted number of households (thousands)	760	16,440	6,740	2,800	9,540	25,980
Total number of households in sample	160	3,600	1,530	690	2,220	5,830
Total number of persons in sample	340	9,600	2,450	1,680	4,130	13,740
Total number of adults in sample	230	7,050	2,430	1,170	3,600	10,650
Weighted average number of persons per household	2.0	2.6	1.6	2.5	1.8	2.3

Commodity or service	Average weekly household expenditure (£)					
1 Food & non-alcoholic drinks	31.90	57.70	42.20	43.90	42.70	52.20
2 Alcoholic drinks, tobacco & narcotics	9.50	12.80	7.10	11.20	8.30	11.20
3 Clothing & footwear	10.10	26.40	9.80	16.00	11.60	20.90
4 Housing (net)[2], fuel & power	42.50	64.80	41.80	50.80	44.40	57.30
5 Household goods & services	11.10	32.30	21.60	17.40	20.40	27.90
6 Health	1.10	5.20	5.80	4.70	5.50	5.30
7 Transport	25.60	74.60	28.40	35.60	30.50	58.40
8 Communication	8.60	13.60	7.80	9.60	8.30	11.70
9 Recreation & culture	19.40	69.80	36.90	38.10	37.20	57.90
10 Education	[9.00]	9.30	0.90	8.20	3.00	7.00
11 Restaurants & hotels	16.00	48.80	18.50	25.30	20.50	38.40
12 Miscellaneous goods & services	14.20	42.50	22.20	22.10	22.20	35.00
1–12 All expenditure groups	199.00	457.70	243.00	283.00	254.70	383.10
13 Other expenditure items	30.00	95.10	32.70	29.20	31.60	71.80
Total expenditure	**229.00**	**552.80**	**275.60**	**312.20**	**286.40**	**455.00**
Average weekly expenditure per person (£) **Total expenditure**	**112.50**	**209.70**	**175.20**	**127.30**	**156.40**	**194.40**

Note: The commodity and service categories are not comparable to those in publications before 2001–02.
Please see page xiii for symbols and conventions used in this report.

1 Includes households where household reference person was on a Government supported training scheme.

2 Excluding mortgage interest payments, council tax and Northern Ireland rates.

ONS, Family Spending 2009,   © Crown copyright 2010

Table A20   **Household expenditure by gross income: the household reference person is a full-time employee, 2009**

based on weighted data and including children's expenditure

	Lowest twenty per cent	Second quintile group	Third quintile group	Fourth quintile group	Highest twenty per cent	All house- holds
Lower boundary of group (£ per week)[1]		235	410	647	985	
Weighted number of households (thousands)	190	1,000	2,500	3,580	4,120	11,380
Total number of households in sample	40	220	550	770	880	2,450
Total number of persons in sample	50	380	1,280	2,150	2,700	6,560
Total number of adults in sample	50	310	950	1,570	2,030	4,910
Weighted average number of persons per household	1.4	1.7	2.3	2.8	3.0	2.6
Commodity or service	Average weekly household expenditure (£)					
1 Food & non-alcoholic drinks	29.50	32.00	47.10	58.20	74.20	58.80
2 Alcoholic drinks, tobacco & narcotics	[5.70]	8.70	11.10	13.50	15.50	13.10
3 Clothing & footwear	[7.20]	10.90	16.90	25.60	43.50	28.60
4 Housing (net)[2], fuel & power	64.80	66.00	66.30	61.30	70.80	66.30
5 Household goods & services	15.40	14.50	22.70	31.60	47.80	33.70
6 Health	[7.80]	2.60	3.40	4.30	8.30	5.50
7 Transport	13.90	34.50	51.60	75.90	116.30	80.50
8 Communication	6.70	8.80	11.50	13.70	16.70	13.80
9 Recreation & culture	25.80	32.70	43.90	65.00	117.20	75.80
10 Education	[3.80]	[7.50]	7.80	4.50	14.80	9.20
11 Restaurants & hotels	17.40	19.80	30.20	43.40	85.20	53.10
12 Miscellaneous goods & services	13.80	19.70	29.40	38.30	69.50	45.60
1–12 All expenditure groups	211.80	257.60	342.00	435.40	679.70	484.00
13 Other expenditure items	33.50	43.70	64.60	87.70	156.00	102.60
Total expenditure	**245.30**	**301.30**	**406.70**	**523.10**	**835.70**	**586.60**
Average weekly expenditure per person (£) **Total expenditure**	**178.80**	**180.80**	**176.40**	**189.80**	**275.70**	**222.40**

Note: The commodity and service categories are not comparable to those in publications before 2001–02.
   Please see page xiii for symbols and conventions used in this report.

1 Lower boundary of 2009 gross income quintile groups (£ per week).

2 Excluding mortgage interest payments, council tax and Northern Ireland rates.

ONS, Family Spending 2009, © *Crown copyright 2010*

Table A21   **Household expenditure by gross income: the household reference person is self–employed, 2007–2009**

based on weighted data and including children's expenditure

	Lowest twenty per cent	Second quintile group	Third quintile group	Fourth quintile group	Highest twenty per cent	All house-holds
Lower boundary of group (gross income : £ per week)[1]		235	410	647	985	
Average weighted number of households (thousands)	150	330	460	470	600	2,010
Total number of households in sample (over 3 years)	110	230	340	340	410	1,440
Total number of persons in sample (over 3 years)	200	590	1,000	1,030	1,300	4,120
Total number of adults in sample (over 3 years)	160	410	700	750	970	2,980
Weighted average number of persons per household	1.8	2.5	2.8	3.0	3.2	2.8
Commodity or service			Average weekly household expenditure (£)			
1 Food & non-alcoholic drinks	37.80	47.10	60.00	67.90	75.80	62.80
2 Alcoholic drinks, tobacco & narcotics	6.50	9.50	13.70	14.20	15.40	13.00
3 Clothing & footwear	9.10	20.70	24.40	24.50	45.30	28.90
4 Housing(net)[2], fuel & power	56.00	63.60	56.50	65.10	65.50	62.00
5 Household goods & services	23.60	33.50	28.70	40.90	59.90	41.00
6 Health	2.60	2.40	5.90	4.20	9.10	5.70
7 Transport	40.30	61.70	67.50	86.90	128.60	87.50
8 Communication	9.90	13.30	14.90	17.90	20.60	16.70
9 Recreation & culture	24.00	42.60	59.60	74.50	118.90	75.80
10 Education	[7.80]	7.00	2.00	10.40	28.00	12.90
11 Restaurants & hotels	25.30	36.30	42.50	55.30	85.50	55.90
12 Miscellaneous goods & services	30.60	29.90	40.60	48.80	68.70	48.60
1–12 All expenditure groups	273.60	367.80	416.20	510.70	721.20	510.80
13 Other expenditure items	61.40	85.10	86.90	120.40	184.60	121.40
Total expenditure	**335.10**	**452.90**	**503.10**	**631.10**	**905.80**	**632.20**
Average weekly expenditure per person (£) **Total expenditure**	**190.60**	**181.90**	**177.90**	**210.70**	**281.80**	**222.00**

Note: The commodity and service categories are not comparable to those in publications before 2001–02.
Please see page xiii for symbols and conventions used in this report.
This table is based on a three year average.

1 Lower boundary of 2009 gross income quintile groups (£ per week).

2 Excluding mortgage interest payments, council tax and Northern Ireland rates.

ONS, Family Spending 2009,   © Crown copyright 2010

Table A22 **Household expenditure by number of persons working, 2009**

based on weighted data and including children's expenditure

	Number of persons working					All house-holds
	None	One	Two	Three	Four or more	
Weighted number of households (thousands)	8,980	7,420	7,740	1,490	350	25,980
Total number of households in sample	2,080	1,670	1,690	310	70	5,830
Total number of persons in sample	3,570	3,690	5,000	1,150	330	13,740
Total number of adults in sample	3,080	2,720	3,620	950	280	10,650
Weighted average number of persons per household	1.7	2.2	2.9	3.8	4.7	2.3
Weighted average age of head of household	65	47	42	49	48	52
Employment status of the household reference person[1]:						
- % working full-time or self-employed	0	65	89	85	89	50
- % working part-time	0	19	10	13	8	9
- % not working	100	15	2	3	3	41
Commodity or service	Average weekly household expenditure (£)					
1 Food & non-alcoholic drinks	38.40	48.30	64.80	80.30	86.80	52.20
2 Alcoholic drinks, tobacco & narcotics	7.80	11.10	13.70	16.00	21.70	11.20
3 Clothing & footwear	9.30	18.40	30.00	50.40	48.40	20.90
4 Housing(net)[2], fuel & power	42.20	64.00	65.70	68.40	68.40	57.30
5 Household goods & services	16.90	29.60	35.50	44.80	35.40	27.90
6 Health	4.50	5.00	6.50	5.60	4.90	5.30
7 Transport	25.50	52.90	88.20	110.10	140.70	58.40
8 Communication	7.40	11.80	14.40	19.60	24.90	11.70
9 Recreation & culture	32.80	53.10	79.20	111.80	99.30	57.90
10 Education	2.30	10.00	8.50	10.30	[12.50]	7.00
11 Restaurants & hotels	17.00	34.70	57.30	74.10	95.30	38.40
12 Miscellaneous goods & services	18.70	33.20	50.50	53.90	73.20	35.00
1–12 All expenditure groups	222.90	372.20	514.20	645.30	711.60	383.10
13 Other expenditure items	28.70	74.70	109.80	106.80	126.20	71.80
Total expenditure	**251.60**	**446.90**	**624.00**	**752.10**	**837.80**	**455.00**
Average weekly expenditure per person (£) **Total expenditure**	**151.20**	**204.80**	**215.50**	**199.80**	**179.40**	**194.40**

Note: The commodity and service categories are not comparable to those in publications before 2001–02.
Please see page xiii for symbols and conventions used in this report.

1 Excludes households where the household reference person was on a Government-supported training scheme.

2 Excluding mortgage interest payments, council tax and Northern Ireland rates.

ONS, Family Spending 2009, © Crown copyright 2010

Table A23   **Household expenditure by age at which the household reference person completed continuous full-time education, 2009**

based on weighted data and including children's expenditure

	Aged 14 and under	Aged 15	Aged 16	Aged 17 and under 19	Aged 19 and under 22	Aged 22 or over
Weighted number of households (thousands)	370	3,550	6,910	4,030	2,680	3,300
Total number of households in sample	100	860	1,560	910	560	710
Total number of persons in sample	230	1,840	4,210	2,430	1,420	1,820
Total number of adults in sample	190	1,590	2,980	1,730	1,050	1,350
Weighted average number of persons per household	2.4	2.2	2.7	2.6	2.5	2.6
Weighted average age of head of household	54	56	45	44	41	41

Commodity or service	Average weekly household expenditure (£)					
1 Food & non-alcoholic drinks	53.90	50.70	54.40	56.70	55.90	58.30
2 Alcoholic drinks, tobacco & narcotics	11.60	12.40	13.40	12.20	13.60	10.00
3 Clothing & footwear	18.90	16.80	23.70	26.50	24.90	29.50
4 Housing(net)[1], fuel & power	45.90	47.30	53.70	62.20	73.20	83.90
5 Household goods & services	19.00	22.40	27.10	31.10	33.30	40.80
6 Health	4.30	5.30	3.60	5.40	7.80	5.50
7 Transport	47.70	49.80	58.40	73.40	79.60	86.70
8 Communication	10.90	10.80	12.60	13.30	13.70	13.90
9 Recreation & culture	42.00	53.90	62.10	68.30	77.00	68.00
10 Education	[1.10]	1.10	3.90	7.70	14.10	24.10
11 Restaurants & hotels	26.50	29.30	38.90	44.80	59.70	58.70
12 Miscellaneous goods & services	22.10	25.90	33.20	40.50	52.10	49.40
1–12 All expenditure groups	304.00	325.60	385.00	442.00	504.90	529.00
13 Other expenditure items	44.30	42.40	69.90	83.10	124.30	117.70
Total expenditure	**348.30**	**368.00**	**455.00**	**525.10**	**629.20**	**646.60**
Average weekly expenditure per person (£) **Total expenditure**	**143.70**	**169.90**	**169.40**	**198.90**	**254.20**	**251.60**

Note: The commodity and service categories are not comparable to those in publications before 2001–02.
       Please see page xiii for symbols and conventions used in this report.

1 Excluding mortgage interest payments, council tax and Northern Ireland rates.

ONS, Family Spending 2009,   © Crown copyright 2010

Table A24   **Household expenditure by socio-economic classification of household reference person, 2009**

based on weighted data and including children's expenditure

	Large employers & higher manag-erial	Higher profess-ional	Lower manag-erial & profess-ional	Inter-mediate	Small employ-ers	Lower super-visory
Weighted number of households (thousands)	1,200	1,700	4,900	1,520	1,460	1,740
Total number of households in sample	260	370	1,050	360	340	370
Total number of persons in sample	770	990	2,760	860	950	1,010
Total number of adults in sample	540	720	2,060	640	690	760
Weighted average number of persons per household	2.9	2.6	2.6	2.4	2.8	2.7
Commodity or service	Average weekly household expenditure (£)					
1 Food & non-alcoholic drinks	71.30	67.30	58.80	50.70	61.50	57.90
2 Alcoholic drinks, tobacco & narcotics	14.60	11.20	13.80	10.60	14.00	14.10
3 Clothing & footwear	43.00	34.40	28.70	22.30	24.90	20.70
4 Housing (net)[3], fuel & power	64.20	74.30	66.10	62.60	60.40	56.00
5 Household goods & services	64.30	44.30	34.00	24.00	27.70	26.70
6 Health	9.30	6.90	5.90	4.90	4.40	3.70
7 Transport	109.20	102.90	82.20	64.20	77.10	67.10
8 Communication	14.90	14.20	14.20	12.20	16.40	13.20
9 Recreation & culture	134.80	84.30	77.60	53.60	63.60	69.30
10 Education	23.40	22.40	7.70	5.70	7.50	4.00
11 Restaurants & hotels	80.60	62.80	58.40	41.20	47.00	38.70
12 Miscellaneous goods & services	69.90	61.40	47.40	36.70	40.70	34.00
1–12 All expenditure groups	699.40	586.30	494.90	388.70	445.20	405.30
13 Other expenditure items	178.20	146.60	104.10	72.80	93.40	76.60
Total expenditure	**877.70**	**732.90**	**599.00**	**461.50**	**538.70**	**481.90**
Average weekly expenditure per person (£) **Total expenditure**	**302.90**	**278.70**	**230.80**	**193.70**	**192.40**	**177.50**

Note: The commodity and service categories are not comparable to those in publications before 2001–02.
    Please see page xiii for symbols and conventions used in this report.

1 Includes those who have never worked.

2 Includes those who are economically inactive.

3 Excludes mortgage interest payments, council tax and Northern Ireland rates.

ONS, Family Spending 2009, © *Crown copyright 2010*

Table A24   **Household expenditure by socio-economic classification of household reference person, 2009 (cont.)**

based on weighted data and including children's expenditure

		Semi-routine	Routine	Long-term unem-ployed[1]	Students	Occupation not stated[2]	All house-holds
Weighted number of households (thousands)		1,990	1,470	510	470	9,000	25,980
Total number of households in sample		450	330	120	90	2,100	5,830
Total number of persons in sample		1,190	900	320	210	3,780	13,740
Total number of adults in sample		860	670	170	170	3,380	10,650
Weighted average number of persons per household		2.6	2.7	2.9	2.5	1.8	2.3
Commodity or service		Average weekly household expenditure (£)					
1	Food & non-alcoholic drinks	52.10	49.80	39.00	41.50	42.50	52.20
2	Alcoholic drinks, tobacco & narcotics	11.80	12.60	8.50	6.00	8.40	11.20
3	Clothing & footwear	19.80	19.70	15.70	26.40	10.80	20.90
4	Housing (net)[3], fuel & power	65.00	65.10	45.00	115.60	41.90	57.30
5	Household goods & services	27.00	21.10	8.90	17.80	20.60	27.90
6	Health	3.40	4.10	6.00	3.20	5.30	5.30
7	Transport	50.00	50.50	14.60	55.20	30.40	58.40
8	Communication	12.70	11.70	7.70	13.50	8.10	11.70
9	Recreation & culture	47.30	46.50	20.10	37.70	36.80	57.90
10	Education	1.80	[1.10]	[2.40]	67.00	1.40	7.00
11	Restaurants & hotels	30.50	30.90	14.70	36.40	19.70	38.40
12	Miscellaneous goods & services	27.60	29.90	13.30	27.00	21.80	35.00
1–12	All expenditure groups	349.00	343.20	196.00	447.40	247.80	383.10
13	Other expenditure items	53.30	55.80	14.80	61.50	31.80	71.80
Total expenditure		**402.30**	**398.90**	**210.90**	**508.80**	**279.60**	**455.00**
Average weekly expenditure per person (£) **Total expenditure**		**152.30**	**149.60**	**73.90**	**200.10**	**159.10**	**194.40**

Note: The commodity and service categories are not comparable to those in publications before 2001–02.
Please see page xiii for symbols and conventions used in this report.

1 Includes those who have never worked.

2 Includes those who are economically inactive.

3 Excludes mortgage interest payments, council tax and Northern Ireland rates.

ONS, Family Spending 2009, © Crown copyright 2010

Table A25   **Expenditure by household composition, 2009**

based on weighted data and including children's expenditure

Commodity or service		Retired households				Non-retired	
		State pension[1]		Other retired		One person	Two adults
		One person	Two adults	One person	Two adults		
Weighted number of households (thousands)		770	400	2,750	2,400	4,000	5,790
Total number of households in sample		150	120	580	610	870	1,270
Total number of persons in sample		150	230	580	1,220	870	2,540
Total number of adults in sample		150	230	580	1,220	870	2,540
Weighted average number of persons per household		1.0	2.0	1.0	2.0	1.0	2.0
Commodity or service		Average weekly household expenditure (£)					
1	Food & non-alcoholic drinks	26.40	47.40	29.40	54.30	25.30	52.00
2	Alcoholic drinks, tobacco & narcotics	2.40	6.10	4.30	11.40	8.70	13.20
3	Clothing & footwear	5.70	7.80	6.70	12.90	9.00	22.60
4	Housing(net)[2], fuel & power	32.70	36.90	40.00	45.50	50.20	65.20
5	Household goods & services	11.60	19.60	16.00	28.60	20.20	31.70
6	Health	4.50	2.50	4.00	8.60	3.00	6.50
7	Transport	7.30	31.80	15.40	40.00	35.10	73.80
8	Communication	5.40	6.40	6.50	8.80	8.00	12.30
9	Recreation & culture	17.00	41.30	24.60	51.70	31.00	69.30
10	Education	[0.00]	-	[0.70]	[0.40]	3.10	5.30
11	Restaurants & hotels	7.30	12.00	11.20	28.40	23.00	48.30
12	Miscellaneous goods & services	11.80	16.70	18.40	26.80	19.30	39.50
1–12	All expenditure groups	132.10	228.40	177.20	317.30	235.60	439.80
13	Other expenditure items	16.80	33.50	25.00	45.00	59.30	89.70
Total expenditure		**148.90**	**261.90**	**202.20**	**362.30**	**294.90**	**529.50**
Average weekly expenditure per person (£) **Total expenditure**		**148.90**	**131.00**	**202.20**	**181.20**	**294.90**	**264.70**

Note: The commodity and service categories are not comparable to those in publications before 2001–02.
        Please see page xiii for symbols and conventions used in this report.

1 Mainly dependent on state pensions and not economically active – see definitions in Appendix B.

2 Excluding mortgage interest payments, council tax and Northern Ireland rates.

ONS, Family Spending 2009,   © Crown copyright 2010

Table A25   **Expenditure by household composition, 2009 (cont.)**

based on weighted data and including children's expenditure

| | | Retired and non-retired households | | | | | | |
| | | One adult | | Two adults | | | Three or more adults | |
		with one child	with two or more children	with one child	with two children	with three or more children	without children	with children
Weighted number of households (thousands)		650	640	2,210	2,100	830	2,320	1,130
Total number of households in sample		160	180	480	500	210	470	240
Total number of persons in sample		320	610	1,450	2,000	1,080	1,560	1,140
Total number of adults in sample		160	180	960	1,000	410	1,560	790
Weighted average number of persons per household		2.0	3.4	3.0	4.0	5.3	3.4	4.8
Commodity or service		Average weekly household expenditure (£)						
1	Food & non-alcoholic drinks	36.70	53.90	62.50	76.50	87.90	75.80	85.90
2	Alcoholic drinks, tobacco & narcotics	8.90	7.90	12.10	13.80	13.60	17.70	15.00
3	Clothing & footwear	15.40	20.30	27.00	32.70	35.40	35.60	50.90
4	Housing(net)[2], fuel & power	57.20	61.50	68.60	59.50	66.80	71.60	68.40
5	Household goods & services	19.10	19.20	35.50	36.20	26.20	38.50	37.60
6	Health	1.30	1.60	4.80	6.80	2.80	6.70	6.30
7	Transport	29.10	31.90	82.00	76.70	82.90	99.40	99.60
8	Communication	9.40	11.90	13.90	14.80	14.70	18.80	20.20
9	Recreation & culture	32.50	39.90	64.80	98.10	70.30	87.70	87.50
10	Education	[4.20]	5.90	9.70	16.90	8.90	19.00	18.10
11	Restaurants & hotels	19.60	29.30	46.20	54.50	48.00	62.50	73.90
12	Miscellaneous goods & services	23.40	32.40	49.70	55.30	44.70	49.70	52.40
1–12	All expenditure groups	256.90	315.70	476.80	541.60	502.30	583.00	615.80
13	Other expenditure items	34.70	49.40	109.80	111.60	92.90	82.00	95.10
Total expenditure		**291.60**	**365.10**	**586.60**	**653.20**	**595.20**	**665.00**	**710.90**
Average weekly expenditure per person (£) **Total expenditure**		**145.80**	**107.10**	**195.50**	**163.30**	**113.20**	**198.10**	**147.60**

Note: The commodity and service categories are not comparable to those in publications before 2001–02.
Please see page xiii for symbols and conventions used in this report.

1 Mainly dependent on state pensions and not economically active – see definitions in Appendix B.

2 Excluding mortgage interest payments, council tax and Northern Ireland rates.

ONS, Family Spending 2009, © Crown copyright 2010

Table A26 **Expenditure of one person retired households mainly dependent on state pensions[1] by gross income quintile group, 2007–2009**

based on weighted data

Commodity or service	Lowest twenty per cent	Second quintile group	Third quintile group	Fourth quintile group	Highest twenty per cent	All house- holds
Lower boundary of group (gross income: £ per week)[2]		235	410	647	985	
Average weighted number of households (thousands)	710	80	0	0	0	800
Total number of households in sample (over 3 years)	460	50	0	0	0	510
Total number of persons in sample (over 3 years)	460	50	0	0	0	510
Total number of adults in sample (over 3 years)	460	50	0	0	0	510
Weighted average number of persons per household	1.0	1.0	1.0	0	0	1.0

Commodity or service	Average weekly household expenditure (£)					
1 Food & non-alcoholic drinks	25.30	22.10	[7.90]	-	-	24.90
2 Alcoholic drinks, tobacco & narcotics	3.30	[2.00]	-	-	-	3.10
3 Clothing & footwear	4.80	[8.70]	[3.00]	-	-	5.00
4 Housing(net)[3], fuel & power	31.60	35.90	[28.90]	-	-	32.20
5 Household goods & services	13.30	14.50	[2.20]	-	-	13.60
6 Health	2.60	3.30	-	-	-	2.80
7 Transport	9.00	7.20	-	-	-	8.80
8 Communication	5.20	5.60	[1.10]	-	-	5.20
9 Recreation & culture	19.00	15.70	[8.30]	-	-	18.70
10 Education	[0.00]	-	-	-	-	[0.00]
11 Restaurants & hotels	6.70	10.10	[2.70]	-	-	7.00
12 Miscellaneous goods & services	12.70	14.60	[3.70]	-	-	12.90
1–12 All expenditure groups	133.30	139.60	[57.70]	-	-	134.30
13 Other expenditure items	17.50	32.10	[5.20]	-	-	18.80
Total expenditure	**150.90**	**171.60**	**[62.90]**	**-**	**-**	**153.10**
Average weekly expenditure per person (£) **Total expenditure**	**150.90**	**171.60**	**[62.90]**	**-**	**-**	**153.10**

Note: The commodity and service categories are not comparable to those in publications before 2001–02.
Please see page xiii for symbols and conventions used in this report.
This table is based on a three year average.

1 Mainly dependent on state pensions and not economically active - see defintions in Appendix B.

2 Lower boundary of 2009 gross income quintile groups (£ per week).

3 Excluding mortgage interest payments, council tax and Northern Ireland rates.

ONS, Family Spending 2009, © *Crown copyright 2010*

Table A27 **Expenditure of one person retired households not mainly dependent on state pensions by gross income quintile group, 2007–2009**

based on weighted data

	Lowest twenty per cent	Second quintile group	Third quintile group	Fourth quintile group	Highest twenty per cent	All house-holds
Lower boundary of group (gross income: £ per week)[1]		235	410	647	985	
Average weighted number of households (thousands)	1,520	910	230	60	10	2,730
Total number of households in sample (over 3 years)	980	600	150	40	10	1,780
Total number of persons in sample (over 3 years)	980	600	150	40	10	1,780
Total number of adults in sample (over 3 years)	980	600	150	40	10	1,780
Weighted average number of persons per household	1.0	1.0	1.0	1.0	1.0	1.0
Commodity or service	Average weekly household expenditure (£)					
1 Food & non-alcoholic drinks	25.80	28.60	33.70	35.70	[18.70]	27.60
2 Alcoholic drinks, tobacco & narcotics	3.70	4.40	7.50	[8.80]	[2.60]	4.40
3 Clothing & footwear	5.50	8.00	8.80	14.50	[8.60]	6.80
4 Housing(net)[2] fuel & power	33.70	38.90	41.10	56.20	[21.70]	36.60
5 Household goods & services	11.70	15.80	32.10	39.90	[17.20]	15.30
6 Health	3.40	4.50	11.30	[10.30]	[0.20]	4.50
7 Transport	8.60	19.30	31.10	36.50	[24.50]	14.80
8 Communication	5.40	6.20	7.70	8.30	[4.70]	6.00
9 Recreation & culture	16.60	28.10	47.50	58.00	[33.70]	24.10
10 Education	[0.00]	[0.80]	[4.20]	[7.10]	-	0.80
11 Restaurants & hotels	7.20	[12.30]	14.00	32.10	[31.30]	10.20
12 Miscellaneous goods & services	12.00	18.70	30.90	48.00	[28.40]	16.60
1–12 All expenditure groups	133.70	[185.70]	269.90	355.30	[191.60]	167.60
13 Other expenditure items	14.80	[30.80]	44.60	182.90	[55.30]	26.70
Total expenditure	**148.50**	**[216.50]**	**314.50**	**538.20**	**[246.80]**	**194.30**
Average weekly expenditure per person (£) **Total expenditure**	**148.50**	**[216.50]**	**314.50**	**538.20**	**370.20**	**194.30**

Note: The commodity and service categories are not comparable to those in publications before 2001–02.
　　　Please see page xiii for symbols and conventions used in this report.
　　　This table is based on a three year average.

1 Lower boundary of 2009 gross income quintile groups (£ per week).

2 Excluding mortgage interest payments, council tax and Northern Ireland rates.

ONS, Family Spending 2009, © Crown copyright 2010

Table A28 **Expenditure of one adult non-retired households by gross income quintile group, 2009**

based on weighted data

Commodity or service	Lowest twenty per cent	Second quintile group	Third quintile group	Fourth quintile group	Highest twenty per cent	All house-holds
Lower boundary of group (gross income £ per week)[1]		235	410	647	985	
Average weighted number of households (thousands)	1,320	900	880	490	270	3,850
Total number of households in sample (over 3 years)	890	620	590	320	160	2,580
Total number of persons in sample (over 3 years)	890	620	590	320	160	2,580
Total number of adults in sample (over 3 years)	890	620	590	320	160	2,580
Weighted average number of persons per household	1.0	1.0	1.0	1.0	1.0	1.0

Commodity or service	Average weekly household expenditure (£)					
1 Food & non-alcoholic drinks	20.70	24.80	26.80	29.90	29.50	24.80
2 Alcoholic drinks, tobacco & narcotics	7.60	7.50	8.70	9.80	9.40	8.20
3 Clothing & footwear	5.00	7.50	11.50	14.40	21.00	9.40
4 Housing(net)[2], fuel & power	37.90	52.40	48.40	54.40	66.10	47.70
5 Household goods & services	8.70	15.50	18.20	31.40	61.70	19.10
6 Health	1.40	2.80	2.80	7.30	4.60	3.10
7 Transport	16.00	32.70	50.20	57.30	97.90	38.80
8 Communication	6.00	8.10	10.10	10.60	11.60	8.40
9 Recreation & culture	16.00	26.80	35.80	41.00	71.10	30.10
10 Education	2.00	[2.10]	1.30	10.70	[6.20]	3.20
11 Restaurants & hotels	10.10	17.20	29.30	34.90	59.70	22.80
12 Miscellaneous goods & services	10.70	17.50	22.90	29.70	47.50	20.00
1–12 All expenditure groups	142.00	214.80	266.00	331.40	486.20	235.40
13 Other expenditure items	17.40	52.20	76.80	106.20	226.80	65.00
Total expenditure	**159.40**	**267.10**	**342.80**	**437.60**	**713.00**	**300.40**
Average weekly expenditure per person (£) **Total expenditure**	**159.40**	**267.10**	**342.80**	**437.60**	**713.00**	**300.40**

Note: The commodity and service categories are not comparable to those in publications before 2001–02.
Please see page xiii for symbols and conventions used in this report.
This table is based on a three year average.

1 Lower boundary of 2009 gross income quintile groups (£ per week).

2 Excluding mortgage interest payments, council tax and Northern Ireland rates.

ONS, Family Spending 2009, © Crown copyright 2010

Table A29 **Expenditure of one adult households with children by gross income quintile group 2007–2009**

based on weighted data and including children's expenditure

	Lowest twenty per cent	Second quintile group	Third quintile group	Fourth quintile group	Highest twenty per cent	All house-holds
Lower boundary of group (gross income £ per week)[1]		235	410	647	985	
Average weighted number of households (thousands)	540	490	240	100	30	1,400
Total number of households in sample (over 3 years)	430	400	200	70	20	1,130
Total number of persons in sample (over 3 years)	1,110	1,150	560	190	60	3,060
Total number of adults in sample (over 3 years)	430	400	200	70	20	1,130
Weighted average number of persons per household	2.5	2.8	2.7	2.5	2.6	2.6
Commodity or service	Average weekly household expenditure (£)					
1 Food & non-alcoholic drinks	36.80	44.90	46.50	51.00	66.40	42.90
2 Alcoholic drinks, tobacco & narcotics	7.70	8.20	9.10	9.70	[8.30]	8.30
3 Clothing & footwear	13.70	21.30	25.20	26.70	[58.00]	20.10
4 Housing(net)[2], fuel & power	46.60	58.10	65.50	68.90	109.30	56.60
5 Household goods & services	14.80	24.40	23.80	31.00	32.20	21.20
6 Health	1.40	1.30	2.50	6.30	[8.10]	2.10
7 Transport	15.50	28.10	45.80	53.80	78.60	29.00
8 Communication	7.80	10.80	15.40	14.50	16.80	10.80
9 Recreation & culture	23.50	36.50	47.10	77.50	173.70	38.70
10 Education	2.50	3.70	2.80	[12.20]	[27.30]	4.00
11 Restaurants & hotels	13.40	20.70	32.20	54.80	47.10	22.90
12 Miscellaneous goods & services	15.40	24.40	45.10	43.00	65.00	26.70
1–12 All expenditure groups	199.20	282.50	361.10	449.40	690.90	283.20
13 Other expenditure items	14.40	39.60	77.10	99.50	165.50	42.80
Total expenditure	**213.60**	**322.10**	**438.20**	**548.90**	**856.40**	**326.00**
Average weekly expenditure per person (£) **Total expenditure**	**85.10**	**114.30**	**165.30**	**221.00**	**325.90**	**123.40**

Note: The commodity and service categories are not comparable to those in publications before 2001–02.
Please see page xiii for symbols and conventions used in this report.
This table is based on a three year average.

1 Lower boundary of 2009 gross income quintile groups (£ per week).

2 Excluding mortgage interest payments, council tax and Northern Ireland rates.

ONS, Family Spending 2009, © Crown copyright 2010

Table A30   **Expenditure of two adult households with children by gross income
quintile group, 2007–2009**

based on weighted data and including children's expenditure

Commodity or service	Lowest twenty per cent	Second quintile group	Third quintile group	Fourth quintile group	Highest twenty per cent	All house- holds
Lower boundary of group (£ per week)[1]		235	410	647	985	
Average weighted number of households (thousands)	210	580	1,090	1,560	1,550	4,990
Total number of households in sample (over 3 years)	140	410	800	1,130	1,120	3,590
Total number of persons in sample (over 3 years)	500	1,620	3,120	4,290	4,300	13,820
Total number of adults in sample (over 3 years)	280	810	1,600	2,260	2,240	7,190
Weighted average number of persons per household	3.6	3.9	3.8	3.8	3.8	3.8
Commodity or service	Average weekly household expenditure (£)					
1 Food & non-alcoholic drinks	50.00	54.90	61.70	68.30	84.60	69.60
2 Alcoholic drinks, tobacco & narcotics	14.50	12.20	11.10	12.30	15.10	13.00
3 Clothing & footwear	14.10	22.90	23.00	30.30	44.10	31.40
4 Housing(net)[2], fuel & power	53.80	67.60	65.20	55.20	64.60	61.60
5 Household goods & services	19.10	23.90	22.40	37.40	61.10	39.10
6 Health	2.60	1.50	3.30	4.70	8.90	5.20
7 Transport	32.40	42.20	55.50	81.00	134.30	85.20
8 Communication	9.40	12.20	13.80	14.80	16.80	14.70
9 Recreation & culture	26.00	41.00	56.60	74.30	121.50	79.20
10 Education	[5.80]	5.40	3.90	4.80	37.00	14.70
11 Restaurants & hotels	23.00	30.60	32.20	47.00	74.90	49.50
12 Miscellaneous goods & services	19.70	26.60	37.10	49.90	84.00	53.70
1–12 All expenditure groups	270.60	341.00	385.70	480.00	746.90	516.80
13 Other expenditure items	29.10	50.40	74.50	118.00	206.90	124.30
Total expenditure	**299.70**	**391.40**	**460.20**	**598.00**	**953.80**	**641.10**
Average weekly expenditure per person (£)
Total expenditure	**83.50**	**99.20**	**120.70**	**158.80**	**250.60**	**168.60**

Note: The commodity and service categories are not comparable to those in publications before 2001–02.
Please see page xiii for symbols and conventions used in this report.
This table is based on a three year average.

1 Lower boundary of 2009 gross income quintile groups (£ per week).

2 Excluding mortgage interest payments, council tax and Northern Ireland rates.

ONS, Family Spending 2009,   © Crown copyright 2010

Table A31   **Expenditure of two adult non-retired households by gross income quintile group, 2007–2009**

based on weighted data

	Lowest twenty per cent	Second quintile group	Third quintile group	Fourth quintile group	Highest twenty per cent	All house-holds
Lower boundary of group (£ per week)[1]		235	410	647	985	
Average weighted number of households (thousands)	360	690	1,390	1,650	1,690	5,790
Total number of households in sample (over 3 years)	250	500	990	1,110	1,110	3,950
Total number of persons in sample (over 3 years)	500	1,000	1,980	2,210	2,220	7,900
Total number of adults in sample (over 3 years)	500	1,000	1,980	2,210	2,220	7,900
Weighted average number of persons per household	2.0	2.0	2.0	2.0	2.0	2.0
Commodity or service	Average weekly household expenditure (£)					
1 Food & non-alcoholic drinks	40.30	45.50	49.50	49.90	56.90	50.70
2 Alcoholic drinks, tobacco & narcotics	11.00	12.40	12.80	13.40	14.20	13.20
3 Clothing & footwear	12.60	14.60	19.00	21.60	36.20	23.90
4 Housing(net)[2], fuel & power	55.10	58.10	56.80	58.20	63.80	59.30
5 Household goods & services	20.40	22.50	31.60	32.60	50.70	35.70
6 Health	3.10	3.90	5.90	5.40	10.80	6.80
7 Transport	30.80	45.40	59.00	76.50	118.30	78.00
8 Communication	8.70	10.60	12.20	13.10	15.20	12.90
9 Recreation & culture	30.40	44.50	51.80	67.70	105.30	69.80
10 Education	[9.80]	[4.00]	1.70	3.70	6.70	4.60
11 Restaurants & hotels	17.90	23.50	32.60	47.80	77.00	48.00
12 Miscellaneous goods & services	17.10	23.20	31.50	37.90	57.30	39.00
1–12 All expenditure groups	257.00	308.20	364.30	427.70	612.40	441.90
13 Other expenditure items	31.30	42.90	61.50	95.80	163.90	97.40
Total expenditure	**288.30**	**351.10**	**425.80**	**523.60**	**776.30**	**539.30**
Average weekly expenditure per person (£) **Total expenditure**	**144.10**	**175.60**	**212.90**	**261.80**	**388.20**	**269.70**

Note: The commodity and service categories are not comparable to those in publications before 2001–02.
Please see page xiii for symbols and conventions used in this report.
This table is based on a three year average.

1 Lower boundary of 2009 gross income quintile groups (£ per week).

2 Excluding mortgage interest payments, council tax and Northern Ireland rates.

ONS, Family Spending 2009,   © Crown copyright 2010

Table A32 **Expenditure of two adult retired households mainly dependent on state pensions[1]**
by gross income quintile group, 2007–2009

based on weighted data

	Lowest twenty per cent	Second quintile group	Third quintile group	Fourth quintile group	Highest twenty per cent	All house-holds
Lower boundary of group (£ per week)[2]		235	410	647	985	
Average weighted number of households (thousands)	190	260	20	0	0	460
Total number of households in sample (over 3 years)	160	230	10	0	0	400
Total number of persons in sample (over 3 years)	320	450	30	0	0	790
Total number of adults in sample (over 3 years)	320	450	30	0	0	790
Weighted average number of persons per household	2.0	2.0	2.0	0	0	2.0

Commodity or service	Average weekly household expenditure (£)					
1 Food & non-alcoholic drinks	45.40	47.10	[52.20]	-	-	46.70
2 Alcoholic drinks, tobacco & narcotics	5.30	8.50	[4.10]	-	-	7.00
3 Clothing & footwear	7.10	9.80	[6.30]	-	-	8.60
4 Housing(net)[3], fuel & power	30.80	37.70	[44.80]	-	-	35.30
5 Household goods & services	13.50	20.30	[13.50]	-	-	17.30
6 Health	2.30	3.60	[4.10]	-	-	3.10
7 Transport	26.90	26.70	[35.30]	-	-	27.50
8 Communication	5.60	6.60	[8.40]	-	-	6.20
9 Recreation & culture	30.00	41.50	[53.70]	-	-	37.60
10 Education	-	[0.30]	-	-	-	[0.20]
11 Restaurants & hotels	10.90	14.30	[25.10]	-	-	13.50
12 Miscellaneous goods & services	16.40	18.40	[17.10]	-	-	17.60
1–12 All expenditure groups	194.20	234.70	[264.60]	-	-	220.70
13 Other expenditure items	31.50	32.50	[50.90]	-	-	31.80
Total expenditure	**225.80**	**267.20**	**[315.60]**	**-**	**-**	**252.40**
Average weekly expenditure per person (£) **Total expenditure**	**112.90**	**133.60**	**[157.80]**	**-**	**-**	**126.20**

Note: The commodity and service categories are not comparable to those in publications before 2001–02.
Please see page xiii for Symbols and conventions used in this report.
This table is based on a three year average.

1 Mainly dependent on the state pensions and not economically active -see defintions in Appendix B.

2 Lower boundary of 2009 gross income quintile groups (£ per week).

3 Excluding mortgage interest payments, council tax and Northern Ireland rates.

ONS, Family Spending 2009, © Crown copyright 2010

Table A33   **Expenditure of two adult retired households not mainly dependent on state pensions by gross income quintile group, 2007–2009**

based on weighted data

Commodity or service	Lowest twenty per cent	Second quintile group	Third quintile group	Fourth quintile group	Highest twenty per cent	All house-holds
Lower boundary of group (£ per week)[1]		235	410	647	985	
Average weighted number of households (thousands)	190	1,010	680	270	100	2,250
Total number of households in sample (over 3 years)	130	800	540	210	80	1,760
Total number of persons in sample (over 3 years)	270	1,600	1,070	430	160	3,520
Total number of adults in sample (over 3 years)	270	1,600	1,070	430	160	3,520
Weighted average number of persons per household	2.0	2.0	2.0	2.0	2.0	2.0
Commodity or service	Average weekly household expenditure (£)					
1 Food & non-alcoholic drinks	44.10	49.40	53.70	62.70	62.00	52.40
2 Alcoholic drinks, tobacco & narcotics	8.40	9.00	9.30	13.30	18.00	9.90
3 Clothing & footwear	7.20	9.00	15.30	20.40	24.40	12.80
4 Housing(net)[2], fuel & power	35.80	39.90	40.50	49.50	64.90	42.00
5 Household goods & services	16.60	19.60	28.90	52.60	83.20	28.80
6 Health	2.90	5.60	9.70	8.60	10.30	7.20
7 Transport	19.00	34.20	48.80	63.70	81.10	42.90
8 Communication	8.20	7.30	8.00	10.50	12.50	8.20
9 Recreation & culture	31.40	41.90	82.00	105.50	120.50	64.10
10 Education	0.00	[0.10]	[0.40]	[2.30]	[1.30]	0.60
11 Restaurants & hotels	12.40	17.90	29.30	51.50	64.40	27.00
12 Miscellaneous goods & services	15.50	19.70	29.20	53.80	89.50	29.20
1–12 All expenditure groups	201.40	253.50	355.20	494.50	632.00	325.30
13 Other expenditure items	14.40	33.50	45.10	93.20	100.80	45.50
Total expenditure	**215.90**	**287.00**	**400.30**	**587.60**	**732.90**	**370.80**
Average weekly expenditure per person (£) **Total expenditure**	**107.90**	**143.50**	**200.10**	**293.80**	**366.40**	**185.40**

Note: The commodity and service categories are not comparable to those in publications before 2001–02.
Please see page xiii for symbols and conventions used in this report.
This table is based on a three year average.

1 Lower boundary of 2009 gross income quintile groups (£ per week).

2 Excluding mortgage interest payments, council tax and Northern Ireland rates.

ONS, Family Spending 2009, © Crown copyright 2010

Table A34   **Household expenditure by tenure, 2009**

based on weighted data and including children's expenditure

	Owners			Social rented from		
	Owned outright	Buying with a mortgage[1]	All	Council[2]	Registered Social Landlord[3]	All
Weighted number of households (thousands)	8,180	9,530	17,720	2,380	2,180	4,550
Total number of households in sample	1,980	2,120	4,100	540	450	990
Total number of persons in sample	3,850	6,010	9,860	1,170	980	2,150
Total number of adults in sample	3,610	4,240	7,850	840	680	1,510
Weighted average number of persons per household	1.9	2.8	2.4	2.2	2.1	2.2
Commodity or service	Average weekly household expenditure (£)					
1 Food & non-alcoholic drinks	51.80	62.00	57.20	40.70	38.00	39.40
2 Alcoholic drinks, tobacco & narcotics	9.30	13.30	11.40	10.70	9.60	10.20
3 Clothing & footwear	17.30	29.20	23.70	13.50	11.40	12.50
4 Housing(net)[6], fuel & power	40.70	41.70	41.20	55.60	63.50	59.40
5 Household goods & services	33.40	34.30	33.90	14.20	15.00	14.60
6 Health	7.20	5.80	6.50	2.90	2.90	2.90
7 Transport	53.80	81.40	68.70	24.90	27.00	25.90
8 Communication	9.80	14.40	12.30	9.40	8.80	9.10
9 Recreation & culture	61.40	77.10	69.90	27.80	28.40	28.10
10 Education	3.40	8.90	6.30	0.80	1.10	0.90
11 Restaurants & hotels	35.50	50.80	43.70	19.50	16.40	18.00
12 Miscellaneous goods & services	35.10	47.10	41.50	15.10	15.20	15.20
1–12 All expenditure groups	358.60	466.00	416.40	235.10	237.30	236.20
13 Other expenditure items	46.20	133.80	93.30	15.10	16.30	15.70
Total expenditure	**404.80**	**599.80**	**509.70**	**250.20**	**253.60**	**251.80**
Average weekly expenditure per person (£) **Total expenditure**	**211.70**	**213.90**	**213.10**	**112.40**	**121.90**	**116.80**

Note: The commodity and service categories are not comparable to those in publications before 2001–02.
     Please see page xiii for symbols and conventions used in this report.

1 Including shared owners (who own part of the equity and pay mortgage, part rent).

2 "Council" includes local authorities, New Towns and Scottish Homes, but see note 3 below.

3 Formerly Housing Associations.

ONS, Family Spending 2009,   © Crown copyright 2010

Table A34   **Household expenditure by tenure, 2009 (cont.)**

based on weighted data and including children's expenditure

| | Private rented[4] | | | | All |
	Rent free	Rent paid, unfurn-ished[5]	Rent paid, furnished	All	tenures
Weighted number of households (thousands)	360	2,600	750	3,710	25,980
Total number of households in sample	80	530	140	740	5,830
Total number of persons in sample	140	1,290	310	1,740	13,740
Total number of adults in sample	120	910	250	1,290	10,650
Weighted average number of persons per household	1.9	2.4	2.3	2.3	2.3
Commodity or service	Average weekly household expenditure (£)				
1 Food & non-alcoholic drinks	46.90	44.30	39.60	43.60	52.20
2 Alcoholic drinks, tobacco & narcotics	8.40	11.70	10.40	11.10	11.20
3 Clothing & footwear	23.40	17.40	18.00	18.10	20.90
4 Housing(net)[6], fuel & power	27.70	134.30	171.70	131.50	57.30
5 Household goods & services	16.20	18.00	8.70	15.90	27.90
6 Health	2.10	2.70	2.50	2.60	5.30
7 Transport	38.80	51.20	47.90	49.30	58.40
8 Communication	8.90	12.00	12.30	11.80	11.70
9 Recreation & culture	50.30	36.60	32.20	37.10	57.90
10 Education	[14.00]	6.00	59.10	17.50	7.00
11 Restaurants & hotels	26.40	40.00	35.90	37.80	38.40
12 Miscellaneous goods & services	19.10	32.20	20.00	28.50	35.00
1–12 All expenditure groups	282.10	406.40	458.20	404.70	383.10
13 Other expenditure items	43.80	33.50	50.00	37.80	71.80
Total expenditure	**325.90**	**439.80**	**508.30**	**442.50**	**455.00**
Average weekly expenditure per person (£)					
Total expenditure	**172.20**	**185.00**	**219.70**	**191.00**	**194.40**

Note: The commodity and service categories are not comparable to those in publications before 2001–02.
        Please see page xiii for symbols and conventions used in this report.

4 All tenants whose accommodation goes with the job of someone in the household are allocated to "rented privately",
   even if the landlord is a local authority or housing association or Housing Action Trust, or if the accommodation is
   rent free. Squatters are also included in this category.

5 "Unfurnished" includes the answers: "partly furnished".

6 Excluding mortgage interest payments, council tax and Northern Ireland rates.

ONS, Family Spending 2009, © Crown copyright 2010

Table A35 **Household expenditure by UK Countries and Government Office Regions, 2007–2009**

based on weighted data and including children's expenditure

	North East	North West	Yorks & the Humber	East Midlands	West Midlands	East	London
Average weighted number of households (thousands)	1,220	3,040	2,140	1,970	2,140	2,260	3,030
Total number of households in sample (over 3 years)	730	1,780	1,500	1,260	1,500	1,580	1,470
Total number of persons in sample (over 3 years)	1,700	4,200	3,530	2,910	3,740	3,690	3,540
Total number of adults in sample (over 3 years)	1,330	3,200	2,680	2,250	2,840	2,860	2,670
Weighted average number of persons per household	2.4	2.4	2.3	2.3	2.5	2.3	2.5

Commodity or service	Average weekly household expenditure (£)						
1 Food & non-alcoholic drinks	45.50	48.80	45.10	49.30	50.80	50.30	52.30
2 Alcoholic drinks, tobacco & narcotics	10.50	12.70	10.30	10.30	11.70	10.40	9.80
3 Clothing & footwear	20.50	22.20	17.60	18.70	22.80	21.10	25.70
4 Housing(net)[1], fuel & power	44.50	46.40	48.50	47.30	48.20	54.20	80.10
5 Household goods & services	28.20	26.30	27.80	25.80	29.40	34.10	32.90
6 Health	3.90	4.40	3.90	6.10	4.60	6.30	7.30
7 Transport	49.00	55.20	51.30	63.30	61.50	67.10	60.80
8 Communication	10.30	11.30	10.30	11.40	11.60	12.50	14.40
9 Recreation & culture	51.20	55.30	53.70	52.30	59.20	61.80	58.10
10 Education	4.90	4.30	3.60	4.10	4.90	5.00	15.30
11 Restaurants & hotels	33.10	37.70	34.40	34.80	36.40	36.70	47.40
12 Miscellaneous goods & services	28.00	34.20	28.90	32.20	35.30	38.90	40.60
1–12 All expenditure groups	329.60	358.80	335.30	355.60	376.50	398.40	444.70
13 Other expenditure items	57.60	71.30	65.40	67.50	69.30	89.30	107.60
Total expenditure	**387.20**	**430.20**	**400.70**	**423.00**	**445.80**	**487.70**	**552.30**
Average weekly expenditure per person (£) **Total expenditure**	**164.10**	**177.80**	**175.70**	**181.50**	**180.60**	**215.40**	**222.60**

Note: The commodity and service categories are not comparable to those in publications before 2001–02.
  Please see page xiii for symbols and conventions used in this report.
  This table is based on a three year average.

1 Excluding mortgage interest payments, council tax and Northern Ireland rates.

ONS, Family Spending 2009, © *Crown copyright 2010*

Table A35   **Household expenditure by UK Countries and Government Office Regions, 2007–2009 (cont.)**

based on weighted data and including children's expenditure

	South East	South West	England	Wales	Scotland	Northern Ireland	United Kingdom
Average weighted number of households (thousands)	3,070	2,490	21,350	1,280	2,370	670	25,670
Total number of households in sample (over 3 years)	2,350	1,520	13,680	820	1,550	1,770	17,810
Total number of persons in sample (over 3 years)	5,670	3,410	32,380	1,860	3,380	4,600	42,220
Total number of adults in sample (over 3 years)	4,370	2,740	24,940	1,490	2,700	3,380	32,510
Weighted average number of persons per household	2.3	2.3	2.4	2.3	2.2	2.7	2.4
Commodity or service	Average weekly household expenditure (£)						
1 Food & non-alcoholic drinks	54.00	52.60	50.30	50.10	48.60	57.30	50.30
2 Alcoholic drinks, tobacco & narcotics	11.00	10.20	10.80	11.30	11.80	14.90	11.10
3 Clothing & footwear	20.80	19.70	21.20	19.00	21.80	34.70	21.50
4 Housing(net)[1], fuel & power	58.10	58.20	55.40	50.30	45.80	45.90	54.00
5 Household goods & services	32.70	31.90	30.10	23.30	27.50	31.70	29.60
6 Health	6.60	5.90	5.60	3.00	4.70	4.50	5.40
7 Transport	75.30	62.60	61.70	52.00	61.10	62.90	61.20
8 Communication	12.40	11.90	12.00	10.00	11.00	14.30	11.80
9 Recreation & culture	66.10	63.20	58.50	57.80	58.30	58.40	58.40
10 Education	9.40	8.10	7.10	5.20	4.30	4.30	6.70
11 Restaurants & hotels	41.90	36.20	38.40	28.80	34.80	46.00	37.80
12 Miscellaneous goods & services	41.30	36.80	36.00	27.80	32.60	38.60	35.30
1–12 All expenditure groups	429.80	397.30	387.10	338.50	362.30	413.60	383.10
13 Other expenditure items	94.10	76.80	80.30	57.60	76.40	72.30	78.60
Total expenditure	**523.90**	**474.10**	**467.50**	**396.10**	**438.70**	**485.80**	**461.70**
Average weekly expenditure per person (£) **Total expenditure**	**224.40**	**204.80**	**197.50**	**173.00**	**203.00**	**183.30**	**196.40**

Note: The commodity and service categories are not comparable to those in publications before 2001–02.
Please see page xiii for symbols and conventions used in this report.
This table is based on a three year average.

1 Excluding mortgage interest payments, council tax and Northern Ireland rates.

ONS, Family Spending 2009, © Crown copyright 2010

Table A36   **Household expenditure as a percentage of total expenditure by UK countries and Government Office Regions, 2007–2009**

based on weighted data and including children's expenditure

	North East	North West	Yorks & the Humber	East Midlands	West Midlands	East	London
Average weighted number of households (thousands)	1,220	3,040	2,140	1,970	2,140	2,260	3,030
Total number of households in sample (over 3 years)	730	1,780	1,500	1,260	1,500	1,580	1,470
Total number of persons in sample (over 3 years)	1,700	4,200	3,530	2,910	3,740	3,690	3,540
Total number of adults in sample (over 3 years)	1,330	3,200	2,680	2,250	2,840	2,860	2,670
Weighted average number of persons per household	2.4	2.4	2.3	2.3	2.5	2.3	2.5

Commodity or service	Percentage of total expenditure						
1 Food & non-alcoholic drinks	12	11	11	12	11	10	9
2 Alcoholic drinks, tobacco & narcotics	3	3	3	2	3	2	2
3 Clothing & footwear	5	5	4	4	5	4	5
4 Housing(net)[1], fuel & power	11	11	12	11	11	11	15
5 Household goods & services	7	6	7	6	7	7	6
6 Health	1	1	1	1	1	1	1
7 Transport	13	13	13	15	14	14	11
8 Communication	3	3	3	3	3	3	3
9 Recreation & culture	13	13	13	12	13	13	11
10 Education	1	1	1	1	1	1	3
11 Restaurants & hotels	9	9	9	8	8	8	9
12 Miscellaneous goods & services	7	8	7	8	8	8	7
1–12 All expenditure groups	85	83	84	84	84	82	81
13 Other expenditure items	15	17	16	16	16	18	19
Total expenditure	100	100	100	100	100	100	100

Note: The commodity and service categories are not comparable to those in publications before 2001–02.
      Please see page xiii for symbols and conventions used in this report.
      This table is based on a three year average.

1 Excluding mortgage interest payments, council tax and Northern Ireland rates.

ONS, Family Spending 2009,   © Crown copyright 2010

Table A36 **Household expenditure as a percentage of total expenditure by UK countries and Government Office Regions, 2007–2009 (cont.)**

based on weighted data and including children's expenditure

	South East	South West	England	Wales	Scotland	Northern Ireland	United Kingdom
Average weighted number of households (thousands)	3,070	2,490	21,350	1,280	2,370	670	25,670
Total number of households in sample (over 3 years)	2,350	1,520	13,680	820	1,550	1,770	17,810
Total number of persons in sample (over 3 years)	5,670	3,410	32,380	1,860	3,380	4,600	42,220
Total number of adults in sample (over 3 years)	4,370	2,740	24,940	1,490	2,700	3,380	32,510
Weighted average number of persons per household	2.3	2.3	2.4	2.3	2.2	2.7	2.4
Commodity or service	Percentage of total expenditure						
1 Food & non-alcoholic drinks	10	11	11	13	11	12	11
2 Alcoholic drinks, tobacco & narcotics	2	2	2	3	3	3	2
3 Clothing & footwear	4	4	5	5	5	7	5
4 Housing(net)[1], fuel & power	11	12	12	13	10	9	12
5 Household goods & services	6	7	6	6	6	7	6
6 Health	1	1	1	1	1	1	1
7 Transport	14	13	13	13	14	13	13
8 Communication	2	3	3	3	3	3	3
9 Recreation & culture	13	13	13	15	13	12	13
10 Education	2	2	2	1	1	1	1
11 Restaurants & hotels	8	8	8	7	8	9	8
12 Miscellaneous goods & services	8	8	8	7	7	8	8
1–12 All expenditure groups	82	84	83	85	83	85	83
13 Other expenditure items	18	16	17	15	17	15	17
Total expenditure	**100**	**100**	**100**	**100**	**100**	**100**	**100**

Note: The commodity and service categories are not comparable to those in publications before 2001–02.
Please see page xiii for symbols and conventions used in this report.
This table is based on a three year average.

1 Excluding mortgage interest payments, council tax and Northern Ireland rates.

ONS, Family Spending 2009,   © Crown copyright 2010

Table A37   **Detailed household expenditure by UK countries and Government Office Regions, 2007–2009**

based on weighted data and including children's expenditure

		North East	North West	Yorks & the Humber	East Midlands	West Midlands	East	London
Average weighted number of households (thousands)		1,220	3,040	2,140	1,970	2,140	2,260	3,030
Total number of households in sample (over 3 years)		730	1,780	1,500	1,260	1,500	1,580	1,470
Total number of persons in sample (over 3 years)		1,700	4,200	3,530	2,910	3,740	3,690	3,540
Total number of adults in sample (over 3 years)		1,330	3,200	2,680	2,250	2,840	2,860	2,670
Weighted average number of persons per household		2.4	2.4	2.3	2.3	2.5	2.3	2.5
Commodity or service		Average weekly household expenditure (£)						
1	**Food & non-alcoholic drinks**	**45.50**	**48.80**	**45.10**	**49.30**	**50.80**	**50.30**	**52.30**
1.1	Food	41.80	44.70	41.70	45.40	46.90	46.30	47.80
1.1.1	Bread, rice and cereals	4.70	4.70	4.40	4.70	5.00	4.60	5.00
1.1.2	Pasta products	0.30	0.40	0.40	0.40	0.30	0.30	0.40
1.1.3	Buns, cakes, biscuits etc.	2.90	3.00	2.80	3.10	3.00	3.20	2.70
1.1.4	Pastry (savoury)	0.70	0.60	0.60	0.70	0.60	0.70	0.60
1.1.5	Beef (fresh, chilled or frozen)	1.60	1.50	1.50	1.40	1.70	1.70	1.40
1.1.6	Pork (fresh, chilled or frozen)	0.50	0.60	0.50	0.70	0.80	0.70	0.60
1.1.7	Lamb (fresh, chilled or frozen)	0.40	0.70	0.50	0.50	0.90	0.60	0.90
1.1.8	Poultry (fresh, chilled or frozen)	1.60	1.90	1.60	1.70	2.10	1.90	2.20
1.1.9	Bacon and ham	0.80	1.10	0.90	0.90	1.00	0.90	0.60
1.1.10	Other meat and meat preparations	5.20	5.40	4.90	4.90	5.10	5.20	4.20
1.1.11	Fish and fish products	2.00	2.10	2.00	2.20	2.30	2.30	3.00
1.1.12	Milk	2.60	2.80	2.60	2.80	2.70	2.40	2.30
1.1.13	Cheese and curd	1.30	1.50	1.40	1.70	1.60	1.80	1.60
1.1.14	Eggs	0.50	0.60	0.50	0.60	0.50	0.60	0.70
1.1.15	Other milk products	1.60	1.70	1.60	1.90	1.70	2.00	1.90
1.1.16	Butter	0.40	0.30	0.30	0.30	0.30	0.30	0.30
1.1.17	Margarine, other vegetable fats and peanut butter	0.40	0.50	0.40	0.50	0.60	0.50	0.40
1.1.18	Cooking oils and fats	0.20	0.20	0.20	0.30	0.30	0.20	0.50
1.1.19	Fresh fruit	2.30	2.50	2.50	2.90	2.70	3.00	3.70
1.1.20	Other fresh, chilled or frozen fruits	0.20	0.30	0.30	0.30	0.30	0.30	0.40
1.1.21	Dried fruit and nuts	0.30	0.40	0.40	0.50	0.40	0.60	0.70
1.1.22	Preserved fruit and fruit based products	0.10	0.10	0.10	0.10	0.10	0.20	0.10
1.1.23	Fresh vegetables	3.10	3.20	3.30	3.70	3.70	3.90	4.80
1.1.24	Dried vegetables	0.00	0.00	0.00	0.00	0.00	0.00	0.10
1.1.25	Other preserved or processed vegetables	1.00	1.00	1.00	1.20	1.10	1.10	1.40
1.1.26	Potatoes	0.90	0.90	0.80	0.90	1.00	0.80	0.80
1.1.27	Other tubers and products of tuber vegetables	1.30	1.30	1.20	1.20	1.40	1.20	0.90
1.1.28	Sugar and sugar products	0.30	0.30	0.30	0.30	0.40	0.30	0.30
1.1.29	Jams, marmalades	0.20	0.30	0.30	0.30	0.40	0.30	0.30
1.1.30	Chocolate	1.30	1.50	1.40	1.60	1.50	1.50	1.30
1.1.31	Confectionery products	0.60	0.60	0.60	0.60	0.70	0.50	0.50
1.1.32	Edible ices and ice cream	0.40	0.40	0.40	0.40	0.50	0.50	0.50
1.1.33	Other food products	2.00	2.20	1.90	2.20	2.30	2.10	2.60
1.2	Non-alcoholic drinks	3.70	4.00	3.40	3.90	3.90	4.00	4.50
1.2.1	Coffee	0.60	0.60	0.60	0.60	0.60	0.60	0.50
1.2.2	Tea	0.40	0.40	0.40	0.50	0.50	0.40	0.40
1.2.3	Cocoa and powdered chocolate	0.10	0.10	0.10	0.10	0.10	0.10	0.10
1.2.4	Fruit and vegetable juices (inc. fruit squash)	0.90	1.10	0.90	1.10	1.00	1.20	1.40
1.2.5	Mineral or spring waters	0.20	0.20	0.10	0.20	0.20	0.20	0.40
1.2.6	Soft drinks (inc. fizzy and ready to drink fruit drinks)	1.60	1.70	1.40	1.50	1.60	1.50	1.70

Note: The commodity and service categories are not comparable to those in publications before 2001–02.
   The numbering system is sequential, it does not use actual COICOP codes.
   Please see page xiii for symbols and conventions used in this report.
   This table is based on a three year average.

ONS, Family Spending 2009, © Crown copyright 2010

Table A37   **Detailed household expenditure by UK countries and Government Office Regions, 2007–2009 (cont.)**

based on weighted data and including children's expenditure

	South East	South West	England	Wales	Scotland	Northern Ireland	United Kingdom
Average weighted number of households (thousands)	3,070	2,490	21,350	1,280	2,370	670	25,670
Total number of households in sample (over 3 years)	2,350	1,520	13,680	820	1,550	1,770	17,810
Total number of persons in sample (over 3 years)	5,670	3,410	32,380	1,860	3,380	4,600	42,220
Total number of adults in sample (over 3 years)	4,370	2,740	24,940	1,490	2,700	3,380	32,510
Weighted average number of persons per household	2.3	2.3	2.4	2.3	2.2	2.7	2.4

Commodity or service	Average weekly household expenditure (£)						
1 Food & non-alcoholic drinks	**54.00**	**52.60**	**50.30**	**50.10**	**48.60**	**57.30**	**50.30**
1.1 Food	49.70	48.70	46.30	46.30	44.30	52.50	46.30
1.1.1 Bread, rice and cereals	4.70	4.70	4.70	4.50	4.80	6.00	4.70
1.1.2 Pasta products	0.40	0.40	0.40	0.40	0.40	0.40	0.40
1.1.3 Buns, cakes, biscuits etc.	3.40	3.40	3.10	3.10	3.10	4.20	3.10
1.1.4 Pastry (savoury)	0.80	0.70	0.70	0.70	0.70	0.60	0.70
1.1.5 Beef (fresh, chilled or frozen)	1.60	1.70	1.60	1.80	1.70	3.10	1.60
1.1.6 Pork (fresh, chilled or frozen)	0.60	0.70	0.60	0.80	0.50	0.80	0.60
1.1.7 Lamb (fresh, chilled or frozen)	0.80	0.70	0.70	0.70	0.30	0.40	0.70
1.1.8 Poultry (fresh, chilled or frozen)	2.10	1.90	1.90	1.80	1.60	2.40	1.90
1.1.9 Bacon and ham	1.00	1.00	0.90	1.00	0.90	1.30	0.90
1.1.10 Other meat and meat preparations	5.40	5.20	5.00	5.50	5.80	6.20	5.20
1.1.11 Fish and fish products	2.50	2.30	2.30	2.10	2.00	1.70	2.30
1.1.12 Milk	2.50	2.70	2.60	2.80	2.50	2.90	2.60
1.1.13 Cheese and curd	2.00	2.00	1.70	1.60	1.50	1.40	1.70
1.1.14 Eggs	0.60	0.60	0.60	0.60	0.60	0.60	0.60
1.1.15 Other milk products	2.10	2.10	1.90	1.80	1.70	2.00	1.90
1.1.16 Butter	0.40	0.40	0.30	0.30	0.40	0.40	0.30
1.1.17 Margarine, other vegetable fats and peanut butter	0.50	0.50	0.50	0.50	0.40	0.50	0.50
1.1.18 Cooking oils and fats	0.30	0.30	0.30	0.30	0.20	0.20	0.30
1.1.19 Fresh fruit	3.30	3.30	3.00	2.90	2.70	3.00	3.00
1.1.20 Other fresh, chilled or frozen fruits	0.30	0.30	0.30	0.30	0.40	0.40	0.30
1.1.21 Dried fruit and nuts	0.60	0.60	0.50	0.50	0.40	0.40	0.50
1.1.22 Preserved fruit and fruit based products	0.10	0.20	0.10	0.10	0.10	0.10	0.10
1.1.23 Fresh vegetables	4.40	4.10	3.90	3.50	2.90	3.10	3.80
1.1.24 Dried vegetables	0.00	0.00	0.00	0.00	0.00	0.00	0.00
1.1.25 Other preserved or processed vegetables	1.30	1.20	1.20	1.10	1.10	1.30	1.20
1.1.26 Potatoes	0.90	0.90	0.90	0.90	0.80	1.40	0.90
1.1.27 Other tubers and products of tuber vegetables	1.30	1.30	1.20	1.30	1.50	1.60	1.30
1.1.28 Sugar and sugar products	0.30	0.30	0.30	0.30	0.30	0.20	0.30
1.1.29 Jams, marmalades	0.30	0.30	0.20	0.30	0.30	0.30	0.20
1.1.30 Chocolate	1.50	1.50	1.50	1.50	1.60	1.70	1.50
1.1.31 Confectionery products	0.60	0.50	0.60	0.60	0.60	0.70	0.60
1.1.32 Edible ices and ice cream	0.50	0.60	0.50	0.50	0.50	0.50	0.50
1.1.33 Other food products	2.50	2.30	2.30	2.20	2.20	2.50	2.30
1.2 Non-alcoholic drinks	4.40	3.90	4.00	3.80	4.30	4.90	4.10
1.2.1 Coffee	0.60	0.60	0.60	0.50	0.60	0.50	0.60
1.2.2 Tea	0.40	0.50	0.40	0.50	0.30	0.40	0.40
1.2.3 Cocoa and powdered chocolate	0.10	0.10	0.10	0.10	0.10	0.00	0.10
1.2.4 Fruit and vegetable juices	1.30	1.10	1.10	1.00	1.10	1.20	1.10
1.2.5 Mineral or spring waters	0.20	0.20	0.20	0.10	0.20	0.30	0.20
1.2.6 Soft drinks	1.70	1.30	1.60	1.60	2.00	2.40	1.60

Note: The commodity and service categories are not comparable to those in publications before 2001–02.

The numbering system is sequential, it does not use actual COICOP codes.

Please see page xiii for symbols and conventions used in this report.

This table is based on a three year average.

ONS, Family Spending 2009,   © Crown copyright 2010

Table A37   **Detailed household expenditure by UK countries and Government Office Regions, 2007–2009 (cont.)**

based on weighted data and including children's expenditure

			North East	North West	Yorks & the Humber	East Midlands	West Midlands	East	London
Commodity or service			Average weekly household expenditure (£)						
2	**Alcoholic drink, tobacco & narcotics**		**10.50**	**12.70**	**10.30**	**10.30**	**11.70**	**10.40**	**9.80**
2.1	Alcoholic drinks		6.20	7.40	5.90	6.10	6.50	6.70	6.00
	2.1.1	Spirits and liqueurs (brought home)	1.00	1.50	0.90	1.10	1.40	1.20	0.90
	2.1.2	Wines, fortified wines (brought home)	2.90	3.70	2.90	3.00	3.10	3.70	3.60
	2.1.3	Beer, lager, ciders and perry (brought home)	2.20	2.20	2.10	1.90	1.90	1.70	1.40
	2.1.4	Alcopops (brought home)	0.10	0.10	0.10	0.10	0.10	0.00	0.00
2.2	Tobacco and narcotics		4.30	5.30	4.40	4.20	5.20	3.60	3.80
	2.2.1	Cigarettes	3.90	4.70	3.80	3.60	4.40	3.00	3.50
	2.2.2	Cigars, other tobacco products and narcotics	0.50	0.60	0.50	0.70	0.80	0.60	0.30
3	**Clothing & footwear**		**20.50**	**22.20**	**17.60**	**18.70**	**22.80**	**21.10**	**25.70**
3.1	Clothing		16.60	17.60	14.40	15.00	18.20	17.20	20.40
	3.1.1	Men's outer garments	4.20	3.80	3.30	4.20	4.50	4.30	5.20
	3.1.2	Men's under garments	0.40	0.30	0.40	0.40	0.30	0.30	0.40
	3.1.3	Women's outer garments	7.70	7.80	6.60	6.20	8.10	8.10	9.50
	3.1.4	Women's under garments	1.00	1.00	0.90	0.90	1.30	1.00	1.00
	3.1.5	Boys' outer garments (5–15)	0.80	0.80	0.60	0.80	1.00	0.70	0.70
	3.1.6	Girls' outer garments (5–15)	0.70	1.30	0.90	0.80	0.90	0.80	0.90
	3.1.7	Infants' outer garments (under 5)	0.70	0.90	0.60	0.60	0.80	0.60	0.70
	3.1.8	Children's under garments (under 16)	0.30	0.50	0.20	0.30	0.30	0.30	0.40
	3.1.9	Accessories	0.60	0.70	0.60	0.60	0.70	0.70	0.80
	3.1.10	Haberdashery, clothing materials and clothing hire	0.10	0.30	0.20	0.10	0.30	0.10	0.20
	3.1.11	Dry cleaners, laundry and dyeing	0.10	0.20	0.20	0.20	0.20	0.30	0.60
3.2	Footwear		3.90	4.60	3.20	3.70	4.60	3.90	5.30
4	**Housing (net)[1], fuel & power**		**44.50**	**46.40**	**48.50**	**47.30**	**48.20**	**54.20**	**80.10**
4.1	Actual rentals for housing		29.10	27.50	28.10	26.00	27.30	28.50	68.10
	4.1.1	Gross rent	29.10	27.20	28.10	25.90	27.30	28.50	68.10
	4.1.2	*less* housing benefit, rebates & allowances rec'd	14.80	12.80	11.40	10.10	12.70	9.20	23.30
	4.1.3	Net rent[2]	14.40	14.40	16.70	15.80	14.60	19.30	44.80
	4.1.4	Second dwelling rent	0.00	0.30	0.10	0.10	0.00	0.00	0.00
4.2	Maintenance and repair of dwelling		5.90	5.50	6.30	6.40	7.30	8.20	8.10
4.3	Water supply and miscellaneous services relating to the dwelling		6.40	7.80	7.10	6.50	6.60	7.70	9.30
4.4	Electricity, gas and other fuels		17.70	18.50	18.40	18.60	19.70	19.10	18.00
	4.4.1	Electricity	8.80	8.60	8.80	8.90	9.30	9.50	8.60
	4.4.2	Gas	8.60	9.20	9.10	8.50	9.60	8.20	9.30
	4.4.3	Other fuels	0.30	0.70	0.50	1.20	0.80	1.40	0.00

Note: The commodity and service categories are not comparable to those in publications before 2001–02.
The numbering system is sequential, it does not use actual COICOP codes.
Please see page xiii for symbols and conventions used in this report.
This table is based on a three year average.

1 Excluding mortgage interest payments, council tax and Northern Ireland rates.

2 The figure included in total expenditure is net rent as opposed to gross rent.

ONS, Family Spending 2009, © Crown copyright 2010

Table A37   **Detailed household expenditure by UK countries and Government Office Regions, 2007–2009 (cont.)**

based on weighted data and including children's expenditure

Commodity or service		South East	South West	England	Wales	Scotland	Northern Ireland	United Kingdom
		Average weekly household expenditure (£)						
2	**Alcoholic drink, tobacco & narcotics**	**11.00**	**10.20**	**10.80**	**11.30**	**11.80**	**14.90**	**11.10**
2.1	Alcoholic drinks	7.20	6.50	6.60	6.40	6.40	6.40	6.50
2.1.1	Spirits and liqueurs (brought home)	1.20	1.20	1.20	1.30	1.70	1.60	1.30
2.1.2	Wines, fortified wines (brought home)	4.20	3.60	3.50	3.20	2.90	2.70	3.40
2.1.3	Beer, lager, ciders and perry (brought home)	1.80	1.60	1.80	1.80	1.70	1.90	1.80
2.1.4	Alcopops (brought home)	0.00	0.00	0.10	[0.00]	0.10	0.20	0.10
2.2	Tobacco and narcotics	3.80	3.80	4.30	4.90	5.40	8.50	4.50
2.2.1	Cigarettes	3.30	2.80	3.70	4.00	4.90	8.10	3.90
2.2.2	Cigars, other tobacco products and narcotics	0.50	1.00	0.60	0.90	0.60	0.40	0.60
3	**Clothing & footwear**	**20.80**	**19.70**	**21.20**	**19.00**	**21.80**	**34.70**	**21.50**
3.1	Clothing	17.10	16.00	17.10	15.40	18.10	27.80	17.40
3.1.1	Men's outer garments	4.40	3.70	4.20	3.60	4.50	6.80	4.30
3.1.2	Men's under garments	0.40	0.30	0.40	0.40	0.30	0.50	0.40
3.1.3	Women's outer garments	7.30	7.50	7.70	7.40	8.20	13.20	7.90
3.1.4	Women's under garments	1.20	1.30	1.10	0.80	1.10	1.30	1.10
3.1.5	Boys' outer garments (5–15)	0.60	0.50	0.70	0.50	0.70	1.30	0.70
3.1.6	Girls' outer garments (5–15)	0.90	0.90	0.90	1.00	0.90	1.70	1.00
3.1.7	Infants' outer garments (under 5)	0.60	0.50	0.70	0.50	0.60	1.10	0.70
3.1.8	Children's under garments (under 16)	0.30	0.30	0.30	0.30	0.30	0.50	0.30
3.1.9	Accessories	0.70	0.60	0.70	0.60	0.90	0.90	0.70
3.1.10	Haberdashery, clothing materials and clothing hire	0.30	0.20	0.20	0.10	0.30	0.20	0.20
3.1.11	Dry cleaners, laundry and dyeing	0.30	0.30	0.30	0.10	0.20	0.30	0.30
3.2	Footwear	3.80	3.60	4.10	3.50	3.70	6.90	4.10
4	**Housing (net)[1], fuel & power**	**58.10**	**58.20**	**55.40**	**50.30**	**45.80**	**45.90**	**54.00**
4.1	Actual rentals for housing	34.10	29.50	34.60	24.50	24.10	23.50	32.80
4.1.1	Gross rent	34.00	29.40	34.50	24.50	24.10	23.40	32.80
4.1.2	*less* housing benefit, rebates & allowances rec'd	10.90	10.00	13.10	9.40	10.40	9.80	12.50
4.1.3	Net rent[2]	23.10	19.40	21.50	15.20	13.70	13.60	20.20
4.1.4	Second dwelling rent	0.10	0.00	0.10	0.00	0.00	0.00	0.00
4.2	Maintenance and repair of dwelling	8.20	10.70	7.50	7.10	5.40	6.20	7.20
4.3	Water supply and miscellaneous services relating to the dwelling	7.70	8.60	7.70	7.60	6.80	0.40	7.40
4.4	Electricity, gas and other fuels	19.00	19.40	18.70	20.40	20.00	25.70	19.10
4.4.1	Electricity	9.40	9.90	9.10	9.70	9.80	10.10	9.20
4.4.2	Gas	8.90	7.00	8.70	8.10	8.70	1.90	8.50
4.4.3	Other fuels	0.70	2.50	0.90	2.50	1.40	13.80	1.40

Note: The commodity and service categories are not comparable to those in publications before 2001–02.
The numbering system is sequential, it does not use actual COICOP codes.
Please see page xiii for symbols and conventions used in this report.
This table is based on a three year average.

1 Excluding mortgage interest payments, council tax and Northern Ireland rates.

2 The figure included in total expenditure is net rent as opposed to gross rent.

ONS, Family Spending 2009, © Crown copyright 2010

Table A37 **Detailed household expenditure by UK countries and Government Office Regions, 2007–2009 (cont.)**

based on weighted data and including children's expenditure

Commodity or service	North East	North West	Yorks & the Humber	East Midlands	West Midlands	East	London
	\multicolumn{7}{}{Average weekly household expenditure (£)}						
5 **Household goods & services**	**28.20**	**26.30**	**27.80**	**25.80**	**29.40**	**34.10**	**32.90**
5.1 Furniture and furnishings, carpets and other floor coverings	17.40	15.10	14.40	12.70	16.60	18.90	18.90
5.1.1 Furniture and furnishings	14.30	11.80	11.20	9.30	13.10	15.00	14.70
5.1.2 Floor coverings	3.10	3.40	3.20	3.40	3.50	3.90	4.30
5.2 Household textiles	1.50	1.30	1.50	1.50	1.50	1.40	1.90
5.3 Household appliances	1.50	2.40	4.80	3.30	2.30	4.20	3.10
5.4 Glassware, tableware and household utensils	1.20	1.10	1.10	1.20	1.20	1.50	1.60
5.5 Tools and equipment for house and garden	1.60	1.90	1.80	2.30	2.30	2.80	1.90
5.6 Goods and services for routine household maintenance	5.10	4.40	4.20	4.90	5.50	5.40	5.50
5.6.1 Cleaning materials	2.00	2.00	2.00	2.30	2.40	2.40	2.20
5.6.2 Household goods and hardware	0.90	1.10	1.00	1.20	1.20	1.20	1.10
5.6.3 Domestic services, carpet cleaning and hire/repair of furniture/furnishings	2.20	1.40	1.20	1.40	1.90	1.80	2.20
6 **Health**	**3.90**	**4.40**	**3.90**	**6.10**	**4.60**	**6.30**	**7.30**
6.1 Medical products, appliances and equipment	2.60	3.40	2.70	3.40	2.90	3.70	3.80
6.1.1 Medicines, prescriptions, healthcare products and equipment	1.30	2.30	1.30	2.40	1.60	1.80	2.10
6.1.2 Spectacles, lenses, accessories and repairs	1.30	1.10	1.30	1.00	1.30	1.90	1.70
6.2 Hospital services	1.30	1.00	1.30	2.80	1.70	2.60	3.60
7 **Transport**	**49.00**	**55.20**	**51.30**	**63.30**	**61.50**	**67.10**	**60.80**
7.1 Purchase of vehicles	15.20	20.60	16.50	25.20	24.00	20.30	17.50
7.1.1 Purchase of new cars and vans	5.20	6.40	5.60	8.70	7.20	6.60	7.00
7.1.2 Purchase of second hand cars or vans	9.60	13.90	10.60	15.60	15.60	12.30	10.00
7.1.3 Purchase of motorcycles and other vehicles	[0.40]	0.40	0.30	0.90	1.20	1.50	0.60
7.2 Operation of personal transport	26.10	26.50	25.80	31.20	30.30	34.30	24.60
7.2.1 Spares and accessories	3.20	1.20	1.60	2.30	1.90	2.20	1.70
7.2.2 Petrol, diesel and other motor oils	17.10	18.40	17.40	20.40	20.80	21.90	14.60
7.2.3 Repairs and servicing	4.10	5.00	4.90	6.10	5.10	7.30	6.40
7.2.4 Other motoring costs	1.70	2.00	1.90	2.30	2.50	2.90	1.90
7.3 Transport services	7.70	8.10	8.90	6.90	7.20	12.40	18.70
7.3.1 Rail and tube fares	1.10	1.40	1.60	1.40	1.10	5.20	4.20
7.3.2 Bus and coach fares	1.80	1.60	1.80	1.10	1.60	0.90	1.20
7.3.3 Combined fares	[0.20]	0.10	0.40	0.20	0.10	1.40	7.10
7.3.4 Other travel and transport	4.70	4.90	5.10	4.30	4.30	5.00	6.30
8 **Communication**	**10.30**	**11.30**	**10.30**	**11.40**	**11.60**	**12.50**	**14.40**
8.1 Postal services	0.30	0.40	0.30	0.40	0.40	0.60	0.50
8.2 Telephone and telefax equipment	0.50	0.70	0.70	0.40	0.60	0.50	0.60
8.3 Telephone and telefax services	9.50	10.20	9.30	10.60	10.60	11.30	13.30

Note: The commodity and service categories are not comparable to those in publications before 2001–02.
The numbering system is sequential, it does not use actual COICOP codes.
Please see page xiii for symbols and conventions used in this report.
This table is based on a three year average.

ONS, Family Spending 2009, © Crown copyright 2010

Table A37   **Detailed household expenditure by UK countries and Government Office Regions, 2007–2009 (cont.)**

based on weighted data and including children's expenditure

Commodity or service	South East	South West	England	Wales	Scotland	Northern Ireland	United Kingdom
	Average weekly household expenditure (£)						
5 Household goods & services	**32.70**	**31.90**	**30.10**	**23.30**	**27.50**	**31.70**	**29.60**
5.1 Furniture and furnishings, carpets and other floor coverings	17.00	16.30	16.40	9.10	15.60	16.80	16.00
5.1.1 Furniture and furnishings	12.50	12.90	12.70	6.90	11.90	12.70	12.40
5.1.2 Floor coverings	4.40	3.40	3.70	2.10	3.70	4.10	3.60
5.2 Household textiles	1.80	1.40	1.50	1.30	1.70	1.90	1.60
5.3 Household appliances	3.70	4.50	3.40	4.50	2.30	3.50	3.30
5.4 Glassware, tableware and household utensils	1.80	1.70	1.40	1.40	1.30	1.40	1.40
5.5 Tools and equipment for house and garden	2.60	2.60	2.20	2.50	1.80	2.50	2.20
5.6 Goods and services for routine household maintenance	5.80	5.40	5.20	4.50	4.80	5.50	5.10
5.6.1 Cleaning materials	2.30	2.30	2.20	2.20	2.00	2.50	2.20
5.6.2 Household goods and hardware	1.30	1.30	1.20	1.10	1.00	1.20	1.10
5.6.3 Domestic services, carpet cleaning and hire/repair of furniture/furnishings	2.10	1.90	1.80	1.20	1.80	1.80	1.80
6 Health	**6.60**	**5.90**	**5.60**	**3.00**	**4.70**	**4.50**	**5.40**
6.1 Medical products, appliances and equipment	3.60	3.30	3.30	2.00	2.50	3.00	3.20
6.1.1 Medicines, prescriptions, healthcare products and equipment	1.90	1.60	1.90	1.20	1.40	2.10	1.80
6.1.2 Spectacles, lenses, accessories and repairs	1.70	1.70	1.40	0.80	1.10	0.90	1.40
6.2 Hospital services	3.00	2.60	2.30	1.00	2.20	1.50	2.20
7 Transport	**75.30**	**62.60**	**61.70**	**52.00**	**61.10**	**62.90**	**61.20**
7.1 Purchase of vehicles	27.50	20.60	21.20	15.60	24.10	17.60	21.10
7.1.1 Purchase of new cars and vans	8.30	5.50	6.80	6.10	8.70	7.50	7.00
7.1.2 Purchase of second hand cars or vans	18.50	14.30	13.70	9.10	14.70	9.80	13.40
7.1.3 Purchase of motorcycles and other vehicles	0.70	0.80	0.70	0.40	0.70	0.30	0.70
7.2 Operation of personal transport	36.40	34.40	30.10	29.70	27.30	35.90	30.00
7.2.1 Spares and accessories	2.90	2.50	2.10	2.10	1.80	2.90	2.10
7.2.2 Petrol, diesel and other motor oils	22.00	21.40	19.30	21.30	18.40	25.90	19.50
7.2.3 Repairs and servicing	8.50	7.70	6.30	4.70	5.30	5.40	6.10
7.2.4 Other motoring costs	3.00	2.70	2.40	1.60	1.80	1.70	2.20
7.3 Transport services	11.40	7.60	10.30	6.70	9.70	9.40	10.10
7.3.1 Rail and tube fares	4.30	2.00	2.70	0.90	2.00	0.70	2.50
7.3.2 Bus and coach fares	0.80	1.00	1.30	1.10	1.60	1.10	1.30
7.3.3 Combined fares	1.10	0.10	1.40	0.10	0.30	0.00	1.20
7.3.4 Other travel and transport	5.10	4.50	5.00	4.70	5.80	7.60	5.10
8 Communication	**12.40**	**11.90**	**12.00**	**10.00**	**11.00**	**14.30**	**11.80**
8.1 Postal services	0.60	0.70	0.50	0.30	0.50	0.40	0.50
8.2 Telephone and telefax equipment	0.40	0.40	0.50	0.70	0.60	0.80	0.60
8.3 Telephone and telefax services	11.40	10.80	10.90	9.00	10.00	13.10	10.80

Note: The commodity and service categories are not comparable to those in publications before 2001–02.
The numbering system is sequential, it does not use actual COICOP codes.
Please see page xiii for symbols and conventions used in this report.
This table is based on a three year average.

ONS, Family Spending 2009, © Crown copyright 2010

Table A37 **Detailed household expenditure by UK countries and Government Office Regions, 2007–2009 (cont.)**

based on weighted data and including children's expenditure

Commodity or service	North East	North West	Yorks & the Humber	East Midlands	West Midlands	East	London
	Average weekly household expenditure (£)						
9 Recreation & culture	**51.20**	**55.30**	**53.70**	**52.30**	**59.20**	**61.80**	**58.10**
9.1 Audio-visual, photographic and information processing equipment	7.30	6.60	7.00	5.40	8.50	7.10	6.10
9.1.1 Audio equipment and accessories, CD players	1.00	1.20	1.20	1.20	1.30	2.20	1.30
9.1.2 TV, video and computers	5.90	4.40	5.10	3.60	5.50	4.00	3.50
9.1.3 Photographic, cine and optical equipment	0.40	0.90	0.60	0.70	1.70	0.80	1.20
9.2 Other major durables for recreation and culture	0.30	1.60	2.10	2.70	3.10	1.90	6.00
9.3 Other recreational items and equipment, gardens and pets	8.90	10.30	9.70	10.20	11.10	11.70	8.00
9.3.1 Games, toys and hobbies	2.00	2.00	1.60	2.10	2.00	2.50	1.50
9.3.2 Computer software and games	1.90	1.60	1.40	1.70	1.70	1.50	1.50
9.3.3 Equipment for sport, camping and open-air recreation	0.90	0.90	1.50	0.70	0.80	1.20	0.80
9.3.4 Horticultural goods, garden equipment and plants	1.70	2.80	1.90	2.70	2.70	2.70	2.30
9.3.5 Pets and pet food	2.40	3.00	3.40	3.20	3.90	3.80	1.90
9.4 Recreational and cultural services	16.60	17.10	15.40	16.00	17.10	19.50	18.30
9.4.1 Sports admissions, subscriptions, leisure class fees and equipment hire	3.80	4.70	4.20	3.90	4.40	6.70	6.50
9.4.2 Cinema, theatre and museums etc.	1.80	1.90	1.40	2.00	1.60	2.40	2.50
9.4.3 TV, video, satellite rental, cable subscriptions, TV licences and the Internet	5.60	6.10	5.60	5.80	5.50	6.30	5.50
9.4.4 Miscellaneous entertainments	0.80	1.20	1.00	1.20	1.00	1.00	1.10
9.4.5 Development of film, deposit for film development, passport photos, holiday and school photos	0.20	0.20	0.30	0.20	0.40	0.30	0.30
9.4.6 Gambling payments	4.50	3.00	2.90	2.90	4.10	2.70	2.30
9.5 Newspapers, books and stationery	5.30	5.90	5.30	5.80	6.30	6.00	5.80
9.5.1 Books	1.30	1.30	1.20	1.20	1.40	1.30	1.70
9.5.2 Diaries, address books, cards etc.	1.50	1.80	1.70	1.80	2.10	1.90	1.70
9.5.3 Newspapers	1.70	1.80	1.50	1.80	1.80	1.90	1.50
9.5.4 Magazines and periodicals	0.80	1.00	0.90	1.00	1.00	0.90	0.90
9.6 Package holidays	12.60	13.80	14.20	12.10	13.10	15.70	13.90
9.6.1 Package holidays – UK	0.60	0.90	1.10	0.80	1.20	1.50	0.50
9.6.2 Package holidays – abroad	12.00	12.90	13.10	11.30	11.90	14.10	13.40
10 Education	**4.90**	**4.30**	**3.60**	**4.10**	**4.90**	**5.00**	**15.30**
10.1 Education fees	4.60	4.00	3.10	3.90	4.60	4.60	14.80
10.2 Payments for school trips, other ad-hoc expenditure	0.30	0.30	0.50	0.20	0.30	0.40	0.50
11 Restaurants & hotels	**33.10**	**37.70**	**34.40**	**34.80**	**36.40**	**36.70**	**47.40**
11.1 Catering services	28.20	30.90	29.30	28.40	29.60	29.40	40.00
11.1.1 Restaurant and café meals	9.90	12.10	11.90	12.20	11.60	13.10	16.50
11.1.2 Alcoholic drinks (away from home)	8.00	8.40	7.30	7.10	7.20	6.80	8.40
11.1.3 Take away meals eaten at home	4.10	4.00	3.80	3.50	4.10	3.60	4.30
11.1.4 Other take-away and snack food	3.90	4.10	4.10	3.40	3.80	4.00	6.30
11.1.5 Contract catering (food) and canteens	2.20	2.30	2.20	2.10	2.90	1.90	4.50
11.2 Accommodation services	5.00	6.80	5.10	6.50	6.90	7.30	7.40
11.2.1 Holiday in the UK	2.10	3.00	2.70	2.90	3.40	3.10	1.90
11.2.2 Holiday abroad	2.80	3.80	2.50	3.50	3.40	4.20	5.40
11.2.3 Room hire	0.00	0.00	0.00	0.00	0.10	0.00	0.10

Note: The commodity and service categories are not comparable to those in publications before 2001–02.
The numbering system is sequential, it does not use actual COICOP codes.
Please see page xiii for symbols and conventions used in this report.
This table is based on a three year average.

ONS, Family Spending 2009, © Crown copyright 2010

Table A37   **Detailed household expenditure by UK countries and Government Office Regions, 2007–2009 (cont.)**

based on weighted data and including children's expenditure

Commodity or service	South East	South West	England	Wales	Scotland	Northern Ireland	United Kingdom
	Average weekly household expenditure (£)						
9 Recreation & culture	**66.10**	**63.20**	**58.50**	**57.80**	**58.30**	**58.40**	**58.40**
9.1 Audio-visual, photographic and information processing equipment	8.50	9.10	7.30	7.40	6.80	8.10	7.30
9.1.1 Audio equipment and accessories, CD players	1.70	1.60	1.40	1.20	1.40	1.50	1.40
9.1.2 TV, video and computers	6.10	7.10	5.00	5.00	5.10	5.90	5.00
9.1.3 Photographic, cine and optical equipment	0.70	0.40	0.90	1.30	0.30	0.70	0.80
9.2 Other major durables for recreation and culture	2.70	3.00	2.80	7.50	2.20	2.10	3.00
9.3 Other recreational items and equipment, gardens and pets	12.30	11.90	10.60	10.00	10.80	11.30	10.60
9.3.1 Games, toys and hobbies	2.10	2.20	2.00	1.70	1.90	2.80	2.00
9.3.2 Computer software and games	1.90	1.40	1.60	0.80	2.20	1.80	1.60
9.3.3 Equipment for sport, camping and open-air recreation	1.10	0.80	1.00	1.00	0.60	1.00	0.90
9.3.4 Horticultural goods, garden equipment and plants	3.10	3.10	2.60	2.40	3.00	2.50	2.60
9.3.5 Pets and pet food	4.10	4.40	3.40	4.10	3.10	3.20	3.40
9.4 Recreational and cultural services	21.60	17.20	17.90	14.40	18.20	19.10	17.70
9.4.1 Sports admissions, subscriptions, leisure class fees and equipment hire	5.40	5.40	5.20	3.30	4.70	5.30	5.00
9.4.2 Cinema, theatre and museums etc.	2.30	2.20	2.10	2.00	2.00	2.40	2.00
9.4.3 TV, video, satellite rental, cable subscriptions, TV licences and the Internet	6.20	5.30	5.80	5.50	6.10	5.80	5.80
9.4.4 Miscellaneous entertainments	1.10	1.50	1.10	0.80	1.10	1.50	1.10
9.4.5 Development of film, deposit for film development, passport photos, holiday and school photos	0.40	0.30	0.30	0.20	0.30	0.30	0.30
9.4.6 Gambling payments	6.20	2.40	3.40	2.70	4.00	3.70	3.40
9.5 Newspapers, books and stationery	6.80	6.80	6.10	5.80	6.60	6.80	6.10
9.5.1 Books	1.80	1.60	1.50	1.20	1.30	1.30	1.40
9.5.2 Diaries, address books, cards etc.	2.20	2.10	1.90	1.70	1.90	1.90	1.90
9.5.3 Newspapers	1.80	2.00	1.80	2.00	2.40	2.60	1.90
9.5.4 Magazines and periodicals	1.00	1.00	1.00	0.90	0.90	1.00	1.00
9.6 Package holidays	14.20	15.30	13.90	12.50	13.70	11.00	13.80
9.6.1 Package holidays – UK	1.10	1.40	1.00	1.00	0.70	0.60	1.00
9.6.2 Package holidays – abroad	13.10	13.90	12.90	11.50	13.10	10.40	12.80
10 Education	**9.40**	**8.10**	**7.10**	**5.20**	**4.30**	**4.30**	**6.70**
10.1 Education fees	9.10	7.80	6.70	4.90	4.10	3.80	6.30
10.2 Payments for school trips, other ad-hoc expenditure	0.30	0.30	0.30	0.30	0.20	0.60	0.30
11 Restaurants & hotels	**41.90**	**36.20**	**38.40**	**28.80**	**34.80**	**46.00**	**37.80**
11.1 Catering services	32.60	28.60	31.30	26.30	29.60	41.30	31.20
11.1.1 Restaurant and café meals	15.20	13.20	13.20	10.50	12.50	15.90	13.10
11.1.2 Alcoholic drinks (away from home)	7.10	6.90	7.50	7.00	7.10	9.10	7.50
11.1.3 Take away meals eaten at home	3.80	3.20	3.80	3.60	4.10	7.00	3.90
11.1.4 Other take-away and snack food	4.00	3.20	4.20	3.50	4.10	6.30	4.20
11.1.5 Contract catering (food) and canteens	2.50	2.10	2.60	1.70	1.80	3.10	2.50
11.2 Accommodation services	9.30	7.60	7.10	2.50	5.20	4.70	6.60
11.2.1 Holiday in the UK	3.70	3.20	2.90	1.40	2.20	1.20	2.70
11.2.2 Holiday abroad	5.50	4.40	4.10	1.10	3.00	3.50	3.80
11.2.3 Room hire	0.00	0.00	0.00	0.00	0.00	0.00	0.00

Note: The commodity and service categories are not comparable to those in publications before 2001–02.
The numbering system is sequential, it does not use actual COICOP codes.
Please see page xiii for symbols and conventions used in this report.
This table is based on a three year average.

ONS, *Family Spending 2009,* © Crown copyright 2010

Table A37   Detailed household expenditure by UK countries and Government Office Regions,
2007–2009 (cont.)

based on weighted data and including children's expenditure

	North East	North West	Yorks & the Humber	East Midlands	West Midlands	East	London
Commodity or service	Average weekly household expenditure (£)						
12 Miscellaneous goods & services	**28.00**	**34.20**	**28.90**	**32.20**	**35.30**	**38.90**	**40.60**
12.1 Personal care	8.90	9.80	9.50	8.70	10.10	10.50	10.50
12.1.1 Hairdressing, beauty treatment	2.50	3.10	3.30	2.50	3.10	3.30	3.10
12.1.2 Toilet paper	0.60	0.70	0.70	0.80	0.80	0.80	0.70
12.1.3 Toiletries and soap	1.70	2.00	1.80	1.90	2.00	2.10	2.30
12.1.4 Baby toiletries and accessories (disposable)	0.50	0.70	0.60	0.60	0.70	0.70	0.70
12.1.5 Hair products, cosmetics and electrical personal appliances	3.50	3.20	3.00	3.00	3.60	3.60	3.60
12.2 Personal effects	2.40	2.80	2.20	2.80	3.10	3.00	4.20
12.3 Social protection	2.80	3.50	2.00	2.40	3.10	3.80	4.20
12.4 Insurance	11.40	14.90	12.90	14.10	15.30	16.00	16.10
12.4.1 Household insurances - structural, contents and appliances	4.40	4.90	4.70	4.90	5.00	5.30	5.30
12.4.2 Medical insurance premiums	0.60	1.20	0.90	1.00	1.60	1.90	2.40
12.4.3 Vehicle insurance including boat insurance	6.30	8.40	7.20	7.90	8.60	8.80	8.20
12.4.4 Non-package holiday, other travel insurance	0.10	0.40	0.10	0.30	0.10	0.10	0.20
12.5 Other services n.e.c	2.40	3.30	2.40	4.10	3.60	5.70	5.60
12.5.1 Moving house	1.10	1.60	1.10	2.70	1.70	2.80	3.30
12.5.2 Bank, building society, post office, credit card charges	0.40	0.40	0.40	0.40	0.50	0.40	0.50
12.5.3 Other services and professional fees	0.90	1.20	0.90	1.00	1.40	2.40	1.70
1-12 All expenditure groups	**329.60**	**358.80**	**335.30**	**355.60**	**376.50**	**398.40**	**444.70**
13 Other expenditure items	**57.60**	**71.30**	**65.40**	**67.50**	**69.30**	**89.30**	**107.60**
13.1 Housing: mortgage interest payments council tax etc.	43.60	47.70	44.20	48.10	50.90	62.20	71.00
13.2 Licences, fines and transfers	2.30	2.90	3.10	3.30	3.20	3.60	3.10
13.3 Holiday spending	4.50	10.90	9.20	7.80	5.90	9.60	18.70
13.4 Money transfers and credit	7.20	9.90	8.90	8.20	9.30	14.00	14.70
13.4.1 Money, cash gifts given to children	0.10	0.10	0.10	0.10	0.10	0.10	0.10
13.4.2 Cash gifts and donations	6.20	8.60	7.50	6.70	7.40	12.30	12.30
13.4.3 Club instalment payments (child) and interest on credit cards	1.00	1.20	1.30	1.40	1.80	1.60	2.40
Total expenditure	**387.20**	**430.20**	**400.70**	**423.00**	**445.80**	**487.70**	**552.30**
14 Other items recorded							
14.1 Life assurance, contributions to pension funds	16.30	18.20	17.20	18.20	18.90	22.50	22.20
14.2 Other insurance inc. friendly societies	0.90	1.10	1.40	1.10	1.20	1.60	0.90
14.3 Income tax, payments *less* refunds	63.10	79.70	66.40	82.80	81.10	104.10	160.60
14.4 National insurance contributions	24.20	25.90	23.40	25.80	26.20	30.50	35.20
14.5 Purchase or alteration of dwellings, mortgages	32.90	36.50	45.10	36.60	49.40	55.90	48.70
14.6 Savings and investments	3.90	5.70	4.60	4.40	5.30	7.10	9.10
14.7 Pay off loan to clear other debt	2.30	2.00	2.20	2.30	2.70	2.10	2.50
14.8 Windfall receipts from gambling etc[3]	2.50	1.80	1.90	1.40	1.70	1.40	1.70

Note: The commodity and service categories are not comparable to those in publications before 2001–02.
The numbering system is sequential, it does not use actual COICOP codes.
Please see page xiii for symbols and conventions used in this report.
This table is based on a three year average.

3 Expressed as an income figure as opposed to an expenditure figure.

ONS, Family Spending 2009,   © Crown copyright 2010

Table A37   **Detailed household expenditure by UK countries and Government Office Regions, 2007–2009 (cont.)**

based on weighted data and including children's expenditure

Commodity or service	South East	South West	England	Wales	Scotland	Northern Ireland	United Kingdom
			Average weekly household expenditure (£)				
12 Miscellaneous goods & services	**41.30**	**36.80**	**36.00**	**27.80**	**32.60**	**38.60**	**35.30**
12.1 Personal care	11.90	10.10	10.10	8.20	9.90	12.80	10.10
12.1.1 Hairdressing, beauty treatment	4.10	3.20	3.20	2.30	3.20	4.10	3.20
12.1.2 Toilet paper	0.80	0.80	0.80	0.80	0.70	0.90	0.80
12.1.3 Toiletries and soap	2.40	2.20	2.10	1.90	1.90	2.60	2.10
12.1.4 Baby toiletries and accessories (disposable)	0.70	0.50	0.70	0.50	0.50	0.90	0.60
12.1.5 Hair products, cosmetics and electrical personal appliances	3.90	3.50	3.40	2.70	3.50	4.20	3.40
12.2 Personal effects	4.40	3.90	3.30	2.00	3.60	2.80	3.30
12.3 Social protection	2.90	3.30	3.20	2.70	3.10	3.40	3.20
12.4 Insurance	16.60	14.70	15.00	12.70	12.00	15.10	14.60
12.4.1 Household insurances – structural, contents and appliances	5.30	5.10	5.00	4.80	4.80	4.20	5.00
12.4.2 Medical insurance premiums	2.60	1.60	1.60	0.70	1.00	1.00	1.50
12.4.3 Vehicle insurance including boat insurance	8.70	7.90	8.10	7.10	6.10	9.70	7.90
12.4.4 Non-package holiday, other travel insurance	0.10	0.20	0.20	0.10	0.20	0.10	0.20
12.5 Other services n.e.c	5.40	4.80	4.30	2.20	4.00	4.50	4.20
12.5.1 Moving house	3.70	2.90	2.50	1.00	1.90	1.10	2.30
12.5.2 Bank, building society, post office, credit card charges	0.50	0.60	0.50	0.40	0.50	0.40	0.50
12.5.3 Other services and professional fees	1.20	1.40	1.40	0.90	1.70	2.90	1.40
1-12 All expenditure groups	**429.80**	**397.30**	**387.10**	**338.50**	**362.30**	**413.60**	**383.10**
13 Other expenditure items	**94.10**	**76.80**	**80.30**	**57.60**	**76.40**	**72.30**	**78.60**
13.1 Housing: mortgage interest payments, council tax etc.	67.20	54.40	55.90	40.40	53.10	39.60	54.40
13.2 Licences, fines and transfers	3.50	3.80	3.30	3.00	2.80	3.60	3.20
13.3 Holiday spending	11.10	8.30	10.30	6.60	8.70	13.90	10.00
13.4 Money transfers and credit	12.20	10.20	10.90	7.60	11.90	15.20	10.90
13.4.1 Money, cash gifts given to children	0.10	0.10	0.10	0.10	0.10	0.20	0.10
13.4.2 Cash gifts and donations	9.90	8.30	9.10	6.10	10.30	14.20	9.20
13.4.3 Club instalment payments (child) and interest on credit cards	2.20	1.80	1.70	1.40	1.50	0.80	1.60
Total expenditure	**523.90**	**474.10**	**467.50**	**396.10**	**438.70**	**485.80**	**461.70**
14 Other items recorded							
14.1 Life assurance, contributions to pension funds	23.80	21.30	20.20	17.60	21.40	17.00	20.10
14.2 Other insurance inc. friendly societies	1.70	1.50	1.30	0.70	1.30	0.80	1.30
14.3 Income tax, payments *less* refunds	117.90	81.00	97.40	70.50	88.20	73.80	94.60
14.4 National insurance contributions	31.70	24.60	28.00	23.40	28.10	24.80	27.70
14.5 Purchase or alteration of dwellings, mortgages	66.10	41.80	47.00	33.70	38.70	35.00	45.20
14.6 Savings and investments	8.50	9.40	6.80	2.50	6.50	3.40	6.50
14.7 Pay off loan to clear other debt	3.80	2.50	2.50	1.50	2.10	0.60	2.40
14.8 Windfall receipts from gambling etc[3]	3.90	1.00	1.90	1.50	2.00	3.00	1.90

Note: The commodity and service categories are not comparable to those in publications before 2001–02.
The numbering system is sequential, it does not use actual COICOP codes.
Please see page xiii for symbols and conventions used in this report.
This table is based on a three year average.

3 Expressed as an income figure as opposed to an expenditure figure.

ONS, Family Spending 2009,   © Crown copyright 2010

Table A38   **Household expenditure by urban/rural areas (GB)[1], 2007–2009**

based on weighted data and including children's expenditure

	Urban	Rural
Average number of weighted households (thousands)	19,540	5,470
Total number of households in sample (over 3 years)	12,340	3,700
Total number of persons in sample (over 3 years)	29,070	8,550
Total number of adults in sample (over 3 years)	22,340	6,790
Weighted average number of persons per household	2.4	2.3

Commodity or service		Average weekly household expenditure (£)	
1	Food & non-alcoholic drinks	49.20	53.60
2	Alcoholic drinks, tobacco & narcotics	10.70	11.90
3	Clothing & footwear	21.20	20.90
4	Housing (net)[2], fuel & power	54.90	52.00
5	Household goods & services	28.30	33.90
6	Health	5.30	5.90
7	Transport	57.00	75.70
8	Communication	11.80	11.60
9	Recreation & culture	56.40	65.80
10	Education	6.50	7.40
11	Restaurants & hotels	37.10	39.30
12	Miscellaneous goods & services	34.40	38.30
1–12	All expenditure groups	372.80	416.30
13	Other expenditure items	77.40	83.70
Total expenditure		**450.20**	**500.00**

Average weekly expenditure per person (£)	Urban	Rural
Total expenditure	**191.20**	**217.00**

Note: The commodity and service categories are not comparable to those in publications before 2001–02.
Please see page xiii for symbols and conventions used in this report.
This table is based on a three year average.

1 Combined urban/rural classification for England & Wales and Scotland – see definitions in Appendix B.

2 Excludes mortgage interest payments, council tax.

ONS, Family Spending 2009, © Crown copyright 2010

Table A.39   Government Office Regions of the United Kingdom

Orkney Islands

Shetland Islands

SCOTLAND

ENGLAND

—— GOR boundary

NORTHERN IRELAND

NORTH EAST

NORTH WEST

YORKSHIRE AND THE HUMBER

EAST MIDLANDS

WEST MIDLANDS

WALES

EAST OF ENGLAND

LONDON

SOUTH EAST

SOUTH WEST

Table A40 Income and source of income by household composition, 2009

based on weighted data

Composition of household	Weighted number of households (000s)	Number of households in the sample (Number)	Disposable (£)	Gross (£)	Wages and salaries	Self employment	Investments	Annuities and pensions¹	Social security benefits²	Other sources
			Weekly household income		Source of income — Percentage of gross weekly household income					
All households	**25,980**	**5,830**	**558**	**683**	**66**	**8**	**3**	**8**	**14**	**1**
Composition of household										
One adult	7,510	1,600	285	350	50	7	3	14	25	1
Retired households mainly dependent on state pensions³	770	150	162	163	-	-	1	5	94	[0]
Other retired households	2,750	580	248	267	-	-	7	39	54	[1]
Non-retired households	4,000	870	335	443	74	11	2	4	8	1
One adult, one child	650	160	265	298	52	[3]	0	[0]	37	7
One adult, two or more children	640	180	345	375	42	[2]	0	[0]	49	6
One man and one woman	8,000	1,880	606	735	61	8	4	13	14	1
Retired households mainly dependent on state pensions³	390	110	271	273	[0]	[0]	1	8	91	-
Other retired households	2,300	590	454	495	11	[1]	7	39	43	0
Non-retired households	5,310	1,180	696	872	74	10	4	7	5	1
Two men or two women	590	110	518	639	74	[2]	4	4	12	3
Two men or two women with children	160	40	469	535	64	[6]	[0]	[0]	26	[3]
One man one woman, one child	2,090	460	737	939	85	6	2	1	6	0
One man one woman, two children	2,080	490	813	1,004	76	14	2	[0]	8	0
One man one woman, three children	660	160	693	858	74	10	1	[0]	15	1
Two adults, four or more children	160	40	626	711	54	[9]	[0]	[1]	33	[3]
Three adults	1,660	340	782	955	72	7	3	8	10	1
Three adults, one or more children	860	180	879	1,072	72	14	1	2	9	2
Four or more adults	660	130	994	1,210	76	9	1	4	7	3
Four or more adults, One or more children	270	60	919	1,118	73	[6]	[4]	[1]	15	2

Note: Please see page xiii for symbols and conventions used in this report.

1 Other than social security benefits.

2 Excluding housing benefit and council tax benefit (rates rebate in Northern Ireland) – see definitions in Appendix B.

3 Mainly dependent on state pension and not economically active – see defintions in Appendix B.

ONS, Family Spending 2009, © *Crown copyright 2010*

Table A41   **Income and source of income by age of household reference person, 2009**

based on weighted data

Age of head of household	Weighted number of house-holds	Number of house-holds in the sample	Weekly household income		Source of income					
			Disposable	Gross	Wages and salaries	Self employment	Investments	Annuities and pensions[1]	Social security benefits[2]	Other sources
	(000s)	Number	£	£	Percentage of gross weekly household income					
Less than 30	2,770	510	470	575	83	4	0	[0]	9	4
30 to 49	9,670	2,110	690	873	79	11	2	0	7	1
50 to 64	6,740	1,640	602	744	68	9	4	9	9	1
65 to 74	3,310	820	423	464	19	4	5	30	41	1
75 or over	3,500	730	307	331	7	[1]	5	32	54	[0]

Please see page xiii for symbols and conventions used in this report.

1 Other than social security benefits.

2 Excluding housing benefit and council tax benefit (rates rebate in Northern Ireland) – see defintions in Appendix B.

ONS, Family Spending 2009, © Crown copyright 2010

Table A42   **Income and source of income by gross income quintile group, 2009**

based on weighted data

Gross income quintile group	Weighted number of house- holds	Number of house- holds in the sample	Weekly household income		Source of income					
			Disposable	Gross	Wages and salaries	Self employment	Investments	Annuities and pensions[1]	Social security benefits[2]	Other sources
	(000s)	Number	£	£	Percentage of gross weekly household income					
Lowest twenty per cent	5,200	1,140	150	153	8	2	2	9	77	2
Second quintile group	5,200	1,220	295	317	28	4	2	17	46	3
Third quintile group	5,190	1,210	453	523	55	6	2	13	21	2
Fourth quintile group	5,200	1,140	660	801	74	7	2	8	8	1
Highest twenty per cent	5,200	1,120	1,233	1,619	79	11	3	4	2	0

Please see page xiii for symbols and conventions used in this report.

1 Other than social security benefits.

2 Excluding housing benefit and council tax benefit (rates rebate in Northern Ireland) – see defintions in Appendix B.

ONS, Family Spending 2009,   © Crown copyright 2010

Table A43   Income and source of income by household tenure, 2009

based on weighted data

Tenure of dwelling	Weighted number of house-holds	Number of house-holds in the sample	Weekly household income		Source of income					
			Disposable	Gross	Wages and salaries	Self employment	Investments	Annuities and pensions[1]	Social security benefits[2]	Other sources
	(000s)	Number	£	£	Percentage of gross weekly household income					
Owners										
Owned outright	8,180	1,980	498	598	42	7	6	21	22	1
Buying with a mortgage[3]	9,530	2,120	778	978	80	10	2	2	5	1
All	17,720	4,100	649	803	67	9	3	9	11	1
Social rented from										
Council[4]	2,380	540	284	312	46	3	0	3	47	1
Registered social landlord[5]	2,180	450	281	310	44	[2]	0	5	47	2
All	4,550	990	283	311	45	3	0	4	47	1
Private rented[6]	360	80	415	491	68	3	3	5	17	4
Rent free	2,600	530	466	569	74	[8]	1	1	14	[2]
Rent paid, unfurnished[7]	750	140	482	589	83	[2]	1	[0]	6	7
Rent paid, furnished	3,710	740	464	565	76	6	1	1	12	3
All										

Please see page xiii for symbols and conventions used in this report.

1 Other than social security benefits.

2 Excluding housing benefit and council tax benefit (rates rebate in Northern Ireland) – see defintions in Appendix B.

3 Including shared owners (who own part of the equity and pay mortgage, part rent).

4 "Council" includes local authorities, new towns, and scottish homes, but see note 5 below.

5 Formerly housing association.

6 All tenants whose accomodation goes with the job of someone in the household are allocated to "rented privately", even if the landlord is a local authority, housing association, or housing action trust, or if the accomodation is rent free. Squatters are also included in this category.

7 'Unfurnished' includes the answers: 'partly furnished'.

ONS, Family Spending 2009, © Crown copyright 2010

Table A44   **Income and source of income by UK Countries and Government Office Regions, 2007–2009**

based on weighted data

Government Office Regions	Weighted number of of house-holds	Total number of house-holds	Weekly household income		Source of income					
			Disposable	Gross	Wages and salaries	Self employment	Investments	Annuities and pensions[1]	Social security benefits[2]	Other sources
	(000s)	Number	£	£	Percentage of gross weekly household income					
United Kingdom	25,670	17,810	558	685	67	9	3	7	13	1
North East	1,220	730	471	561	66	8	2	6	17	1
North West	3,040	1,780	507	616	66	7	2	8	16	1
Yorkshire and the Humber	2,140	1,500	471	565	67	7	2	7	16	1
East Midlands	1,970	1,260	511	625	66	7	4	7	14	1
West Midlands	2,140	1,500	523	634	66	8	3	7	15	1
East	2,260	1,580	592	732	70	9	3	7	11	1
London	3,030	1,470	738	940	71	9	6	5	8	1
South East	3,070	2,350	640	797	67	11	3	8	10	1
South West	2,490	1,520	539	648	60	10	4	10	15	1
England	21,350	13,680	568	698	67	9	4	7	13	1
Wales	1,280	820	488	585	63	9	3	8	17	1
Scotland	2,370	1,550	521	640	69	7	3	8	13	1
Northern Ireland	670	1,770	522	627	65	10	2	6	16	1

Please see page xiii for symbols and conventions used in this report.

This table is based on a three year average.

1 Other than social security benefits.

2 Excluding housing benefit and council tax benefit (rates rebate in Northern Ireland) – see defintions in Appendix B.

ONS, Family Spending 2009,   © Crown copyright 2010

Table A45   Income and source of income by GB urban/rural area, 2007–2009

based on weighted data

	Weighted number of house-holds	Total number of house-holds	Weekly household income		Source of income					
			Disposable	Gross	Wages and salaries	Self employment	Investments	Annuities and pensions[1]	Social security benefits[2]	Other sources
GB urban rural areas	(000s)	Number	£	£	Percentage of gross weekly household income					
Urban	19,540	12,340	546	671	68	8	3	7	13	1
Rural	5,470	3,700	605	743	62	11	5	9	12	1

Please see page xiii for symbols and conventions used in this report.

This table is based on a three year average.

1 Other than social security benefits.

2 Excluding housing benefit and council tax benefit (rates rebate in Northern Ireland) – see definitions in Appendix B.

ONS, Family Spending 2009,   © Crown copyright 2010

Table A46   **Income and source of income by socio-economic classification, 2009**

based on weighted data

NS-SEC Group[3]	Weighted number of house-holds (000s)	Number of house-holds in the sample Number	Weekly household income Disposable £	Gross £	Wages and salaries	Self employment	Investments	Annuities and pensions[1]	Social security benefits[2]	Other sources
					Percentage of gross weekly household income					
Large employers/higher managerial	1,200	260	1,174	1,647	87	8	2	1	2	0
Higher professional	1,700	370	1,032	1,341	76	15	3	3	2	0
Lower managerial and professional	4,900	1,050	755	965	87	4	2	2	4	1
Intermediate	1,520	360	543	664	80	4	1	5	9	1
Small employers	1,460	340	678	748	22	61	3	4	9	1
Lower supervisory	1,740	370	596	738	89	1	1	2	6	1
Semi-routine	1,990	450	444	526	78	[1]	1	4	15	1
Routine	1,470	330	469	560	82	[0]	1	3	13	1
Long-term unemployed[4]	510	120	202	204	[10]	[1]	[0]	[1]	85	[3]
Students	470	90	377	437	62	[8]	1	-	8	22
Occupation not stated[5]	9,000	2,100	325	352	12	1	6	30	50	1

Note: Please see page xiii for symbols and conventions used in this report.

1 Other than social security benefits.

2 Excluding housing benefit and council tax benefit (rates rebate in Northern Ireland) – see definitions in Appendix B.

3 National Statistics Socio–economic classification (NS–SEC) – see defintions in Appendix B.

4 Includes those who have never worked.

5 Includes those who are economically inactive – see defintions in Appendix B.

ONS, Family Spending 2009,   © Crown copyright 2010

Table A47   **Income and source of income, 1970 to 2009**

	Weighted number of house-holds	Number of house-holds in the sample	Weekly household income[1]				Source of income					
			Current prices		Constant prices		Wages and salaries	Self employment	Investments	Annuities and pensions[2]	Social security benefits[3]	Other sources
			Disposable	Gross	Disposable	Gross						
	(000s)	Number	£	£	£	£	Percentage of gross weekly household income					
1970		6,390	28	34	328	396	77	7	4	3	9	1
1980		6,940	115	140	367	449	75	6	3	3	13	1
1990		7,050	258	317	437	537	67	10	6	5	11	1
1995-96		6,800	307	381	437	542	64	9	5	7	14	2
1996-97		6,420	325	397	452	552	65	9	4	7	14	1
1997-98		6,410	343	421	462	567	67	8	4	7	13	1
1998-99[4]	24,660	6,630	371	457	484	596	68	8	4	7	12	1
1999-2000	25,340	7,100	391	480	502	617	66	10	5	7	12	1
2000-01	25,030	6,640	409	503	510	627	67	9	4	7	12	1
2001-02[5]	24,450	7,470	442	541	544	664	68	8	4	7	12	1
2002-03	24,350	6,930	453	552	546	665	68	8	3	7	12	1
2003-04	24,670	7,050	464	570	544	668	67	9	3	7	13	1
2004-05	24,430	6,800	489	601	556	682	68	8	3	7	13	1
2005-06	24,800	6,790	500	616	554	682	67	8	3	7	13	1
2006[6]	24,790	6,650	521	642	562	692	67	9	3	7	12	1
2006[7]	25,440	6,650	515	635	556	685	67	9	3	7	13	1
2007	25,350	6,140	534	659	552	682	67	8	4	7	13	1
2008	25,690	5,850	582	713	579	709	67	9	4	7	12	1
2009	25,980	5,830	558	683	558	683	66	8	3	8	14	1

Note: Please see page xiii for symbols and conventions used in this report.

1 Does not include imputed income from owner-occupied and rent-free households.

2 Other than social security benefits.

3 Excluding housing benefit and council tax benefit (rates rebate in Northern Ireland) and their predecessors in earlier years – see Appendix B.

4 Based on weighted data from 1998–99.

5 From 2001–02 onwards, weighting is based on the population estimates from the 2001 census.

6 From 1998–99 to this version of 2006, figures shown are based on weighted data using non-reponsive weights based on the 1991 Census and population figures from the 1991 and 2001 Censuses.

7 From this version of 2006, figures shown are based on weighted data using updated weights, with non-response weights and poulation figures based on the 2001 Census.

ONS, Family Spending 2009, © *Crown copyright 2010*

Table A48 **Characteristics of households, 2009**

based on weighted data

	% [1] of all house-holds	Weighted number of house-holds (000s)	House-holds in sample (number)		% [1] of all house-holds	Weighted number of house-holds (000s)	House-holds in sample (number)
Total number of households	100	25,980	5,830	**Composition of household (cont)**			
				Four adults	2	530	110
Size of household							
One person	29	7,510	1,600	Four adults, one child	1	140	30
Two persons	36	9,240	2,160	Four adults, two or more children	[0]	70	20
Three persons	17	4,290	940				
Four persons	13	3,370	770	Five adults	[0]	100	20
Five persons	5	1,170	270				
Six persons	1	270	60	Five adults, one or more children	[0]	40	..
Seven persons	[0]	70	20				
Eight persons	[0]	30	..	All other households without children	[0]	30	..
Nine or more persons	[0]	20	..	All other households with children	[0]	20	..
Composition of household							
One adult	29	7,510	1,600	**Number of economically active persons in household**			
Retired households mainly dependent on state pensions[2]	3	770	150	No person	31	8,030	1,890
Other retired households	11	2,750	580	One person	29	7,550	1,710
Non-retired households	15	4,000	870	More than one person	40	10,400	2,230
One man	13	3,380	710	Two persons	32	8,230	1,780
Aged under 65	9	2,370	470	Three persons	7	1,730	360
Aged 65 and over	4	1,010	250	Four persons	1	380	80
One woman	16	4,130	890	Five persons	[0]	50	..
Aged under 60	5	1,360	340	Six or more persons	[0]	10	..
Aged 60 and over	11	2,770	550				
One adult, one child	2	650	160	Households with married women	48	12,550	2,970
One man, one child	[0]	100	20	Households with married women			
One woman, one child	2	550	140	economically active	27	7,060	1,620
One adult, two or more children	2	640	180	With no dependent children	14	3,670	830
One man, two or more children	[0]	30	..	With dependent children	13	3,390	790
One woman, two or more children	2	600	170	One child	6	1,550	350
				Two children	5	1,430	340
One man, one woman	31	8,000	1,880	Three children	1	360	90
Retired households mainly dependent on state pensions[2]	1	390	110	Four or more children	[0]	50	10
Other retired households	9	2,300	590	Households with married women			
Non-retired households	20	5,310	1,180	not economically active	21	5,490	1,350
Two men or two women	2	590	110	With no dependent children	16	4,160	1,050
				With dependent children	5	1,330	300
Two adults with children	20	5,140	1,190	One child	2	520	110
One man one woman, one child	8	2,090	460	Two children	2	490	120
Two men or two women, one child	0	110	30	Three children	1	250	60
One man one woman, two children	8	2,080	490	Four or more children	0	80	20
Two men or two women, two children	[0]	20	10				
One man one woman, three children	3	660	160	**Economic status of household reference person**			
Two men or two women, three children	[0]	20	..	Economically active	63	16,440	3,600
Two adults, four children	0	130	30	Employee at work	53	13,640	2,980
Two adults, five children	[0]	20	..	Full-time	44	11,380	2,450
Two adults, six or more children	[0]	10	..	Part-time	9	2,260	530
Three adults	6	1,660	340	Government-supported training	[0]	30	..
Three adults with children	3	860	180	Unemployed	3	760	160
Three adults, one child	2	570	120	Self-employed	8	2,010	460
Three adults, two children	1	231	51				
Three adults, three children	[0]	29	..	Economically inactive	37	9,540	2,220
Three adults, four or more children	[0]	33	..				

Note: Please see page xiii for symbols and conventions used in this report.

1 Based on weighted number of households.

2 Mainly dependent on state pensions and not economically active – see definitions in Appendix B.

ONS, Family Spending 2009, © Crown copyright 2010

Table A48   **Characteristics of households, 2009 (cont.)**

based on weighted data

	%[1] of all house-holds	Weighted number of house-holds (000s)	House-holds in sample (number)		%[1] of all house-holds	Weighted number of house-holds (000s)	House-holds in sample (number)
Age of household reference person				**GB urban/rural areas (over 3 years)**			
15 and under 20 years	[0]	90	20	GB Urban	78	19,540	4,110
20 and under 25 years	4	920	160	GB rural	22	5,470	1,230
25 and under 30 years	7	1,750	330				
30 and under 35 years	8	1,960	430				
35 and under 40 years	9	2,360	520	**Tenure of dwelling[5]**			
40 and under 45 years	11	2,770	590	Owners			
				Owned outright	32	8180	1980
45 and under 50 years	10	2,580	580	Buying with a mortgage	37	9,530	2,120
50 and under 55 years	9	2,330	530	All	68	17,720	4,100
55 and under 60 years	9	2,300	580	Social rented from			
				Council	9	2,380	540
60 and under 65 years	8	2,100	530	Registered social landlord	8	2,180	450
65 and under 70 years	7	1,690	430	All	18	4,550	990
70 and under 75 years	6	1,620	400	Private rented			
				Rent free	1	360	80
75 and under 80 years	6	1,500	330	Rent paid, unfurnished	10	2,600	530
80 and under 85 years	5	1,180	260	Rent paid, furnished	3	750	140
85 and under 90 years	2	590	110	All	14	3,710	740
90 years or more	1	220	40				
				Households with durable goods			
Government Office Regions and Countries				Car/van	76	19,730	4,540
2007–2009 (3 year average)				One	43	11,280	2,620
United Kingdom	100	25,670	5,940	Two	26	6,740	1,550
				Three or more	7	1,710	370
North East	5	1,220	240				
North West	12	3,040	590	Central heating, full or partial	95	24650	5560
Yorkshire and the Humber	8	2,140	500	Fridge-freezer or deep freezer	97	25,220	5,660
				Washing machine	96	24,850	5,610
East Midlands	8	1,970	420	Tumble dryer	58	15,190	3,490
West Midlands	8	2,140	500	Dishwasher	39	10,160	2,420
East	9	2,260	530	Microwave oven	93	24,110	5,420
London	12	3,030	490	Telephone	88	22,950	5,180
South East	12	3,070	780	Mobile phone	81	20,940	4,590
South West	10	2,490	510	Video recorder	61	15,880	3,660
				DVD Player	90	23,260	5,220
England	83	21,350	4,560	Satellite receiver[6]	86	22,250	5,020
Wales	5	1,280	270	Compact disc player	84	21,870	4,930
Scotland	9	2,370	520	Home computer	75	19,580	4,340
Northern Ireland	3	670	590	Internet connection	71	18,470	4,080
Socio-economic classification							
of household reference person							
Higher managerial and professional	11	2,900	630				
Large employers/higher managerial	5	1,200	260				
Higher professional	7	1,700	370				
Lower managerial and professional	19	4,900	1,050				
Intermediate	6	1,520	360				
Small employers	6	1,460	340				
Lower supervisory	7	1,740	370				
Semi-routine	8	1,990	450				
Routine	6	1,470	330				
Long-term unemployed[3]	2	510	120				
Students	2	470	90				
Occupation not stated[4]	35	9,000	2,100				

Note: Please see page xiii for symbols and conventions used in this report.

1 Based on weighted number of households.

2 Mainly dependent on state pensions and not economically active – see definitions in Appendix B.

3 Includes those who have never worked.

4 Includes those who are economically inactive – see definitions in Appendix B.

5 See footnotes in Table A34.

6 Includes digital and cable receivers.

ONS, Family Spending 2009, © *Crown copyright 2010*

Table A49 Characteristics of persons, 2009

based on weighted data

	Males				Females				All persons		
	Percentage[1] of		Weighted number of persons (000s)	Persons in the sample (number)	Percentage[1] of		Weighted number of persons (000s)	Persons in the sample (number)	Percentage[1] of	Weighted number of persons (000s)	Persons in the sample (number)
	all males	all persons			all females	all persons			all persons		
All persons	*100*	*49*	**29,660**	**6,590**	*100*	*51*	**31,130**	**7,150**	*100*	**60,800**	**13,740**
Adults	*78*	*38*	**23,240**	**5,070**	*79*	*40*	**24,550**	**5,580**	*79*	**47,780**	**10,650**
Persons aged under 60	*58*	*28*	17,190	3,520	*56*	*29*	17,300	3,900	*57*	34,480	7,410
Persons aged 60 or under 65	*6*	*3*	1,730	450	*7*	*3*	2,010	510	*6*	3,750	960
Persons aged 65 or under 70	*5*	*2*	1,350	350	*4*	*2*	1,330	350	*4*	2,680	700
Persons aged 70 or over	*10*	*5*	2,970	750	*13*	*6*	3,910	820	*11*	6,880	1,580
Children	*22*	*11*	**6,430**	**1,520**	*21*	*11*	**6,580**	**1,570**	*21*	**13,010**	**3,090**
Children under 2 years of age	*3*	*1*	820	190	*3*	*2*	900	210	*3*	1,720	390
Children aged 2 or under 5	*4*	*2*	1,030	260	*3*	*2*	1,010	260	*3*	2,040	520
Children aged 5 or under 16	*13*	*6*	3,790	900	*13*	*7*	3,940	930	*13*	7,730	1,820
Children aged 16 or under 18	*3*	*1*	790	190	*2*	*1*	750	170	*3*	1,530	360
Economic activity											
Persons active (aged 16 or over)	*57*	*28*	16,840	3,530	*46*	*23*	14,180	3,190	*51*	31,020	6,720
Persons not active	*43*	*21*	12,820	3,060	*55*	*28*	16,950	3,960	*49*	29,780	7,020
Men 65 or over and women 60 or over	*13*	*6*	3,830	980	*21*	*11*	6,410	1,470	*17*	10,240	2,450
Others (Including children under 16)	*30*	*15*	8,990	2,080	*34*	*17*	10,550	2,490	*32*	19,540	4,570

Note: Please see page xiii for symbols and conventions used in this report.

1 Based on weighted number of households.

ONS, Family Spending 2009, © Crown copyright 2010

Table A50   **Percentage of households with durable goods 1970 to 2009**

	Car/van	Central heating[1]	Washing machine	Tumble dryer	Dish-washer	Micro-wave	Telephone	Mobile phone	Video recorder	DVD Player	Satellite receiver[2]	Cd player	Home computer	Internet connection
1970	52	30	65	--	--	--	35	--	--	--	--	--	--	--
1975	57	47	72	--	--	--	52	--	--	--	--	--	--	--
1980	60	59	79	--	--	--	72	--	--	--	--	--	--	--
1985	63	69	83	--	--	--	81	--	30	--	--	--	13	--
1990	67	79	86	--	--	--	87	--	61	--	--	--	17	--
1994-95	69	84	89	50	18	67	91	--	76	--	--	46	--	--
1995-96	70	85	91	50	20	70	92	--	79	--	--	51	--	--
1996-97	69	87	91	51	20	75	93	16	82	--	19	59	27	--
1997-98	70	89	91	51	22	77	94	20	84	--	26	63	29	--
1998-99	72	89	92	51	24	80	95	26	86	--	27	68	32	9
1998-99[3]	72	89	92	51	23	79	95	27	85	--	28	68	33	10
1999-2000	71	90	91	52	23	80	95	44	86	--	32	72	38	19
2000-01	72	91	93	53	25	84	93	47	87	--	40	77	44	32
2001-02[4]	74	92	93	54	27	86	94	64	90	--	43	80	49	39
2002-03	74	93	94	56	29	87	94	70	90	31	45	83	55	45
2003-04	75	94	94	57	31	89	92	76	90	50	49	86	58	49
2004-05	75	95	95	58	33	90	93	78	88	67	58	87	62	53
2005-06	74	94	95	58	35	91	92	79	86	79	65	88	65	55
2006[5]	76	95	96	59	38	91	91	80	82	83	71	88	67	59
2006[6]	74	95	96	59	37	91	91	79	82	83	83	70	87	67
2007	75	95	96	57	37	91	89	78	75	86	77	86	70	61
2008	74	95	96	59	37	92	90	79	70	88	82	86	72	66
2009	76	95	96	58	39	93	88	81	61	90	86	84	75	71

Note: Please see page xiii for symbols and conventions used in this report.

-- Data not available.

1 Full or partial.

2 Includes digital and cable receivers.

3 From this version of 1998–99, figures shown are based on weighted data and including children's expenditure.

4 From 2001–02 onwards, weighting is based on the population figures from the 2001 census.

5 From 1998–99 to this version of 2006, figures shown are based on weighted data using non-response weights based on the 1991 Census and population figures from the 1991 and 2001 Census.

6 From this version of 2006, figures shown are based on weighted data using updated weights, with non-response weights and population figures based on the 2001 Census.

ONS, Family Spending 2009, © Crown copyright 2010

Table A51   **Percentage[1] of households with durable goods by income group and household composition, 2009**

based on weighted data and including children's expenditure

	Central heating[2]	Washing machine	Tumble dryer	Micro-wave	Dish-washer	CD player
All households	**95**	**96**	**58**	**93**	**39**	**84**
Gross income decile group						
Lowest ten per cent	93	82	37	88	10	63
Second decile group	93	90	41	90	16	73
Third decile group	93	93	50	94	22	73
Fourth decile group	95	98	53	93	27	86
Fifth decile group	95	97	59	93	30	87
Sixth decile group	95	98	62	93	39	90
Seventh decile group	95	100	66	95	45	90
Eighth decile group	96	99	68	95	57	91
Ninth decile group	97	100	70	94	65	92
Highest ten per cent	97	99	78	93	80	96
Household composition						
One adult, retired households[3]	89	84	37	83	16	54
One adult, non-retired households	93	90	44	92	23	82
One adult, one child	96	98	56	95	23	82
One adult, two or more children	96	99	72	95	34	85
Two adults, retired households[3]	91	97	50	90	20	76
Two adults, non-retired households	95	98	62	93	47	90
Two adults, one child	97	99	67	93	52	87
Two adults, two or more children	97	99	74	95	56	90
All other households without children	93	96	60	96	40	88
All other households with children	99	100	73	95	55	86

	Home computer	Internet connection	Tele-phone	Mobile phone	Satellite receiver[4]	DVD Player
All households	**75**	**71**	**88**	**81**	**86**	**90**
Gross income decile group						
Lowest ten per cent	38	30	67	67	68	72
Second decile group	41	35	83	62	74	75
Third decile group	58	54	86	73	82	83
Fourth decile group	68	60	88	79	84	90
Fifth decile group	79	73	89	81	88	93
Sixth decile group	85	80	90	87	90	93
Seventh decile group	93	89	93	87	91	96
Eighth decile group	96	95	94	87	92	96
Ninth decile group	99	97	96	91	94	98
Highest ten per cent	98	97	97	92	93	98
Household composition						
One adult, retired households[3]	15	9	97	40	63	53
One adult, non-retired households	68	60	70	84	78	89
One adult, one child	78	70	61	85	86	95
One adult, two or more children	85	79	78	89	92	97
Two adults, retired households[3]	37	32	100	65	82	84
Two adults, non-retired households	89	86	90	87	90	96
Two adults, one child	95	91	89	89	93	97
Two adults, two or more children	96	93	92	91	94	98
All other households without children	91	87	87	92	88	94
All other households with children	91	88	86	83	92	95

Note: Please see page xiii for symbols and conventions used in this report.

1 See table A52 for number of recording households.

2 Full or partial.

3 Mainly dependent on state pensions and not economically active – see Appendix B.

4 Includes digital and cable receivers.

ONS, Family Spending 2009, © Crown copyright 2010

Table A52   **Percentage of households with cars by income group, tenure and household composition 2009**

based on weighted data

	One car/van	Two cars/vans	Three or more cars/vans	All with cars/vans	Weighted number of house-holds (000s)	House-holds in the sample (number)
All households	*43*	*26*	*7*	*76*	25,980	5,830
Gross income decile group						
Lowest ten per cent	*29*	*[3]*	*[0]*	*33*	2,600	560
Second decile group	*40*	*3*	*[1]*	*44*	2,600	580
Third decile group	*51*	*8*	*[1]*	*60*	2,600	600
Fourth decile group	*66*	*10*	*[1]*	*78*	2,600	620
Fifth decile group	*56*	*19*	*4*	*79*	2,600	610
Sixth decile group	*53*	*28*	*4*	*86*	2,600	600
Seventh decile group	*48*	*37*	*8*	*92*	2,600	580
Eighth decile group	*38*	*49*	*9*	*96*	2,600	560
Ninth decile group	*28*	*53*	*15*	*96*	2,600	560
Highest ten per cent	*24*	*49*	*22*	*96*	2,600	550
Tenure of dwelling[1]						
Owners						
Owned outright	*50*	*23*	*7*	*81*	8,180	1,980
Buying with a mortgage	*42*	*41*	*10*	*93*	9,530	2,120
All	*46*	*33*	*8*	*87*	17,720	4,100
Social rented from						
Council	*34*	*6*	*[1]*	*40*	2,380	540
Registered social landlord[2]	*36*	*6*	*[2]*	*44*	2,180	450
All	*35*	*6*	*[1]*	*42*	4,550	990
Private rented						
Rent free	*43*	*[19]*	*[3]*	*65*	360	80
Rent paid, unfurnished	*44*	*19*	*[4]*	*67*	2,600	530
Rent paid, furnished	*34*	*[9]*	*[5]*	*47*	750	140
All	*42*	*17*	*4*	*63*	3,710	740
Household composition						
One adult, retired mainly dependent on state pensions[3]	*34*	*[1]*	*-*	*35*	770	150
One adult, other retired	*40*	*[1]*	*[0]*	*42*	2,750	580
One adult, non-retired	*60*	*5*	*[0]*	*65*	4,000	870
One adult, one child	*54*	*[2]*	*-*	*56*	650	160
One adult, two or more children	*59*	*[3]*	*-*	*62*	640	180
Two adults, retired mainly dependent on state pensions[3]	*67*	*[13]*	*[1]*	*81*	400	120
Two adults, other retired	*62*	*18*	*[1]*	*82*	2,400	610
Two adults, non-retired	*40*	*42*	*5*	*87*	5,790	1,270
Two adults, one child	*36*	*47*	*6*	*89*	2,090	460
Two adults, two children	*38*	*50*	*5*	*93*	2,080	490
Two adults, three children	*46*	*38*	*[5]*	*88*	660	160
Two adults, four or more children	*46*	*[29]*	*-*	*75*	160	40
Three adults	*24*	*38*	*26*	*88*	1,660	340
Three adults, one or more children	*25*	*37*	*27*	*89*	860	180
All other households without children	*[12]*	*30*	*46*	*88*	660	130
All other households with children	*28*	*26*	*27*	*81*	420	100

Note: Please see page xiii for symbols and conventions used in this report.

1 See footnotes in Table A34.

2 Formerly housing association.

3 Mainly dependent on state pensions and not economically active - see Appendix B.

ONS, Family Spending 2009, © Crown copyright 2010

Table A53   **Percentage of households with durable goods by UK Countries and Government Office Regions, 2007–2009**

based on weighted data

	North East	North West	Yorks and the Humber	East Midlands	West Midlands	East	London
Average weighted number of households (thousands)	1,220	3,040	2,140	1,970	2,140	2,260	3,030
Total number of households in sample (over 3 years)	730	1,780	1,500	1,260	1,500	1,580	1,470
Percentage of households by Government Office Region and Country							
Car/van	68	73	72	78	77	83	64
One	43	42	43	45	44	45	45
Two	21	25	24	27	26	29	15
Three or more	4	6	5	7	7	9	4
Central heating full or partial	98	95	95	95	95	97	93
Fridge-freezer or deep freezer	98	97	96	97	97	97	97
Washing machine	96	96	96	96	95	96	94
Tumble dryer	58	59	60	58	64	61	45
Dishwasher	27	32	33	38	35	43	38
Microwave	93	94	94	94	94	91	87
Telephone	87	88	85	88	89	93	89
Mobile phone	76	78	79	84	85	81	81
DVD player	90	90	86	89	89	88	85
Satellite receiver[1]	83	87	81	81	82	81	77
CD player	85	86	83	88	86	88	82
Home computer	67	71	68	71	71	76	77
Internet connection	61	64	61	63	65	71	72

	South East	South West	England	Wales	Scotland	Northern Ireland	United Kingdom
Weighted number of households (thousands)	3,070	2,490	21,350	1,280	2,370	670	25,670
Total number of households in sample (over 3 years)	2,350	1,520	13,680	820	1,550	1,770	17,810
Percentage of households by Government Office Region and Country							
Car/van	81	82	76	75	71	77	75
One	42	44	44	44	44	43	44
Two	31	31	26	25	23	27	25
Three or more	8	7	6	6	4	7	6
Central heating full or partial	95	94	95	94	96	98	95
Fridge-freezer or deep freezer	97	97	97	97	96	96	97
Washing machine	96	96	96	96	97	98	96
Tumble dryer	60	61	58	59	58	60	58
Dishwasher	46	43	38	33	38	49	38
Microwave	90	92	92	95	92	93	92
Telephone	91	92	89	89	89	84	89
Mobile phone	81	85	81	49	84	56	79
DVD Player	89	87	88	86	89	81	88
Satellite receiver[1]	82	82	82	78	85	82	82
CD player	87	88	86	87	84	80	86
Home computer	77	73	73	68	72	64	72
Internet connection	72	68	67	61	65	57	66

Note: Please see page xiii for symbols and conventions used in this report.
      This table is based on a three year average.

1 Includes digital and cable receivers.

ONS, Family Spending 2009, © *Crown copyright 2010*

Table A54

Percentage of households by size, composition and age in each gross income decile group, 2009

based on weighted data

	Lowest ten per cent	Second decile group	Third decile group	Fourth decile group	Fifth decile group	Sixth decile group	Seventh decile group	Eighth decile group	Ninth decile group	Highest ten per cent	All households
Lower boundary of group (£ per week)		158	235	315	410	520	647	796	985	1,348	
Weighted number of households (thousands)	2,600	2,600	2,600	2,600	2,600	2,600	2,600	2,600	2,600	2,600	25,980
Number of households in the sample	560	580	600	620	610	600	580	560	560	550	5,830
Size of household											
One person	80	62	40	32	25	18	12	9	5	6	29
Two persons	17	24	38	44	42	46	42	35	38	29	36
Three persons	[3]	9	9	13	14	19	23	25	24	27	17
Four persons	[0]	4	6	6	12	13	17	24	23	26	13
Five persons	[0]	[1]	5	[3]	5	3	5	6	8	8	5
Six or more persons	[0]	[0]	[1]	[2]	[2]	[1]	[1]	[2]	[2]	4	2
All sizes	100	100	100	100	100	100	100	100	100	100	100
Household composition											
One adult, retired mainly dependent on state pensions[1]	17	10	[2]	[0]	-	-	-	-	-	-	3
One adult, other retired	22	35	24	13	7	[3]	[1]	[1]	[0]	[1]	11
One adult, non-retired	41	17	14	19	18	15	11	8	5	5	15
One adult, one child	9	4	3	3	[3]	[1]	[1]	[1]	[0]	[0]	2
One adult, two or more children	[1]	5	6	5	[3]	[2]	[1]	[0]	[1]	[0]	2
Two adults, retired mainly dependent on state pensions[1]	[1]	5	6	3	[1]	[0]	-	-	-	-	2
Two adults, other retired	[0]	7	17	24	16	13	6	5	[2]	[1]	9
Two adults, non-retired	7	9	13	14	21	32	35	29	35	28	22
Two adults, one child	[1]	[3]	[3]	5	7	11	11	14	12	14	8
Two adults, two children	-	[2]	[2]	4	8	8	13	15	13	15	8
Two adults, three children	[0]	[1]	[3]	[2]	3	[2]	4	4	4	[3]	3
Two adults, four or more children	-	-	[1]	[1]	[1]	[1]	[1]	[1]	[1]	[1]	1
Three adults	[1]	[2]	[2]	4	4	6	11	9	12	13	6
Three adults, one or more children	[0]	[1]	[2]	[2]	[3]	[3]	3	5	7	7	3
All other households without children	-	[0]	[0]	[1]	[2]	[2]	[2]	4	6	9	3
All other households with children	[1]	[0]	[2]	[1]	[1]	[2]	[2]	[2]	[2]	[3]	2
All compositions	100	100	100	100	100	100	100	100	100	100	100
Age of household reference person											
15 and under 20 years	[2]	[1]	[0]	-	[0]	[0]	-	-	-	-	[0]
20 and under 25 years	7	[4]	[3]	[4]	5	6	[4]	[1]	[1]	[1]	4
25 and under 30 years	5	7	5	8	6	8	8	9	7	5	7
30 and under 35 years	5	[2]	8	5	7	8	10	11	11	8	8
35 and under 40 years	5	5	5	7	9	9	11	11	15	13	9
40 and under 45 years	8	4	6	7	7	11	13	18	17	16	11
45 and under 50 years	6	4	5	7	11	11	11	12	14	19	10
50 and under 55 years	8	6	6	5	7	9	10	11	12	16	9
55 and under 60 years	10	5	6	7	9	9	11	10	11	11	9
60 and under 65 years	9	8	9	8	10	9	9	7	6	6	8
65 and under 70 years	5	10	9	11	8	6	8	4	3	[2]	7
70 and under 75 years	7	9	12	11	9	5	[3]	4	[1]	[1]	6
75 and under 80 years	7	13	11	10	5	5	[2]	[2]	[1]	[1]	6
80 and under 85 years	10	12	10	6	4	[2]	[1]	[1]	[0]	[0]	5
85 and under 90 years	6	8	[2]	[3]	[2]	[2]	-	[1]	[0]	-	2
90 years or more	[2]	[2]	[2]	[1]	[0]	[0]	-	-	-	[0]	1
All ages	100	100	100	100	100	100	100	100	100	100	100

Note: Please see page xiii for symbols and conventions used in this report.

1 Mainly dependent on state pensions and not economically active – see Appendix B.

ONS, Family Spending 2009, © Crown copyright 2010

Table A55 **Percentage of households by economic activity, tenure and socio-economic classification in each gross income decile group, 2009**

based on weighted data

	Lowest ten per cent	Second decile group	Third decile group	Fourth decile group	Fifth decile group	Sixth decile group	Seventh decile group	Eighth decile group	Ninth decile group	Highest ten per cent	All households
Lower boundary of group (£ per week)		158	235	315	410	520	647	796	985	1,348	
Weighted number of households (thousands)	2,600	2,600	2,600	2,600	2,600	2,600	2,600	2,600	2,600	2,600	25,980
Number of households in the sample	560	580	600	620	610	600	580	560	560	550	5,830
Number of economically active persons in household											
No person	72	75	59	44	26	16	8	6	[2]	[2]	31
One person	26	20	31	43	47	39	32	22	15	16	29
Two persons	[2]	4	9	13	23	40	51	57	62	55	32
Three persons	[1]	[1]	[1]	[1]	[3]	4	8	13	16	20	7
Four or more persons	-	-	-	-	-	[0]	[2]	[2]	5	8	2
All economically active persons	100	100	100	100	100	100	100	100	100	100	100
Tenure of dwelling[1]											
Owners											
Owned outright	26	39	44	41	40	33	27	23	19	23	32
Buying with a mortgage	7	8	12	21	29	43	53	59	67	68	37
All	33	48	56	62	69	75	80	83	86	90	68
Social rented from											
Council	25	18	16	11	8	5	4	[2]	[1]	[1]	9
Registered social landlord[2]	22	20	13	9	8	[3]	[3]	[3]	[2]	[0]	8
All	47	38	29	20	16	9	7	5	[3]	[1]	18
Private rented											
Rent free	[3]	[1]	[2]	[1]	[1]	[1]	[2]	[1]	[1]	[1]	1
Rent paid, unfurnished	14	10	9	13	11	11	8	10	8	5	10
Rent paid, furnished	[3]	[3]	[3]	[3]	[3]	5	[2]	[1]	[3]	[2]	3
All	20	14	15	18	15	16	12	12	12	9	14
All tenures	100	100	100	100	100	100	100	100	100	100	100
Socio-economic classification											
Higher managerial and professional											
Large employers/higher managerial	-	[0]	[0]	[0]	[1]	[3]	[2]	6	11	22	5
Higher professional	[0]	[1]	[1]	[0]	[3]	[3]	10	11	13	24	7
Lower managerial and professional	[3]	[2]	6	11	15	19	27	31	41	34	19
Intermediate	[2]	[2]	4	6	9	9	9	8	6	[3]	6
Small employers	[2]	3	5	6	7	9	7	7	7	4	6
Lower supervisory	[2]	[0]	[3]	4	9	11	13	12	8	5	7
Semi-routine	5	5	10	11	12	10	10	8	4	[2]	8
Routine	[3]	5	5	5	9	9	9	5	4	[1]	6
Long-term unemployed[3]	9	3	[3]	[2]	[1]	[0]	-	-	-	-	2
Students	[4]	[2]	[3]	[2]	[2]	[2]	[0]	[0]	[2]	[1]	2
Occupation not stated[4]	69	76	60	51	32	23	14	11	5	5	35
All occupational groups	100	100	100	100	100	100	100	100	100	100	100

Note: Please see page xiii for symbols and conventions used in this report.

1 See footnotes in Table A34.

2 Formerly housing association.

3 Includes those who have never worked.

4 Includes those who are economically inactive - see definitions in Appendix B.

ONS, Family Spending 2009, © *Crown copyright 2010*

Methodology

Description and response rate of the survey

The survey

A household expenditure survey has been conducted each year in the UK since 1957. From 1957 to March 2001 the Family Expenditure and National Food Surveys (FES and NFS) provided information on household expenditure patterns and food consumption. In April 2001 these surveys were combined to form the Expenditure and Food Survey (EFS).

In 2008 selected Government household surveys, on which the Office for National Statistics (ONS) leads, were combined into one Integrated Household Survey (IHS) – known as the Continuous Population Survey in the public domain. In anticipation of this, the EFS moved to a calendar-year basis in January 2006. The EFS questionnaire became known as the Living Costs and Food (LCF) module of the IHS in 2008, to accommodate the insertion of a core set of IHS questions. In addition to the LCF, the other surveys initially incorporated into the IHS were the General Household Survey (GHS) and the Omnibus Survey (OMN), (these surveys are now called the General Lifestyle Survey (GLF) and Opinions Survey (OPN) respectively) and the English Housing Survey (EHS). In 2009 the Labour Force Survey (LFS) and the Life Opportunities Survey (LOS) also joined the IHS.

The LCF is a voluntary sample survey of private households. The basic unit of the survey is the household. The LCF (in line with other Government household surveys) uses the harmonised definition of a household: A household comprises one person or a group of people who have the accommodation as their only or main residence and (for a group): *either share at least one meal a day **or** share the living accommodation, that is, a living room or sitting room* (see 'Definitions'). The previous definition (used on the FES) differed from the harmonised definition by requiring both common housekeeping **and** a shared living room.

Each individual aged 16 and over in the household visited is asked to keep diary records of daily expenditure for two weeks. Information about regular expenditure, such as rent and mortgage payments, is obtained from a household interview along with retrospective information on certain large, infrequent expenditures such as those on vehicles. Since 1998–99 the results have also included information from simplified diaries kept by children aged between 7 and 15. The effects of including children's expenditure were shown in Appendix F of Family Spending for 1998–99 and again for 1999–2000. Inclusion of the data is now a standard feature of the survey.

Detailed questions are asked about the income of each adult member of the household. In addition, personal information such as age, sex and marital status is recorded for each household member. Paper versions of the computerised household and income questionnaires can be obtained from ONS at the address given in the Introduction.

The survey is continuous, interviews being spread evenly over the year to ensure that seasonal effects are covered. From time to time changes are made to the information sought. Some changes reflect new forms of expenditure or new sources of income, especially benefits. Others are the result of new requirements by the survey's users. An important example is the re-definition of housing costs for owner occupiers in 1992 (see 'Changes in definitions, 1991 to 2009').

The sample design

The LCF sample for Great Britain is a multi-stage stratified random sample with clustering. It is drawn from the Small Users file of the Postcode Address File (PAF) – the Post Office's list of addresses. All Scottish offshore islands and the Isles of Scilly are excluded from the sample because of excessive interview travel costs. Postal sectors are the primary sample unit. 638 postal sectors are randomly selected after being arranged in strata defined by Government Office Regions (sub-divided into metropolitan and non-metropolitan areas) and two 2001 Census variables – socio-economic group of head of household and ownership of cars. These census variables were new stratifiers originally introduced for the 1996–97 survey, and updated following the results of the 2001 Census. The Northern Ireland sample is drawn as a random sample of addresses from the Land and Property Services Agency list.

Response to the survey

Great Britain

Around 11,482 households were selected in 2009 for the LCF in Great Britain, however, it is not possible to get full response. A small number of households cannot be contacted at all, and in other households one or more members decline to co-operate. 5,019 households in Great Britain co-operated fully in the survey in 2009; that is they answered the household questionnaire and all adults in the household answered the full income questionnaire and kept the expenditure diary. A further 204 households provided sufficient information to be included as valid responses. The overall response rate for the 2009 LCF was 50 per cent in Great Britain. This represented a 1 percentage point decrease in response from the 2008 survey year.

Details of response are shown in the following table.

Response in 2009 - Great Britain

		No of households or addresses	Percentage of effective sample
i.	Sampled addresses	11,482	-
ii.	Ineligible addresses: businesses, institutions, empty, demolished/derelict	1,198	-
iii.	Extra households (multi-household addresses)	82	-
iv.	Total eligible (that is i less ii, plus iii)	10,366	100.0
v.	Co-operating households (which includes 204 partials)	5,223	50.4
vi.	Refusals	3,752	36.2
vii.	Households at which no contact could be obtained	1,391	13.4

Northern Ireland

In the Northern Ireland survey, the eligible sample was 1,084 households. The number of co-operating households who provided usable data was 602, giving a response rate of 56 per cent. This represents an increase of 2 percentage points from the 2008 survey year. Northern Ireland is over-sampled in order to provide a large enough sample for some separate analysis. The weighting procedure compensates for the over-sampling.

The fieldwork

The fieldwork is conducted by the Office for National Statistics (ONS) in Great Britain, and by the Northern Ireland Statistics and Research Agency (NISRA) of the Department of Finance and Personnel in Northern Ireland, using almost identical questionnaires. Households at the selected addresses are visited and asked to co-operate in the survey. In order to maximise response, interviewers make at least four separate calls, and sometimes many more, at different times of day on households which are difficult to contact. Interviews are conducted by Computer Assisted Personal Interviewing (CAPI) using portable computers. During the interview information is collected about the household; certain regular payments such as rent, gas, electricity and telephone accounts; expenditure on certain large items (for example vehicle purchases over the previous 12 months); and income. Each individual aged 16 and over in the household is asked to keep a detailed record of expenditure every day for two weeks. Children aged between 7 and 15 are also asked to keep a simplified diary of daily expenditure. In 2009 a total of 1,512 children aged between 7 and 15 in responding households in the UK were asked to complete expenditure diaries; 232, or about 15 per cent, did not do so. This number includes both refusals and children who had no expenditure during the two weeks. Information provided by all members of the household is kept strictly confidential. Each person aged 16 and over in the household who keeps a diary (and whose income information is collected) is subsequently paid £10, as a token of appreciation. Children who keep a diary are given a £5 payment.

In the last two months of the 1998–99 survey, as an experiment, a small book of postage stamps was enclosed with the introductory letter sent to every address. Response seemed to increase as a result of this experiment and it has become a permanent feature of the survey. It is difficult to quantify the exact effect on response but the cognitive work that was carried out as part of the EFS development indicated that it was having a positive effect.

A new strategy for reissues was adopted in 1999–2000 and has continued since. Addresses where there had been no contact or a refusal, but were judged suitable for reissue, were accumulated to form complete batches consisting only of reissues. The interviewers dealing with them were specially selected and given extra briefing. In 2009 some 34 addresses were reissued, of which 14 were converted into responding households. This increased the overall response rate by 0.1 percentage points.

Eligible response

Under LCF rules, a refusal by just one person to respond to the income section of the questionnaire invalidates the response of the whole household. Similarly, a refusal by the household's main shopper to complete the two-week expenditure diary also results in an invalid response.

While questions about general household affairs are put to all household members or to the household representative person (HRP), questions about work and income are put to the individual members of the household. Where a member of the household is not present during the household interview, another member of the household (for example a spouse) may be able to provide information about the absent person. The individual's interview is then identified as a proxy interview.

In 2001–02, the EFS began including households that contained a proxy interview. In that year, 12 per cent of all responding households contained at least one proxy interview. In 2009 the percentage of responding households with a proxy interview was 21 per cent. Analysis of the 2002–03 data revealed that the inclusion of proxy interviews increased response from above average income households. For the 2002–03 survey, the average gross normal weekly household income was some 3 percentage points higher than it would have been if proxy interviews had not been accepted. The analysis showed a similar difference for average total expenditure.

Reliability

Great care is taken in collecting information from households, and comprehensive checks are applied during processing so that errors in recording and processing are minimised. The main factors that affect the reliability of the survey results are sampling variability, non-response bias and some incorrect reporting of certain items of expenditure and income. Measures of sampling variability are given alongside some results in this report and are discussed in detail in 'Standard errors and estimates of precision'.

The households which decline to respond to the survey tend to differ in some respects from those which co-operate. It is therefore possible that their patterns of expenditure and income also differ. A comparison was made of the households responding in the 1991 FES with those not responding, based on information from the 1991 Census of Population (A comparison of the Census characteristics of respondents and non-respondents to the 1991 FES by K Foster, ONS Survey Methodology Bulletin No. 38, Jan 1996). Results from the study indicate that response was lower than average in Greater London, higher in non-metropolitan areas, and that non-response tended to increase with increasing age of the head of the household – up to age 65. Households that contained three or more adults, or where the head was born outside the United Kingdom or was classified to an ethnic minority group, were also more likely than others to be non-responding. Non-response was also above average where the head of the household had no post-school qualifications, was self-employed, or was in a manual social class group. The data were re-weighted to compensate for the main non-response biases identified from the 1991 Census comparison, as described in 'Weighting'. ONS has completed a similar comparative exercise with the 2001 Census data, which resulted in an update of the non-response weights for the estimates for 2007 onwards.

Checks are included in the CAPI program, which are applied to the responses given during the interview. Other procedures are also in place to ensure that users are provided with high quality data. For example, quality control is carried out to ensure that any outliers are genuine, and checks are made on any unusual changes in average spending compared with the previous year.

When aspects of the survey change, rigorous tests are used to ensure the proposed changes are sensible and work both in the field and on the processing system. For example, in 1996–97 an improved set of questions was introduced on income from self-employment. This was developed by focus groups and then tested by piloting before being introduced into the main survey.

Income and expenditure balancing

The LCF is designed primarily as a survey of household expenditure on goods and services. It also gathers information about the income of household members, and is an important and detailed source of income data. However, it is not possible to draw up a balance sheet of income and expenditure either for individual households or groups of households.

The majority of expenditure information collected relates to the two-week period immediately following the interview, whereas income components can refer to a much longer period (the most recent 12 months). LCF income does not include withdrawal of savings; loans and money received in payment of loans; receipts from maturing insurance policies; proceeds from the sale of assets (such as a car); and winnings from betting or windfalls, such as legacies. Despite this, recorded expenditure might reflect these items, as well as the effects of living off savings, using capital, borrowing money or income – either recent or from a previous period.

Hence, there is no reason why income and expenditure should balance. In fact measured expenditure exceeds measured income at the bottom end of the income distribution. However, this difference cannot be regarded as a reliable measure of savings or dis-saving.

For further information of what is included in income on the LCF see 'Income headings'.

Imputation of missing information

Although LCF response is generally based on complete households responding, there are areas in the survey for which missing information is imputed. This falls into two broad categories:

(i)   Specific items of information missing from a response. These missing values are imputed on a case by case basis using other information collected in the interview. The procedure is used, for example, for council tax payments and for interest received on savings

(ii)   Imputation of a complete diary case. Where a response is missing a diary from a household member, this information is imputed using information from respondents with similar characteristics

Uses of the survey

LCF expenditure data

Retail Prices Index – The main reason, historically, for instituting a regular survey on expenditure by households has been to provide information on spending patterns for the Retail Prices Index (RPI). The RPI plays a vital role in the uprating of state pensions and welfare benefits and in general economic policy and analysis. The RPI measures the change in the cost of a selection of goods and services representative of the expenditure of the vast majority of households. The pattern of expenditure gradually changes from one year to the next, and the composition of the basket needs to be kept up-to-date. Accordingly, regular information is required on spending patterns and much of this is supplied by the Living Costs and Food (LCF) module of the Integrated Household Survey (IHS). The expenditure weights for the general RPI need to relate to people within given income limits, for which the LCF is the only source of information.

Household expenditure and Gross Domestic Product (GDP*)* – LCF data on spending are an important source used in compiling national estimates of household final consumption expenditure which are published regularly in United Kingdom National Accounts (ONS Blue Book). Household final consumption expenditure estimates feed into the National Accounts and estimates of GDP. They also provide the weights for the Consumer Price Index (CPI), and for Purchasing Power Parities (PPPs) for international price comparisons. LCF data are also used in the estimation of taxes on expenditure, in particular VAT.

Regional accounts – LCF expenditure information is one of the sources used by ONS to derive regional estimates of consumption expenditure. It is also used in compiling some of the other estimates for the regional accounts.

The Statistical Office of the European Communities (Eurostat) collates information from family budget surveys conducted by the member states. The LCF is the UK's contribution to this. The UK is one of only a few countries with such a regular, continuous and detailed survey.

Other Government uses – The Department of Energy and Climate Change and the Department for Transport both use LCF expenditure data in their own fields relating to, for example, energy, housing, cars and transport. Several other Government publications include LCF expenditure data, such as *Social Trends, Regional Trends* and the *Social Focus* series.

Non-Government uses – There are also numerous users outside Central Government, including academic researchers and business and market researchers. One example is an academic study that has used LCF data as part of a wider study, to obtain a clear picture of utility expenditure patterns across the European Union.

LCF income data

Redistribution of income – LCF information on income and expenditure is used to study how Government taxes and benefits affect household income. The Government's interdepartmental tax benefit model is based on the LCF and enables the economic effects of policy measures to be analysed across households. This model is used by HM Treasury and HM Revenue and Customs to estimate the impact on different households of possible changes in taxes and benefits.

Non-Government users – As with the expenditure data, LCF income data are also studied extensively outside Government. In particular, academic researchers in the economic and social science areas of many universities use the LCF. For example the Institute for Fiscal Studies uses LCF data in research it carries out both for Government and on its own account to inform public debate.

Other LCF data

The Department for Environment, Food and Rural Affairs (Defra) publishes separate reports using LCF data on food expenditure to estimate consumption and nutrient intake.

The Department for Transport uses LCF data to monitor and forecast levels of car ownership and use, and in studies on the effects of motoring taxes.

Note: Great care is taken to ensure complete confidentiality of information and to protect the identity of LCF households. Only anonymised data are supplied to users.

Standard errors and estimates of precision

The LCF is a sample of households and not a census of the whole population. Therefore, the results are liable to differ to some degree from those that would have been obtained if every single household had been covered. Some of the differences will be systematic, in that lower proportions of certain types of household respond than of others. That aspect is discussed in 'Description and response rate of the survey' and 'Weighting'. This section discusses the effect of sampling variability; in other words, the effect of differences in expenditure and income between the households in the sample and in the whole population that arise from random chance. The degree of variability will depend on the sample size and how widely particular categories of expenditure (or income) vary between households. The sampling variability is smallest for the average expenditure of large groups of households on items purchased frequently and when the level of spending does not vary greatly between households. Conversely, it is largest for small groups of households, and for items purchased infrequently or for which expenditure varies considerably between households. A numerical measure of the likely magnitude of such differences (between the sample estimate and the value of the entire population) is provided by the quantity known as the standard error.

The calculation of standard errors takes into account the fact that the LCF sample is drawn in two stages, first a sample of areas (primary sampling units) then a sample of addresses within each of these areas. The main features of the sample design are described in 'Description and response rate of the survey'. The calculation also takes account of the effect of weighting. The two-stage sample increases sampling variability slightly, but the weighting reduces it for some items.

Standard errors for detailed expenditure items are presented in relative terms in Table A1 (standard error as a percentage of the average to which it refers). As the calculation of full standard errors is complex, this is the only table where they are shown. Tables B1 and B2 in this section show the design factor (DEFT), a measure of the efficiency of the survey's sample design. The DEFT is calculated by dividing the 'full' standard error by the standard error that would have applied if the survey had used a simple random sample ('simple method').

Table B1 Percentage standard errors of expenditure of households and number of recording households, 2009

Commodity or service	Weighted average weekly household expenditure (£)	Percentage standard error		Percentage standard error	Households recording expenditure	
		Simple method	Design factor (DEFT)	Full method	Recording households in sample	Percentage of all households
All expenditure groups	383.10	1.0	1.1	1.1	5,825	100
Food and non-alcoholic drinks	52.20	0.8	1.0	0.8	5,799	100
Alcoholic drink, tobacco & narcotics	11.20	2.1	1.0	2.0	3,650	63
Clothing and footwear	20.90	2.2	1.1	2.4	3,911	67
Housing, fuel and power	57.30	1.2	1.2	1.5	5,799	100
Household goods and services	27.90	3.3	1.2	4.1	5,357	92
Health	5.30	6.4	1.0	6.5	2,962	51
Transport	58.40	1.8	1.1	1.9	4,950	85
Communication	11.70	1.1	1.1	1.3	5,485	94
Recreation and culture	57.90	3.2	0.9	2.8	5,769	99
Education	7.00	8.5	1.4	11.8	456	8
Restaurants and hotels	38.40	2.1	1.3	2.7	5,100	88
Miscellaneous goods and services	35.00	2.1	1.1	2.3	5,692	98

ONS, Family Spending 2009, © Crown copyright 2010

Table B2 Percentage standard errors of income of households and numbers of recording households, 2009

Source of income	Weighted average weekly household income (£)	Percentage standard error		Percentage standard error	Households recording income	
		Simple method	Design factor (DEFT)	Full method	Recording households in sample	Percentage of all households
Gross household income	683	1.3	1.1	1.4	5,815	100
Wages and salaries	453	1.8	0.9	1.6	3,486	60
Self-employment	57	6.8	1.2	8.5	672	12
Investments	19	7.4	1.1	7.9	2,842	49
Annuities and pensions (other than social security benefits)	52	3.7	0.8	2.9	1,802	31
Social security benefits	95	1.4	0.7	1.0	4,339	75
Other sources	7	7.0	1.2	8.4	738	13

ONS, Family Spending 2009, © Crown copyright 2010

Using the standard errors – confidence intervals

A common use of standard errors is in calculating 95 per cent confidence intervals. Simplifying a little, these can be taken to mean that there is only a 5 per cent chance that the true population value lies outside the 95 per cent confidence interval, which is calculated as 1.96 times the standard error on either side of the mean. For example, the average expenditure on food and non-alcoholic drinks is £52.20 and the corresponding percentage standard error (full method) is 0.8 per cent. The amount either side of the mean for 95 per cent confidence is then:

1.96 x (0.8 ÷100) x £52.20 = £0.80 (rounded to nearest 10p)
Lower limit is 52.20 – 0.80 = £51.40 (rounded to nearest 10p)
Upper limit is 52.20 + 0.80 = £53.00 (rounded to nearest 10p)

Similar calculations can be carried out for other estimates of expenditure and income. The 95 per cent confidence intervals for main expenditure categories are given in **Table B3**.

Table B3   95 per cent confidence intervals for average household expenditure, 2009

Commodity or service	Weighted average weekly household expenditure (£)	95% confidence interval	
		Lower limit	Upper limit
All expenditure groups	**383.10**	**374.60**	**391.70**
Food and non-alcoholic drinks	52.20	51.30	53.00
Alcoholic drink, tobacco & narcotics	11.20	10.70	11.60
Clothing and footwear	20.90	19.90	21.90
Housing, fuel and power	57.30	55.60	59.00
Household goods and services	27.90	25.70	30.20
Health	5.30	4.60	6.00
Transport	58.40	56.20	60.60
Communication	11.70	11.40	11.90
Recreation and culture	57.90	54.70	61.00
Education	7.00	5.40	8.60
Restaurants and hotels	38.40	36.40	40.40
Miscellaneous goods and services	35.00	33.50	36.60

ONS, Family Spending 2009, © Crown copyright 2010

Calculation of standard errors – confidence intervals
Simple method

This formula treats the LCF sample as though it had arisen from a much simpler design with no multi-stage sampling, stratification, differential sampling or non-response weights. The weights are used but only to estimate the true population standard deviation in what is, in fact, a weighted design. The method of calculation is as follows: Let n be the total number of responding households in the survey, x_r the expenditure on a particular item of the r-th household, w_r be the weight attached to household r, and $\bar{x}$ the average expenditure per household on that item (averaged over the n households). Then the standard error $\bar{x}$, *sesrs*, is given by:

$$sesrs = \sqrt{\frac{\sum_{r=1}^{n} w_r (x_r - \bar{x})^2}{(n-1)\sum_{r=1}^{n} w_r}}$$

Full method

In fact, the sample in Great Britain is a multi-stage, stratified, random sample described further in 'Description and response rate of the survey'. First a sample of areas, the Primary Sampling Units (PSUs), is drawn from an ordered list. Then within each PSU a random sample of households is drawn. In Northern Ireland, however, the sample is drawn in a single stage and there is no clustering. The results are also weighted for non-response and calibrated to match the population separately by sex, by 5-year age ranges, and by region, as described in 'Weighting'.

The method for calculating complex standard errors for the weighted estimates used on this survey is quite complex. First, methods are applied that take account of the clustering, stratification and differential sampling (and initial non-response weights) used in the design. These are then modified to allow for the calibration weighting used on the survey. The exact formulae also depend on whether standard errors are being estimated for an estimated total or a mean or proportion. Here the method for a total is outlined.

Consecutive PSUs in the ordered list are first grouped into pairs or triples, at the end of a regional stratum. The standard error of a weighted total is estimated by:

$$sedes = \sqrt{\sum_{h} \frac{k_h}{k_h - 1} \sum_{i} (x_{hi} - \bar{x}_h)^2}$$

where the h denotes the stratum (PSU pairs or triples), k_h is the number of PSUs in the stratum h (either 2 or 3), the x_{hi} is the weighted total in PSU i and the $\bar{x}_h$ is the mean of these totals in stratum h. Further details of this method of estimating sampling errors are described in *A Sampling Errors Manual* (B Butcher and D Elliot, ONS 1987).

The effect of the calibration weighting is calculated using a jackknife linearisation estimator. It uses the formula given above but with each household's expenditure, x_r, replaced by a residual from a linear regression of expenditure on the number of people in each household in each of the region and age by sex categories used in the weighting.

The formulae have been expressed in terms of expenditures on a particular item, but of course they can also be applied to expenditures on groups of items, commodity groups and incomes from particular sources.

Definitions

Major changes in definitions since 1991 are described in 'Changes to definitions, 1991 to 2009'. Changes made between 1980 and 1990 are summarised in Appendix E of Family Spending 1994–95. For earlier changes see Annex 5 of Family Expenditure Survey 1980.

Household

A household comprises one person or a group of people who have the accommodation as their only or main residence and (for a group):

> *Either share at least one meal a day*
>
> *or*   *share the living accommodation, that is, a living room or sitting room*

Resident domestic servants are included. The members of a household are not necessarily related by blood or marriage. As the survey covers only private households, people living in hostels, hotels, boarding houses or institutions are excluded. Households are included if some or all members are not British subjects, however information is not collected from households containing members of the diplomatic service of another country or members of the United States armed forces.

Retired households

Retired households are those where the household reference person is retired. The household reference person is defined as retired if they are 65 years of age or more and male, or 60 years of age or more and female, and economically inactive. Therefore, if for example a male household reference person is aged over 65 years of age, but working part-time or waiting to take up a part-time job, this household would not be classified as a retired household. For analysis purposes two categories are used in this report:

- 'A retired household mainly dependent upon state pensions' is one in which at least three-quarters of the total income of the household is derived from national insurance retirement and similar pensions, including housing and other benefits paid in supplement to or instead of such pensions. The term 'national insurance retirement and similar pensions' includes national insurance disablement and war disability pensions, and income support in conjunction with these disability payments

- 'Other retired households' are retired households which do not fulfil the income conditions of 'retired household mainly dependent upon state pensions' because more than a quarter of the household's income derives from other sources. For example, occupational retirement pensions and/or income from investments, or annuities .

Household reference person (HRP)

From 2001–02 the concept of household reference person (HRP) was adopted on all government-sponsored surveys in place of head of household. The household reference person is the householder who:
- owns the household accommodation, or
- is legally responsible for the rent of the accommodation, or
- has the household accommodation as an emolument or perquisite, or
- has the household accommodation by virtue of some relationship to the owner who is not a member of the household.

If there are joint householders the household reference person will be the one with the higher income. If the income is the same, then the eldest householder is taken.

Members of household

In most cases the members of co-operating households are easily identified as the people who satisfy the conditions in the definition of a household, see above, and are present during the record-keeping period. However, difficulties of definition arise where people are temporarily away from the household or else spend their time between two residences. The following rules apply in deciding whether or not such persons are members of the household:

- married persons living and working away from home for any period are included as members, provided they consider the sampled address to be their main residence. In general, other people (such as relatives, friends and boarders) who are either temporarily absent or who spend their time between the sampled address and another address, are included as members if they consider the sampled address to be their main residence. However, there are exceptions which override the subjective main residence rule:

  i.   Children under 16 years of age away at school are included as members;

  ii.   Older persons receiving education away from home, including children aged 16 and 17, are excluded unless they are at home for all or most of the record-keeping period;

  iii. Visitors staying temporarily with the household, and others who have been in the household for only a short time are treated as members, provided they will be staying with the household for at least one month from the start of record-keeping.

Household composition

A consequence of these definitions is that household compositions quoted in this report include some households where certain members are temporarily absent, for example, a 'two-adult and children' household where one parent is temporarily away from home.

Adult

In the report, persons who have reached the age of 18 are classed as adults. In addition, those aged 16 to 18 who are not in full-time education, or who are married, are classed as adults.

Children

In the report, persons who are under 18 years of age, in full-time education and have never been married are classed as children.

However, in the definition of clothing, clothing for persons aged 16 years and over is classified as clothing for men and women; clothing for those aged 5 to 15 as clothing for boys and girls; and clothing for those under five as babies clothing.

Main Diary Keeper (MDK)

The MDK is the person in the household who is normally responsible for most of the food shopping. This includes people who organise and pay for the shopping although they do not physically do the shopping themselves.

Spenders

Household members aged 16 and over, excluding those who, for special reasons, are not capable of keeping diary record-books, are described as spenders.

Absent spenders

If a spender is absent for longer than 7 days they are defined as an 'absent spender'. Absent spenders do not keep a diary and consequently are not eligible for the monetary gift that is paid to diary keepers.

Non spenders

If a household member is completely incapable of contributing to the survey by answering questions or keeping a diary, then they are defined as a 'non-spender'. However, incapable people living on their own cannot be designated as non-spenders as they comprise the whole expenditure unit. If this is the case, the interviewer should enlist the help of the person outside of the household who looks after their interests. If there is no-one able or willing to help, the address should be coded as incapable.

Economically active

These are persons aged 16 and over who fall into the following categories:

- **Employees at work** – those who at the time of interview were working full-time or part-time as employees or were away from work on holiday. Part-time work is defined as normally working 30 hours a week or less (excluding meal breaks) including regularly worked overtime.

- **Employees temporarily away from work** – those who, at the time of interview, had a job but were temporarily absent due to, for example, illness, temporary lay-off, or strike.

- **Government supported training schemes** – those participating in government programmes and schemes who, in the course of their participation, receive training such as Employment Training, and including those who are also employees in employment.

- **Self-employed** – those who, at the time of interview, said they were self-employed.

- **Unemployed** – those who, at the time of interview, were out of employment and have sought work within the last four weeks and were available to start work within two weeks, or were waiting to start a job already obtained.

- **Unpaid family workers** – those working unpaid for their own or a relative's business. In this report, unpaid family workers are included under economically inactive in analyses by economic status (Tables A19 and A48) because insufficient information is available to assign them to an economic status group.

Economically inactive

- **Retired** – persons who have reached national insurance retirement age (60 and over for women; 65 and over for men) and are not economically active.

- **Unoccupied** – persons under national insurance retirement age who are not working, nor actively seeking work. This category includes certain self-employed persons such as mail order agents and baby-sitters who are not classified as economically active.

National Statistics Socio-economic classification (NS-SEC)

From 2001 the National Statistics Socio-economic classification (NS-SEC) was adopted for all official surveys, in place of Social Class based on Occupation and Socio-economic group. NS-SEC is itself based on the Standard Occupational Classification 2000 (SOC2000) and details of employment status. Although NS-SEC is an occupationally based classification, there are procedures for classifying those not in work.

The main categories used for analysis in Family Spending are:

1   Higher managerial and professional occupations, sub-divided into:
         1.1   Large employers and higher managerial occupations
         1.2   Higher professional occupations
2   Lower managerial and professional occupations
3   Intermediate occupations
4   Small employers and own account workers
5   Lower supervisory and technical occupations
6   Semi-routine occupations
7   Routine occupations
8   Never worked and long-term unemployed
9   Students
10   Occupation not stated
11   Not classifiable for other reasons

The long-term unemployed are defined as those unemployed and seeking work for 12 months or more. Members of the armed forces, who were assigned to a separate category in Social Class, are included within the NS-SEC classification. Individuals that have retired within the last 12 months are classified according to their employment. Other retired individuals are assigned to the 'Not classifiable for other reasons' category.

Socio-economic classification (SE-SEC) Regions

These are the Government Office Regions as defined in 1994. See the region map on page 116 of Appendix A for more details.

Urban and rural areas

This classification introduced in 2005/06 replaces the previous Department for Transport, Local Government and the Regions (DTLR) 1991 Census-based urban and rural classification, which was used in previous editions of *Family Spending*. The new classification is applied across Great Britain and is an amalgamation of the Rural and Urban Classification 2004 for England and Wales and the Scottish Executive Urban Rural Classification. These classifications are based on 2001 Census data and have been endorsed as the standard National Statistics Classifications for identifying urban and rural areas across GB. In broad terms, an area is defined as urban or rural depending on whether the population falls inside a settlement of 10,000 or more. For further details concerning these classifications please refer to the Office for National Statistics (ONS) website: www.statistics.gov.uk/geography/nrudp.asp.

Expenditure

Any definition of expenditure is to some extent arbitrary, and the inclusion of certain types of payment is a matter of convenience or convention depending on the purpose for which the information is to be used. In the tables in this report, total expenditure represents current expenditure on goods and services. Total expenditure, defined in this way, excludes those recorded payments that are really savings or investments: for example, purchases of national savings certificates, life assurance premiums, and contributions to pension funds. Similarly, income tax payments, national insurance contributions, mortgage capital repayments and other payments for major additions to dwellings are excluded. Expenditure data are collected in the diary record-book and in the household schedule. Informants are asked to record in the diary any payments made during the 14 days of record-keeping, whether or not the goods or services paid for have been received. Certain types of expenditure which are usually regular though infrequent, such as insurance, licences and season tickets, and the periods to which they relate, are recorded in the household schedule as well as regular payments such as utility bills.

The cash purchase of motor vehicles is also entered in the household schedule. In addition, expenditure on some items purchased infrequently (thereby being subject to high sampling errors) has been recorded in the household schedule using a retrospective recall period of either 3 or 12 months. These items include carpets, furniture, holidays and some housing costs. In order to avoid duplication, all payments shown in the diary record-book which relate to items listed in the household or income schedules are omitted in the analysis of the data, irrespective of whether there is a corresponding entry on the latter schedules. Amounts paid in respect of periods longer than a week are converted to weekly values.

Expenditure tables in this report show the 12 main commodity groups of spending and these are broken down into items which are numbered hierarchically (see 'Changes to definitions, 1991 to 2009' which details a major change to the coding frame used from 2001–02). Table A1 shows a further breakdown in the items themselves into components which can be separately identified. The items are numbered as in the main expenditure tables and against each item or component the average weekly household expenditure and percentage standard error is shown.

Qualifications which apply to this concept of expenditure are described in the following paragraphs:

- **Goods supplied from a household's own shop or farm**
  Spenders are asked to record and give the value of goods obtained from their own shop or farm, even if the goods are withdrawn from stock for personal use without payment. The value is included as expenditure.

- **Hire purchase and credit sales agreements, and transactions financed by loans repaid by instalments**
  Expenditure on transactions under hire purchase or credit sales agreements, or financed by loans repaid by instalments, consists of all instalments that are still being paid at the date of interview, together with down payments on commodities acquired within the preceding three months. These two components (divided by the periods covered) provide the weekly averages which are included in the expenditure on the separate items given in the tables in this report.

- **Club payments and budget account payments, instalments through mail order firms and similar forms of credit transaction**
  When goods are purchased by forms of credit other than hire purchase and credit sales agreement, the expenditure on them may be estimated either from the amount of the instalment which is paid or from the value of the goods which are acquired. Since the particular commodities to which the instalment relates may not be known, details of goods

ordered through, for example, clubs or mail order firms, during the month prior to the date of interview, are recorded in the household schedule. The weekly equivalent of the value of the goods is included in the expenditure on the separate items given in the tables in this report. This procedure has the advantage of enabling club transactions to be related to specific articles. Although payments into clubs, etc. are shown in the diary record-book, these entries are excluded from expenditure estimates.

- **Credit card transactions**

  From 1988 purchases made by credit card or charge card have been recorded in the survey on an acquisition basis rather than the formerly used payment basis. Thus, if a spender acquired an item (by use of credit/charge card) during the two week survey period, the value of the item would be included as part of expenditure in that period whether or not any payment was made in this period to the credit card account. Payments made to the card account are ignored. However any payment of credit/charge card interest is included in expenditure if made in the two week period.

- **Income Tax**

  Amounts of income tax deducted under the Pay as you earn (PAYE) scheme or paid directly by those who are employers or self-employed are recorded (together with information about tax refunds). For employers and the self-employed the amounts comprise the actual payments made in the previous 12 months and may not correspond to the tax due on the income arising in that period, for example if no tax has been paid but is due or if tax payments cover more than one financial year. However, the amounts of tax deducted at source from some of the items which appear in the Income Schedule are not directly available. Estimates of the tax paid on bank and building society interest and amounts deducted from dividends on stocks and shares are therefore made by applying the appropriate rates of tax. In the case of income tax paid at source on pensions and annuities, similar adjustments are made. These estimates mainly affect the relatively few households with high incomes from interest and dividends, and households including someone receiving a pension from previous employment.

- **Rented dwellings**

  Expenditure on rented dwellings is taken as the sum of expenditure on a number of items such as rent, council tax, and water rates. For local authority tenants the expenditure is gross rent less any rebate (including rebate received in the form of housing benefit), and for other tenants it is gross rent less any rent allowance received under statutory schemes including the Housing Benefit Scheme. Rebate on Council Tax or rates (Northern Ireland) is deducted from expenditure on Council Tax or rates. Receipts from sub-letting part of the dwelling are not deducted from housing costs but appear (net of the expenses of the sub-letting) as investment income.

- **Rent-free dwellings**

  Rent-free dwellings are those owned by someone outside the household and where either no rent is charged or the rent is paid by someone outside the household. Households whose rent is paid directly to the landlord by the DWP do not live rent-free. Payments for Council Tax for example are regarded as the cost of housing. Rebate on rates (Northern Ireland)/Council Tax/water rates(Scotland) (including rebate received in the form of housing benefit), is deducted from expenditure on rates/Council Tax/water rates. Receipts from sub-letting part of the dwelling are not deducted from housing costs but appear (net of the expenses of the sub-letting) as investment income.

- **Owner-occupied dwellings**
  In the LCF, payments for water rates, ground rent, fuel, maintenance and repair of the dwelling, among other items, are regarded as the cost of housing. Receipts from letting part of the dwelling are not deducted from housing costs but appear (net of the expenses of the letting) as investment income. Mortgage capital repayments and amounts paid for the outright purchase of the dwelling or for major structural alterations are not included as housing expenditure, but are entered under 'other items recorded', as are Council Tax, rates (Northern Ireland) and mortgage interest payments. Structural insurance is included in 'Miscellaneous goods and services'.

- **Second-hand goods and part-exchange transactions**
  The survey expenditure data are based on information about actual payments and therefore include payments for second-hand goods and part-exchange transactions. New payments only are included for part-exchange transactions, that is the costs of the goods obtained less the amounts allowed for the goods which are traded in. Receipts for goods sold or traded in are not included in income.

- **Business expenses**
  The survey covers only private households and is concerned with payments made by members of households as private individuals. Spenders are asked to state whether expenditure that has been recorded on the schedules includes amounts that will be refunded as expenses from a business or organisation or that will be entered as business expenses for income tax purposes, for example rent, telephone charges, travelling expenses and meals out. Any such amounts are deducted from the recorded expenditure.

Income

The standard concept of income in the survey is, as far as possible, that of gross weekly cash income current at the time of interview, that is before the deduction of income tax actually paid, national insurance contributions and other deductions at source. However, for a few tables a concept of disposable income is used, defined as gross weekly cash income less the statutory deductions and payments of income tax (taking refunds into account) and national insurance contributions. Analysis in Chapter 3 of this volume and some other analyses of LCF data use 'equivalisation' of incomes: in other words adjustment of household income to allow for the different size and composition of each household. For more information see Chapter 3 of this volume. The cash levels of certain items of income (and expenditure) recorded in the survey by households receiving supplementary benefit were affected by the Housing Benefit Scheme introduced in stages from November 1982. From 1984 housing expenditure is given on a strictly net basis and all rent/council tax rebates and allowances and housing benefit are excluded from gross income.

Although information about most types of income is obtained on a current basis, some data, principally income from investment and from self-employment, are estimated over a 12-month period.

The following are excluded from the assessment of income:

- money received by one member of the household from another (for example housekeeping money, dress allowance, children's pocket money) other than wages paid to resident domestic servants;

- withdrawals of savings, receipts from maturing insurance policies, proceeds from sale of financial and other assets (such as houses, cars, and furniture), winnings from betting, lump-sum gratuities and windfalls such as legacies.;

- the value of educational grants and scholarships not paid in cash.;

- the value of income in kind, including the value of goods received free and the abatement in cost of goods received at reduced prices, and of bills paid by someone who is not a member of the household;

- loans and money received in repayment of loans.

Details are obtained of the income of each member of the household. The income of the household is taken to be the sum of the incomes of all its members. The information does not relate to a common or a fixed time period. Items recorded for periods greater than a week are converted to a weekly value.

Particular points relating to some components of income are as follows:

- **Wages and salaries of employees**

  The normal gross wages or salaries of employees are taken to be their earnings. These are calculated by adding to the normal 'take home' pay amounts deducted at source, such as income tax payments, national insurance contributions and other deductions (for example payments into firm social clubs, superannuation schemes, works transport, and benevolent funds). Employees are asked to give the earnings actually received including bonuses and commission the last time payment was made and, if different, the amount usually received. It is the amount usually received that is regarded as the normal take-home pay. Additions are made so as to include in normal earnings the value of occasional payments, such as bonuses or commissions received quarterly or annually. One of the principal objects in obtaining data on income is to enable expenditure to be classified in ranges of normal income. Average household expenditure is likely to be based on the long-term expectations of the various members of the household as to their incomes rather than be altered by short-term changes affecting individuals. Hence, if employees have been away from work without pay for 13 weeks or less, they are regarded as continuing to receive their normal earnings instead of social security benefits, such as unemployment or sickness benefit, that they may be receiving. Otherwise, normal earnings are disregarded and current short-term social security benefits taken instead. Wages and salaries include any earnings from subsidiary employment as an employee and the earnings of HM Forces.

- **Income from self-employment**

  Income from self-employment covers any personal income from employment other than as an employee: for example, as a sole trader, professional or other person working on his own account or in partnership, including subsidiary work on his own account by a person whose main job is as an employee. It is measured from estimates of income or trading profits, after deduction of business expenses but before deduction of tax, over the most recent 12-month period for which figures can be given. Should either a loss have been made or no profit, income would be taken as the amounts drawn from the business for own use or as any other income received from the job or business. Persons working as mail order agents or baby-sitters, with no other employment, have been classified as unoccupied rather than as self-employed, and the earnings involved have been classified as earnings from 'other sources' rather than self-employment income.

- **Income from investment**

  Income from investments or from property, other than that in which the household is residing, is the amount received during the 12 months immediately prior to the date of the initial interview. It includes receipts from sub-letting part of the dwelling (net of the expenses of the sub-letting). If income tax has been deducted at source the gross amount is estimated by applying a conversion factor during processing.

- **Social security benefits**

  Income from social security benefits does not include the short-term payments such as unemployment or sickness benefit, received by an employee who has been away from work for 13 weeks or less, and who is therefore regarded as continuing to receive his normal earnings as described on page 140.

Quantiles

The quantiles of a distribution divide it into a number of equal parts; each of which contains the same number of households. In Family Spending, quantiles are applied to both household expenditure and income distributions.

For example, the median of a distribution divides it into two equal parts, so that half the households in a distribution of household income will have income more than the median, and the other half will have income less than the median. Similarly, quartiles, quintiles and deciles divide the distribution into four, five and ten equal parts respectively.

Most of the analysis in Family Spending is done in terms of quintile groups and decile groups.

In the calculation of quantiles for this report, zero values are counted as part of the distribution.

Income headings

Headings used for identifying 2009 income information

Source of Income

References in tables	Components separately identified	Explanatory notes
a. Wages and salaries	Normal 'take-home' pay from main employment 'Take-home' pay from subsidiary employment Employees' income tax deduction Employees' National Insurance contribution Superannuation contributions deducted from pay Other deductions	(i) In the calculation of household income in this report, where an employee has been away from work without pay for 13 weeks or less his normal wage or salary has been used in estimating his total income instead of social security benefits, such as unemployment or sickness benefits that he may have received. Otherwise such benefits are used in estimating total income (see notes at reference e). (ii) Normal income from wages and salaries is estimated by adding to the normal 'take-home' pay deductions made at source last time paid, together with the weekly value of occasional additions to wages and salaries (see page 137). (iii) The components of wages and salaries, for which figures are separately available, amount in total to the normal earnings of employees, regardless of the operation of the 13 week rule in note (i) above. Thus the sum of the components listed here does not in general equal the wages and salaries figure in tables of this report.

Income headings

Headings used for identifying 2009 income information

Source of income

b. Self-employment	Income from business or profession, including subsidiary self-employment	The earnings or profits of a trade or profession, after deduction of business expenses but before deduction of tax.
c. Investments	Interest on building society shares and deposits Interest on bank deposits and savings accounts including National Savings Bank Interest on ISAs Interest on Gilt-edged stock and War Loans Interest and dividends from stocks, shares, bonds, trusts, PEPs, debentures and other securities Rent or income from property, after deducting expenses but inclusive of income tax (including receipts from letting or sub-letting part of own residence, net of the expenses of the letting or sub-letting). Other unearned Income	
d. Annuities and pensions, other than social security	Annuities and income from trust or covenant Pensions from previous employers Personal pensions	
e. Benefits	Child benefit Guardian's allowance Carer's allowance (formerly Invalid care allowance) Retirement pension (National Insurance) or old person's pension Pension credit Widow's pension/bereavement allowance or widowed parent's allowance War disablement pension or war widow/widower's pension Severe disablement allowance Care component of disability living allowance Mobility component of disability living allowance Attendance allowance Job seekers allowance Winter fuel allowance Cold Weather Payment Income support Working tax credit Child tax credit Incapacity benefit	(i) The calculation of household income in this report takes account of the 13 week rule described at reference a, note (i). (ii) The components of social security benefits, for which figures are separately available, amount in total to the benefits received in the week before interview. That is to say, they include amounts that are discounted from the total by the operation of the 13 week rule in note (i). Thus the sum of the components listed here differs from the total of social security benefits used in the income tables of this report. (iii) Housing Benefit is treated as a reduction in housing costs and not as income.

Income headings

Headings used for identifying 2009 income information

Source of income

Statutory sick pay (from employer)

Industrial injury disablement benefit

Maternity allowance

Statutory maternity pay

Statutory paternity pay

Statutory adoption pay

Health in pregnancy grant

Any other benefit including lump sums and grants

Social security benefits excluded from Income
calculation by 13 week rule.

f. Other sources   Married person's allowance from husband/wife
temporarily away from home

Alimony or separation allowances;
allowances for foster children, allowances from
members of the Armed Forces or Merchant Navy,
or any other money from friends or relatives,
other than husbands outside the household

Benefits from trade unions, friendly societies etc.
other than pensions

Value of meal vouchers

Earnings from intermittent or casual work over
12 months, not included in a or b above

Student loans and money scholarships received
by persons aged 16 and over and aged under
16

Other income for children under 16   e.g. from spare time jobs or income from
Trusts or investments

STANDARD STATISTICAL REGION

GOVERNMENT OFFICE REGION

STANDARD STATISTICAL REGION		GOVERNMENT OFFICE REGION
NORTH	Cleveland Durham Northumberland Tyne and Wear	NORTH EAST
	Cumbria	
NORTH WEST	Cheshire Greater Manchester Lancashire Merseyside	NORTH WEST
YORKSHIRE AND HUMBERSIDE	Humberside North Yorkshire South Yorkshire West Yorkshire	YORKSHIRE AND THE HUMBER
EAST MIDLANDS	Derbyshire Leicestershire Lincolnshire Northamptonshire Nottinghamshire	EAST MIDLANDS
WEST MIDLANDS	Hereford and Worcester Shropshire Staffordshire Warwickshire West Midlands	WEST MIDLANDS
EAST ANGLIA	Cambridgeshire Norfolk Suffolk	EAST OF ENGLAND
	Bedfordshire Essex Hertfordshire	
	Greater London	LONDON
SOUTH EAST	Berkshire Buckinghamshire East Sussex Hampshire Isle of Wight Kent Oxfordshire Surrey West Sussex	SOUTH EAST
SOUTH WEST	Avon Cornwall Devon Dorset Gloucestershire Somerset Wiltshire	SOUTH WEST

Change in definitions, 1991 to 2009

1991

No significant changes.

1992

Housing – Imputed rent for owner occupiers and households in rent-free accommodation was discontinued. For owner occupiers this had been the rent they would have had to pay themselves to live in the property they own, and for households in rent-free accommodation it was the rent they would normally have had to pay. Until 1990 these amounts were counted both as income and as a housing cost. Mortgage interest payments were counted as a housing cost for the first time in 1991.

1993

Council Tax – Council Tax was introduced to replace the Community Charge in Great Britain from April 1993.

1994-95

New expenditure items – The definition of expenditure was extended to include two items previously shown under 'other payments recorded'. These were:
• gambling payments, and
• mortgage protection premiums.

Expenditure classifications – A new classification system for expenditures was introduced in April 1994. The system is hierarchical and allows more detail to be preserved than the previous system. New categories of expenditure were introduced and are shown in detail in Table 7.1. The 14 main groups of expenditure were retained, but there were some changes in the content of these groups.

Gambling Payments – data on gambling expenditure and winnings are collected in the expenditure diary. Previously these were excluded from the definition of household expenditure used in the FES. The data are shown as memoranda items under the heading 'Other payments recorded' on both gross and net bases. The net basis corresponds approximately to the treatment of gambling in the National Accounts. The introduction of the National Lottery stimulated a reconsideration of this treatment. From April 1994, (gross) gambling payments have been included as expenditure in 'Leisure Services'. Gambling winnings continued to be noted as a memorandum item under 'Other items recorded'. They are treated as windfall income. They do not form a part of normal household income, nor are they subtracted from gross gambling payments. This treatment is in line with the PRODCOM classification of the Statistical Office of the European Communities (SOEC) for expenditure in household budget surveys.

1995-96

Geographical coverage – The FES geographical coverage was extended to mainland Scotland north of the Caledonian Canal.

Under 16s diaries – Two-week expenditure diaries for 7 to 15-year-olds were introduced following three feasibility pilot studies which found that children of that age group were able to cope with the task of keeping a two-week expenditure record. Children are asked to record everything they buy with their own money but to exclude items bought with other people's money. Purchases are coded according to the same coding categories as adult diaries except for meals and snacks away from home which are coded as school meals, hot meals and snacks, and cold meals and snacks. Children who keep a diary are given a £5 incentive payment. A refusal to keep an under 16's diary does not invalidate the household from inclusion in the survey.

Pocket money given to children is still recorded separately in adult diaries, and money paid by adults for school meals and school travel is recorded in the Household Questionnaire. Double counting is eliminated at the processing stage.

Tables in *Family Spending* reports did not include the information from the children's diaries until the 1998–99 report. Appendix F in the 1998–99 and 1999–2000 reports show what difference the inclusion made.

1996-97

Self-employment –- The way in which information about income from self-employment is collected was substantially revised in 1996–97 following various tests and pilot studies. The quality of such data was increased but this may have lead to a discontinuity. Full details are shown in the Income Questionnaire, available from the address in the introduction.

Cable/satellite television – Information on cable and satellite subscriptions is now collected from the household questionnaire rather than from the diary, leading to more respondents reporting this expenditure.

Mobile phones – Expenditure on mobile phones was previously collected through the diary. From 1996–97 this has been included in the questionnaire.

Job seekers allowance (JSA) – Introduced in October 1996 as a replacement for Unemployment Benefit and any Income Support associated with the payment of Unemployment Benefit. Receipt of JSA is collected with NI Unemployment Benefit and with Income Support. In both cases the number of weeks a respondent has been in receipt of these benefits is taken as the number of weeks receiving JSA in the last 12 months and before that period the number of weeks receiving Unemployment Benefit/Income Support.

Retrospective recall – The period over which information is requested has been extended from 3 to 12 months for vehicle purchase and sale. Information on the purchase of car and motorcycle spare parts is no longer collected by retrospective recall. Instead expenditure on these items is collected through the diary.

State benefits – The lists of benefits specifically asked about was reviewed in 1996–97. See the Income Questionnaire for more information.

Sample stratifiers – New stratifiers were introduced in 1996–97 based on standard regions, socio-economic group and car ownership.

Government Office Regions – Regional analyses are now presented using the Government Office Regions (GORs) formed in 1994. Previously all regional analyses used Standard Statistical Regions (SSRs). For more information see Appendix F in the 1996–97 report.

1997-98

Bank/Building society service charges – Collection of information on service charges levied by banks has been extended to include building societies.

Payments from unemployment/redundancy insurances – Information is now collected on payments received from private unemployment and redundancy insurance policies. This information is then incorporated into the calculation of income from other sources.

Retired households – The definition of retired households has been amended to exclude households where the head of the household is economically active.

Rent-free tenure – The definition of rent-free tenure has been amended to include those households for which someone outside the household, except an employer or an organisation, is paying a rent or mortgage on behalf of the household.

National Lottery – From February 1997 expenditure on National lottery tickets was collected as three separate items: tickets for the Wednesday draw only, tickets for the Saturday draw only and tickets for both draws.

1998-99

Children's income – Three new expenditure codes were introduced: pocket money to children; money given to children for specific purposes and cash gifts to children. These replaced a single code covering all three categories.

Main job and last paid job – Harmonised questions were adopted.

1999-2000

Disabled Persons Tax Credit replaced Disability Working Allowance and **Working Families Tax Credit** replaced Family Credit from October 1999.

2000-01

Household definition – the definition was changed to the harmonised definition which has been in use in the Census and nearly all other government household surveys since 1981. The effect is to group together into a single household some people who would have been allocated to separate households on the previous definition. The effect is fairly small but not negligible.

Up to 1999–2000 the FES definition was based on the pre-1981 Census definition and required members to share eating and budgeting arrangements as well as shared living accommodation.

The definition of a household was:

- One person or a group of people who have the accommodation as their only or main residence, and (for a group) share the living accommodation, that is a living or sitting room, **and** share meals together (or have common housekeeping)

The harmonised definition is less restrictive:

- One person or a group of people who have the accommodation as their only or main residence and (for a group) share the living accommodation, that is a living or sitting room **or** share meals together or have common housekeeping.

The effect of the change is probably to increase average household size by 0.6 per cent.

Question reductions – A thorough review of the questionnaire showed that a number of questions were no longer needed by government users. These were cut from the 2000–01 survey to reduce the burden on respondents. The reduction was fairly small but it did make the interview flow better. All the questions needed for a complete record of expenditure and income were retained.

Redesigned diary – The diary was redesigned to be easier for respondents to keep and to look cleaner. The main change of substance was to delete the column for recording whether each item was purchased by credit, charge or shop card.

Ending of MIRAS – Tax relief on interest on loans for house purchase was abolished from April 2000. Questions related to MIRAS were therefore dropped. They included some that were needed to estimate the amount if the respondent did not know it. A number were retained for other purposes, however, such as the amount of the loan still outstanding which is still asked for households paying a reduced rate of interest because one of them works for the lender.

2001-02

Expenditure and Food Survey (EFS) introduced, replacing the Family Expenditure and National Food Surveys (FES and NFS)

Household reference person – this replaced the previous concept of head of household. The household reference person is the householder, that is the person who:
- owns the household accommodation, or
- is legally responsible for the rent of the accommodation, or
- has the household accommodation as an emolument or perquisite, or
- has the household accommodation by virtue of some relationship to the owner who is not a member of the household.

If there are joint householders the household reference person is the one with the higher income. If the income is the same, then the eldest householder is taken.

A key difference between household reference person and head of household is that the household reference person must always be a householder, whereas the head of household was always the husband, who might not even be a householder himself.

National Statistics Socio-economic classification (NS-SEC) – the National Statistics Socio-economic Classification (NS-SEC) was adopted for all official surveys, in place of social class based on occupation and socio-economic group. NS-SEC is itself based on the Standard Occupational Classification 2000 (SOC2000) and details of employment status.

The long-term unemployed, which fall into a separate category, are defined as those unemployed and seeking work for 12 months or more. Members of the armed forces, who were assigned to a separate category in social class, are included within the NS-SEC classification. Residual groups that remain unclassified include students and those with inadequately described occupations.

COICOP – From 2001–02, the **C**lassification **O**f **I**ndividual **CO**nsumption by **P**urpose (COICOP/HBS, referred to as COICOP in this volume) was introduced as a new coding frame for expenditure items. COICOP has been adapted to the needs of Household Budget Surveys (HBS) across the EU and, as a consequence, is compatible with similar classifications used in national accounts and consumer price indices. This allows the production of indicators which are comparable Europe-wide, such as the Harmonised Indices of Consumer Prices (computed for all goods as well as sub-categories such as food and transport). The main categorisation of spending used in this volume (namely 12 categories relating to food and non-alcoholic beverages; alcoholic beverages, tobacco and narcotics; clothing and footwear; housing, fuel and power; household goods and services; health, transport; communication; recreation and culture; education; restaurants and hotels; and miscellaneous goods and services) is only comparable between the two frames at a broad level. Table 4.1 in this volume has been produced by mapping COICOP to the FES 14 main categories. However the two frames are not comparable for any smaller categories, leading to a break in trends between 2000–01 and 2001–02 for any level of detail below the main 12-fold categorisation. A complete listing of COICOP and COICOP plus (an extra level of detail added by individual countries for their own needs) is available on request from the address in the introduction.

Proxy interviews – While questions about general household affairs are put to all household members or to a main household informant, questions about work and income are put to the individual members of the household. Where a member of the household is not present during the household interview, another member of the household (for example, spouse) may be able to provide information about the absent person. The individual's interview is then identified as a *proxy* interview. From 2001–02 the EFS began accepting responses that contained a proxy interview.

Short income – From 2001–02 the EFS accepted responses from households that answered the short income section. This was designed for respondents who were reluctant to provide more detailed income information.

2002-03

Main shopper – At the launch of the EFS in April 2001, the respondent responsible for buying the household's main shopping was identified as the 'main diary keeper'. From 2002–03, this term was replaced by the 'main shopper'.

The importance of the main shopper is to ensure that we have obtained information on the bulk of the shopping in the household. Without this person's co-operation we have insufficient information to use the other diaries kept by members of the household in a meaningful way. The main shopper must therefore complete a diary for the interview to qualify as a full or partial interview. Without their participation, the outcome will be a refusal no matter who else is willing to complete a diary.

2003-04

Working Tax Credit replaced Disabled Persons Tax Credit and Working Families Tax Credit from April 2003.

Pension Credit replaced Minimum Income Guarantee from October 2003.

Child Tax Credit replaced Children's Tax Credit and Childcare Tax Credit from April 2003.

2004-05

No significant changes.

2005-06

Urban and rural definition – A new urban and rural area classification based on 2001 Census data has been introduced onto the EFS dataset and is presented in Tables A38, A45 and A48 of this publication. The classification replaces the Department for Transport, Local Government and the Regions (DTLR) 1991 Census-based urban and rural classification that was used in previous editions of *Family Spending*. The new classification is the standard National Statistics classification for identifying urban and rural areas in England and Wales, and Scotland. Please refer to 'Definitions' for further details.

Motor vehicle road taxation refunds – Questions on road tax refunds were inadvertently omitted from the 2005–06 questionnaire. Within the Appendix A tables of the 2005–06 report, the heading for category 13.2.3 'Motor vehicle road taxation payments less refunds' has been changed to reflect this omission.

Purchase of vehicles – During April to December 2005 respondents who had sold a vehicle were not asked whether they had bought that same vehicle in the previous year. This was corrected from January 2006, but means that some expenditure on vehicles may have been missed.

2006

No significant changes.

2007

An improvement to the imputation of mortgage interest payments has been implemented and applied to 2006 and 2007 data in this publication, which should lead to more accurate figures. This will also lead to a slight discontinuity.

An error was discovered in the derivation of mortgage capital repayments which was leading to double counting. This has been amended for the 2006 and 2007 data in this publication, which will cause a minor discontinuity.

2008

The LCF question used to derive the student category for NS-SEC B was changed in 2008 due to the introduction of the Integrated Household Survey (IHS). Prior to the IHS, respondents were asked if they were currently in full-time education and those who responded yes to this question were classified as students. Since 2008, respondents have been asked if they are enrolled on any full-time or part-time education course and those who respond 'yes' have then been asked to select the course they are attending from a set of options. Respondents who select any of the full-time course options have been classified as students under NS-SEC. This more stringent definition of full-time student has resulted in a decrease in the number of people classified as students.

2009

Gas & electricity payment methods – Following consultation with the Department for Energy and Climate Change (DECC), the payment methods have been updated for the gas and electricity questions. This has brought the LCF questions in line with those on the EHS. This may cause a slight discontinuity in the data.

A question was added to capture the take up of the Health in Pregnancy grant, a benefit introduced in April 2009.

A question capturing Cold Weather Payments was included from July 2009 onwards.

Weighting

Since 1998–99 the survey has been weighted to reduce the effect of non-response bias and produce population totals and means. The weights are produced in two stages. First, the data are weighted to compensate for non-response (sample-based weighting). Second, the sample distribution is weighted so that it matches the population distribution in terms of region, age group and sex (population-based weighting).

Sample based weighting using the Census

Weighting for non-response involves giving each respondent a weight so that they represent the non-respondents that are similar to them in terms of the survey characteristics. From 1998–99 the EFS used results from the 1991 Census-linked study of non-respondents to carry out non-response weighting[1]. From 2007 onwards the EFS/LCF non-response classes and weights have been annually updated using 2001 Census-linked data.

The Census-linked studies matched Census addresses with the sampled addresses of some of the large continuous surveys, including FES for the1991 link study and EFS for the 2001 link study. In this way it was possible to match the address details of the respondents as well as the non-respondents with corresponding information gathered from the Census for the same address. The information collected during the 1991 and then the 2001 Census/FES/EFS matching work was then used to identify the types of households that were being under-represented in the survey.

For the 1991 Census-based non-response weights, a combination of household variables were analysed with the software package AnswerTree (using the chi-squared statistics CHAID)[2] to identify which characteristics were most significant in distinguishing between responding and non-responding households. These characteristics were sorted by the program to produce 10 weighting classes with different response rates. For the updated 2001 Census-based non-response weights, a combination of household variables were analysed using a mixed model approach. The mixed model is a combined approach to modelling, designed to benefit from the underlying statistical model of logistic regression as well as utilising AnswerTree. Updated weighting classes were produced, using this analysis, to further improve non-response weighting from 2007.

Population-based weighting

The second stage of the weighting adjusts the non-response weights so that weighted totals match population totals. As the LCF sample is based on private households, the population totals used in the weighting need to relate to people living in private households. The population totals used are the most up-to-date official figures available; from 2006 onwards, these totals have been population projections based on estimates rolled forward from the 2001 Census. These estimates used exclude residents of institutions not covered by the EFS/LCF, such as those living in bed-and-breakfast accommodation, hostels, residential homes and other institutions.

The non-response weights were calibrated[3] so that weighted totals matched population totals for males and females in different age groups and for regions. An important feature of the population-based weighting is that it is done by adjusting the factors for households not individuals.

The weighting is carried out separately for each quarter of the survey. The main reason is that sample sizes vary more from quarter to quarter than in the past. This is due to reissuing addresses after an interval of a few months where there had previously been no contact or a refusal to a new interviewer. This results in more interviews in the later quarters of the year than in the first quarter. Quarterly weighting, therefore, counteracts any potential bias from the uneven spread of interviews through the year. Quarterly weighting also results in small sample numbers in some of the age/sex categories that were used in previous years. The categories have therefore been widened slightly to avoid this.

Table B4   The effect of weighting on expenditure, 2009

Commodity or service	Average weekly household expenditure		Absolute difference	Percentage difference
	Unweighted	Weighted as published		
All expenditure groups	**383.10**	**383.10**	**0.03**	*0.0*
Food and non-alcoholic drinks	53.40	52.20	−1.23	*−2.3*
Alcoholic drink, tobacco & narcotics	11.60	11.20	−0.47	*−4.0*
Clothing and footwear	21.80	20.90	−0.83	*−3.8*
Housing, fuel and power	54.30	57.30	2.99	*5.5*
Household goods and services	28.10	27.90	−0.16	*−0.6*
Health	5.40	5.30	−0.15	*−2.7*
Transport	58.70	58.40	−0.31	*−0.5*
Communication	11.60	11.70	0.10	*0.8*
Recreation and culture	58.80	57.90	−0.98	*−1.7*
Education	6.00	7.00	0.94	*15.6*
Restaurants and hotels	38.00	38.40	0.37	*1.0*
Miscellaneous	35.30	35.00	−0.23	*−0.7*
Weekly household income:				
Disposable	554	558	4	*0.8*
Gross	673	683	10	*1.5*

ONS, Family Spending 2009, © Crown copyright 2010

Effects of weighting on the data

Table B4 shows the effects of the weighting by comparing unweighted and weighted data from 2009.

The weighting increased the estimate of total average expenditure by 3 pence a week. It had the largest impact on average weekly expenditure on education, increasing the estimate by 15.6 per cent. It also increased the estimate for housing, fuel and power by 5.5 per cent and decreased the estimate for alcoholic drink, tobacco and narcotics by 4 per cent. It reduced the estimate of spending on clothing and footwear by 3.8 per cent and the estimate of spending on household goods and services by 0.6 per cent. Weighting also increased the estimates of average income, by £4 a week (0.8 per cent) for disposable household income and by £10 a week (1.5 per cent) for gross household income, which is the income used in most tables in the report.

Weighting also has an effect on the variance of estimates. In an analysis on the 1999–2000 data, weighting increased variance slightly for some items and reduced it for others. Overall the effect was to reduce variance slightly.

Further information

Further information on the method used to produce the weights is available from the contacts given on page ii of this publication.

1 See Foster, K. (1994) *Weighting the FES to compensate for non-response, Part 1: An investigation into Census-based weighting schemes*, London: OPCS.
2 CHAID is an acronym that stands for Chi-squared Automatic Interaction Detection. As is suggested by its name, CHAID uses chi-squared statistics to identify optimal splits or groupings of independent variables in terms of predicting the outcome of a dependent variable, in this case response.
3 Implemented by the CALMAR software package before 2007 and GES for 2006–08 (updated weights).

Table B7 Index to tables in reports on the Family Expenditure Survey in 1999–00 to 2000–01 and the Living Costs and Food Survey 2001–02 to 2009

2009 tables		Table numbers in reports for									
		2008	2007	2006	2005–06	2004–05	2003–04	2002–03	2001–02[1]	2000–01	1999–2000
Detailed expenditure and place of purchase											
A1	Detailed expenditure with full-method standard errors	A1	A1	A1	A1	A1	A1	7.1	7.1	7.1	7.1
A2	Expenditure on alcoholic drink by type of premises	A2	A2	A2	A2	A2	A2	7.2	7.2	7.2	7.2
A3	Expenditure on food by place of purchase	A3	A3	A3	A3	A3	A3	7.3	7.3	7.3	7.3
..	Expenditure on alcoholic drink by place of purchase	..	..	..	..	..	..	-	-	-	7.4
A4	Expenditure on selected items by place of purchase	A4	A4	A4	A4	A4	A4	7.4	7.4	7.4	-
..	Expenditure on petrol, diesel and other motor oils by place of purchase	..	..	..	..	..	..	-	-	-	7.5
..	Selected household goods and personal goods and services by place of purchase	..	..	..	..	..	..	-	-	-	7.6
..	Selected regular purchases by place of purchase	..	..	..	..	..	..	-	-	-	7.7
A5	Expenditure on clothing and footwear by place of purchase	A5	A5	A5	A5	A5	A5	7.5	7.5	7.5	7.8
Expenditure by income											
A6	Main items by gross income decile	A6	A6	A6	A6	A6	A6	1.1	1.1	1.1	1.1
A7	Percentage on main items by gross income decile	A7	A7	A7	A7	A7	A7	1.2	1.2	1.2	1.2
A8	Detailed expenditure by gross income decile	A8	A8	A8	A8	A8	A8	1.3	1.3	1.3	1.3
..	(Housing expenditure in each tenure group)	..	..	..	..	..	..	-	-	-	-
A9	Main items by disposable income decile	A9	A9	A9	A9	A9	A9	1.4	1.4	1.4	1.4
A10	Percentage on main items by disposable income decile	A10	A10	A10	A10	A10	A10	1.5	1.5	1.5	1.5
Expenditure by age and income											
A11	Main items by age of HRP	A11	A11	A11	A11	A11	A11	2.1	2.1	2.9	-
..	Main items by age of head of household	..	..	..	..	..	..	-	-	2.1	2.1
A12	Main items as a percentage by age of HRP	A12	A12	A12	A12	A12	A12	2.2	2.2	2.2	2.2
A13	Detailed expenditure by age of HRP	A13	A13	A13	A13	A13	A13	2.3	2.3	2.3	2.3
A14	Aged under 30 by income	A14	A14	A14	A14	A14	A14	2.4	2.4	2.4	2.4
A15	Aged 30 and under 50 by income	A15	A15	A15	A15	A15	A15	2.5	2.5	2.5	2.5
A16	Aged 50 and under 65 by income	A16	A16	A16	A16	A16	A16	2.6	2.6	2.6	2.6
A17	Aged 65 and under 75 by income	A17	A17	A17	A17	A17	A17	2.7	2.7	2.7	2.7
A18	Aged 75 or over by income	A18	A18	A18	A18	A18	A18	2.8	2.8	2.8	2.8
Expenditure by socio-economic characteristics											
A19	By economic activity status of HRP	A19	A19	A19	A19	A19	A19	3.1	3.1	3.9	-
..	By economic activity status of HoH	..	..	..	..	..	..	-	-	3.1	3.1
..	By occupation	..	..	..	..	..	..	-	-	3.2	3.2
A20	HRP is a full-time employee by income	A20	A20	A20	A20	A20	A20	3.2	3.2	3.3	3.3
A21	HRP is self-employed by income	A21	A21	A21	A21	A21	A21	3.3	3.3	3.4	3.4
..	By social class	..	..	..	..	..	..	-	-	3.5	3.5
A22	By number of persons working	A22	A22	A22	A22	A22	A22	3.4	3.4	3.6	3.6
A23	By age HRP completed continuous full-time education	A23	A23	A23	A23	A23	A23	3.5	3.5	3.7	3.7
..	By occupation of HRP	..	..	..	..	..	..	-	-	3.8	-
A24	By socio-economic class of HRP	A24	A24	A24	A24	A24	A24	3.6	3.6	-	-
Expenditure by composition, income and tenure											
A25	Expenditure by household composition	A25	A25	A25	A25	A25	A25	4.1	4.1	4.1	4.1
A26	One adult retired households mainly dependent on state pensions	A26	A26	A26	A26	A26	A26	4.2	4.2	4.2	4.2
A27	One adult retired households not mainly dependent on state pensions	A27	A27	A27	A27	A27	A27	4.3	4.3	4.3	4.3
A28	One adult non-retired	A28	A28	A28	A28	A28	A28	4.4	4.4	4.4	4.4
A29	One adult with children	A29	A29	A29	A29	A29	A29	4.5	4.5	4.5	4.5
A30	Two adults with children	A30	A30	A30	A30	A30	A30	4.6	4.6	4.6	4.6

Notes

.. Tables do not appear in these publications

1 Household Reference Person (HRP) replaced Head Of Household (HOH) in 2001–02

Table B7   Index to tables in reports on the Family Expenditure Survey in 1999–00 to 2000–01 and the Living Costs and Food Survey 2001–02 to 2009 (cont.)

2009 tables		Table numbers in reports for									
		2008	2007	2006	2005–06	2004–05	2003–04	2002–03	2001–02¹	2000–01	1999–2000
Expenditure by composition, income and tenure (cont.)											
A31	Two adults non-retired	A31	A31	A31	A31	A31	A31	4.7	4.7	4.7	4.7
A32	Two adults retired mainly dependent on state pensions	A32	A32	A32	A32	A32	A32	4.8	4.8	4.8	4.8
A33	Two adults retired not mainly dependent on state pensions	A33	A33	A33	A33	A33	A33	4.9	4.9	4.9	4.9
A34	Household expenditure by tenure	A34	A34	A34	A34	A34	A34	4.10	4.10	4.10	4.10
..	Household expenditure by type of dwelling	..	..	..	..	..	..	-	-	-	-
Expenditure by region											
A35	Main items of expenditure by GOR	A35	A35	A35	A35	A35	A35	5.1	5.1	5.1	5.1
A36	Main items as a percentage of expenditure by GOR	A36	A36	A36	A36	A36	A36	5.2	5.2	5.2	5.2
A37	Detailed expenditure by GOR	A37	A37	A37	A37	A37	A37	5.3	5.3	5.3	5.3
..	(Housing expenditure in each tenure group)	..	..	..	..	..	..	-	-	-	-
..	Expenditure by type of administrative area	..	..	..	..	..	..	-	-	5.4	5.4
A38	Expenditure by urban/rural areas (GB only)	A38	A38	A38	A38	A38	A38	5.4	5.4	5.5	-
Household income											
A40	Income by household composition	A40	A40	A40	A40	A40	A40	8.1	8.1	8.1	8.1
A41	Income by age of HRP	A41	A41	A41	A41	A41	A41	8.2	8.2	8.10	-
..	By age of head of household	..	..	..	..	..	..	-	-	8.2	8.2
A42	Income by income group	A42	A42	A42	A42	A42	A42	8.3	8.3	8.3	8.3
A43	Income by household tenure	A43	A43	A43	A43	A43	A43	8.4	8.4	8.4	8.4
..	Income by economic status of HoH	..	..	..	..	..	..	-	-	8.5	8.5
..	Income by occupational grouping of HoH	..	..	..	..	..	..	-	-	8.6	8.6
A44	Income by GOR	A44	A44	A44	A44	A44	A44	8.5	8.5	8.7	8.7
A45	Income by GB urban/rural areas	A45	A45	A45	A45	A45	A45	8.6	8.6	8.8	-
A46	Income by socio-economic class	A46	A46	A46	A46	A46	A46	8.7	-	-	-
A47	Income 1970 to 2009	A47	A47	A47	A47	A47	A47	8.8	8.7	8.9	8.8
..	Income by economic activity status of HRP	..	..	..	..	..	..	-	-	8.11	-
..	Income by occupation of HRP	..	..	..	..	..	..	-	-	8.12	-
Households characteristics and ownership of durable goods											
A48	Household characteristics	A48	A48	A48	A48	A48	A48	9.1	9.1	9.1	9.1
A49	Person characteristics	A49	A49	A49	A49	A49	A49	9.2	9.2	9.2	9.2
A50	Percentage with durable goods 1970 to 2009	A50	A50	A50	A50	A50	A50	9.3	9.3	9.3	9.3
A51	Percentage with durable goods by income group & hhld composition	A51	A51	A51	A51	A51	A51	9.4	9.4	9.4	9.4
A52	Percentage with cars	A52	A52	A52	A52	A52	A52	9.5	9.5	9.5	9.5
A53	Percentage with durable goods by UK Countries and Government Office Regions	A53	A53	A53	A53	A53	A53	9.6	9.6	9.6	9.6
A54	Percentage by size, composition, age, in each income group	A54	A54	A54	A54	A54	A54	9.7	9.7	9.7	9.7
..	Percentage by occupation, economic activity, tenure in each income group	..	..	..	..	..	..	-	-	9.8	9.8
A55	Percentage by economic activity, tenure and socio-economic class in each income group	A55	A55	A55	A55	A55	A55	9.8	9.8	-	-
	Output Area Classification										
A56	Average weekly household expenditure by OAC supergroup	A56	5.3	..	..	..	..	..	..	..	..
A57	Average weekly household expenditure by OAC group	A57	5.4	..	..	..	..	..	..	..	..
A58	Average gross normal weekly household income by OAC supergroup	A58	5.4	..	..	..	..	..	..	..	..
Trends in household expenditure (moved to Chapter 4)											
4.1	FES main items 1994–95 – 2009	4.1	4.1	4.1	4.1	4.1	4.1	6.1	6.1	6.1	6.1
4.2	FES as a percentage of total expenditure 1994–95 – 2009	4.2	4.2	4.2	4.2	4.2	4.2	6.2	6.2	6.2	6.2
..	by Region	..	..	..	..	..	..	-	-	6.3	6.3
4.3	COICOP main items 2003–04 to 2009	4.3	4.3	4.3	4.3	..	..	..	..	..	..
4.4	COICOP as a percentage of total expenditure 2003–04 to 2009	4.4	4.4	4.4	4.4	..	..	..	..	..	..
4.5	Household expenditure 2003–04 to 2009 COICOP based current prices	4.5	..	..	..	..	..	..	..	..	..

Notes

..   Tables do not appear in these publications

1   Household Reference Person (HRP) replaced Head Of Household (HOH) in 2001–02

KYKSHOCK 3

9 music animations
Sjeng Schupp & Michiel van Dyk
and guests

De Buitenkant

Kijkshock3 is Sjeng Schupp and Michiel van Dijk's second book+dvd. This musician/artist duo is well known for its wayward music animations, short films around hilarious situations and tragic characters. The animated films, with original compositions, are specially made for theatre, with live accompaniment from a five-piece band. This dvd comprises all the animations/compositions from the duo's third theatre production, Kijkshock3, which toured the theatres in 2008-2009.

The capricious and absurd universe of Schupp & Van Dijk has its own logic, which you must inhabit in order to experience. To get an idea of what's going on in the heads of the makers, the accompanying book gives a look behind the scenes, with stills, sketches and associative material.

For Kijkshock3 Schupp & Van Dijk invited like-minded artists to also make music animations – eddie d with Eric de Clercq, Frans Schupp with Jasper le Clercq and Marijke Bovens with Michiel van Dijk. All the animators have their own language but they seem to understand each other perfectly.

And then there's the music, seamlessly intertwining with the image. It dips into the jazz idiom, flirts with the classics or looks to the minimalists. The band's unusual instrumentation comprises reeds, drums, bass, violin and accordion. Plus the 'Wulli', as the duo fondly refers to the Wurlitzer piano. That's how you can have a small line-up and still manage to sound distinctive. And surprising – how do you get a seventies sound on accordion? The instrumentalists are also special. They're musical multilinguists and always in for adventure on stage. That comes through on the dvd, recorded semi-live by the band. The music welds the films together to create a whole that can best be experienced by playing the dvd in its entirety, with the book at hand.

With thanks to the Dutch Film Foundation who helped to make the publication of this book+dvd possible.   <<

Published by De Buitenkant, The Netherlands
www.uitgeverijdebuitenkant.nl
ISBN: 978-94-909-1305-2
First edition February 2011

Entire contents © Vinex Productions, Hilversum, NL
www.vinexproductions.nl

Distribution:
Coen Sligting Bookimport - Amsterdam, NL
Idea Books (representative abroad) - Amsterdam, NL
Centraal boekhuis - Culemborg, NL
De Filmfreak - Amsterdam - www.filmfreaks.nl

Cover art: Sjeng Schupp - Amsterdam, NL
Graphic design: Frans Schupp - Amsterdam, NL

Kijkshock3 is het tweede boek+dvd van Sjeng Schupp en Michiel van Dijk. Dit muzikaal/beeldend duo staat bekend om zijn eigenzinnige muziek-animaties. Korte films over hilarische situaties en tragische personages. Bijzonder is dat de animaties, met eigen composities, zijn gemaakt voor het theater. Live op het podium begeleid door een vijfkoppige band. Op deze dvd staan alle animaties/composities van hun derde theatervoorstelling Kijkshock3, waarmee zij in het seizoen 2008-2009 langs de theaters toerden.

In het grillige en absurdistisch universum van Schupp & Van Dijk heerst een eigen logica. Om het te ondergaan, moet je er in gaan wonen. Het begeleidend boek biedt een kijkje in de keuken. Er staan stills, schetsen en associatief materiaal in van de makers. Dat geeft enig idee wat zich in het hoofd van het duo afspeelt.

Voor Kijkshock 3 hebben Schupp & Van Dijk geestverwanten uitgenodigd om ook een muziek-animatie te maken; eddie d met Eric de Clercq, Frans Schupp met Jasper le Clercq en Marijke

Bovens met Michiel van Dijk. Alle animators spreken een eigen taal, maar zij lijken elkaar uitstekend te verstaan.

En er is de muziek. De muziek beweegt zich soepel door het beeld. Bedient zich nu eens van het jazz-idioom, flirt dan met de klassieken of zoekt toenadering tot de minimalisten. De band kent een bijzondere bezetting: rieten, slagwerk, bas, viool en accordeon. Plus het gebruik van de 'Wulli', zoals het duo de Wurlitzer piano liefkozend noemt. Zo lukt het om met een kleine bezetting toch onderscheidend te zijn. En verrassend, want hoe krijg je een seventies sound met een accordeon? Ook de instrumentalisten zijn bijzonder. Ze spreken meerdere muzikale talen. Als podiummensen altijd in voor een avontuurtje. Het avontuurlijke klinkt door op de dvd, die semi-live door de band is opgenomen. De muziek smeedt de films aaneen. Een eenheid die het beste tot zijn recht komt door dvd in één keer af te spelen, met het boek in de buurt.

Bij deze danken wij het Nederlands Fonds voor de Film voor het mede mogelijk maken van de uitgave van dit boek+dvd.   <<

Everything is possible

Sometimes you miss a link.

Sometimes we only had an ending.

Sometimes you have to kill your darlings.

Sometimes we are shameless.

Sometimes it stalls.

 Sometimes you don't know you're thinking about it.

Sometimes you hear a page turn.

Sometimes we had too much time.

Sometimes the music came first.

Sometimes it suddenly starts flowing.

By Marijke Bovens

In de filmpjes mag alles

Soms mis je een bruggetje.

Soms hadden we alleen een einde.

Soms moet je je darlings killen.

Soms zijn we schaamteloos.

Soms stagneert het.

Soms weet je niet dat je nadenkt.

Soms hoor je een bladzijde omslaan.

Soms hadden we te veel tijd.

Soms was er eerst de muziek.

Soms is er opeens de flow

A conversation with Schupp & Van Dijk has lots of sometimeses, occasionally a never ('we never use a storyboard') and rarely an always ('we always edit together'). That's because every film is different.

A film usually arises from a detail. One of the duo has a beginning, a vague image, a sudden passion for an era (the 70's in Broes), or a persistent interval in his head. Then the traffic gets into gear. Sketches, drawings, music fragments, associations, links and brilliant ideas shoot to and fro. One of them makes something and the other reacts to it. 'We're lucky we have the same taste,' says Van Dijk laconically, 'you don't come across that very often.' Schupp: 'We work intuitively and we talk a lot.'

Anything goes in the films. Van Dijk: 'You're allowed to do anything.' Schupp: 'As long as it works.' But in one respect they are strict, with themselves and with others: 'If it's too long and the material isn't good enough, then it quickly becomes pretentious.' Five minutes is the norm, though they go on to talk at length about a half-hour long project they're working on at the moment.

The film takes on its definite form in the editing phase. That's when the rhythm emerges. They shuffle, extend and cut endlessly. Here the image has to take a back seat to the music, there the music has to anticipate the plot, elsewhere an essential film cue has to be built in to give the musicians holdfast – it's performed live after all.

It's a cast-iron formula, the combination of live music and film. Music played live creates tension, you're there and you don't know how it's going to end up. Van Dijk: 'For the dvd we've approached the live situation as closely as possible. We recorded everyone at the same time with a minimum of dubs and retakes. Sometimes you hear less pleasing bits. I'm attached to them. The musicians can let go enjoy themselves. The flow, that's what it's about. Schupp: 'Chet Baker and his false teeth.'   <<

Een gesprek met Schupp & Van Dijk telt vele somsen, af en toe een nooit ('we gebruiken nooit een storyboard') en zelden een altijd ('we editen altijd samen'). Want elk filmpje is anders.

Meestal ontstaat een filmpje vanuit een detail. Een van beiden heeft een beginnetje. Een vaag beeld, een plotselinge liefde voor een tijdperk (de jaren 70 in Broes), of een hardnekkig interval in het hoofd. En dan komt het verkeer op gang. Schetsjes, tekeningen, muziekfragmenten , associaties dwarsverbanden en lumineuze ideeën flitsen heen en weer. De één maakt iets en de ander reageert er op. 'We hebben mazzel dat we dezelfde smaak hebben', zegt Van Dijk laconiek, 'dat kom je niet vaak tegen'. Schupp: 'We gaan intuïtief te werk en we praten heel veel.'

In de filmpjes mag alles. Van Dijk: 'Je kunt je alles veroorloven.' Schupp: 'Als het maar werkt'. Maar in één opzicht zijn ze streng, voor zichzelf en voor anderen: 'Als het te lang is en het materiaal is niet goed genoeg, dan wordt het snel te pretentieus'. Vijf minuten is de norm, om vervolgens uitgebreid te vertellen over het half uur durende project dat zij nu onder handen hebben.

In de editfase krijgt elke film zijn definitieve vorm. Dan ontstaat het ritme. Eindeloos wordt geschoven, verlengd en ingekort. Hier moet het beeld een beetje inzakken om de muziek de ruimte te geven, daar moet de muziek anticiperen op de plot en weer ergens anders moet een onmisbare beeldcue ingebouwd worden om de muzikanten houvast te geven . Het is tenslotte live.   >>

Voor elk filmpje is een unieke compositie geschreven, de meeste door Van Dijk. Het is een ijzersterke formule, de combinatie van live-muziek met beeld. De levende muziek roept spanning op, je bent er bij en je weet niet hoe het af gaat lopen. Van Dijk: 'Voor de dvd hebben we de live-situatie zo dicht mogelijk benaderd. Met zijn allen tegelijk opnemen met zo min mogelijk dubs en reparaties. Je hoort soms de minder fraaie randjes. Daar ben ik aan gehecht. De muzikanten mogen uithalen, genieten. De flow, daar draait het om.' Schupp: 'Chet Baker en zijn kunstgebit.' <<

studio sessions

Photography:

Michiel van Dijk

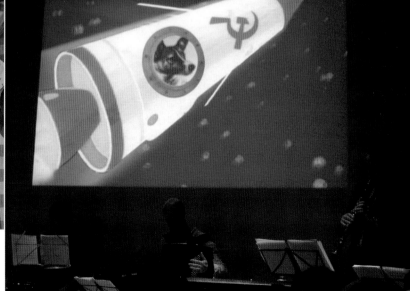

Photography:

Elisabeth Melchior (1, 5, 6)

Peter de Groot (2, 3, 4, 7)

kijkshock live

Laika

Animation: Frans Schupp
Music: Jasper le Clercq

6:24 min

The film is about Laika the dog, as first living being shot into space by the Soviet Union in 1957. In the film Laika sees his dog's life flash before him. Or does the film take place in the head of an old man who fantasises about his lost dog?

The film is a moving collage, a collection of photos and drawn elements. The music also has the character of a collage, reinforcing the images or adding an atmosphere of its own. The film's design breathes the atmosphere of the Soviet Union of the 1950s, as does the music. The melancholy Russian sounding melodies serve to intensify the sad fate of Laika.

De film handelt over het hondje Laika, dat in 1957 door de Sovietunie als eerste levende wezen de ruimte in werd gelanceerd. In de film ziet Laika zijn hondenleven aan zijn geestesoog voorbijkomen. Of zou de film zich in het hoofd van een oude man afspelen, die fantaseert over zijn verloren geraakte hond?

De film is een bewegende collage van foto's en getekende elementen. Ook de muziek heeft een collage-achtig karakter. Soms versterkt die het beeld, soms voegt de muziek juist een eigen sfeer toe. De vormgeving van de film ademt de sfeer van de Sovietunie uit de jaren vijftig van de vorige eeuw. De muziek sluit daarbij aan met Russisch klinkende weemoedige melodieën. En versterkt daardoor de tristesse van het lot van Laika.

Lounge

Animation: Sjeng Schupp
Music: Michiel van Dijk

4:21 min

Lounge is a hallucinatory whirlwind of endlessly morphing images.
Starting point of the film is the music. The plan was to have no plan, the animations were made one to one with the music. The film's strength lies in its intuitiveness. The images resulted from a continual process of association and fantasising with lines, scribbles, forms and figures merging and emerging. The music is fairly uniform with a propulsive drive, allowing the animation to take the stage.

Lounge is een hallicunerende wervelwind van beelden die eindeloos door morfen.
Het uitgangspunt van de film is de muziek. Zonder een echt vooropgezet plan is deze animatiefilm één op één op de muziek gemaakt. De kracht van deze film zit hem in het intuïtieve. Het beeldmateriaal is ontstaan uit eindeloos door-associëren en fantaseren op lijnen, krabbels, vormen en figuren die in elkaar opgaan en uit elkaar ontstaan. De muziek is vrij eenvormig maar met voorwaartse drive, hierdoor krijgt de animatie alle ruimte zich te exposeren.

Kapsalon Hair Saloon

Animation: Sjeng Schupp
Music: Bart Lelivelt

2:05 min

This absurdist film is about a bald man who uses hairdos to pep up his personality. The hairdos belong to famous people, contemporary and historic, and are formed by the smoke from his pipe. It doesn't have the desired effect, and the man eventually settles for his own bald self.

The music is an improvisation on accordion. The accordion's 'blowing' refers to that of the man as he inhales his smoke and blows it out. The improvisation follows the film fairly literally: when the hairdos shoot by, the accordion plays up-tempo and continually threatens to spin out of control.

Deze absurdistische film toont een kale man die door middel van kapsels zijn persoonlijkheid wil opvijzelen. De kapsels zijn van bekende persoonlijkheden uit heden en verleden en worden gevormd door de rook uit zijn pijp. Dit leidt echter niet tot de gewenste bevrediging. Uiteindelijk kiest de man toch voor zijn eigen kale ik.

De muziek is een improvisatie op accordeon. Het geblaas van de accordeon refereert aan dat van de man die zijn rook in en uitblaast. De improvisatie volgt de film vrij letterlijk: wanneer de kapsels voorbijschieten gaat ook de accordeon in uptempo spelen en dreigt constant dol te draaien.

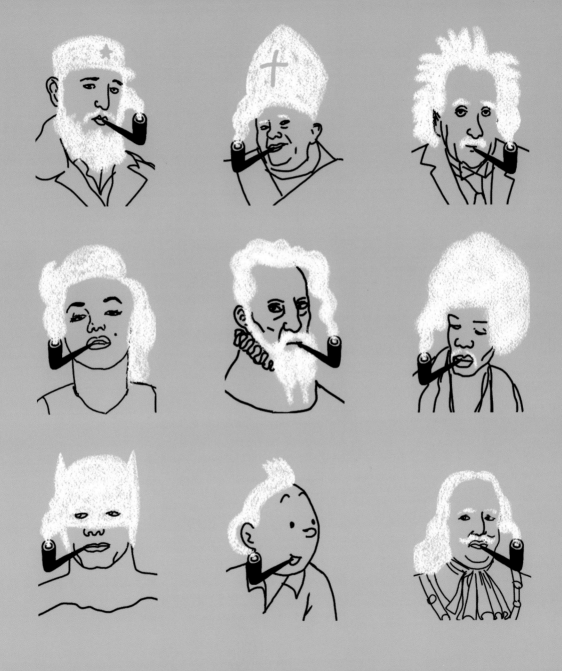

Cuore

Animation: eddie d
Music: Eric de Clercq

5:15 min

In Cuore (Italian for heart) the Beautiful People who define our media landscape come to the fore. This work shows the preoccupation of television makers – and many others – with a certain type of person, seemingly chosen on the basis of looks rather than brains. The actors in this drama include Paris Hilton, the cast of a reality show and a fitness trainer.

Cuore is a musical video collage, a video opera if you like, where found footage is seamlessly integrated with Eric de Clercq's music.

The music is direct and physical, written for a pop band with a strange line-up: no guitars, but virtuoso accordion and violin, grunting baritone sax and recalcitrant bass and drums. Cuore is also an homage to the music of Captain Beefheart.

In Cuore (Italiaans voor 'hart') laten de Mooie Mensen die het beeld in ons medialandschap bepalen flink van zich horen. Het werk toont de preoccupatie van de televisiemakers – en vele anderen – met een bepaald model mens dat eerder geselecteerd lijkt op uiterlijk dan op herseninhoud. Onder andere Paris Hilton, de cast van een realityshow en een fitnesstrainer zijn de acteurs in dit menselijk drama. Cuore is een muzikale videocollage, een video-opera zo u wilt, waarin found footage elementen naadloos geïntegreerd zijn met de muziek van Eric de Clercq.

De muziek is direct en fysiek, geschreven voor een popband met een vreemde bezetting: geen gitaren maar wel virtuoze accordeon en viool, een knorrende baritonsax en tegendraadse bas en drums. Cuore is ook een eerbetoon aan de muziek van Captain Beefheart

Doggy style

Animation: Sjeng Schupp
Music: Hans van der Meer

2:38 min

Doggy style is one big loop, an absurd life cycle of continually being born and eaten. Drummer Hans van der Meer improvises to the cadence created by the repetition of image and sound.

Doggy style is één grote loop. Een absurde levenscyclus van geboren en weer opgegeten worden. De slagwerker Hans van der Meer improviseert op de cadans die ontstaat door de herhaling van beeld en geluid.

5

These days there's always stuff going on everywhere.

Pas de duck

Animation: Sjeng Schupp
Music: Michiel van Dijk

3:30 min

In *Pas de duck* , a dance/music animated film, a cheeky duck sets out to prove that he is the best dancer. His annoying behaviour costs him dearly, but this daffy duck has the last word in the end.
Each dancing figure that appears in the film has its own musical theme. A disruptive funky groove related to the duck' main theme plays in the background of these individual themes. In this way the dance battle is reflected in the music and on screen.

De film Pas de duck is een dans/muziek-animatiefilm waarin een brutale eend wil laten zien dat hij de beste danser is. Zijn irritante gedrag komt hem duur te staan, maar uiteindelijk heeft deze vreemde eend in de bijt toch nog het laatste woord.
Elk dansend figuur dat in de film voorkomt heeft zijn eigen muzikale thema. De thema's worden begeleid door een verstorende funky groove die gerelateerd is aan het hoofdthema van de eend. Op deze manier komt de dance-battle zowel tot uitdrukking in de muziek als op het filmdoek.

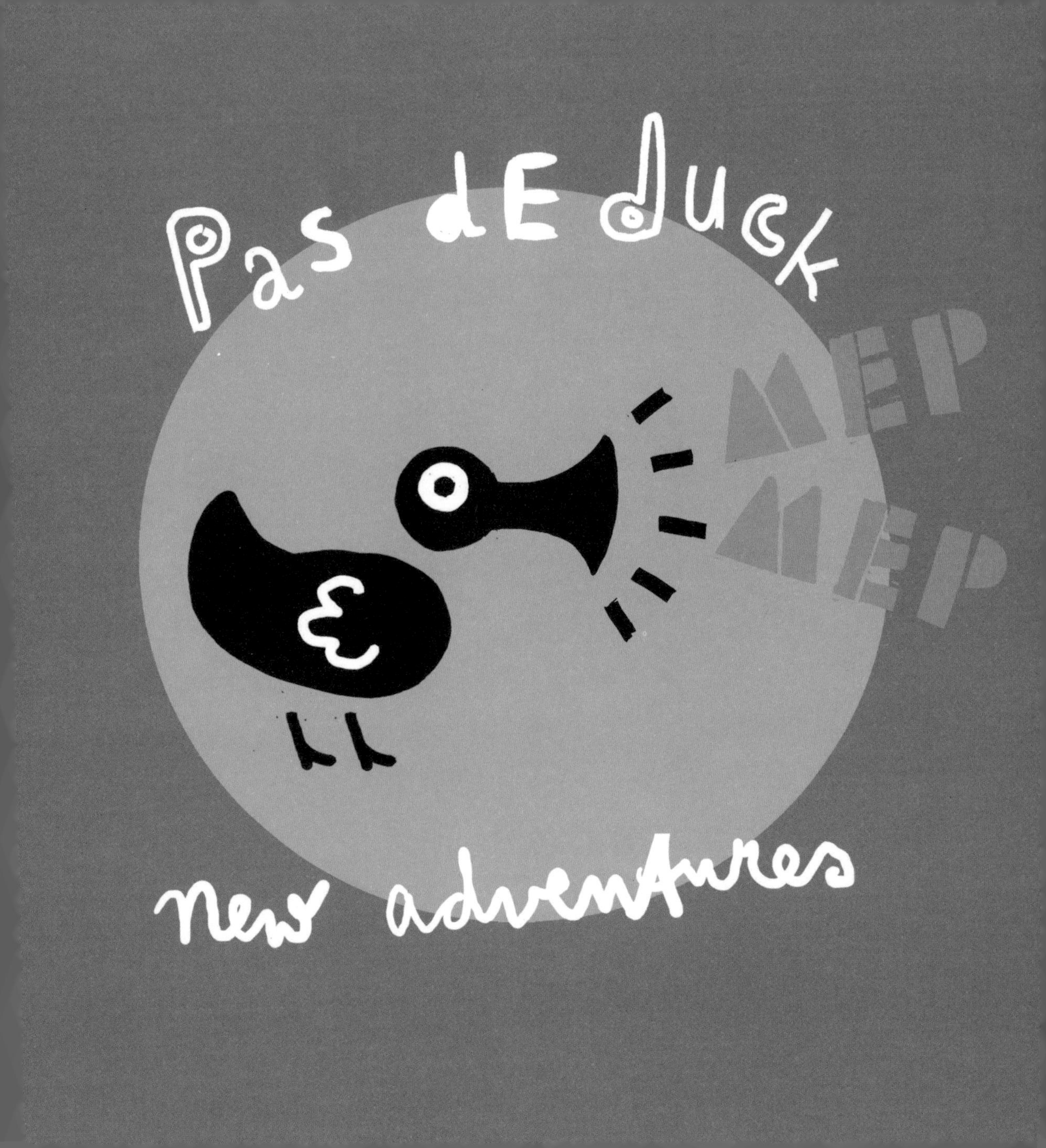
Pas dE duck
MEEP
MEEP
new adventures

© Sjeng Schupp

I was not

Animation: Marijke Bovens
Music: Michiel van Dijk

5:45 min

7

A story that begins with a firm 'Here I am' ends on a shaky 'I was not'. Narcissus is fascinated by the compelling but elusive face that appears on the water's surface. He leans over so eagerly that he loses his balance and sinks in the bottomless depths. After an enormous struggle he comes up again, only to perceive that the outside world is unmoved. The film's tempo varies greatly, from nightmarish sequences to dreamy moments. This is reflected in the composition, which closely follows the film but is not programmatic. A bizarre up-tempo bebop theme accompanies the bad trip; in the dreamy parts the music's tempo is altogether open and still.

Het verhaal begint met een stevig 'Hier ben ik' en eindigt in een wankel 'I was not' – losjes gebaseerd op de mythe van Narcissus. Narcissus is gefascineerd door het dwingende maar ongrijpbare gezicht dat aan de oppervlakte verschijnt. Zo gretig buigt hij zich voorover dat hij zijn evenwicht verliest en in een peilloze diepte zinkt. Na veel geworstel komt ie weer boven, om te merken dat de buitenwereld onverstoorbaar is. Het tempo van de film wisselt van nachtmerrie-achtige sequenties tot dromerige momenten. Dit wordt weerspiegeld in de compositie, die het beeld nauwlettend volgt zonder illustratief te worden. Wanneer de muziek in hoog tempo een vreemd jazzy bebopthema laat horen, bevinden we ons in de bad trip en onder de dromerige gedeelten ligt het tempo in de muziek totaal stil en helemaal open.

Brainwatch

Animation: Sjeng Schupp
Music: Michile van Dijk

6:20 min

Travel through the human brain, destination dark recesses. Brainwatch is an endless zoom through a man's thoughts where you are confronted with a whole gamut of fantasies. At first they are positive. After a while the viewer goes through an imaginary door into the brain's caverns. In the end the man believes he is rid of his darker thoughts, but the question is: is he now in his thoughts or are the thoughts in him?

The music for Brainwatch begins up-tempo but changes to minimal music as soon as we are in the brain. The endless zoom, combined with minimal repetitive music, produces a hovering effect in the simple black-and-white pictogram-like line drawings.

Reis door het menselijk brein, met als eindbestemming de donkere krochten. Brainwatch is een eindeloze zoom door de gedachtenwereld van een man waarbij de meest uiteenlopende hersenspinsels op je af komen. In eerste instantie zijn deze spinsels positief. Na verloop van tijd gaat de kijker door een fictieve deur waarachter zich de krochten van het brein bevinden. Uiteindelijk denkt de man af te zijn van zijn donkere gedachten, maar de vraag is of hij zich nu in zijn gedachten bevindt of dat de gedachten zich in hem bevinden.

De muziek van Brainwatch begint in uptempo maar zodra we in het brein zijn beland transformeert de muziek naar minimalmusic. Door de eindeloze zoom in combinatie met de minimale repeterende muziek gaan de eenvoudige zwart-wit lijntekeningen, bijna pictogrammen, zweven.

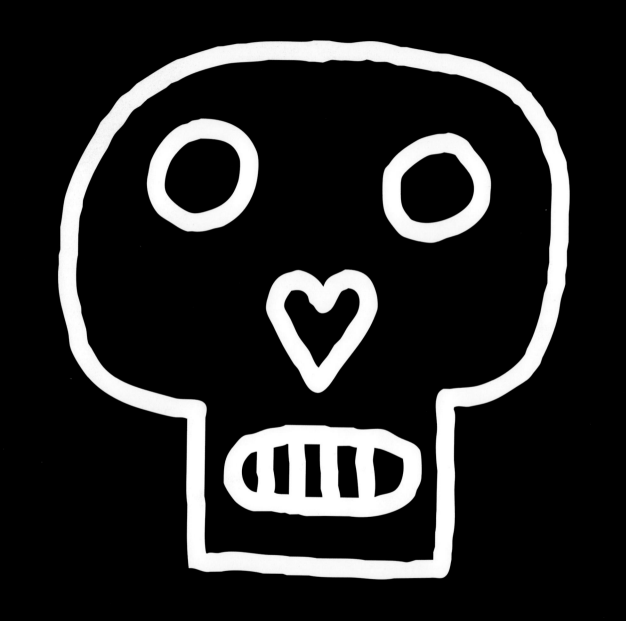

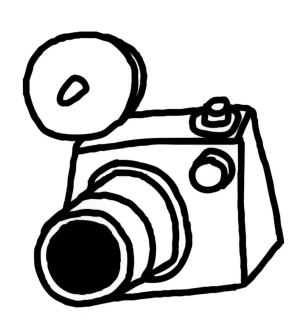

Broes

Animation: Sjeng Schupp
Music: Michiel van Dijk

5:05 min

A man pays a visit to an old Zen Buddhist sage, who gives him wise advice so that he can develop special powers. After a series of increasingly crazy fights the man comes to the conclusion that he has attained his highest state of being; it wasn't him who fought, but the higher powers.
The film parody *Broes* is an ode to seventies' B movie and its music, in semi widescreen.

Een man bezoekt een oude wijze zenboeddhist. Deze geeft hem wijze raad zodat de man in kwestie speciale krachten kan ontwikkelen. Na een serie steeds gekker wordende gevechten komt de man tot de slotconclusie dat hij de hoogste staat van het zijn heeft bereikt; het was niet hij die vocht maar de hogere machten.
De filmparodie Broes is een ode aan de jaren zeventig B-film en filmmuziek. Dit alles in semibreedbeeld.

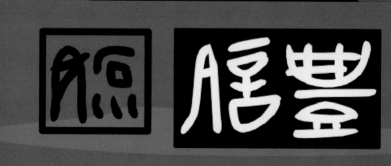

Animators and composers

Frans Schupp is a graphic designer and illustrator, designing books, posters, flyers and websites. Many of his clients work in the cultural sector. Frans has also made two animated films: *Great Ocean*, his debut film from 2006, and *Laika*, 2008. *www.fransschupp.nl*

Michiel van Dijk studied classical saxophone with Leo van Oosterom and jazz saxophone with John Ruocco at the Royal Conservatory of The Hague. He has played with almost all the renowned orchestras and ensembles of the Netherlands. He has composed and arranged for various theatre productions and ensembles. Van Dijk has also composed the music for Vinex Productions' twenty music/animation films. *www.michielvandijk.info*

Marijke Bovens works as an artist, art historian and journalist. She trained as a teacher at d'Witte Leli, and has followed studies at the universities of Amsterdam, Utrecht and Leiden (art history and philosophy) and the Jan van Eyck Akadamie in Maastricht. She paints portraits on commission and exhibits regularly. As freelance journalist she writes about culture, architecture and art for diverse magazines. *www.marijkebovens.nl*

eddie d graduated in 1991 from the Media Art Department of the AkI (art academy) in Enschede. His work comprises photos, videos and video/computer installations. Recurring themes are rhythm, deconstruction of language and the relationship between image and sound. The videos are usually musical compositions where d builds rhythmic structures using his meticulous montage technique. His work is regarded as the standard within this video art genre. *www.eddied.nu*

Sjeng Schupp is illustrator, animator and musician. He has done illustrations for various newspapers, CD covers, posters, flyers, children's books and schoolbooks. The twenty independent animated films that he has made until now have been shown at many international festivals. He plays double bass and bass guitar in renowned classical and contemporary music ensembles. *www.sjengschupp.nl*

Jasper le Clerq studied jazz violin at the Rotterdam Conservatory under Michael Gustorff and Thijs Kramer (classical). He works (or has worked) with extremely diverse ensembles, theatre companies and bands. As a member of the very successful Zapp String Quartet he tours throughout the world. Le Clercq has arranged and composed for various bands and ensembles, and written music for film and theatre. *www.jasperleclercq.nl*

Eric de Clercq completed his composition studies at the Rotterdam Conservatory with Gilius van Bergeijk, Peter-Jan Wagemans and Klaas de Vries. For his often uncompromising music Eric de Clercq makes frequent use of literary texts, electronics and unusual instrumentation. He has written for such prominent national and international ensembles as the Schönberg Ensemble, LOOS and Ensemble Aleph. *www.ericdeclercq.nl*